SOCIAL BEHAVIOR IN AUTISM

CURRENT ISSUES IN AUTISM
Series Editors: Eric Schopler and Gary B. Mesibov

University of North Carolina School of Medicine
Chapel Hill, North Carolina

AUTISM IN ADOLESCENTS AND ADULTS
Edited by Eric Schopler and Gary B. Mesibov

COMMUNICATION PROBLEMS IN AUTISM
Edited by Eric Schopler and Gary B. Mesibov

THE EFFECTS OF AUTISM ON THE FAMILY
Edited by Eric Schopler and Gary B. Mesibov

SOCIAL BEHAVIOR IN AUTISM
Edited by Eric Schopler and Gary B. Mesibov

SOCIAL BEHAVIOR IN AUTISM

Edited by
Eric Schopler
and
Gary B. Mesibov

University of North Carolina School of Medicine
Chapel Hill, North Carolina

PLENUM PRESS • NEW YORK AND LONDON

Library of Congress Cataloging in Publication Data

Main entry under title:

Social behavior in autism.

(Current issues in autism)
Based on the 5th annual TEACCH conference, held in 1984.
Includes bibliographies and index.
1. Autistic children—Rehabilitation. 2. Social skills in children. 3. Autism—Patients—Rehabilitation. 4. Social skills. I. Schopler, Eric. II. Mesibov, Gary B. III. University of North Carolina at Chapel Hill. Dept. of Psychiatry. Division TEACCH. IV. Series. [DNLM: 1. Autism—in infancy & childhood-congresses. 2. Behavior Therapy—in infancy & childhood-congresses. 3. Social Behavior—in infancy & childhood-congresses. WM 203.5 S678 1984]
RJ506.A9S63 1986 618.92′8982 85-28344
ISBN 0-306-42163-1

A Division of Plenum Publishing Corporation
233 Spring Street, New York, N.Y. 10013

Printed in the United States of America

To the North Carolina children and adults who struggle with the social problems in autism

Contributors

ROBERT B. CAIRNS, Department of Psychology, University of North Carolina, Chapel Hill, North Carolina 27514

NANCY DALRYMPLE, Developmental Training Center, Indiana University, Bloomington, Indiana 47405

GERALDINE DAWSON, Department of Psychology, University of Washington, Seattle, Washington 98195

ANNE M. DONNELLAN, School of Education, University of Wisconsin-Madison, Madison, Wisconsin 53706

LARRY GALPERT, Department of Psychology, University of Washington, Seattle, Washington 98195

WENDY C. GAMBLE, College of Human Development, Pennsylvania State University, University Park, Pennsylvania 16802

DEBORAH G. GARFIN, Department of Psychology, North Texas State University, Denton, Texas 76203

WILLARD W. HARTUP, Institute of Child Development, University of Minnesota, Minneapolis, Minnesota 55455

JOYCE HENNING, Developmental Training Center, Indiana University, Bloomington, Indiana 47405

PATRICIA HOWLIN, Institute of Psychiatry, De Crespigny Park, Denmark Hill, London SE5 8AF, England

BEVERLY A. KILMAN, San Diego Regional Center for the Developmentally Disabled, San Diego, California 92123

PETER KNOBLOCK, School of Education, Syracuse University, Syracuse, New York 13210

ANNETTE M. LA GRECA, Department of Psychology, University of Miami, Miami, Florida 33101

ROBERT LEHR, Department of Psychology, State University of New York, Cortland, New York 13045

CATHERINE LORD, Department of Psychology, Glenrose Hospital, Edmonton, Alberta T5G 0B7, Canada

SUSAN M. McHALE, College of Human Development, Pennsylvania State University, University Park, Pennsylvania 16802

GARY B. MESIBOV, Division TEACCH, University of North Carolina, Chapel Hill, North Carolina 27514

J. GREGORY OLLEY, Division TEACCH, University of North Carolina, Chapel Hill, North Carolina 27514

CLARA CLAIBORNE PARK, Department of English, Williams College, Williamstown, Massachusetts 01267

MICHAEL F. SANCILIO, Institute of Child Development, University of Minnesota, Minneapolis, Minnesota 55455

ERIC SCHOPLER, Division TEACCH, University of North Carolina, Chapel Hill, North Carolina 27514

AMITTA SHAH, Medical Research Council Social Psychiatry Unit, Institute of Psychiatry, De Crespigny Park, Denmark Hill, London SE5 8AF, England

WENDY L. STONE, Mailman Center for Child Development, University of Miami School of Medicine, Miami Florida 33101

FRED R. VOLKMAR, Child Study Center, Yale University, New Haven, Connecticut 06510

LORNA WING, Medical Research Council Social Psychiatry Unit, Institute of Psychiatry, De Crespigny Park, Denmark Hill, London SE5 8AF, England

MARIAN WOOTEN, Millbrook Elementary School, 1520 Millbrook Road, Raleigh, North Carolina 27609

Preface

An important component of Division TEACCH's mandate from the Department of Psychiatry of the University of North Carolina School of Medicine and the North Carolina State Legislature is to conduct research aimed toward improving the understanding of developmental disabilities such as autism and to train the professionals who will be needed to work with this challenging population. An important mechanism to help meet these goals is our annual conference on topics of special importance for the understanding and treatment of autism and related disorders.

As with the preceding books in this series entitled Current Issues in Autism, this most recent volume is based on one of these conferences. The books are not, however, simply published proceedings of conference papers. Instead, certain conference participants were asked to develop chapters around their presentations, and other national and international experts whose work is beyond the scope of the conference but related to the conference theme were asked to contribute manuscripts as well. These volumes are intended to provide the most current knowledge and professional practice available to us at this time.

This volume is the culmination of our Fifth Annual TEACCH Conference on the problems of social behavior and autism. Although researchers and clinicians have been fascinated by the social aloofness and peculiarities of autistic youngsters ever since the syndrome was first identified, until recently very little research or clinical effort was devoted toward understanding and remedying these deficits. Recent attempts to better integrate autistic people into community activities have stimulated greater attention to these important problems. This volume places in context the most important data, theoretical ideas, and clinical perspectives. Although no single work can include everything that is being done in this area, we believe that the information in this volume is the most current report on the state of the art in this area, and will be most useful to professionals and parents concerned with understanding and helping people with autism.

ERIC SCHOPLER
GARY B. MESIBOV

Acknowledgments

Any undertaking of this scope can only be accomplished with the cooperation of numerous people. It is our pleasure to acknowledge our many sources of assistance. First, our thanks to Janet Martin, who was instrumental in organizing the conference that was the starting point for this book. Although we have had many conference organizers in the five years that we have hosted these events, none has been as thorough, capable, and pleasant as Janet. Our secretarial and typing needs were met competently and cheerfully by Judy Carter, Deana Betterton, and Eunice Hernandez. John Swetnam provided most valuable editorial assistance in strengthening individual chapters and helping to manage the overall product. We also want to thank our TEACCH colleagues for their most thoughtful and stimulating ideas on social behavior and autism.

Most important, this book, as well as all our efforts in the TEACCH Program, could not have materialized without the assistance of the families of autistic people in North Carolina, the state legislature, and the support of the Department of Psychiatry of the University of North Carolina School of Medicine at Chapel Hill. These families continue to impress upon us the difficulty of their plight and the heroism of their struggle. We in North Carolina are indeed fortunate to live in a state where the legislative and university structures have been committed to the study and amelioration of this complex handicap.

E.S.
G.B.M.

Contents

Chapter 1

INTRODUCTION TO SOCIAL BEHAVIOR IN AUTISM 1

Eric Schopler and Gary B. Mesibov

Overview 1
Historical Perspective 2
Overview of the Book 6
Summary 10
References 10

Part I: Overview of Issues in Social Development

Chapter 2

SOCIAL DEVELOPMENT: RECENT THEORETICAL TRENDS AND RELEVANCE FOR AUTISM 15

Robert B. Cairns

Current Trends in Developmental Theory 16
Relevance for Autism 25
Concluding Comment 29
References 30

Chapter 3

THE DEVELOPMENT OF SOCIAL SKILLS IN CHILDREN 35

Wendy L. Stone and Annette M. La Greca

Introduction 35
Social Behavior and Play 37

Communication Skills 47
Summary and Conclusions 54
References 56

Chapter 4

CHILDREN'S FRIENDSHIPS 61

Willard W. Hartup and Michael F. Sancilio

What Are Friendships? 61
Why Are Friends Important? 63
Individual Differences 65
Friendship Variations 69
Conclusion 76
References 77

Chapter 5

SOCIAL GROWTH IN AUTISM: A PARENT'S PERSPECTIVE 81

Clara Claiborne Park

Early Years 82
Social Development and Speech 84
Modifying Behavior a Click at a Time 86
Points and Motivation 87
"Is This Praise?" 88
A Full School Day at Last 89
Reaching for Adulthood 90
Learning about Emotions 90
Finding the Right Word 91
Toward Social Sensitivity 92
Toward Consciousness of Self and Other 93
Social Behavior and Speech 95
Where is Jessy Now? 96
Looking Ahead 97
References 98

Part II: Social Problems of Autistic People

Chapter 6

AN OVERVIEW OF SOCIAL BEHAVIOR IN AUTISM 103

Patricia Howlin

Definitions of Social Skills in Children 103
The Assessment of Social Behavior 104
The Assessment of Children with Learning Handicaps 107
The Nature of the Social Deficit in Autism 108
Approaches to the Assessment of the Social Handicap in Autism 110
Early Development 110
Studies of Older Children 117
Implications for Treatment 123
Summary 125
References 126

Chapter 7

COMMUNICATION AS A SOCIAL PROBLEM IN AUTISM 133

Deborah G. Garfin and Catherine Lord

Relationship between Communication and Social Relations 134
What Children Communicate About 135
Comprehension 136
Production 142
Summary and Conclusions 148
References 149

Chapter 8

COGNITIVE IMPAIRMENTS AFFECTING SOCIAL BEHAVIOR IN AUTISM 153

Amitta Shah and Lorna Wing

General Cognitive Ability and Social Behavior 154
Specific Social Impairments 158
Specific Cognitive Impairments 161
Speculations 166
References 167

Chapter 9

COMPLIANCE, NONCOMPLIANCE, AND NEGATIVISM 171

Fred R. Volkmar

Issues in the Definition of Compliance, Noncompliance, and "Negativism" 171
Perspectives from Child Development Research 173
Clinical Issues 175
Research Studies 178
Intervention Strategies 182
Summary 184
References 185

Part III: Major Issues and Theoretical Perspectives

Chapter 10

MAINSTREAMING HANDICAPPED CHILDREN IN PUBLIC SCHOOL SETTINGS: CHALLENGES AND LIMITATIONS 191

Susan M. McHale and Wendy C. Gamble

The Foundations of Mainstreamed School Programs 191
Mainstream School Programs 192
The Efficacy of Mainstream School Programs: Problems and Successes 193
Strategies to Enhance the Effectiveness of Mainstream Programs 205
Conclusions 207
References 208

Chapter 11

BEHAVIORAL APPROACHES TO SOCIAL SKILL DEVELOPMENT IN AUTISM: STRENGTHS, MISAPPLICATIONS, AND ALTERNATIVES 213

Anne M. Donnellan and Beverly A. Kilman

The Curriculum Development Triad 216
Contributions of Behavioral, Functional, and Developmental Approaches 216

Problems with Ignoring Behavioral, Functional, or Developmental Approaches 217
Integration of Approaches 218
An Integrated Social Skills Curriculum 219
Behavioral Approaches—Strengths 219
Behavioral Approaches—Misapplications 221
Developmental, Functional, and Behavioral Considerations in Developing Social Skills Curricula 224
Conclusion 231
References 231

Chapter 12

A DEVELOPMENTAL MODEL FOR FACILITATING THE SOCIAL BEHAVIOR OF AUTISTIC CHILDREN 237

Geraldine Dawson and Larry Galpert

Introduction 237
Early Social Development in Normal Infants 239
Social Deficits of Autistic Children 244
Implications of Early Social Deficits for Development 247
A Developmental Approach to intervention 249
Illustration of a Developmental Intervention 251
Limitations of a Developmental Approach 253
References 256

Part IV: Programs for Developing Social Behaviors in Autism

Chapter 13

A COGNITIVE PROGRAM FOR TEACHING SOCIAL BEHAVIORS TO VERBAL AUTISTIC ADOLESCENTS AND ADULTS 265

Gary B. Mesibov

Introduction 265
Targeted Deficits 266
Program 272
Other Aspects 277

Summary and Future Directions 279
References 280

Chapter 14

A MODEL FOR MAINSTREAMING AUTISTIC CHILDREN: THE JOWONIO SCHOOL PROGRAM 285

Peter Knoblock and Robert Lehr

Jowonio School Design 285
Emphasizing Diversity 287
Individualizing Instruction 291
A Social Systems Perspective 295
An Empirical Approach 298
Summary 301
References 302

Chapter 15

SOCIAL SKILLS TRAINING FOR ELEMENTARY SCHOOL AUTISTIC CHILDREN WITH NORMAL PEERS 305

Marian Wooten and Gary B. Mesibov

Introduction 305
Setting 306
Concepts 307
Initial Stages of the Play Group 308
Current Play Groups 309
Objectives 309
Teacher and Pupil Preparation 310
Play Group Structure 312
Activities 313
General Play Group Rules 316
Follow-Up 317
Additional Benefits 318
Conclusions 318
References 319

Chapter 16

A GUIDE FOR DEVELOPING SOCIAL AND LEISURE PROGRAMS FOR STUDENTS WITH AUTISM 321

Joyce Henning and Nancy Dalrymple

Overview 321
Teaching Self-Care and Academic Skills 324
Teaching Interpersonal Skills 325
Teaching Social Communication Skills 328
Teaching Leisure Skills 330
Teaching Community Skills 333
Summary 336
Examples 337
References 349

Chapter 17

THE TEACCH CURRICULUM FOR TEACHING SOCIAL BEHAVIOR TO CHILDREN WITH AUTISM 351

J. Gregory Olley

Social Skills Curricula and Autism 353
Development of the TEACCH Curriculum 353
Assessment of Social Skills 356
Involving Parents 365
Setting Priorities 365
Designing Activities 367
Example 368
Conclusion 370
References 371

INDEX 375

1

Introduction to Social Behavior in Autism

ERIC SCHOPLER and GARY B. MESIBOV

OVERVIEW

Although the incidence of autism as compared with similar disabilities is relatively low, it has received a disproportionately large amount of attention from clinicians and researchers. This is in part because of the severity of the disability and its potentially devastating effects and human suffering. However, the desire to reduce costs and alleviate human pain do not totally account for the interest that the autism syndrome has generated. There is also a fascination with these youngsters and a desire to know more about their puzzling disorder.

Of all the autism symptoms none has attracted more interest and fascination than the peculiarities of social and interpersonal relationships. In fact, the term *autism* itself reflects the centrality of this concept and its prominence in the eyes of the first person to name the syndrome (Kanner, 1943). Given the importance of these social problems, it is ironic that they still represent the least understood and studied of the various aspects of autism (Rutter & Schopler, 1978; Schopler & Mesibov, 1983). This is no doubt because the subtleties and complex variables constituting social relationships are difficult to study in all types of children, not only those with autism. Research in biomedical areas, characteristics, communicative functions, and education is more voluminous because these areas seem more amenable to direct empirical investigations. Nevertheless, the social

ERIC SCHOPLER and GARY B. MESIBOV • Division TEACCH, University of North Carolina, Chapel Hill, North Carolina, 27514.

problems of these youngsters persist and become more compelling as the children identified in early childhood grow into adolescence and adulthood, and programs for handicapped children begin to emphasize community interactions.

The purpose of this book is to help fill this most important gap in the literature on autism. The social problems and skills of autistic youngsters and adults will be addressed by identifying relevant issues from studies of normal development, social problems in autism, and remediation efforts with this population. In this chapter, we will begin with a historical perspective, followed by an analysis of the major trends also reflected in this book.

HISTORICAL PERSPECTIVE

As most students of autism well know, the syndrome was first identified by Leo Kanner's (1943) description of 11 case studies. However, many people do not fully appreciate the authenticity of his descriptions and the extraordinary depth of his understanding, given that he was writing over 40 years ago about a group of youngsters that had never before been recognized as a distinct population. Kanner immediately realized the importance and pervasiveness of their interpersonal deficits: "There is from the start an *extreme autistic aloneness* that, whenever possible, disregards, ignores, shuts out anything that comes to the child from the outside. Direct physical contact or such motion or noise as threatens to disrupt the aloneness is either treated 'as if it weren't there' or, if this is no longer sufficient, resented painfully as distressing interference" (p. 33). Kanner noted that this extreme social isolation was present at birth, and he attributed this deficit more to biological than to emotional factors: "The children's aloneness from the beginning of life makes it difficult to attribute the whole picture exclusively to the type of the early parental relations with our patients. We must, then, assume that these children have come into the world with innate inability to form the usual, biologically provided affective contact with people, just as other children come into the world with innate physical or intellectual handicaps" (pp. 42–43).

In his seminal work, Kanner further analyzed and described these social difficulties. He noted that autistic children could interact with objects so that this deficit primarily involved interpersonal relationships. Kanner described these children as more interested in pictures than in the people they represented as one example of the uniquely problematic aspect of interpersonal relationships. He later described their appropriate and effective relationships to objects, "our children are able to establish and maintain an excellent, purposeful, and 'intelligent' relation to objects that do not threaten to interfere with their aloneness, but are from the start anxiously and tensely impervious to people, with whom for a long time they do not have any kind of direct affective contact" (Kanner, 1943, p. 41).

Although these children relate effectively to objects rather than people, the problem was not simply, according to Kanner, their lack of awareness. He described these children as aware of others, but choosing to restrict their interactions. If intruded upon by another person, they would form a temporary relationship, but a detached one with only part of the person (e.g., hand, foot) rather than with the whole person.

In describing differences between autism and schizophrenia, Kanner described autistic children as extremely aloof from the beginning of life, as compared with the schizophrenic children whose first observable manifestations were preceded by at least 2 years of average development followed by very gradual changes.

Another important observation of Kanner's (1943) was to note the beginnings of social developmental patterns and their changes, as his children grew older. Although they continued to desire aloneness and sameness, an increasing emergence from solitude was observed as well as an acceptance of at least some people. "While the schizophrenic tries to solve his problem by stepping out of the world of which he has been a part and with which he has been in touch, our children gradually *compromise* by extending cautious feelers into a world in which they have been total strangers from the beginning" (pp. 41–42).

Kanner and his colleagues followed up their original sample approximately 30 years later (Kanner, 1971; Kanner, Rodriguez, & Ashenden, 1972) and corroborated their initial impression that sociability increased as autistic children grow older. However, their original clients remained extremely aloof and continued to experience significant difficulties in interpersonal relationships. The follow-up studies also revealed that the autistic people with the best outcomes were those most aware of their differences from nonhandicapped peers and desirous of changing to more appropriate patterns of behavior.

With the exception of Kanner's ongoing research, there was little progress in the understanding of social behavior and autism for several decades. The 1950s and 1960s were dominated by psychoanalytic theorists, arguing that autism represented a schizophrenic withdrawal from reality. Therapeutic efforts focused on either separating parents and children, providing free outlets for emotional expression, or demonstrating that the inappropriate behaviors of autistic children were purposefully oppositional and negative. Given our current understanding of autism, it is not surprising that most of these approaches were not productive.

Bettelheim (1967) was one of the major psychoanalytic theorists advocating for the removal of autistic children from their families. Arguing that cold and rejecting parents were the main cause of autism in their children, he advocated for the development of residential programs. According to Bettelheim these were essential because autistic children must be removed from unconscious parental hostility in order to undo the autistic processes and establish more appropriate behaviors.

The emphasis in the 1950s and 1960s on psychoanalytic theory also resulted in numerous open-ended therapeutic approaches. Play therapy and unstructured groups (Speers & Lansing, 1965) became a common therapeutic intervention for the children accompanied by individual psychotherapy for the parents. Most of the unstructured therapeutic interventions following these psychodynamic formulations resulted in less rather than more appropriate behaviors on the part of the children (Schopler, Brehm, Kinsbourne, & Reichler, 1971). Although many still advocate such intervention techniques, the overwhelming evidence indicates that autism is a neurological rather than a psychogenic disability, and that unstructured, play therapy approaches are quite inappropriate (American Psychiatric Association, 1980; DeMyer, 1979; Rimland, 1964; Rutter & Schopler, 1978).

Motivational theories were also common during these decades. Although he is not a psychoanalytic theorist, Cowan's work (Cowan, Hoddinott, & Wright, 1965) illustrates this area of inquiry. Cowan attempted to identify autistic children who were unwilling, rather than unable, to emit correct responses. In his studies an experimenter modeled appropriate behavior by selecting certain objects of a particular color and placing them in a box. The experimenter rewarded herself with popcorn for enacting this behavior. During the first part of the study, children were then rewarded for placing any objects in the box, regardless of whether they were the ones requested. The results showed that two subjects had perfect scores, responding correctly on each trial. The other ten achieved scores that were significantly lower than would be expected even by chance. Cowan postulated that the children were able to differentiate because their scores were even lower than what would be predicted by chance, and hence they must have been responding incorrectly on purpose. Unfortunately, the data did not accurately reflect this interpretation and in fact ignored the difficulty that autistic children have in relatively unstructured imitative tasks.

From a theoretical perspective some of the behaviorists were not too different from the psychogeneticists. Rather than blaming unconscious parental motives, some of them blamed the children's autism on the inappropriate reinforcement history provided by parents (Ferster, 1961). Nevertheless, behavior modification began to replace the more psychodynamic interpretations (Lovaas, Schaeffer, & Simmons, 1965). These approaches became popular quite rapidly because the behavioral changes they produced were more dramatically effective than results reported by the psychodynamic theorists. However, despite the rapid advances resulting from these operant approaches, research on social behaviors and relationships were not affected to any significant degrees during the 1960s.

The early 1970s ushered in extensive new research on social behaviors in autism. In addition to the already mentioned follow-up studies by the Kanner group, Rutter's (1970) outcome data on his older clients suggested similar positive changes in social development. Rutter's (1970) data focused on the 64 children seen at the Maudsley Hospital. Socially, approximately one-third of this group was judged as showing a fair to good adjustment at follow-up, although only 1 of the 64 was judged as relatively normal and independent. Most of those with fair to good adjustments were able to function relatively independently, but their relationships with others were superficial and sporadic. No one in the group was married and only very few had heterosexual friendships. Similar to subjects in the Kanner follow-up, those who had made the most progress showed an increased interest in others and a desire to have friends, although they lacked the necessary social skills. One of the major clinical implications of both the Kanner and Rutter follow-up studies was that autistic children showed an increased interest and awareness of others during adolescence. Their problem became increasingly a lack of social skills rather than a lack of social interest. These studies also contributed to the recognition that the social problems of autistic persons could not readily be separated from their cognitive and their communication handicaps. Although these handicaps appear hopelessly intertwined from a clinical perspective, they can, fortunately, be separated conceptually. Hence, we have published separate volumes on communication (Schopler & Mesibov, 1985) and social issues.

Following the publication of the outcome studies in the early 1970s there has been an increasing interest in older autistic people and especially their social and interpersonal adjustments (Mesibov, 1983; Schopler & Mesibov, 1983; Wing, 1983). These publications have further verified what Rutter and Kanner described about autistic people's increasing interest in social interactions with age, and also their remaining social deficits.

The 1970s and 1980s have also brought two other new developments that have had continuing impact. First was Wing's (1983) classification of subgroups based on the child's social problems. Her three groups were designated as aloof, passive, and active but odd. The aloof group of autistic individuals were described as cut off from others. Although they can learn to tolerate the presence of other people, most of them continue to want and need to be by themselves at frequent intervals. This social aloofness was associated with severe impairments of verbal and nonverbal communication. Behavioral disturbances such as aggression, destructiveness, and self-injury were particularly common in this group.

Wing's passive group was defined as the easiest to manage and integrate into social units. Most of them are able to imitate to some extent, although they lack understanding of social contacts and meanings. In general, this group showed a willingness to participate in group activities and they generally tended to have higher skills than those described as aloof.

Wing's third, and potentially most difficult, group comprised those described as active but odd. Those in this group demand social attention because of their lengthy monologues and repetitive questioning. People find interacting with this group rather unpleasant because they feel compelled to reply but soon learn that the more they respond, the more the initial demands are repeated. At this point, the implications of the Wing classification system are not altogether clear. However, her system is widely known and could have an impact on future diagnostic classifications in psychiatry.

The other major new development is the suggestion that social deficits could be the primary difficulties in autism (Fein, Waterhouse, Lucci, & Snyder, 1985; Rutter, 1983). Lord (1985) has elaborated on this notion, suggesting that comprehension deficits in autistic people result from their inability to understand social meanings and to abstract general rules. Further support comes from the research recently reviewed by Hermelin and O'Connor (1985).

This new emphasis on the centrality of social problems in autism makes this volume especially timely and important. Some basic research supports this notion, and its major theoretical implications will be described and reviewed. The book has been organized to present the current state of the art as comprehensively as possible.

OVERVIEW OF THE BOOK

This volume includes four major sections designed to provide the comprehensive coverage needed to accomplish the goals of this book. Part I presents an overview of the major issues. This section includes chapters on normal development that have important implications for working with autistic children. We endorse the increasing awareness that a thorough understanding of normal developmental processes is of basic importance to the understanding of developmental difficulties such as autism. Hence, the chapter by Cairns offers a lucid review of some major developmental theories. He reminds us of the limits such theoretical formulations have had for the study of developmental pathology. In so doing, he points the way to closer relevance between developmental theory and clinical application.

Friendship for autistic people presents formidable barriers that can be better understood from the study of normal friendship patterns of development. Hartup and Sancilio present an admirable review of research in this area defining friendship as reciprocity and commitment within a relationship among equals. They proceed to describe how friends accept and support one another, have fun together, confide, share, trust, and understand. They also explain why these are important for the emergence and development of certain competencies such as cooperation, impulse control, and self-knowledge. Important correlations between friendship and personal adaptation are described along with a discussion of variations in friendship patterns. The latter might be especially important for those working with autistic clients because many of their interpersonal relationships will differ significantly from normal patterns.

Stone and La Greca present an analysis of social skill development in normal children and the implications for autism. They identify social play and communication as especially significant. Because play is so critical for peer interaction and represents an important deficit in autism, it is an important area for intervention efforts. Stone and La Greca describe ways of analyzing play skills developmentally and offer some concrete suggestions, such as teaching physical proximity as an important first step. They also trace the normal development of social communication. Because this is another important deficit in autism, it is important to understand its implications for social relationships. They demonstrate how communication skills are important for signaling intention, conveying messages, and regulating turn-taking behavior. They show that these become problematic areas with autistic children, even in those who do develop language.

Despite the important limitations of autistic children, Stone and La Greca provide some specific useful suggestions. They show that if we understand the lack of developmental processes in autistic children, we can develop alternative methods for communicating and receiving messages, taking turns, and providing information.

Clara Park concludes Part I with astute and perceptive insights from her own experience. Throughout her chapter, Park nicely combines the continuity of her daughter Jessy's development with normal young adults while also pointing out significant discrepancies. She provides sharply observed anecdotes demonstrating how abstract and slippery social concepts can be, and how these create obstacles for autistic people. Some of her informative examples of how the social context determines appropriate behaviors and how difficult these are to identify include the following: Is one insulted when you scream? Does screaming hurt people's feelings? Is stealing a napkin really stealing? Is it the same as stealing money? These living examples lend a third dimension to the scholarly descriptions of autism characteristics and greatly facilitate the reader's understanding.

Part II is a review of social problems of autism. Howlin's chapter offers a comprehensive outline of assessment issues in social behavior such as sociometric techniques, behavioral techniques, and analogue tasks. She then describes how such techniques have been used to study social play and interaction. She discusses the implications of this work for autistic people, emphasizing the importance of reciprocity and flexibility. In emphasizing the interactive nature of social relationships, Howlin's chapter points to an important new area of research. Her concluding observation is one that researchers in this area should carefully consider. "From these studies it is clear that, although the frequency of many of the social behaviors shown by autistic children is not necessarily low, there are marked problems in the organization of these behaviors. In particular, the two qualities that appear to be essential for successful peer relations are lacking. These are the ability to relate in a positive and reciprocal way with peers and the ability to adapt interpersonal skills to the ever-changing demands of the social situation."

Garfin and Lord's chapter describes the relationships between communication and social deficits in autistic people. As these are the two major defining features of autism, this chapter is especially critical for tracing the interaction of these deficits and their effects. Reciprocity is stressed by these authors, as is the concept of social motivation. Students of this area will be especially interested in their discussion of comprehension, a very important deficit in autistic people that is not usually discussed because of its complexity and the difficulties in assessing and understanding this pervasive deficit.

Lorna Wing is one of the pioneer investigators and most astute clinical observers of social problems in autism. Shah and Wing examine important connections between cognitive and social deficits. In their chapter they identify the problem as a failure to use the physical mechanisms of gesture, facial expressions, and speech in social interactions, rather than the absence of these. They also describe the lack of neurological organization in these youngsters, essential for the development of normal social skills. "Thus, many of the more subtle social and communication skills in which autistic children show abnormalities appear to be well established in normal infants at a very early stage in life, and are very possibly innate. Early theories suggesting that the social interaction problems in autism are due to the child's conscious and deliberate emotional withdrawal now seem most likely to be incorrect. A more acceptable explanation is that autistic children lack the neurological organization necessary for the development of normal social skills."

Volkmar's chapter on compliance is a most important contribution to this volume. Given the historical image of the autistic child as intentionally noncompliant (Cowan *et al.*, 1965) and the persistence of this interpretation, Volkmar's explanation is especially timely. His ability to explain these behaviors and reinterpret the problem as lack of understanding and conceptual ability has profound clinical implications for those working with these youngsters. This chapter and its interpretation of noncompliant behavior is long overdue.

Part III addresses the major issues and theoretical perspectives that are dominant in the field of social behavior and autism. Mainstreaming is an important concept that many people blindly apply to all handicapped children in all situations. However, McHale and Gamble critically evaluate this concept, concluding that the literature is far from clear in its overwhelming endorsement of totally mainstreamed programs for all autistic children. In fact, they point out that if not carefully understood and structured, many mainstreaming efforts can be more harmful than beneficial to the autistic children involved.

As with other aspects of learning in autistic children, behavioral approaches have been the most widely used in teaching autistic children. Anne Donnellan and Beverly Kilman describe the strengths and limitations of these approaches. Kilman's social training program in San Diego is used as a case example to demonstrate the application of these principles.

Chapter 12 by Dawson and Galpert expertly describes a developmental model for facilitating social behavior in autistic children. Although this perspective has more recently been applied to social behavior than has the behavioral approach, many chapters in this book outline its importance and potential impact. They discuss the implications for research and clinical interventions, and their work promises to be an important model for researchers and clinicians in the years ahead. Moreover, in the long run, developmental models are likely to have more important implications for understanding autism than the behavioral approaches that have dominated the field today.

One of the organizing principles in our compilation of these volumes is our assumption that research derives its primary significance from its application to clinical practice. Therefore, our final section is devoted to clinical programs that use many of the important research findings of the first three sections. Mesibov describes his social cognitive model and how he has translated this into an ongoing social skills training program. He describes how social deficits in a group of high-level, verbal autistic adolescents and adults can be remedied. His model has been followed by leading clinicians and researchers around the country and promises to be of interest to those working directly with verbal autistic youngsters.

Knoblock and Lehr discuss one of the oldest and most intensively studied programs for mainstreaming autistic youngsters, Jowonio School. Readers will learn about the program's guiding philosophy, management, and problem-solving processes. Those who think that mainstreaming simply involves putting handicapped and nonhandicapped children together will learn that a successful program requires considerably more effort than that. The chapter by Wooten and Mesibov again makes this important point, this time with a classroom program in a public school. Their understanding of the issues involved in mainstreaming autistic children, attention to detail, and ability to deal with the nonhandicapped students and teachers are indeed impressive and again show that mainstreaming can be effective but requires considerable skill, knowledge, and effort.

The final chapters by Henning and Dalrymple and Olley demonstrate how research on social behavior can be translated into classroom curricula. These efforts address a wide variety of needs and will be adaptable to most populations of autistic children. These chapters should be especially valuable for teachers wanting assistance in developing specific social skills training programs for their classrooms.

SUMMARY

Because of the interest investigators have shown in the social behavior problems of autistic people and the centrality of these deficits, it is surprising that so little has been written about this important problem. However, the complexity of social interactions and the subtleties of these deficits have made this a difficult area to study. In this volume leading researchers and clinicians discuss general issues in social development, problems confronting autistic youngsters and adults, major theoretical perspectives, and programs that are developing from this knowledge base. This work is timely and projects useful guidelines for the study and remediation of this most important problem during the next decade.

REFERENCES

American Psychiatric Association. (1980). *Diagnostic and statistical manual* (3rd ed.). Washington, DC: Author.

Bettelheim, B. (1967). *The empty fortress.* New York: Free Press.

Cowan, P. A., Hoddinott, B. A., & Wright, B. A. (1965). Compliance and resistance in the conditioning of autistic children: An exploratory study. *Child Development, 36,* 913–923.

DeMyer, M. K. (1979). *Parents and children in autism.* Washington, DC: Winston.

Fein, D., Waterhouse, L., Lucci, D., & Snyder, D. (1985). Cognitive subtypes in developmentally disabled children: A pilot study. *Journal of Autism and Developmental Disorders, 15,* 77–95.

Ferster, C. B. (1961). Positive reinforcement and behavioral deficits of autistic children. *Child Development, 32,* 437–456.

Hermelin, B., & O'Connor, N. (1985). Inner language and nonverbal communication in autism. In E. Schopler & G. B. Mesibov (Eds.), *Communication problems in autism.* New York: Plenum Press.

Kanner, L. (1943). Autistic disturbance of affective contact. *Nervous Child, 2,* 217–250.

Kanner, L. (1971). Follow-up study of eleven children originally reported in 1943. *Journal of Autism and Childhood Schizophrenia, 1,* 119–145.

Kanner, L., Rodriguez, A., & Ashenden, B. (1972). How far can autistic children go in matters of social adaptation? *Journal of Autism and Childhood Schizophrenia, 2,* 9–33.

Lord, C. (1985). The comprehension of language and autism. In E. Schopler & G. B. Mesibov (Eds.), *Communication problems in autism.* New York: Plenum Press.

Lovaas, O. I., Schaeffer, B., & Simmons, J. Q. (1965). Experimental studies in childhood schizophrenia: Building social behavior in autistic children by use of electric shock. *Journal of Experimental Research in Personality, 1,* 99–109.

Mesibov, G. B. (1983). Current perspectives and issues in autism and adolescence. In E. Schopler & G. B. Mesibov (Eds.), *Autism in adolescents and adults* (pp. 37–53). New York: Plenum Press.

Rimland, B. (1964). *Infantile autism*. New York: Appleton-Century-Crofts.

Rutter, M. (1970). Autistic children: Infancy to adulthood. *Seminars in Psychiatry, 2,* 435–450.

Rutter, M. (1983). Cognitive deficits in the pathogenesis of autism. *Journal of Child Psychology and Psychiatry, 24,* 513–531.

Rutter, M., & Schopler, E. (Eds.). (1978). *Autism: A reappraisal of concepts and treatment*. New York: Plenum Press.

Schopler, E., & Mesibov, G. B. (Eds.). (1983). *Autism in adolescents and adults*. New York: Plenum Press.

Schopler, E., & Mesibov, G. B. (Eds.). (1985). *Communication problems in autism*. New York: Plenum Press.

Speers, R. W., & Lansing, C. (1965). *Group therapy in childhood psychosis*. Chapel Hill, NC: University of North Carolina Press.

Wing, L. (1983). Social and interpersonal needs. In E. Schopler & G. B. Mesibov (Eds.), *Autism in adolescents and adults* (pp. 337–354). New York: Plenum Press.

I

Overview of Issues in Social Development

2

Social Development

Recent Theoretical Trends and Relevance for Autism

ROBERT B. CAIRNS

A reexamination of the social development of autistic children and adolescents from the perspective of general developmental theory potentially can yield benefits for both practice and theory. On the one hand, it may identify areas for innovation in treatment and education if one keeps an openness to fresh options. On the other hand, it can cast into relief shortcomings of theory that are subtle or overlooked if one is limited to normal social development. An informed approach to the matter calls for a critical appreciation of both the promise for the future and the pitfalls of the past.

The record indicates there have been plenty of pitfalls in the brief history of autism. General models of behavioral development can claim only mixed success in the initial efforts to identify the causes and effective treatment. The psychoanalytic emphasis on parental personality as the primary causal factor—that emotionally cold, rejecting, intellectual, and compulsive adults produce autistic children—has been hard to put away, despite compelling negative evidence (e.g., Cantwell, Baker, & Rutter, 1978; McAdoo & DeMyer, 1978). Similarly, the social learning view that the developmental course of autism may be sharply modified or reversed by the brief application of behavior modification techniques can be challenged. Rapid short-term therapeutic gains may be demonstrated, but serious problems have been encountered in maintaining and generalizing the effects (e.g., Hingtgen & Bryson, 1972; Lord & O'Neill, 1983). Nor have provocative and cogent ethological theories of the autistic process

ROBERT B. CAIRNS • Department of Psychology, University of North Carolina, Chapel Hill, North Carolina 27514.

(e.g., Tinbergen, 1974; Tinbergen & Tinbergen, 1972) solved the problem of etiology.

Nonetheless, remarkable progress on understanding the disorder and modifying its course has been made over the past 15 years (see Rutter & Schopler, 1978; Schopler & Mesibov, 1983). The advances have been both positive (in demonstrating which treatment approaches are likely to work, and why) and negative (in demonstrating which theories of etiology have slight merit, or none at all). While much of the progress can be traced to the outcomes of clinical research and its cogent analysis, the work cannot be dissociated from general theoretical considerations and the methodologies they support. For example, the ethological study of autistic children has clearly advanced our understanding of the behavioral processes involved in autism (e.g., Hutt & Hutt, 1970). In addition, the systematic application of modeling and reinforcement procedures has provided directions for the short-term modification of some aspects of autistic behavior (e.g., Dawson & Galpert, Chapter 12, this volume). And the studies of families with autistic children have provided critical information about the impact that autistic children have upon their parents and siblings, despite the original focus on parent→child effects.

This chapter on contemporary views of social development is divided into two parts. The first part summarizes seven constructs which have become central to social development theory over the past decade and which may be of some importance in understanding disorders of childhood and adolescence (cf. Cairns, 1979; Hetherington, 1983; Maccoby, 1980; Youniss, 1980). This section comes first because it may help organize some of the themes common to the chapters in this volume. The second part of the chapter has a different, more speculative aim. Because of the absence of a firm bridge between recent theoretical statements of normal social development and the problems of atypical development, some comments are offered on the theoretical constructs and the problems of autism defined in this volume and related works in this series (e.g., Rutter & Schopler, 1978; Schopler & Mesibov, 1983).

CURRENT TRENDS IN DEVELOPMENTAL THEORY

Contemporary developmental investigators are not, for the most part, a doctrinaire lot. They are willing to sample ideas from any orientation if they seem to provide insights that are relevant to the task. So what might be loosely called the modern developmental theory is a mixed bag of ideas, centered around themes that have been lifted from five different orientations (see A. Baldwin, 1980; Cairns, 1979). It is an untidy synthesis, but it has advantages over more rigorous treatment in terms of apparent applicability and flexibility. For instance, most contemporary investigators share both an interest in the issues of attachment theory, on the one hand, and the organizational aspects of developmental psychobiology, on the other. Similarly, life-cycle and life-span developmental approaches provide a framework for integrating the macrosocial issues of a sociological perspective with those of individual human development (Baltes & Brim, 1983; Bronfenbrenner, 1979; Elder, 1975).

What have been accepted as "new trends" in the field are ideas that have been lifted from one or more of the above orientations and juxtaposed to the common core, often in a patchwork fashion. There are certain advantages in this selection procedure because the most attractive proposals of the most prominent theories can be wedded into a single orientation. There are also dangers. One of the primary problems is that the logical coherence of the synthesis is typically assigned a lesser priority than its apparent flexibility. Given enough concepts, any phonemenon can be "explained." The hazard is a real one for developmental analyses because substantive progress in the area requires precision in empirical prediction, not illusions of explanatory breadth.

The strategy I will adopt in describing the theoretical trends relevant to autistic disorders will be to organize them within the framework provided by developmental psychobiology. Despite an immediate cost in being constrained to a single framework, there should be some gains in preserving the coherence of the concepts and in providing guides for their empirical validation. Its suitability for the present integration task follows on two counts, one general and one specific. The general one concerns the explicit commitment of the theory to understanding behavior from an ontogenetic, holistic perspective (Kuo, 1967; Schneirla, 1966), including the proposal that cognitive, emotional, and social accommodations are inextricably related. The second count follows from what has been learned about the biological contributors to some aspects of autism. The emerging consensus on the etiology of autism has implicated various psychobiological contributors—genetic (Folstein & Rutter, 1978), biochemical (Ritvo, Rabin, Yuwiler, Freeman, & Geller, 1978), and neurological (DeLong, 1978). There is, however, only modest information on precisely how the various biological correlates may mediate autistic outcomes.

As it turns out, many of the ideas of developmental psychobiology are familar to contemporary investigators by virtue of their having been incorporated piecemeal into the "common core" of developmental theory.* Seven interlocked

*The original statements by Kuo (1967) and Schneirla (1966) should be read as basic introductions to the orientation. See Gottlieb (1976, 1983), Levine (1982), Sameroff (1983), and Cairns (1979) for a general overview of psychobiology from four different but compatible perspectives. Gottlieb (1983) focuses on perinatal development, Levine (1982) emphasizes hormonal–behavioral interactions, Sameroff (1983) addresses its relation to learning and systems theory, and Cairns (1979) extends the orientation to social development in human beings.

psychobiological concepts capture much of what is "new" in recent social development theory. These are (1) social reciprocity, (2) structure-function bidirectionality, (3) embeddedness of social patterns, (4) developmental plasticity of interchanges, (5) developmental integration and heterochronies, (6) ontogenetic functionalism, and (7) concepts of the self and reality.

Social Synchrony and Social Reciprocity

Social reciprocity occurs when the acts of two or more persons support each other in a relationship and their actions become similar to each other (Cairns, 1979). This kernel concept of social interchange is one of two primary types of social synchrony (i.e., where one person's actions are coordinated with and supportive of the actions of other persons). But not all reciprocal relationships are happy ones, a point that Patterson (1982) has made in his analysis of coercive families. In some of the more distressful relationships of life, aggression begets aggression, and negative interactional patterns may escalate into disastrous ones.

Within a developmental psychobiological framework, primitive social reciprocities are presumed to become established because of basic biobehavioral synchronies in the neonatal period. There is thus an interpersonal bias in behavioral responding from the very beginning of the neonatal period. In normal development, the social acts of others have been seen as playing a role in behavioral organization because they are (a) readily enmeshed with the ongoing behaviors of the child and (b) more compelling (i.e., salient, intrusive) than are nonsocial events (Bowlby, 1958; Cairns, 1966, 1972, 1979). The latter criterion presupposes the synchronous development of normal sensory capacities and attentional processes in the infant and the adult. Failures in sensory-attentional development at this early stage should be reflected in anomolies in social responding and its by-products (e.g, social reciprocity, social synchrony, imitation, and social attachment patterns). These behavioral "by-products" are considered to have special relevance for autism (see Dawson & Galpert, Chapter 12, this volume). As noted by Rutter (1978), deficiencies in social attachment, imitation, and reciprocation (as reflected in difficulties in such homely activities as playing "pat-a-cake") are characteristic of children diagnosed as autistic.

Structure-Function Bidirectionality

Structure-function bidirectionality refers to mutuality of relations between biology and behavior. This concept may be contrasted with biobehavioral accounts of behavior that are essentially monodirectional or reductionistic in explanation, where biological "constraints" are considered primary for learning and most everything else about behavior. Within monodirectional models, social patterns are explained in terms of biological factors, and the biological factors are further reduced to "ultimate" causes (e.g., evolutionary or population genetic events). So "violent" and "aggressive" behavior is explained in terms of genetic, hormonal, or neurological substrates (e.g., Eibl-Eibesfeldt, 1975; Lorenz, 1966). The reductionistic strategy—going downward from observed social behavior to identify genetic determinants—still describes much of what is current in behavioral biology and sociobiology (e.g., Dawkins, 1976; Wilson, 1975).

Structure-function bidirectionality looks at both sides of causation, insisting on the dual importance of biobehavior and behavioral biology. While not denying the impact of biological states on behavior, it points as well to the roles that the social behavior patterns may play in the organization of biological states. These biological states include those of the individual as well as those of other persons with whom he/she interacts. A simple example of such bidirectionality occurs in the normal mother–infant breast-feeding interaction. The suckling actions of the infant produces multiple effects, including changes in the neurohormonal states of the mother. By exteroceptive stimulation, the infant triggers further prolactin and oxytocin manufacture and thereby "designs" the maternal condition of the mother and helps keep her in that state of maternal preparedness. Such bidirectional relations are not limited to the neonatal period but continue to operate throughout the life-span. Some of the more notable instances of function-to-structure feedback patterns occur during adolescence (in sexual maturation and performance) and senescence (in maintenance or decay of cognitive functions).

Behavior patterns thus can serve to organize internal states as well as vice versa. In this regard, behavior is seen as the leading edge of adaptation, an organismic function that is highly flexible and responsive to changing internal and external conditions. For example, physically aggressive actions—directed toward the elimination of especially obnoxious social stimulation—require the recruitment of phasic hormonal and physiological states to support and maintain the action. If successful, the violence will set the stage for the performance of nonaggressive maintenance actions, and the internal organization of tonic states (Cairns, 1972; Schneirla, 1966). Perhaps the most general instances of the bidirectional organization of behavior and biology may be found in sexual reproduction and its coordination in females and males (Lehrman, 1961). More to the point, the channelization of behavioral actions into rigidly defined sequences is a characteristic of adult patients with brain damage. This behavioral stereotypy can serve multiple functions, including the gaiting of behavioral acts so as to not overload the person's reduced capabilities for information processing. On this score, the "insistence on sameness" may be functional for neurologically impaired children (Wing, 1978). A preference for stereotypy could reflect an individual's efforts to maintain an acceptable level of external stimulation.

Social Embeddedness

The concept of a "social matrix" (J. M. Baldwin, 1897) implies the embeddedness of individuals within a system of social relationships. In developmental analyses, the microsocial system may be as small as the family or as diverse as the classroom (Bronfenbrenner, 1979). To the extent that distinctive dyadic adaptations are required by a given person with other persons within such systems, the relations among all remaining members are likely to be affected. Beyond the reciprocal actions that occur within any dyadic unit, the social system itself may support rules for interaction that can serve to reinforce and maintain behavior patterns.

Given that developmental changes in members of a family system require realignments of relationships, the interactional patterns over time are necessarily dynamic and modifiable over time. But changes in individual patterns may arise from nondevelopmental sources as well. Whatever the roots of change, significant modifications in the behavior of individuals are likely to be reflected throughout the social system, and possibly to be resisted by it. The conservative bias of family systems—to maintain continuity within familial relationships and to preserve the integrity of the system itself—can create problems for any intervention plan that does not involve the family as a unit.

Developmental Plasticity of Interchanges

Within a psychobiological framework, behavior is the leading edge of biological adaptation to the environment. Accordingly, social behavior patterns constitute the features of organismic adaptation that are rapid, short-term, rapidly programmed, and relatively reversible. The universality and availability of these adaptations in ontogeny belie their complexity and importance. In this context, the several mechanisms of social learning are appropriately viewed as techniques to fine-tune behavior to specific relationships and settings. As such, they are time-bound processes. One of the mistakes of traditional views of social learning has been to saddle these short-term constructs with the burden of accounting for personality formation across the life-span (Cairns, 1979; Cairns & Cairns, 1985; Kuo, 1967).

Why should interactions be dynamic and plastic? Within a developmental framework, social change is inevitable from infancy to childhood to adolescence and adulthood. It would be maladaptive for individuals to maintain, unchanged, specific patterns of interchange in any relationship over ontogeny. What would be an appropriate reaction pattern for the 3-year-old would be grossly pathological if it persisted in the 13-year-old. Relationships demand realignment, and interactional patterns require adjustment over ontogeny. Because of such developmental reversibilities, the concept of hierarchical organization may not be as relevant for social interactions as for morphology and cognitive patterns. Over the lifetime, social patterns require elimination as well as addition. This subtractive and revisionary aspect of social development is less prominent in morphological and cognitive development.

Given the diversity of the relationships in which children become involved and the multiple roles that they fill over time, social adaptations are hardly unitary at any developmental stage. To the extent that there are severe limits on the cognitive functioning of children in development, there should be limits on interchange plasticity and transfer to new relationships. All this is to say that it is folly to assume that successful short-term training for seriously handicapped children will automatically be translated into long-term gains. On the contrary, just the opposite should be anticipated. Continued and patient support should be expected in each concrete relationship and setting in order for the changes to become consolidated in new relationships.

Developmental Integration, Heterochrony, and Developmental Delay

Developmental integration concerns the ontogenetic process by which the systems of the organism are coordinated to bring about optimal adaptation. Consider, for instance, the question of what determines the quality of children's social interchanges: their cognitive capabilities, their emotional-affective reactivity, their morphological-maturational status, or their prior learning and familial experience? Few contemporary investigators would deny that it is all of the above, including the nature of the interactions among those factors. So far, so good, except that answer begs the basic question of how these factors are integrated in the course of ontogeny. It is hardly sufficient to implicate multiple factors without taking the next, more difficult, step of attempting to indicate how they are joined to achieve particular adaptational goals.* An essential problem of social behavior ontogeny is to outline how these components are weighted differentially within persons over development.

*This was the essential insight of Binet and Henri (1895) in their criticism of the then-dominant "sensory elements" model of intelligence. Binet and Henri argued, in effect, that the key to diagnosis, prediction, and treatment lay in understanding the rules of combination, not in the assessment of component elements. A similar criticism may be offered of contemporary "elementary" studies of emotion, cognition, and social learning. Consider that one is successful in demonstrating that each of these factors, taken alone, has an effect on social behavior. Such demonstrations would constitute only the first step toward scientific understanding or social application. The major problem is to determine how the components are uniquely combined in an adaptative, functioning person.

A related issue concerns the matter of primacy. Which of the above factors is primary in the integration and sets the pace for social development? Within the framework of developmental psychobiology, cognitive and emotional and experiential factors are necessarily intertwined. Each contributes to the momentary status of the organismic system, and the system-as-a-unit provides direction for further adaptation (cf. Bertalanffy, 1933/1962). This is to not say that each contributes equally to the long-term direction of the system as a whole. On the contrary, there is ample evidence from studies of nonhuman mammals that specifiable biological factors are primary in mediating the effects of very early experience, and that variations in the social environment must be extraordinary and extreme in order to influence long-term development (e.g., Henderson, 1980). To arrive at answers about causation, the developmental investigator obviously must be concerned with which factors call the shots in serving as pacemakers for autistic disorders. But regardless of which factors are primary, the developmental concept of bidirectionality promotes attention to the interplay of cognitive, hormonal, and neurological factors in the expression of autistic features.

In the special case of developmental disabilities or delays, limits in a given domain should place limits on the rate of change and adaptation in the total organismic system (de Beer, 1958). However, the delays need not be uniform in all components. For instance, some special problems arise in autistic disorders because there are developmental heterochronies* in some aspects of cognitive growth relative to morphological maturation and emotional development. Such heterochronies—or variations from the normal course in developmental onset and timing of the key behavioral functions—can produce uncommon problems in social and sexual adaptation at puberty. The ontogenetic calendar for sexual and physical maturation may be normal while the developmental timing for advances in cognitive processing may be retarded (Adams & Sheslow, 1983). Such adolescents will not be simply "delayed" in development; rather, they

*A comment on the use of the term *heterochrony* in evolutionary biology and embryology is in order. As employed by de Beer (1958), heterochrony refers to the developmental emergence of a characteristic in the descendant species that is divergent from the timing of its emergence in the ancestral species. This usage in evolutionary biology extends back to Spencer (1881) and Haeckel (1880). Heterochronies can be of two sorts: more rapid appearance in the descendant species than the ancestral one (i.e., *acceleration*) or delayed appearance in the descendant species (i.e., *neoteny*). These concepts have figured importantly in theories on the relationship between development and evolution since Haeckel's (1880) Biogenetic Law that "ontogeny recapitulates phylogeny." De Beer (1958) and others have argued that the "law" should be stated the other way around, because neoteny or extended immaturity (as opposed to acceleration or early maturity) is the more likely route to evolutionary reorganization through variations in ontogeny. In the present context, developmental heterochrony is employed without a direct relation to its usage in evolutionary biology, borrowing from an even earlier usage in embryology to refer to the emergence of a process or characteristic at an abnormal time in individual development.

present a distinctive configuration of component cognitive and maturational processes. Within the cognitive domain, the classical hallmark of autism was the normal patterning of nonverbal functioning with the deficient development of communication functions. Although this distinctive feature is no longer considered to be critical (e.g., Rutter, 1978), the general point is that it is the combination of properties—no single or salient "deviant" characteristic—that defines the adaptive unit.*

Ontogenetic Functionalism

Social behavior has, as a first priority, the accommodation of persons to their immediate circumstances and relationships (Cairns, 1979). Accordingly, the lessons learned about interaction at one stage of ontongeny are not necessarily valid for subsequent ones, and the actions wholly adaptive in one relationship may be grossly inappropriate if they occur in another setting or relationship. On this count, *social* development differs from *language* development. In language, the rules to which the young child is exposed do not have to be significantly amended. The early lessons are clearly relevant for subsequent accommodations, and children extend and refine most aspects of linguistic communication over development. The rules for correct performance are absolute. But in social development, there are clear developmental reversals. Children must extinguish or reverse most aspects of previously acquired social interactions. The infant that becomes distressed by maternal separation or fearful of strangers could hardly persist in these behaviors in later childhood or adolescence. The acts that were once appropriate and adaptative are no longer. Ontogenetic functionalism permits both outcomes, and it thus may be contrasted with the more traditional view of ontogenetic preparation, where early social experiences are judged primarily in terms of their presumed utility for later adaptations. The difference in emphasis—on contemporary accommodations or anticipated adaptations—is a nontrivial one, for it addresses the key matter of what might be the linkages between early experiences and mature behavior. The development of social behavior patterns is not necessarily cumulative or hierarchical in nature, and it does not necessarily progress toward higher levels of perfection.

The assumption of ontogenetic function also raises the question of why any demonstrably maladaptive behaviors persist. For example, if social behaviors are supposed to be functional, then why do most autistic children adopt social

*Binet and Simon (1914) extended the "combinational" concept of intelligence to the issue of whether "retarded" pupils were simply "delayed" in development. Their answer was no. Consistent with the idea that it is the configuration that counts—as opposed to the salient deficiency—Binet and Simon (1914) argued that "retarded" students had distinctive capabilities that were qualitatively different from those of younger children of the same mental age.

patterns that seem to be grossly ill-suited for normal social exchange? The answer to this question requires attention to the matter of what the priorities are in adaptation, and the extent to which the adaptational requirements of autistic children differ from those of nonautistic persons. For instance, the interaction patterns of autistic children, while deviant from the norm, may be in keeping with cognitive resources they have available. While not optimal for the general society, the social adaptations of autistic children could preserve resources that they have for maintaining internal integration and biological balance. As in any treatment process, one should attempt to understand what services a given social pattern is performing for the individual before intervening or attempting to change it. In this regard, the stereotypy and nonreciprocity found in the social adaptations of most autistic children and adolescents could serve a basic function in minimizing environmental change. More advantageous patterns may be learned under special conditions of environmental buffering and support (see Dawson & Galpert, Chapter 12, this volume; Hutt & Hutt, 1970).

One other corollary of ontogenetic functionalism concerning the persistence of early experience should be noted. A reasonable goal in child-rearing and education is to prepare children and adolescents for adult social adaptation. However, it cannot be assumed even in normal development that the early lessons on social interactions will be preserved, or that there will be a hierarchical integration of early and later adaptative experience. On the contrary, the task of social retention, generalization, and adaptation is an ongoing process that presumably requires reinstatement and revision at each of the stages of development. This corollary has significant implications for the design and implementation of social training programs appropriate for each developmental stage.

Concepts of the Self and Reality

The concept of the self outlined by J. M. Baldwin (1897) has been rediscovered by modern developmental theory (e.g., Bandura, 1977; Lewis & Brooks-Gunn, 1978; Selman, 1980; Youniss, 1980), and one may wonder why it was lost in the first place. Clearly one's thoughts of one's competencies and expectations for future success should play a significant role in guiding both actions and interactions. Now that fresh work over the past 10 years has proceeded on the emergence of the self, the knotty theoretical and empirical issues associated with the concept have also resurfaced. A major issue has been the curious lack of relationship between most of the "self" assessments and other, objective means of assessing the social adaptation of the individual (Cairns & Cairns, 1981, 1985). Depending on the measures of "self" that are employed, the relations among the self, others' assessments of the self, and measures of behavioral reality may be negligible, modest, or robust. Further exploration of these phenomena have suggested that the concepts of the self need not be veridical in order to be functional (e.g., Cairns & Cairns, 1985; Wallwork, 1982). In ontogeny, the integration and self-organization of the individual should emerge first.

On the special matter of autism, relatively little attention has been given to the self-concepts or self-appraisals of autistic children and adolescents. Studies of self-recognition in young autistic persons show relatively few differences in comparisons with nonautistic children, but there are qualitative differences in "self-conscious" or "coy" reactions (see Dawson & Galpert, Chapter 12, this volume). But "self-recognition" seems to be a far distance from the essence of the self-concept, which must include beliefs about one's competencies, abilities, and one's identity as a human being. Nonetheless, it seems unwise to conclude that (a) such concepts do not exist in autistic children simply because they are difficult to assess, or that (b) self-concepts do not serve for autistic children adaptational functions that parallel those of normal children.

What is a self-concept good for? At this juncture, our answer must be speculative. It has been proposed that, in normal children, concepts of the self serve two general functions (Cairns & Cairns, 1985). These are (1) to enhance internal organismic balance and promote personal integration, and (2) to provide a veridical assessment of the external world, including the basis for accurate predictions about one's competencies in social relationships and physical adaptation circumstances. The former function reduces the likelihood of internal stress and dysfunction and enhances intraorganismic integration; the latter function reduces the likelihood of social embarrassment or physical harm and enhances social adaptation.

These two adaptational demands—internal integration and external adaptation—are ordinarily in a state of dynamic tension. The private thoughts that one harbors about oneself as effective and competent may be at odds with the impressions that other persons have about one's effectiveness and competencies. In autism, the discrepancies should be great, unless the autistic child has a very poor view of himself/herself. Under these conditions, it might be reasonable to expect that functions of internal integration could be given higher priority than social accommodation, and the discrepant "social" or "consensual validation" information could be shut out or discarded. What then happens in autistic children would be essentially the same as in other "normal" children, but the resultant discrepancies may seem more extreme.

RELEVANCE FOR AUTISM

Except for psychoanalytic models and behavior modification procedures, mainstream contemporary theories of social development have given only modest attention to issues of atypical development. And the one systematic theory addressed to the origins of developmental psychopathology—object relations or attachment theory (Ainsworth, 1972; Bowlby, 1969, 1973)—appears to have only peripheral relevance for understanding the roots of autistic disorders. As observed earlier (e.g., Hingtgen & Bryson, 1972; Rutter & Schopler, 1978; Schopler, 1983), it appears unlikely that autistic outcomes may be attributed to early psychogenic factors, including variations in the quality of the maternal–infant relationship. Nonetheless, information about the maternal–infant interaction and nature of social bonding (and *non*social bonding) may be useful in identifying dimensions of social responsiveness at various developmental stages. The attachment relationship need not be seen as causative in order to be useful, both in diagnosis and in planning.

The current concepts suggest profitable directions to follow in understanding the various forms of autistic disorders. In exploring these theoretical implications, it seems reasonable to employ Rutter's (1978) outline of the distinguishing criteria of autism, namely, "(1) an onset before the age of 30 months; (2) impaired social development which has a number of special characteristics and which is out of keeping with the child's intellectual level; (3) delayed and deviant language development which also has certain defined features and which is out of keeping with the child's intellectual level; and (4) 'insistence on sameness' as shown by stereotyped play patterns, abnormal preoccupations, or resistance to change" (p. 19). These diagnostic and classification criteria may be employed, as Rutter (1978) observes, without prejudgment on other major questions, including the matter of whether autism is a single disease entity or a syndrome with multiple causes, or the extent to which neurological anomalies are involved in the disorder. Although good leads have been established toward answering both questions, there is still a distance to travel before the science can claim a complete understanding of childhood autism.

Early Onset

The diagnostic criterion for autism of onset prior to 30 months strongly implicates the presence of neurological dysfunctions for certain forms of the disorder. To the extent that early social responding is in part dependent upon basic sensory and attentional capabilities, one would expect various social anomalies among children with serious neurological abnormalities. It should be noted that the formation of maternal–infant attachment patterns does not require, in most species, a very high level of cognitive/intellectual functioning. On the contrary, both comparative and cross-cultural studies underscore the robustness of the phenomenon, under a wide range of rearing and handling conditions. Mammalian species with only modest reputations for cognitive achievement form persistent, strong, and intense social attachments to their mothers prior to weaning (e.g. goats, sheep), with nonhuman primates and canines providing close competition (Cairns, 1966). Similarly, there is strong evidence for the cross-cultural universality of attachment patterns in human societies (Ainsworth, 1967; Bowlby, 1969; Kagan, 1976). This process occurs under a wide range of rearing conditions, and it is linked to bonds that occur to the father, to siblings, and to inanimate objects.

Disturbances or delays in such a fundamental process suggests basic attentional, emotional, and/or cognitive deficits. There remains some debate about the exact nature of the disturbances in the mother–child interaction (Sigman & Ungerer, 1984). Moreover, the propensity of autistic children to become attached to inanimate objects would strongly argue against the view that these children are incapable of forming some types of social attachments, in childhood or later. Viewed from the perspective of persons who deal with the child (including the parents and other caretakers), the child's relative lack of responsiveness may itself promote further distance in relationships, and an unhappy cycle of increasing disengagement. At least some of these outcomes seem avoidable, to the extent that parents can benefit from forewarning about the nature of the problem and its anticipated course.

Impaired Social Development

One of the concerns in dealing with social problems of autistic adolescents and young adults has been the developmental emergence of sexual and aggressive patterns and the problems associated with their expression (Flavell, 1983; Melone & Lettick, 1983). The social/sexual difficulties are posed by developmental heterochronies, where biological and morphological characteristics proceed in a normal developmental trajectory despite the retardation of cognitive and interactional skills. How to provide direction for appropriate and acceptable social behavior? According to the humane and reasonable practices described in Schopler and Mesibov (1983), one key is to deal with the issues in a pragmatic and concrete fashion, focusing on the day-to-day skills required for adapting to specific contexts and relationships.

More generally, it is not that autistic children and adolescents are unable to acquire some rudimentary skills of social accommodation. Rather, most autistic children differ from nonautistic ones in terms of the investment that seems necessary for acquisition of the most basic patterns of interchange, and in the plasticity of the accommodations over time and over settings (Rutter, 1978). It is not a total failure of social reciprocity but a failure in the level and spontaneity of reciprocity that normally occurs. This observation suggests that the difficulty lies not merely in performance but in the social learning processes by which these skills are acquired, generalized, and fitted to particular contexts. Accordingly, it is not sufficient to provide training in a given setting and to expect "normal" transfer to new relationships. In social skills, as in occupational ones, the educational task requires attention to the several settings of application. The modest developmental plasticity in social adaptation of autistic persons suggests, in addition, that the treatment/educational programs should be programmed for the life-course, not merely in early childhood or in adolescence.

A comment is called for on the various forms of "peer therapy" that have proved to be useful in providing at least short-term gains for autistic children (McHale, 1979). Why is the procedure successful, and what are its limits? These matters are discussed later in this volume (Hartup & Sancilio, Chapter 4). It may be noted that there seems to be scant basis for believing that the special age-developmental status of the other person is the necessary factor in heightening adaptation. Rather, the key for this form of educational therapy is probably the same as for other forms—namely, the willingness to fit one's actions, behaviors, and communications to a level that is effective and appropriate for the autistic patient. It is probably not the demographic identification (age, sex, or race) of the "other" that is the critical element so much as it is her/his social adaptational characteristics. Any successful treatment plan would seem to call for readjustments by the "other" that are fitted to the special learning needs and social plasticity limitations of the autistic child within the "zone of proximal development" (Valsiner, 1984). One possible hazard of peer therapy is that it can be transmuted on occasion into peer ridicule. Normal children under minimal supervision have remarkable capacities for both help and harm, and not all "peers" are suited for the task of therapy.

Delayed and Deviant Language Development

It is hard to imagine that social development in humans proceeds independently of language development, or vice versa. Nonetheless, theory building relevant to these two domains has progressed as if the theorists lived in different lands. And they have, as far as empirical research beyond infancy is concerned. So the covergence of the social and language dysfunctions of autism may provide fresh insight for the broader question of how these domains may be integrated theoretically. For our present purposes, it is informative that studies of language and communication needs of autistic children and adolescents emphasize the problems of ensuring that a given communication is useful (Lord & O'Neill, 1983). Intervention programs have been most successful in demonstrating that a variety of methods for teaching autistic youngsters are effective in establishing skills. However, it is less clear that these skills—once acquired—can be employed flexibly and productively by autistic adolescents to communicate something that they wish another person to know. This problem of functional flexibility is similar to the one encountered in social behavior establishment and intervention. In this regard, Lord and O'Neill (1983) comment: "Facilitating this process [of language development] requires careful consideration of with whom the adolescent is communicating and what he has to say. It is this kind of consideration that we have barely begun" (p. 75).

Insistence on Sameness

This characteristic of the autistic syndrome identified by Kanner (1943) refers to a variety of stereotyped behaviors and routines. These routines often lead to an intense attachment to inanimate objects in childhood and compulsive preoccupations with bus routes, numbers, and colors in adolescence and adulthood (Rutter, 1978). Such attachment may be viewed, in Tolman's (1932) terms, as a "behavior support" around which action patterns become rigidly organized. Loss of such an external support leads to disruption and distress, in a process not unlike that associated with the separation-distress phenomenon of normal infancy (Cairns, 1966, 1972). In the broader view, stereotyped actions may be seen as the by-product of an adaptive behavioral process. Given limited cognitive and/or integrative capabilities, autistic children may impose order on an otherwise disorderly and disorganizing social environment. And if the order cannot be achieved through stereotyped actions, Richer (1978) suggests that the autistic child may withdraw in order to minimize social stimulation. In an insightful discussion of this issue, Wing (1978) observes that the classically autistic child "cannot cope with novelty, so [he] obtains his enjoyment from constant repetition of the same activities and experiences, and his sense of security from the maintenance of the familiar environment and routine, in obsessive detail" (p. 41).

In addition to whatever behavior-organizing services may be met by the stereotypy, an impaired neurological apparatus may directly promote behavioral rigidity and repetition. In this regard, the absence of normal central inhibitory controls in autism could lead to the rigid recurrence and stereotypy of action patterns. In the extreme, these acts may become self-injurious. Both possibilities—the organizing effects of this "insistence on sameness" and the possible lack of inhibitory controls—deserve exploration in further studies of autistic children.

CONCLUDING COMMENT

Remarkable advances have been made in our understanding of the causes and course of autism over the past 15 years, as summarized in the present volume and related works (Rutter & Schopler, 1978; Schopler & Mesibov, 1983). Many of the more important insights have arisen in the course of helping autistic children and their families deal with the concrete tasks of living. Empirical studies of the developmental pattern and its course have permitted researchers to dismiss as inadequate most of the theoretical proposals that attracted attention to the syndrome in the first place. The emerging developmental interpretation emphasizes the integrity of organismic functioning, even for children who differ greatly from the norm in their capabilities for cognitive integration.

Although our understanding of autistic disorders—or disorder—is far from complete, the progress that has been achieved points to a couple of lessons for developmental psychology. The first is that psychological theories of social development cannot afford to continue to give short shrift to the biological contributions to behavior. Failure to take into account the configuration of morphological-physiologial-neurological contributors to social development virtually guarantees an incomplete and inadequate account. This essential point has been emphasized by writers as disparate as Schneirla (1966), Kuo (1967), McGraw (1948), Gesell (1928), and Bell (1968). Once these contributions were outlined in a developmental-organismic model, most of the theoretical "trends" cited in this chapter were inevitable. Perhaps this is also why a developmental psychobiological account offers a coherent framework for the integration of the emerging findings on autism. The neurological and cognitive integration deficits that have now been broadly implicated in the disorder demand a theoretical model that does not ignore these features of the body and the mind.

The second lesson is related to the first, and concerns the appropriate relationship involving application, research, and theory. Alfred Binet (Binet & Simon, 1908) offered a brief statement on this matter in response to the criticism that he was "opposed, with blind infatuation, to all theory. . . ." In rejoinder, Binet wrote: "In our opinion, the ideal of the scientific method must be a combination of theory and of experimentation. Such a combination is well defined in the following formula: prolonged meditation upon facts gathered at first hand" (p. 1).

The "formula" served Binet well in his time, and I suspect that it is still valid. The combination remains a key for solving the remaining puzzles of social development, including autism. Our task remains to describe with precision the applied implications of the ontogenetic perspective.

REFERENCES

Adams, W. V., & Sheslow, D. V. (1983). A developmental perspective of adolescence. In E. Schopler & G. B. Mesibov (Eds.), *Autism in adolescents and adults* (pp. 11–36). New York: Plenum Press.

Ainsworth, M. D. S. (1967). *Infancy in Uganda: Infant care and the growth of love*. Baltimore: Johns Hopkins University Press.

Ainsworth, M. D. S. (1972). Attachment and dependency: A comparison. In J. L. Gewirtz (Ed.), *Attachment and dependency*. New York: Wiley.

Baldwin, A. (1980). *Theories of child development* (rev. ed.). New York: Wiley.

Baldwin, J. M. (1897). *Social and ethical interpretations in mental development: A study in social psychology*. New York: Macmillan.

Baltes, P. B., & Brim, O., Jr. (Eds.). (1983). *Advances in life-span developmental psychology* (Vol. 5). New York: Wiley.

Bandura, A. (1977). *Social learning theory*. Englewood Cliffs, NJ: Prentice-Hall.

Bell, R. Q. (1968). A reinterpretation of the direction of effects in studies of socialization. *Psychological Review, 75,* 81–95.

Bertalanffy, L. V. (1962). *Modern theories of development: An introduction to theoretical biology*. New York: Harper. (Original work published 1933)

Binet, A., & Henri, V. (1895). La psychologie individuelle. *L'Année Psychologique, 2,* 411–465.

Binet, A., & Simon, T. (1908). Le développement de l'intelligence chez les enfants. *L'Année Psychologique, 14,* 1–94.

Binet, A., & Simon, T. (1914). *Mentally defective children* (W. B. Drummond, Trans.). London: Edward Arnold.

Bowlby, J. (1958). The nature of the child's tie to his mother. *International Journal of Psychoanalysis, 39,* 350–373.

Bowlby, J. (1969). *Attachment and loss. Vol. 1: Attachment*. New York: Basic Books.

Bowlby, J. (1973). *Attachment and loss. Vol. 2: Separation*. New York: Basic Books.

Bronfenbrenner, U. (1979). *The ecology of human development: Experiments by nature and design*. Cambridge, MA: Harvard University Press.

Cairns, R. B. (1966). Attachment behavior of mammals. *Psychological Review, 73,* 409–426.

Cairns, R. B. (1972). Attachment and dependency: A psychobiological and social learning synthesis. In J. L. Gewirtz (Ed.), *Attachment and dependency*. New York: Wiley.

Cairns, R. B. (1979). *Social development: The origins and plasticity of interchanges*. San Francisco: Freeman.

Cairns, R. B., & Cairns, B. D. (1981). Self-reflections: An essay and commentary on "Social cognition and the acquisition of self." *Developmental Review, 1,* 171–180.

Cairns, R. B., & Cairns, B. D. (1985). Toward a developmental theory of interactions: Four issues of adolescent aggression. In D. Olweus, J. Block, & M. Radke-Yarrow (Eds.), *Development of antisocial and prosocial behavior* (pp. 315–342). New York: Wiley.

Cantwell, D. P., Baker, L., & Rutter, M. (1978). Family factors. In M. Rutter & E. Schopler (Eds.), *Autism: A reappraisal of concepts and treatment* (pp. 269–296). New York: Plenum Press.

Dawkins, R. (1976). *The selfish gene*. Oxford: Oxford University Press.

de Beer, G. (1958). *Embryos and ancestors* (3rd ed.). London: Oxford University Press.

DeLong, G. R. (1978) A neuropsychologic interpretation of infantile autism. In M. Rutter & E. Schopler (Eds.), *Autism: A reappraisal of concepts and treatment* (pp. 207–217). New York: Plenum Press.

Eibl-Eibesfeldt, I. (1975). *Ethology: The biology of behavior* (2nd ed.). New York: Holt, Rinehart & Winston.

Elder, G. H., Jr. (1975). Age differentiation and the life course. *Annual Review of Sociology, 1,* 165–190.

Flavell, J. E. (1983). The management of aggressive behavior. In E. Schopler & G. B. Mesibov (Eds.), *Autism in adolescents and adults* (pp. 187–222). New York: Plenum Press.

Folstein, S., & Rutter, M. (1978). A twin study of individuals with infantile autism. In M. Rutter & E. Schopler (Eds.), *Autism: A reappraisal of concepts and treatment* (pp. 219–241). New York: Plenum Press.

Gesell, A. (1928). *Infancy and human growth*. New York: Macmillan.

Gottlieb, G. (1976). Conceptions of prenatal development. *Psychological Review, 83,* 899–912.

Gottlieb, G. (1983). The psychobiological approach to developmental issues. In M. M. Haith & J. J. Campos (Vol. Eds.) & P. H. Mussen (Gen. Ed.), *Infancy and developmental psychobiology, Vol. 2: Handbook of child psychology* (4th ed., pp. 1–26). New York: Wiley.

Haeckel, E. (1880). *History of creation.* New York: Appleton.

Henderson, N. D. (1980). Effects of early experience upon the behavior of animals: The second twenty-five years of research. In E. C. Simmel (Ed.), *Early experience and early behavior: Implications for social development* (pp. 39–77). New York: Academic Press.

Hetherington, M. (Vol. Ed.). (1983). *Socialization, personality, and social development* (Vol. 3). In P. H. Mussen (Gen. Ed.), *Handbook of child psychology* (4th ed.). New York: Wiley.

Hingtgen, J. N., & Bryson, C. Q. (1972). Recent developments in the study of early childhood psychoses: Infantile autism, childhood schizophrenia and related disorders. *Schizophrenia Bulletin, 5,* 8–53.

Hutt, S. J., & Hutt, C. (1970). *Direct observation and measurement of behavior.* Springfield, IL: Charles C Thomas.

Kagan, J. (1976). Emergent themes in human development. *American Scientist, 64,* 186–196.

Kanner, L. (1943). Autistic disturbances of affective contact. *Nervous Child, 2,* 217–250.

Kuo, Z-Y. (1967). *The dynamics of behavioral development: An epigenetic view.* New York: Random House.

Lehrman, D. S. (1961). Hormonal regulation of parental behavior in birds and infrahuman animals. In W. C. Young (Ed.), *Sex and internal secretions* (pp. 1268–1382). (3rd ed.). Baltimore: Williams and Wilkins.

Levine, S. (1982). Psychobiology and the concept of development. *Minnesota symposia on child psychology, 15,* 28–53.

Lewis, M., & Brooks-Gunn, J. (1978). *Social cognition and the acquisition of the self.* New York: Plenum Press.

Lord, C., & O'Neill, P. J. (1983). Language and communication needs of adolescents with autism. In E. Schopler & G. B. Mesibov (Eds.), *Autism in adolescents and adults* (pp. 57–77). New York: Plenum Press.

Lorenz, K. Z. (1966). *On aggression.* New York: Harcourt, Brace and World, 1966.

Maccoby, E. E. (1980). *Social development: Psychological growth and the parent–child relationship.* New York: Harcourt Brace Jovanovich.

McAdoo, W. G., & DeMyer, M. K. (1978). Personality characteristics of parents. In M. Rutter & E. Schopler (Eds.), *Autism: A reappraisal of concepts and treatment* (pp. 251–267). New York: Plenum Press.

McGraw, M. B. (1948). Maturation of behavior. In L. Carmichael (Ed.), *Manual of child psychology.* New York: Wiley.

McHale, S. M. (1979). *Changes in the play and communicatory behavior of autistic and nonhandicapped children as a function of repeated peer interaction.* Unpublished doctoral dissertation, University of North Carolina.

Melone, M. B., & Lettick, A. L. (1983). Sex education at Benhaven. In E. Schopler & G. B. Mesibov (Eds.), *Autism in adolescents and adults* (pp. 169–186). New York: Plenum Press.

Patterson, G. R. (1982). *Coercive family process.* Eugene, OR: Castallia Press.

Richer, J. (1978). The partial noncommunication of culture to autistic children—An application of human ethology. In M. Rutter & E. Schopler (Eds.), *Autism: A reappraisal of concepts and treatment* (pp. 47–61). New York: Plenum Press.

Ritvo, E. R., Rabin, K., Yuwiler, A., Freeman, B. J., & Geller, E. (1978). Biochemical and hematologic studies: A critical review. In M. Rutter & E. Schopler (Eds.), *Autism: A reappraisal of concepts and treatment* (pp. 163–183). New York: Plenum Press.

Rutter, M. (1978). Diagnosis and definition. In M. Rutter & E. Schopler (Eds.), *Autism: A reappraisal of concepts and treatment* (pp. 1–25). New York: Plenum Press.

Rutter, M., & Schopler, E. (Eds.). (1978). *Autism: A reappraisal of concepts and treatment.* New York: Plenum Press.

Sameroff, A. J. (1983). Developmental systems: Contexts and evolution. In P. H. Mussen (Gen. Ed.) & W. Kessen (Vol. Ed.), *Handbook of child psychology, Vol. 1: History, theory, and methods* (pp. 237–294). New York: Wiley.

Schopler, E. (1983). Introduction: Can an adolescent or adult have autism? In E. Schopler & G. B. Mesibov (Eds.), *Autism in adolescents and adults* (pp. 1–11). New York: Plenum Press.

Schopler, E., & Mesibov, G. B. (Eds.). (1983). *Autism in adolescents and adults*. New York: Plenum Press.

Selman, R. L. (1980). *The growth of interpersonal understanding: Developmental and clinical analyses*. New York: Academic Press.

Sigman, M., & Ungerer, J. (1985) Attachment behaviors in autistic children. *Journal of Autistic and Developmental Disorders, 14*, 231–244.

Spencer, H. (1881). *Illustrations of universal progress; a series of discussions*. New York: Appleton.

Tinbergen, N. (1974). Ethology and stress diseases. *Science 185*, 20–26.

Tinbergen, E. A., & Tinbergen, N. (1972). Early childhood autism: An etiological approach. In *Advances in ethology, 10,* Supplement to *Journal of Comparative Ethology*. Berlin and Hamburg: Verlag Paul Parry.

Tolman, E. C. (1932). *Purposive behavior in animals and men*. New York: Century.

Valsiner, J. (1984). Construction of the zone of proximal development in adult–child joint action: The socialization of meals. In B. Rogoff & J. V. Wertsch (Eds.), *Children's learning in the "zone of proximal development." New directions for child development* (Vol. 23, pp. 65–76). San Francisco: Jossey-Bass.

Wallwork, E. (1982). Religious development. In J. M. Broughton & D. J. Freeman-Moir (Eds.), *The cognitive developmental psychology of James Mark Baldwin: Current theory and research in genetic epistemology* (pp. 335–388). Norwood, NJ: Ablex.

Wilson, E. O. (1975). *Sociobiology*. Cambridge, MA: Harvard University Press.

Wing, L. (1978). Social, behavioral, and cognitive characteristics: An epidemiological approach. In M. Rutter & E. Schopler (Eds.), *Autism: A reappraisal of concepts and treatment* (pp. 27–45). New York: Plenum Press.

Youniss, J. (1980). *Parents and peers in social development*. Chicago: University of Chicago Press.

3

The Development of Social Skills in Children

WENDY L. STONE and ANNETTE M. LA GRECA

INTRODUCTION

In recent years, there has been a tremendous surge of interest in the development of children's peer relationships and social competence. Although children's peer interactions have been the focus of considerable attention since the 1930s and 1940s, this area is now being explored with renewed vigor by clinical, developmental, and behavioral investigators.

Much of the current impetus for this avenue of exploration has been derived from relatively recent studies that underscore the importance of children's peer relationships for emotional functioning and later psychological adjustment. The work of Cowen (Cowen, Pederson, Babigian, Izzo, & Trost, 1973) and Roff (Roff, Sells, & Golden, 1972) and their colleagues has been particularly instrumental in this regard. For instance, children who demonstrated difficulties in peer relationships during the early elementary school years were found to have a higher incidence of emotional maladustment in later years, when compared to children with more satisfactory peer relationships (Cowen *et al.*, 1973). Moreover, other investigators have noted the high stability of peer reputations (both positive and negative) over periods ranging from several weeks or months to several years (e.g., Bryan, 1976; Coie & Dodge, 1983). Together, these two avenues of investigation point to the importance of early intervention for children with peer relationship difficulties and the need for more detailed information on

WENDY L. STONE • Mailman Center for Child Development, University of Miami School of Medicine, Miami, Florida 33101. ANNETTE M. LA GRECA • Department of Psychology, University of Miami, Miami, Florida 33101.

normal social development. In this context, research on children's social competence has blossomed.

Although many definitions have been offered for the concepts of "social competence" and "social skills" (e.g., Hops, 1983; McFall, 1982), we generally endorse the views espoused by Putallaz and Gottman (1982). These authors defined social competence as "those aspects of social behavior that are important with respect to preventing physical illness or psychopathology in children and adults" (p. 7). That is, only those social behaviors that have been demonstrated to predict psychological risk should be considered in the area of social competence. We further emphasize "social skills" as the positive or adaptive behaviors within this broad domain of social behavior.

Social Skills and Autism

It is well accepted that children with autism experience considerable difficulty with normal social skills and peer interactions (Rutter, 1978a). In fact, difficulties with social development and problems with social relationships are hallmarks of autism and are among the chief defining characteristics of this pervasive developmental disorder (American Psychiatric Association, 1980).

In light of these known social problems for autistic children, and considering the aforementioned literature underscoring the importance of social relationships for psychological functioning, the purpose of the present chapter is to review some of the findings on the development of social skills in normal or nonhandicapped youngsters. The intent of such a review is to provide a framework of normally occurring social skills that could then be utilized in intervention efforts with autistic children.

Given the breadth of the area of social skills, this review is intended to be selective rather than exhaustive in focus. Our discussion will be limited primarily to children of preschool and elementary school ages (approximately 3 through 12 years). The review will draw largely from observational studies of children's peer interactions, thus emphasizing the *behavioral* aspects of interactions with *peers*. Furthermore, although both positive and negative social behaviors contribute to the child's overall social functioning, our emphasis will be on the positive skills that may be of interest in promoting and encouraging social development. In particular, we will focus on two main areas of social skills—play skills and peer communication. Both types of skills are essential for sustained positive peer interactions among preschool and elementary school children. Moreover, both areas have been recognized as severe problems for children with autism (Ferrari, 1982). It is our hope that an overview of these two main areas of social skills will provide the interested professional with initial resource material for developing successful social intervention programs for autistic children.

SOCIAL BEHAVIOR AND PLAY

In addition to its pure intrinsic value, play with peers serves many extrinsic functions within the context of human development. Social play provides a forum for learning and practicing cognitive skills such as problem solving, verbal skills such as conversation, motor skills, and socialization skills such as conflict resolution and prosocial behavior (Rubin, Fein, & Vandenberg, 1983). Not only is play the initial vehicle for promoting social participation, but it also forms the basis for initiating and maintaining social relationships throughout the preschool and elementary school years.

Given such developmental importance, it is not surprising that investigators have found play to occur earlier in a child's development than was previously suspected. In reviewing the developmental literature, we will focus first on social behaviors that occur within the context of peer play, and then will discuss specific hierarchies that characterize children's play behaviors at different ages. This dual focus reflects the distinct orientations of the existing literature on play.

Developmental Overview

Throughout early childhood, there is a developmental trend toward more frequent and sustained peer interactions, with social play behaviors increasing in the degree to which they involve reciprocity, verbal communication, and complex game-playing skills. To a large extent, changes in play skills are mediated by the continuous development of cognitive abilities, such as verbal fluency, symbolic thought, and imaginative capacities.

In addition to age influences, play behaviors are also dependent upon and reflective of many other variables. Environmental factors, such as prior experience with peers (Howes, 1983), physical presence of the mother (Field, 1979), classroom structure (Tremblay, Hendrickson, Strain, & Shores, 1980), and the kinds of toys and play materials available (Redman & La Greca, 1983), all have been found to influence the level and type of children's play behavior. Other variables, such as socioeconomic level (Rubin, Maioni, & Hornung, 1976) and sex of the child and of the play partner (Greenwood, Walker, Todd, & Hops, 1981), also have proved important.

Infancy and Toddler Years

Recent evidence suggests that social play behaviors appear as early as the first year of an infant's life. Hartup (1983) notes that infant–infant interactive behaviors appear in a relatively consistent order: First to emerge is looking or visual regard of the other infant's face, followed by reaching and touching, and later by coordinated social acts. This evolution of social behavior with peers parallels the types of interactive behaviors that children display with their mothers and with inanimate objects.

The earliest social interactions with peers often have a focus on objects and the manipulation of the physical environment. For instance, infants as young as 6 to 10 months have been found to demonstrate social behaviors with peers that include offering and exchanging toys, mutual object manipulation, and physical imitation using toys and objects. However, these emerging play behaviors are brief and fleeting in infancy, and often unrelated to the actions of the partner (Eckerman, Whatley, & Kutz, 1975; Vandell & Wilson, 1982). The most frequent interactions are observed when babies are placed within extremely close proximity; even under such intensive circumstances, the frequency of these brief social contacts (a few seconds in duration) averages only about once every 2 minutes (Finkelstein, Dent, Gallagher, & Ramey, 1978).

During the second year of life, peer interactions typically become more lengthy, frequent, and complex. The initial stages of true interaction appear, as toddlers begin to relate and coordinate their own behavior with that of their social partners (Eckerman & Stein, 1982). Positive and negative affective displays during peer interactions also emerge at this time (Ross & Goldman, 1976). Longer play interchanges (sequences of two or more units) now occur, accompanied by mutual visual regard (Mueller & Brenner, 1977) and often within the context of social games. Ross (1982) defines social games as "the mutual involvement of two partners and the repeated enactment of related game roles in a turn-alternation pattern" (p. 509). Simple imitation games predominate at the beginning of this period, while complementary and reciprocal game roles increase in frequency as children approach their second birthday (Ross, 1982).

Although studies examining behavioral aspects of peer preferences among infants and toddlers have been nearly nonexistent, one study (Lee, 1973) of 8- to 10-month-olds did suggest that qualitative, rather than quantitative, differences in an infant's social behavior are related to peer preference. In this study, babies were observed in a day-care setting, and one infant who was consistently approached by others was compared to a child who was avoided. The preferred infant was observed to be more responsive to social contacts and engaged in more reciprocal interactions with the other infants. Thus, even at very early ages, the behavioral dimensions of "responsiveness to others" and "reciprocity" in social interactions appear to be important indicators of a child's likability.

Preschool Years

During the preschool years, children's developing social skills emerge more clearly. The frequency of peer interactions increases over this period, and positive social behaviors consistently occur with much greater frequency than negative ones. Moreover, positive social behaviors appear to be reciprocal in nature; children who initiate more positive social contacts also are the recipients of more social bids from peers (Hartup, 1983; Hartup, Glazer, & Charlesworth, 1967).

Many different types of social behaviors are subsumed under the generic heading of "positive social behavior," also referred to as "positive reinforcement" with peers, including (a) giving positive attention and approval (e.g., laughing, smiling), (b) giving affection and personal acceptance, (c) submission (e.g., sharing, compromising), and (d) token giving (e.g., spontaneously giving objects, such as toys) (Charlesworth & Hartup, 1967). Observations of children's behavior during peer play have disclosed that, in particular, the frequency of smiling and laughing, playing with peers, sharing, and cooperative acts all increase during the preschool years (Hartup, 1983; Radke-Yarrow, Zahn-Waxler, & Chapman, 1983). Moreover, good eye contact and physical proximity during peer interchanges are apparent at this age (Mueller, 1972; Savitzky & Watson, 1975).

New and qualitatively different play patterns are exhibited, as children develop social pretend skills. Although solitary pretense may begin as young as 12 to 13 months with self-directed pretend gestures (e.g., simulating drinking from a toy baby bottle), pretend play with peers does not typically appear before the age of 3 (McCune-Nicolich, 1981). In social pretense, or sociodramatic play, children "undertake roles and imitate in action and verbally the role figures; they use make-believe to change the function of objects, to evoke imaginary situations, and to describe nonperformed activities; they interact with other children (mostly one or two only) whenever they have an opportunity, and cooperate in the elaboration of the theme; they are able to sustain the game for relatively long periods" (Smilansky, 1968, p. 40).

The key elements of pretend play are thus imitative behavior, make-believe, and interaction. Language skills are crucial for structuring as well as maintaining social pretend play, from the first step of establishing the situation as one of "pretend" to the labeling of specific roles, actions, and situations that enables mutual theme development (Garvey, 1974). Social pretense has been found to be a generally enjoyable activity, associated with positive social behaviors and emotional expression (Fein, 1981).

Between the ages of 3 and 6, sociodramatic play increases in frequency as well as complexity (Fein, 1981). One aspect of increasing complexity pertains to the type of roles enacted. Younger children's role relationships are always self-referenced, or tied closely to real-life experiences (e.g., child in relation to parent). In contrast, older children are able to adopt role relationships that extend beyond their personal experiences to those observed in others (e.g., husband in relation to wife). The degree of reciprocity in the role play also increases with age. Younger children are more likely to enact their roles independently, without reference to the other, while older children's roles are more adapted to and integrated with each other (Fein, 1981).

Training Studies. Many social play behaviors emerge during the preschool years, raising the issue of which behaviors to promote in order to enhance children's social effectiveness. Initial social intervention studies with preschoolers emphasized increasing the frequency of the children's peer interactions (e.g., Allen, Hart, Buell, Harris, & Wolf, 1964). However, unless one also attends to the *quality* of the social interaction, this approach can produce undesirable results, such as by inadvertently increasing the frequency of negative or aggressive peer behaviors (Kirby & Toler, 1970).

A more productive approach has been to focus on increasing positive social behaviors, since a rather extensive body of literature supports the importance of positive social interactions for peer acceptance (see Hartup, 1983, for a review). Consequently, several studies by Strain and his colleagues have been aimed at promoting "positive social behaviors" during peer play (e.g., Strain, 1977; Strain, Shores & Timm, 1977). Others have targeted specific types of positive social behaviors for intervention; those that have been stressed most often in peer intervention efforts with preschoolers include smiling and laughing with peers (Keller & Carlson, 1974), sharing (Barton & Bevirt, 1981), giving affection or praise (Rogers-Warren & Baer, 1976), and joining or entering ongoing peer activities (Evers & Schwarz, 1973; O'Connor, 1969).

Social play behaviors that have a high probability of eliciting a positive reaction from peers appear to be especially suitable goals for social intervention. In a recent study (Tremblay, Strain, Hendrickson, & Shores, 1981), preschoolers' play behaviors were recorded in sequential fashion so that socially effective behaviors could be identified (i.e., behaviors that met with a positive response from peers). Using this approach, several play behaviors were identified that were associated with a greater than 50% chance of receiving a positive peer response. These behaviors were rough and tumble play (92%), sharing (79%), play organizer (67%), assistance (63%), and affection (56%). Interestingly, some of the behaviors that occurred most frequently (verbal commands and statements) were not found to be socially effective. This highlights the importance of considering the social impact of children's peer play behaviors; it may be tempting to view the most frequent behaviors as the most important when, in fact, this may not be the case.

Following a careful assessment along these lines, socially effective play behaviors can be translated into appropriate goals for preschool social intervention efforts. Strain and colleagues (Hendrickson, Strain, Tremblay, & Shores, in press) recently have achieved considerable success in improving the peer interactions of behaviorally disordered children by focusing on such behaviors during treatment.

Elementary School Years

Still further quantitative and qualitative changes can be observed in the peer play behavior of elementary-school-age children. As children enter school, peer contacts expand substantially. Although older children interact more frequently with peers, and these contacts continue to be predominantly positive in nature, the general category of "positive social behavior" belies the growing complexity and sophistication of children's social skills. Unfortunately, there are many gaps in our knowledge of older children's social skills because observational studies examining the specific parameters of elementary school children's peer play behavior have been few and far between. Moreover, direct comparison with the literature on preschoolers is difficult, at best, since studies have not systematically compared preschool and elementary school children.

It does appear that responsiveness to others and reciprocity in peer interactions are aspects of social functioning that appear in early childhood, and continue to maintain importance for older children (Gottman, Gonso, & Rasmussen, 1975). In fact, during the elementary school years, children become much more adept at adapting their behavior to their social partner's needs (Hartup, 1983).

Other available literature suggests that sharing and other prosocial behaviors (e.g, helping, cooperation) increase in middle childhood and play an important role in peer relationships (Radke-Yarrow *et al.*, 1983). However, the specific behavioral strategies children employ appear to become more complex across the 6- to 12-year age range. For example, self-reports of how they would offer assistance to another child differed for kindergarten versus third-grade children (Melburg, McCabe, & Kobasigawa, 1980, as reported by Hartup, 1983). The younger children typically offered direct assistance, while the older children varied their helping behavior according to situational constraints. Similar changes have been noted in children's ideas about peer conflict resolution (Wiley, 1983). Observational studies in naturalistic settings that document these changes are very much in need.

Concomitant with the developing independence and maturity of elementary school children, effective social functioning may require greater skill at initiating peer contacts. The ability to enter ongoing peer activities and to extend invitations to peers appears to be an important social task for the elementary school child to master (Asher, 1983; Gottman *et al.*, 1975). Not surprisingly, several recent studies have been focused on "peer entry" behaviors in an effort to determine effective joining tactics (e.g., Dodge, 1983; Putallaz, 1983).

For instance, Putallaz and Gottman (1981) examined the peer-group entry strategies of popular and unpopular children. Second and third graders were observed as they entered a play dyad. In this "entry" situation, popular children differed from the unpopular group in that they were less disagreeable, and less likely to ask questions for information, talk about themselves, and state their feelings or opinions. In essence, the popular children did not draw attention to themselves when joining peers, but rather attempted to fit into the dyad's frame of reference.

More recently, Dodge and colleagues (Dodge, Schlundt, Schocken, & Delugach, 1983) observed group-entry behaviors in previously unacquainted second-grade boys. Play groups, consisting of eight boys, met for eight 1-hour sessions over a 2-week period. Successful peer-group entry strategies were determined by calculating the conditional probabilities of various entry behaviors or "tactics." The tactics that had high probability of meeting with positive peer responses were deemed to be "successful."

The results suggested that a particularly successful peer-group entry strategy involved first waiting and hovering around peers, then mimicking the peer-group's activity (e.g., playing ball), and finally making a statement about the group or the activity. These findings are consistent with those of Putallaz and Gottman (1981), in that the successful joining strategy was one that preserved the *status quo* of the group, rather than drawing attention to the entering child.

Continued work of this nature, which attempts to delineate behavioral components of important social behaviors and relate these components to other indices of social success, will be of considerable interest. Much has yet to be accomplished in terms of understanding qualitative changes in social skills that occur during the elementary school years.

Training Studies. Unlike the intervention programs for preschoolers that often concentrated on very broad behavioral categories (e.g., positive social behavior) or a single specific skill area (e.g., sharing), attempts to improve the social skills of elementary school children generally have been more detailed and comprehensive, focusing on multiple skill areas. This comprehensive approach largely reflects the growing complexity of social interactions among older children.

Although, most certainly, the content of an intervention program should be tailored to the kinds of social problems the participants are experiencing, comprehensive programs do highlight skill areas that appear to contribute to positive peer interactions among middle elementary school children. Most social skills training efforts with this age group have emphasized skills involved in (a) *participating in peer activities,* such as entering groups or joining others (Gresham & Nagle, 1980), and extending invitations to peers (Gottman, Gonso, & Schuler, 1976), and (b) *maintaining positive peer interactions,* such as through sharing and cooperative play (Oden & Asher, 1977), giving support, attention, or help to peers (Ladd, 1981), and giving compliments or verbal praise (La Greca & Santogrossi, 1980). In addition to these skill areas, many intervention programs included *training in conversation skills,* an area that will be considered in the next section of this chapter.

Existing social skills intervention studies provide an overview of developmentally important peer interaction skills. However, the components of these interaction skills have not been delineated empirically. A more detailed appreciation of the complexities and components of peer-oriented behavior is needed for training to be truly effective. As we begin to gather more specific information on the behavioral components of the various skill areas that contribute to positive peer relationships, greater refinement in our training programs should be forthcoming.

Play Hierarchies

Many investigators of the development of children's play skills have focused on identifying predominant forms of play in different age groups. This research is very important for understanding children's social behavior because different forms of play may be more or less conducive to social participation and require certain social skills. For example, sociodramatic play (play with peers that involves an enactment of social roles) is common among 4- to 6-year-olds. A child who does not possess the cognitive or social skills needed for this type of play may be seriously limited in his/her opportunities for participation in peer activities.

Research on the development of children's play skills was inspired by an early observational study of play in preschoolers that distinguished between peer interaction and several degrees of social participation (Parten, 1932). Parten's sequential social stages consisted of unoccupied behavior, onlooker behavior, solitary play, parallel activity (independent play near other children with similar materials), associative play (unorganized group play), and cooperative or organized (group) play.

In a sample of preschoolers, Parten (1932) observed a developmental play sequence; younger children (2- to 3-year-olds) engaged more frequently in less interactive play types (i.e., solitary and parallel play), while older children (3- to 4 1/2-year-olds) engaged in more interactive and organized play in groups (i.e., associative and cooperative play). In addition to the cross-sectional data, a progression from solitary and parallel play to associative and cooperative play was also observed over the several-month course of study.

Subsequent investigations of preschool play interactions employing Parten's social participation categories have supported transitions from solitary to group play with increasing age (e.g., Smith, 1978). However, the most striking result of this line of research is the finding that all types of play can be found at all preschool ages (Bakeman & Brownlee, 1980; Barnes, 1971). This has led to recent attempts to make further differentiations within social participation categories. Rather than focusing purely on degree of interaction, a number of investigators have derived developmental play hierarchies that nest cognitive or behavioral characteristics within categories of solitary and interactive play.

Two such play hierarchies have been devised for very young children (18 to 42 months) and represent a downward extension and modification of Parten's approach. For instance, Howes (1980) describes a five-level peer-play scale with ascending levels reflecting changes along two dimensions: increasing complexity of social exchanges, and increasing complexity in use of objects and activities. At Level I, children engage in parallel play, without eye contact or peer-directed behavior. Level II involves parallel play with mutual regard, and Level III involves simple social play in which a peer-directed behavior occurs along with visual regard. Level IV play consists of complementary or reciprocal action and mutual gaze and awareness. At the final stage, Level V, children engage in "both contingent social behaviors and complementary actions" (Howes, 1980, p. 371). In a sample of children between approximately 1 1/2- and 3 1/2-years-old, Howes has found the scale to be sensitive to length of experience with peers, rather than to age.

Another social-cognitive play hierarchy, focused more on symbolic, pretend play, was developed by Fein, Moorin, and Enslein (1982) for toddlers and younger preschoolers. Their model described a progressive coordination of cognitive (i.e., pretend) and social behaviors, yielding the following 11-step developmental sequence: onlooker, solitary functional play, solitary pretend play, social functional play, social pretend play, solitary transformations, solitary play communications, social transformations, social play communication, solitary external agent, and social external agent. The two social levels (solitary and group) again derive from Parten (1932), and five cognitive levels from Piaget (1962). At each successive cognitive stage, solitary precedes social play, since the latter is presumably more complex and demanding. The authors report this scale to be sensitive to age as well as to peer group experience for children between approximately 1 1/2 and 3 1/2 years of age.

Play hierarchies such as these provide some developmental guidelines for the type of play activities to anticipate and encourage in very young children. For preschool-aged children (approximately ages 3 through 7), a more sophisticated social-cognitive play hierarchy has been developed by Rubin and his colleagues (e.g., Rubin *et al.*, 1976; Rubin, Watson, & Jambor, 1978). This hierarchy combines Parten's six social play categories with four cognitive play categories derived from Piaget (1962) and described by Smilansky (1968). The cognitive play stages are functional play (simple muscular movements with or without objects), constructive play (manipulation of objects to create or construct something), dramatic (or pretend) play, and games-with-rules. This yields combined social-cognitive play categories, such as solitary-functional play, parallel-constructive play, group-dramatic play, and so on.

Some efforts have been made to relate these play categories to independent indices of children's social functioning. In one recent study, Rubin (1982) compared the play behavior of preschoolers who were classified as either socially withdrawn, normal, or sociable. The socially withdrawn children were observed to participate in less dramatic play and fewer social games than the other two groups. These results are consonant with previous findings by Rubin and Maioni (1975) with 3 1/2- to 4 1/2-year-old children; popular preschoolers were observed to engage in more dramatic play and less functional play than unpopular children. Still more recent efforts with kindergarten and first-grade children (Rubin & Daniels-Beirness, 1983) have disclosed peer popularity to be positively related to parallel-constructive play and group play and game activities, and negatively related to solitary-dramatic and solitary-functional play.

The picture that emerges from this line of research is that socially skilled children typically participate in the more socially and cognitively sophisticated forms of play. Socially effective preschoolers appear to engage in more socially oriented dramatic play and social games, and less functional play. As children approach the early elementary school years, group play and game activities become important, while all forms of solitary play, with the exception of solitary-constructive play, appear with lower frequency among socially competent children.

This research suggests that, in addition to social behaviors during play, the form of play behavior may be an important consideration for promoting children's social effectiveness. For instance, children in the early elementary school grades who exhibit difficulties with group play activities may be more likely to encounter serious limitations in their abilities to participate in peer activities than preschool-aged children, for whom group play is a less frequent occurrence.

Very little is known about the forms of play that predominate during the elementary school years, and how various play activities are related to children's social competence, with one major exception. Excellent physical abilities or athletic skills in males appear to be related to peer likability (McGraw & Tolbert, 1953; see also Hartup, 1983).

Despite the general paucity of research on play activities among older children, a handful of studies have examined sex differences in peer activity preferences, obtaining some rather interesting results. Lever (1976, 1978), for example, found that males may be more inclined to engage in organized, large-group play activities (e.g., baseball) than females. In contrast, females tend to prefer more intimate one-to-one and small group activities (e.g., listening to records together). These findings are consonant with the work of Waldrop and Halverson (1975), which also points to the importance of "extensive" or group-oriented play activities for males and the more "intensive" one-to-one interactions for females.

Implications for Autism

We have seen that with cognitive maturity and peer experience the normal child's play skills grow from the object-focused, fleeting behavioral exchanges of infancy and toddlerhood to more lengthy, complex, and symbolic interactions of the preschool and elementary school years—interactions that demand an increasing level of turn taking and reciprocity. The subtle mechanics underlying these gradual transformations still remain a question and subject to theoretical debate.

Whatever the processes involved, it is clear that autistic children have severely deficient social behaviors and play skills. For example, the play behavior of children with autism is typically stereotyped and repetitive rather than symbolic or imaginative (Wing, Gould, Yeates, & Brierly, 1977). Even when pretend behavior occurs, it is repetitive and invariant, unlike the creative and ever-changing pretense of nonautistic children (Rutter, 1978a). Moreover, autistic children have been observed to engage in peer interactions very infrequently, and the limited contact they have is generally negative in nature (Strain & Cooke, 1976). Thus, the presence of appropriate social skills and play behaviors appears to be extremely limited in many autistic children.

Vandell and Wilson (1982) delineated certain prerequisite behaviors facilitating beginning peer interactions in toddlers: mutual visual regard, mutual object manipulation, and imitation. It is easy to see how even at this basic level, many autistic children would have difficulty. Absence or unusual use of eye contact, rigid and sterotyped use of objects, and weak imitation skills are among those that characterize the autistic youngster (Rutter, 1978a). Furthermore, the developmental literature presumes a tolerance for physical proximity of peers, which is not always present in autistic children.

In designing intervention programs for play skills, one may benefit from borrowing the literature's dual focus on the form as well as the content of play activities. For example, in teaching a new play behavior, such as tolerating physical proximity, initial instruction might occur within a parallel play situation with just one other child. In this setting social demands and interaction would be at a minimum. Later training might then take place in developmentally more advanced play contexts, such as groups.

In a similar vein, developmentally earlier play skills should be mastered before later ones are taught. Once physical proximity has been accomplished, for example, the next series of sequential steps might be observing and attending to the other child, engaging in brief nonverbal contacts such as giving objects or mutual object play, and taking turns within simple routines. Initial social encounters are likely to be more successful if concrete objects or toys—rather than eye contact—serve as a focus for interaction. Furthermore, it appears that social responsiveness may be more easily taught than social intiation. For instance,

Strain, Kerr, and Ragland (1979) were able to increase the social participation of autistic children by teaching nonhandicapped peers to initiate play activities with the autistic children.

Just as physical proximity might need to be taught as a prerequisite play skill, other "pretraining" tasks might need to be tackled prior to, or in conjunction with, social training activities with peers. For example, mutual object play often presumes knowledge of appropriate object use and/or adequate imitation skills. Consequently, task analysis and careful assessment should precede social training with peers.

Since play forms a critical basis for peer participation, it may be of interest to teach or promote play skills that are compatible with those of peers or likely playmates. Certainly this can become very complicated with autistic children who are cognitively delayed, as is true in approximately 70% of the cases (Dawson & Mesibov, 1983). Seemingly, the cognitive play level of the autistic child should be reasonably well matched with that of the peer playmate for sustained interaction to occur. This may necessitate the pairing of chronologically younger partners with autistic children.

As social games become more complex in the later preschool and elementary school years, communication skills become increasingly important for social interaction. This represents yet another hurdle for autistic children given their well-documented language and communication handicaps (Ricks & Wing, 1976). The role of communication skills in children's peer interactions will be considered further in the next section.

COMMUNICATION SKILLS

Communication has been cited as the foundation of social interaction (Ross, Lollis, & Elliot, 1982). As a social behavior, it serves the purpose of establishing and maintaining interpersonal contact. This section will describe the development of communication skills within the context of children's peer interactions.

Developmental Overview

As with play, the study of communication development in young children has largely followed the lines of Piaget. Piaget (1926) characterized the communication of young children as egocentric, or nonsocial. Until the age of 7, children were believed to be essentially unable to communicate socially, due to their inability to take another's perspective into account or adapt their messages to the needs and characteristics of the listener. More recently, Piaget's view has been challenged by the accumulation of empirical data revealing children to demonstrate social communication long before the age of 7 (Schmidt & Paris, 1984). As with most developmental skills, distinct communication tasks become prominent at different ages.

Verbal and nonverbal communication skills change substantially in quantitative and qualitative ways over the early childhood years. Peer communication during the toddler and early preschool years is primarily directed at gaining peers' attention and setting the stage for play activities. During middle childhood, there is much greater emphasis on conversation skills and verbal discourse as an accompaniment to play and as a peer activity in its own right. By adulthood, conversation skills play a critical role in social interactions with other peer adults. Consequently, children who display communication deficits are likely to encounter increasing difficulty with the important social skills of initiating and maintaining peer contacts as they get older.

Infancy and Toddler Years

One of the first communicative tasks is that of obtaining the attention of a peer listener (Keane & Conger, 1981). The importance of this skill is underlined by the finding that listener attention is highly predictive of communicative success in 2-year-olds (Mueller, Bleier, Krakow, Hegedus, & Cournoyer, 1977), as well as 3 1/2- to 5 1/2-year-olds (Mueller, 1972). In infancy this skill has been studied primarily by observing how babies interact with familiar adults, rather than with peers. By the age of 9 to 10 months, infants have been found to initiate communication through eye contact, physical gestures, and vocalizations. Babies are able to use their voices to attract attention, express emotion, and engage in social exchanges with familiar adults (Ricks & Wing, 1976). Infants as young as 10 months have also been observed to elicit attention by pointing at the same time as vocalizing and looking at their mothers (Leung & Rheingold, 1981). These early infant initiations are generally limited to requesting objects or actions, rejecting offered objects or activities, and calling attention to objects (Paul & Cohen, 1982). In the earliest peer communicative interchanges, objects in the infant's physical environment also play a prominent role in their provision of an initial, concrete focus for shared attention (Keenan & Klein, 1975).

During the second and third years of life, speech develops rapidly and becomes a new tool for eliciting attention. Nevertheless, eye contact, nonverbal gestures, and physical objects maintain their importance in initiating communication. A study by Wellman and Lempers (1977) illustrates the various behaviors used by 2-year-olds to elicit peer attention to toys or objects in the room. The most frequent behaviors observed, along with their percentage occurrences, were verbalizing (64%), looking at the listener (72%), pointing to the object (45%), and showing the object (55%). These authors found that a high proportion of the initiations (78%) were successful, in that they met with responses from peers.

In spite of its increasing importance in the toddler years, the use of speech has its limitations in eliciting peer attention. For example, although 2- and 3-year-olds are often capable of using specific verbal attention-getting techniques such as calling their partner's name and ending sentences with tag questions (e.g., "OK?"), these more advanced behaviors are rarely employed (Schmidt & Paris, 1984) before the age of 5. Furthermore, verbalizations are not always understood, and their use seems to be restricted to particular types of communicative overtures. This was illustrated in the following study.

In a sample of 20- to 22-month-olds, Ross and colleagues (1982) found that 43% of the communicative overtures to peers employed meaningful vocalizations. Three types of overtures frequently accompanied by vocalizations were showing objects, requesting objects, and protesting. Although the verbal mode was often used alone, it was not always the best understood in this young sample; comprehension for some overtures (e.g., requesting objects and protesting) was higher when gestures were used alone or in combination with the utterance. Overall, comprehension of these overtures in toddler peers was high, ranging from 60 to 70%.

Mueller *et al.* (1977) examined more closely the relationship between verbal initiations and responses in a similarly aged sample (21- to 23-month-olds). As mentioned above, listener attention (as evidenced by visual or physical orientation toward the speaker) was found to be most predictive of listener responses. Two speaker behaviors that also predicted listener responses were looking at the receiver and selecting listener-relevant topics (i.e., content related to the listener's activity rather than the speaker's). Verbal listener responses increased over the year from 27 to 65%, as speakers improved in selecting listener-relevant content and both speaker and listener increased their visual attention to each other.

Paralleling the beginning stages of turn-taking and reciprocity in social play, 2- and 3-year-old speakers demonstrate an emerging ability to adjust their utterances according to listener responses and feedback. Speakers have been found to recommunicate messages not receiving suitable responses (Keenan & Klein, 1975). Recommunications, however, were not always well adapted to the listener's needs; second messages to peers were just as likely to be redundant as to include more information. Furthermore, recommunications occurred in only half of the instances that their initial messages met with no response from peers (Wellman & Lempers, 1977).

At the same time that speakers are refining their initiation skills, it seems that listener responses are also becoming modified. Following a pair of twins, aged 2 years 9 months, over a 1-year period, Keenan and Klein (1975) observed qualitative differences in predominant listener responses. Initially, responses involved simple repetition of the speaker's utterances or the rhyming of nonsense syllables. Later in the year, however, the listener was able to accomplish the more sophisticated communicative task of adding new information to the topic (or object) referred to by the speaker. Of course, caution must be exerted in interpreting and generalizing these results, due to the restricted sample.

Preschool Years

Having established the ability to secure the listener's attention and response, the 3- to 5-year-old communicator now bears the onus of adapting subsequent speech to the listener's needs or feedback. Both observational and experimental studies have found preschoolers to adapt their speech in response to listener feedback as well as to specific personal characteristics (e.g., age, cognitive level, linguistic level) of listeners. To examine the effect of age of listener upon speaker utterances, Shatz and Gelman (1973) analyzed the speech of 4-year-olds when paired with 2-year-olds, peers, and adults. As anticipated, speakers used shorter utterances and more attentional utterances (e.g., "Look," "Hey") with 7-year-old partners than with adult partners. Furthermore, the younger 2-year-olds received more short utterances and more visual attention-holders than the older 2-year-olds. Speech to peers was similar to that used with adult partners. Masur (1978) extended these findings by classifying 2-year-old listeners as high verbal or low verbal on the basis of their mean length of utterances. Four-year-old speakers were found to differentially adjust their speech to these two groups of listeners, producing longer utterances to the more verbal listeners. Preschool children have also been found to adjust their speech according to the speech characteristics of same-aged partners (Garvey & Ben-Debba, 1974) and the needs of developmentally delayed partners (Guralnick & Paul-Brown, 1984).

Preschool children also are becoming more adept at providing adaptive responses to listener feedback. In recommunicating unclear messages, 4-year-olds have been found to include additional information 66% of the time (Spilton & Lee, 1977). However, speaker adaptation was dependent upon the explicitness of the feedback received; specific questions from the listener were most likely to lead to adaptive speaker responses. The ability to respond to more general verbal feedback and implicit nonverbal feedback (e.g., a puzzled facial expression) is usually seen only in older children (Schmidt & Paris, 1984).

Mutual engagement of communicative partners is common in this age group, with verbal initiations eliciting peer attention or responses 77 to 85% of the time (Garvey, 1975; Mueller, 1972). Early conversational ploys and routines begin to appear, ostensibly to secure listener attention and involvement. One such ploy is the "summons–answer" routine, which involves the following three steps: Speaker summons listener (e.g., "Hey, Sue"); listener answers (e.g., "Yeah?"); speaker then produces the reason for the summons (e.g., "Look at this") (Garvey & Hogan, 1973). Improved language ability within this time span is evidenced in older preschoolers using more words per utterance (Garvey & Ben Debba, 1974), longer communicative sequences (Garvey & Hogan, 1973), and more indirect and complete forms of requests (e.g., questions rather than direct imperatives) (Garvey, 1975) compared to their younger counterparts.

Although verbal communications occur frequently among preschoolers during peer interactions, nonverbal behaviors seem to maintain an important role in eliciting positive and sustained peer responses. In a recent study of preschool children's social interactions (Tremblay *et al.*, 1981), the most frequent behaviors were not the ones that had the highest probabilities of meeting with positive peer responses. Although four of the five most frequently occurring behaviors were verbal (statements, commands, questions, and vocal attention), only "questions" received a positive response from peers more than 50% of the time. One other verbal behavior, "play organizer" (e.g, "Let's play house"), had a high probability of eliciting a positive peer response (67%), though this was a relatively uncommon behavior. By contrast, several motor/gestural behaviors frequently received positive peer responses (rough-and-tumble play, sharing, offering assistance, and showing affection).

Asking questions and making "play organizer" statements thus seem to be important verbal communication skills for preschool children. Further corroboration of the importance of "play organizer" statements is provided by Strain and colleagues (Strain, 1977; Strain *et al.*, 1977), who found that a successful strategy for improving the peer participation of withdrawn preschoolers involved training peers to initiate "play organizer" statements toward the withdrawn/target children.

The limited success of the other verbal/communication behaviors in the Tremblay *et al.* (1981) study may have resulted from failure to supplement verbal initiations with nonverbal cues (e.g., eye contact, gestures). In fact, the authors noted that visual or physical orientation toward peers was often absent during verbal behaviors, and this absence might have accounted, in part, for their low level of effectiveness. Other investigators (e.g., Mueller & Lucas, 1975) have also found visual orientation to be an important predictor of peer responses to verbal initiations in young children.

Elementary School Years

By the time they attend kindergarten or early elementary school, children are refining their verbal and nonverbal communication skills, and incorporating them into the context of peer interactions much more extensively. Nonverbal communication skills become increasingly more effective as children become better at comprehending or "reading" nonverbal cues in others (e.g., facial expressions, body movements, voice intonation) (Girgus & Wolf, 1975) and also display a more sophisticated use of nonverbal behaviors in their own peer contacts. For instance, children in the early elementary grades have been observed to display more social gazing, more mutual eye contact, and a greater proportion of eye contact during speaking and listening than preschoolers (Levine & Sutton-Smith, 1973).

Verbally, children are becoming more effective and responsive as both speakers and listeners. In the role of speaker, elementary school children become more adept at eliciting attention and feedback from listeners, and are able to respond appropriately to explicit verbal feedback (such as questions) and adapt their speech to the listener's needs (Karabenick & Miller, 1977). Listeners usually respond to verbal as well as nonverbal initiations and are beginning to provide verbal feedback spontaneously when messages are unclear. Through the elementary years, listeners become better able to spontaneously provide accurate verbal feedback; at the same time, speakers learn to respond to implicit nonverbal feedback, such as a puzzled facial expression (Schmidt & Paris, 1984). Subtle aspects of conversational congruence, such as pausing, also develop within this period (Welkowitz, Cariffe, & Feldstein, 1976).

During the elementary school years, communication skills contribute to sustained peer interactions in at least two main ways. Communication skills play an important role in regulating peer contacts, such as by initiating play and resolving conflict. In addition, social conversation becomes important in its own right as a shared peer activity. The main focus, however, in the observational literature has been on the social communication skills that regulate peer activities.

Observations of children's social conversation during seminaturalistic peer interactions reveal a growing verbal sophistication in the ways children resolve conflict. For instance, Putallaz and Gottman (1981) compared the dyadic peer interactions of popular and unpopular children. During the dyadic interactions, second and third graders played a word-naming game and were observed through a one-way mirror. Popular children were found to be less disagreeable, more likely to provide reasons or cite rules when they did disagree with others, and more likely to suggest constructive alternatives when criticizing peers. This suggests that socially effective (or popular) children demonstrate assertive communication skills in conflict situations. Such verbal strategies contrast sharply with those of younger children, who rely to a greater extent upon physically aggressive means of resolving conflict (e.g., hitting) or enlist the help of adults as mediators (Wiley, 1983).

Less is known about children's conversation as a social activity. Bonney (1955) found that popular children tended to engage in more verbal discourse with peers than did unpopular children. Other research (Reisman & Shorr, 1978) indicates that children with good social relationships are more likely to "ask questions" and "talk more" than those with poor social interactions. Still other work suggests that training conversation skills, often in conjunction with teaching other social skills, can lead to improvements in children's acceptance from peers (e.g., Bierman & Furman, 1984; Oden & Asher, 1977).

Judging by the kinds of skills that have been included in intervention studies, successful social conversation appears to involve reciprocity, turn taking, and responsiveness to others—dimensions that parallel important aspects of social play. Specifically, the conversation skills that have been emphasized with elementary-school-aged children include *asking questions* of others, particularly open-ended questions (Minkin *et al.*, 1976); *talking and sharing information* about oneself (La Greca & Mesibov, 1981); giving *suggestions and advice* (Ladd, 1981); and *displaying an active interest* in the conversation by maintaining eye contact or giving positive feedback (La Greca & Santogrossi, 1980). Sticking to a topic of conversation and generating topics for conversation also were included in one intervention study with learning-disabled children (La Greca & Mesibov, 1981).

Implications for Autism

Deviant language and communication development is one of the most significant of the cognitive and behavioral difficulties characterizing autism. Autistic children are typically late beginning to speak, and approximately half never develop meaningful speech at all. Those who do often demonstrate abnormalities in usage as well as delivery. In addition to problems with speech production and comprehension, nonverbal communicative behaviors, such as the use of gestures and eye contact, often fail to develop (Rutter, 1978b). Consequently, many autistic children would be expected to have difficulty performing even the earliest communicative tasks of infancy. In fact, Curcio (1978) found that a sample of nonverbal autistic children never pointed to or showed objects to elicit attention, a common communicative behavior in normal infants and toddlers.

During the toddler and preschool years, communication skills become important for signaling and understanding intention, determining and conveying messages, and initiating and regulating the alternation of turns (Ross, 1982). More sophisticated skills become apparent in children of elementary school age, when social conversation increasingly becomes a peer activity in its own right. Even in those autistic children who acquire the ability to apply grammar correctly and speak in complete sentences, conversation is often restricted to the use of stereotyped phrases and the exchange of concrete pieces of information about limited topics of interest (Ricks & Wing, 1976). Consequently, one might anticipate increasing difficulty in their ability to participate in peer activities as autistic children get older.

With these serious limitations in mind, initial social goals for autistic children might be directed toward teaching responsiveness to communicative overtures from peers, rather than initiation of communication. Social responsiveness has been found to proceed on a developmental continuum, from mere physical orientation to the peer partner, to attending to the overture, to echoing or imitating the communication, and finally to adding more information to the topic at hand. Each of the later tasks can be performed verbally or through an alternate communication system (e.g., signing, writing, gesturing), depending upon the communicative level of the child. As with play, this type of training activity can be facilitated by prompting nonhandicapped peers to initiate interactions using simple verbal statements (e.g., "Let's play").

Promoting the initiation of communication is likely to prove more difficult for an autistic child who receives little intrinsic satisfaction from eliciting the social attention of others in his/her environment. Nonverbal overtures leading to an immediate, tangible response may therefore be more easily taught than those for which the only environmental response is a smile or a nod. For example, early communicative training may focus on teaching a child to point to a favorite food treat in order to receive a taste. While a good deal of physical prompting may be necessary at first, eventually the visual presence of the food may be the only stimulus required to generate a self-initiated pointing response. By receiving such immediate, tangible reinforcement for communicating, the child, it is hoped, will learn the beneficial nature of the process of initiating communication.

Following from the developmental literature, more advanced communication training activities for more verbal autistic children might focus on reciprocity and turn-taking in social discourse, decoding nonverbal feedback such as facial expressions, and utilizing appropriate inflections and intonations in speech.

SUMMARY AND CONCLUSIONS

This chapter has reviewed the development of social skills by focusing on two primary areas: play skills and peer communication. These particular areas were chosen for their importance in initiating and maintaining positive peer relationships as well as their particular relevance for autistic populations. Although they encompass distinct domains of social development, the interdependence of play and communication should be evident from the foregoing discussion. Communication is important in initiating, defining, and regulating play activities, and by the same token, play often serves as the initial focus for communicative efforts. On a larger scale, the interrelationships between these aspects of social development may serve to remind us of the continuity and interface of all areas of development and growth. Just as social growth is influenced by the domains of environment and cognitive ability, it also serves to further shape and define these same areas.

By definition, autism involves impaired social development. However, the manifestation of social deficits varies from individual to individual, and can range from extreme resistance to intrusion and social avoidance, to shallow social awareness, interest, and relating skills. Likewise, component abilities such as play and communication can also be exhibited to different degrees from one autistic child to the next. For example, while some autistic children fail to develop either speech or nonverbal systems of communication, others are fully capable of speaking in complete and grammatically correct sentences. This has enormous implications for the design of social skills programs for autistic children.

As with any population, the first step in facilitating social development in autistic children is to carefully assess areas of strength and weakness. This is best accomplished by analyzing social behaviors in terms of specific component skills. The importance of a developmental approach to assessment cannot be overstated. An understanding of normal social development is essential for identifying normative patterns and sequences, clarifying the relative importance of specific behaviors at different ages, elucidating changes in the manifestation of a given behavior over time, and providing information about the contexts in which the behavior is likely to occur for different age groups. The assessment should also include an evaluation of the social effectiveness (i.e., ability to elicit positive peer responses) of specific social skills with respect to the relevant peer group.

In working with autistic children, it is important to tailor social objectives and activities to the individual child. Specific questions that should be addressed include these: What is the child's cognitive and developmental level? What are the particular manifestations of social and language impairments in this child? How do other autistic behaviors interfere with his/her social functioning? What specific behaviors are most in need of remediation? Which underlying skills are present or absent? Which social skills would be of greatest functional significance for the child? Is he/she currently performing this skill in any social context?

While the above questions can be answered with information gleaned from a careful assessment, a number of other questions and issues relevant to this population have no easy solutions. First is the troublesome issue of generalization. Once a social behavior has improved in the training context, how can its transfer to other situations be facilitated? Difficult to accomplish with normal populations, generalization can be expected to be even more problematic for individuals in whom this is a specific cognitive deficit. A second issue involves selecting an appropriate peer group for comparison and training when chronological age and mental age are discrepant. What are the relative advantages of each as guideposts for selecting training goals and activities?

It is hoped that these issues become resolved as more and more investigators adopt a developmental approach to assessing, understanding, and enhancing social skills in autistic children.

ACKNOWLEDGMENTS

The preparation of this paper was supported in part by the Mailman Foundation and the Florida Diagnostic and Learning Resources System through a state general revenue appropriation for evaluation services in exceptional student education.

REFERENCES

Allen, K. E., Hart, B., Buell, J. S., Harris, F. R., & Wolf M. M. (1964). Effects of social reinforcement of isolate behavior of a nursery school child. *Child Development, 35,* 511–518.

American Psychiatric Association. (1980). *Diagnostic and statistical manual of mental disorders* (3rd ed.). Washington, DC: Author.

Asher, S. R. (1983). Social competence and peer status: Recent advances and future directions. *Child Development, 54,* 1427–1434.

Bakeman, R., & Brownlee, J. R. (1980). The strategic use of parallel play: A sequential analysis. *Child Development, 51,* 873–878.

Barnes, K. E. (1971). Preschool play norms: A replication. *Developmental Psychology, 5,* 99–103.

Barton, E. J., & Bevirt, J. (1981). Generalization of sharing across groups. Assessment of group composition with preschool children. *Behavior Modification, 5,* 503–522.

Bierman, K. L., & Furman, W. (1984). The effects of social skills training and peer involvement on the social adjustment of preadolescents. *Child Development, 55,* 151–162.

Bonney, M. E. (1955). Social behavior differences between second-grade children of high and low sociometric status. *Journal of Educational Psychology, 48,* 481–495.

Bryan, T. H. (1976). Peer popularity of learning disabled children: A replication. *Journal of Learning Disabilities, 9,* 307–311.

Charlesworth, R., & Hartup, W. (1967). Positive social reinforcement in the nursery school peer group. *Child Development, 38,* 993–1002.

Coie, J. D., & Dodge, K. A. (1983). Continuities and changes in children's social status: A five-year longitudinal study. *Merrill-Palmer Quarterly, 29,* 261–282.

Cowen, E. L., Pederson, A., Babigian, H., Izzo, L. D., & Trost, M. A. (1973). Long-term follow-up of early detected vulnerable children. *Journal of Consulting and Clinical Psychology, 41,* 438–446.

Curcio, F. (1978). Sensorimotor functioning and communication in mute autistic children. *Journal of Autism and Childhood Schizophrenia, 8,* 281–292.

Dawson, G., & Mesibov, G. B. (1983). In C. E. Walker & M. C. Roberts (Eds.), *Handbook of clinical child psychiatry* (pp. 543–572). New York: Wiley.

Dodge, K. A. (1983). Behavioral antecedents of peer social status. *Child Development, 54,* 1386–1399.

Dodge, K. A. Schlundt, D. C. Schocken, I., & Delugach, J. D. (1983). Social competence and chlidren's sociometric status: The role of peer group entry strategies. *Merrill-Palmer Quarterly, 29,* 309–336.

Eckerman, C. O., & Stein, M. R. (1982). The toddler's emerging interactive skills. In K. H. Rubin & H. S. Ross (Eds.), *Peer relationships and social skills in childhood* (pp. 41–71). New York: Springer-Verlag.

Eckerman, C. O., Whatley, J. L., & Kutz, S. L. (1975). Growth of social play with peers during the second year of life. *Developmental Psychology 11,* 42–49.

Evers, W. L., & Schwarz, J. C. (1973). Modifying social withdrawal in preschoolers: The effects of filmed modeling and teacher praise. *Journal of Abnormal Child Psychology, 1,* 248–256.

Fein, G. G. (1981). Pretend play in childhood: An integrative review. *Child Development, 52,* 1095–1118.

Fein, G. G., Moorin, E. R., & Enslein, J. (1982). Pretense and peer behavior: An intersectoral analysis. *Human Development, 25,* 392–406.

Ferrari, M. (1982). Childhood autism: Deficits of communication and symbolic development. I. Distinctions from language disorders. *Journal of Communication Disorders, 15,* 191–208.

Field, T. (1979). Games parents play with normal and high-risk infants. *Child Psychiatry and Human Development, 10,* 41–48.

Finkelstein, N. W., Dent, C., Gallagher, K., & Ramey, C. T. (1978). Social behavior of infants and toddlers in a daycare environment. *Developmental Psychology, 14,* 257–262.

Garvey, C. (1974). Some properties of social play. *Merrill-Palmer Quarterly, 20,* 163–180.

Garvey, C. (1975). Requests and responses in children's speech. *Journal of Child Language, 2,* 41–63.

Garvey, C., & Ben Debba, M. (1974). Effects of age, sex, and partner on children's dyadic speech. *Child Development, 45,* 1159–1161.

Garvey, C., & Hogan, R. (1973). Social speech and social interaction: Egocentrism revisited. *Child Development, 44,* 562–568.

Girgus, J. S., & Wolf, J. (1975). Age changes in the ability to encode social class. *Developmental Psychology, 11,* 118.

Gottman, J. M., Gonso, J., & Rasmussen, B. (1975). Social interaction, social competence, and friendship in children. *Child Development, 46,* 709–718.

Gottman, J. M., Gonso, J., & Schuler, P. (1976). Teaching social skills to isolated children. *Journal of Abnormal Child Psychology, 4,* 179–198.

Greenwood, C. R., Walker, H. M., Todd, N. M., & Hops, H. (1981). Normative and descriptive analysis of preschool free play social interaction rates. *Journal of Pediatric Psychology, 6,* 343–367.

Gresham, F. M., & Nagle, R. J. (1980). Social skills training with children: Responsiveness to modeling and coaching as a function of peer orientation. *Journal of Consulting and Clinical Psychology, 48,* 718–729.

Guralnick, M. J., & Paul-Brown, D. (1984). Communicative adjustments during behavior-request episodes among children at different developmental levels. *Child Development, 55,* 911–919.

Hartup, W. W. (1983). Peer relations. In P. H. Mussen (Ed.), *Handbook of child psychology* (Vol. 4, pp. 103–196). New York: Wiley.

Hartup, W. W., Glazer, J. A., & Charlesworth, R. (1967). Peer reinforcement and sociometric status. *Child Development, 38,* 1017–1024.

Hendrickson, J. M., Strain, P. S., Tremblay, A., & Shores, R. E. (in press). Functional effects of peer social intiations on withdrawn preschool children. *Behavioral Modification.*

Hops, H. (1983). Children's social competence and skill: Current research practices and future directions. *Behavioral Therapy, 14,* 3–18.

Howes, C. (1980). Peer play scale as an index of complexity of peer interaction. *Developmental Psychology, 16,* 371–372.

Howes, C. (1983). Patterns of friendship. *Child Development, 54,* 1041–1053.

Karabenick, J. D., & Miller, S. A. (1977). The effects of age, sex, and listener feedback on grade school children's referential communication. *Child Development, 48,* 678–683.

Keane, S. P., & Conger, J. C. (1981). The implications of communication development for social skills training. *Journal of Pediatric Psychology, 6,* 369–381.

Keenan, E. O., & Klein, E. (1975). Coherency in children's discourse. *Journal of Psycholinguistic Research, 4,* 365–380.

Keller, M. G., & Carlson, P. M. (1974). The use of symbolic modeling to promote social skills in children with low levels of social responsiveness. *Child Development, 45,* 912–919.

Kirby, F. D., & Toler, Jr., H. C. (1970). Modification of preschool isolate behavior: A case study. *Journal of Applied Behavior Analysis, 3,* 309–314.

Ladd, G. W. (1981). Effectiveness of a social learning method for enhancing children's social interaction and peer acceptance. *Child Development, 52,* 171–178.

La Greca, A. M., & Mesibov, G. B. (1981). Facilitating interpersonal functioning with peers in learning-disabled children. *Journal of Learning Disabilities, 14,* 197–199, 238.

La Greca, A. M., & Santogrossi, D. A. (1980). Social skills training with elementary school students: A behavioral group approach. *Journal of Consulting and Clinical Psychology, 48,* 220–228.

Lee, L. C. (1973, August). *Social encounters of infants: The beginnings of popularity.* Paper presented at the meeting of the International Society for the Study of Behavioral Development, Ann Arbor, MI.

Leung, E. H. L., & Rheingold, H. L. (1981). Development of pointing as a social gesture. *Developmental Psychology, 17,* 215–220.

Lever, J. (1976). Sex differences in the games children play. *Social Problems, 23,* 478–487.

Lever, J. (1978). Sex differences in the complexity of children's play and games. *American Sociological Review, 43,* 471–483.

Levine, M. H. & Sutton-Smith, B. (1973). Effects of age, sex, and task on visual behavior during dyadic interaction. *Developmental Psychology, 9,* 400–405.

Masur, E. F. (1978). Preschool boys' speech modifications: The effect of listeners' linguistic levels and conversational responsiveness. *Child Development, 49,* 924–927.

McCune-Nicolich, L. (1981). Toward symbolic functioning: Structure of early pretend games and potential parallels with language. *Child Development, 52,* 785–797.

McFall, R. M. (1982). A review and reformulation of the concept of social skills. *Behavioral Assessment, 4,* 1–33.

McGraw, L. W., & Tolbert, J. W. (1953). Sociometric status and athletic ability of junior high school boys. *Research Quarterly, 24,* 72–80.

Minkin, N., Braukmann, C. J., Minkin, B. L., Timbers, G. D., Timbers, B. J., Fixsen, D. L., Phillips, E. L., & Wolf, M. M. (1976). The social validation and training of conversational skills. *Journal of Applied Behavioral Analysis, 9,* 127–139.

Mueller, E. (1972). The maintenance of verbal exchanges between young children. *Child Development, 43,* 930–938.

Mueller, E., Bleier, M., Krakow, J., Hegedus, K., & Cournoyer, P. (1977). The development of peer verbal interaction among two-year old boys. *Child Development, 48,* 284–287.

Mueller, E., & Brenner, J. (1977). The origins of social skills and interaction among playgroup toddlers. *Child Development, 48,* 854–861.

Mueller, E. and Lucas, T. (1975). A developmental analysis of peer interaction among toddlers. In M. Lewis & L. Rosenblum (Eds.), *Peer relations and friendship.* New York: Wiley.

O'Connor, R. D. (1969). Modification and social withdrawal through symbolic modeling. *Journal of Applied Behavior Analysis, 2,* 15–22.

Oden, S., & Asher, S. R. (1977). Coaching children in social skills for friendship making. *Child Development, 48,* 495–506.

Parten, M. B. (1932). Social participation among pre-school children. *Journal of Abnormal and Social Psychology, 27,* 243–269.

Paul, R., & Cohen, D. J. (1982). Communication development and its disorders: A psycholinguistic perspective. *Schizophrenia Bulletin, 8,* 279–293.

Piaget, J. (1926). *The language and thought of the child.* New York: Harcourt & Brace.

Piaget, J. (1962). *Play, dreams, and imitation in childhood.* New York: Norton.

Putallaz, M. (1983). Predicting children's sociometric status from their behavior. *Child Development, 54,* 1417–1426.

Putallaz, M., & Gottman, J. M. (1981). An interactional model of children's entry into peer groups. *Child Development, 52,* 986–994.

Putallaz, M., & Gottman, J. M. (1982). Conceptualizing social competence in children. In P. Karoly & J. J. Steffen (Eds.), *Advances in child behavior analysis and therapy* (Vol. 2, pp. 1–37). New York: Gardner Press.

Radke-Yarrow, M., Zahn-Waxler, C., & Chapman, M. (1983). Children's prosocial dispositions and behavior. In P. H. Mussen (Ed.), *Handbook of child psychology* (Vol. 4, pp. 469–545). New York: Wiley.

Redman, T. A., & La Greca, A. M. (1983). *Sex differences in children's social and play behavior: The effects of play settings.* Unpublished manuscript, University of Miami.

Reisman, J. M., & Shorr, S. I. (1978). Friendship claims and expectations among children and adults. *Child Development, 49,* 913–916.

Ricks, D. M., & Wing, L. (1976). Language, communication, and the use of symbols. In L. Wing (Ed.), *Early childhood autism* (pp. 93–134). London: Pergamon Press.

Roff, M., Sells, S. B., & Golden, M. M. (1972). *Social adjustment and personality development in children.* Minneapolis: University of Minnesota Press.

Rogers-Warren, A., & Baer, D. M. (1976). Correspondence between saying and doing: Teaching children to share and praise. *Journal of Applied Behavior Analysis, 9,* 335–354.

Ross, H. S. (1982). Establishment of social games among toddlers. *Developmental Psychology, 18,* 509–518.

Ross, H. S., & Goldman, B. M. (1976). Establishing new social relations in infancy. In T. Alloway, L. Krames, & P. Pliner (Eds.), *Advances in communication and affect* (Vol. 4). New York: Plenum Press.

Ross, H. S., Lollis, S. P., & Elliot, C. (1982). Toddler–peer communication. In K. H. Rubin & H. S. Ross (Eds.), *Peer relationships and social skills in childhood* (pp. 73–98). New York: Springer-Verlag.

Rubin, K. H. (1982). Social and social-cognitive developmental characteristics of young isolate, normal, and sociable children. In K. H. Rubin & H. S. Ross (Eds.), *Peer relationships and social skills in childhood* (pp. 353–374). New York: Springer-Verlag.

Rubin, K. H., & Daniels-Beirness, T. (1983). Concurrent and predictive correlates of sociometric status in kindergarten and grade 1 children. *Merrill-Palmer Quarterly, 29,* 337–351.

Rubin, K. H., Fein, G. G., & Vandenberg, B. (1983). Play. In P. H. Mussen (Ed.), *Handbook of child psychology* (Vol. 3, pp. 693–774). New York: Wiley.

Rubin, K. H., & Maioni, T. L. (1975). Play preference and its relationship to egocentrism, popularity and classification skills in preschoolers. *Merrill-Palmer Quarterly, 21,* 171–179.

Rubin, K. H., Maioni, T. L., & Hornung, M. (1976). Free-play behaviors in middle and lower class preschoolers: Parten and Piaget revisited. *Child Development, 47,* 414–419.

Rubin, K. H., Watson, K. S., & Jambor, T. W. (1978). Free-play behavior in preschool and kindergarten children. *Child Development, 49,* 534–536.

Rutter, M. (1978a). Diagnosis and definition. In M. Rutter & E. Schopler (Eds.), *Autism: A reappraisal of concepts and treatment* (pp. 1–25). New York: Plenum Press.

Rutter, M. (1978b). Language disorder and infantile autism. In M. Rutter & E. Schopler (Eds.), *Autism: A reappraisal of concepts and treatment* (pp. 85–104). New York: Plenum Press.

Savitzky, J. C., & Watson, M. J. (1975). Patterns of proxemic behavior among preschool children. *Representative Research in Social Psychology, 6,* 109–113.

Schmidt, C. R., & Paris, S. G. (1984). The development of verbal communicative skills in children. In H. W. Reese (Ed.), *Advances in Child Development and Behavior, 18,* 1–47.

Shatz, M., & Gelman, R. (1973). The development of communication skills: Modifications in the speech of young children as a function of the listener. *Monographs of the Society for Research in Child Development, 38*(5, Serial No. 152).

Smilansky, S. (1968). *The effects of sociodramatic play on disadvantaged preschool children.* New York: Wiley.

Smith, P. K. (1978). A longitudinal study of social participation in preschool children: Solitary and parallel play reexamined. *Developmental Psychology, 14,* 517–523.

Spilton, D., & Lee, L. C. (1977). Some determinants of effective communication in four-year olds. *Child Development, 48,* 968–977.

Strain, P. S. (1977). An experimental analysis of peer social initiations on the behavior of withdrawn preschool children: Some training and generalization effects. *Journal of Abnormal Child Psychology, 5,* 445–455.

Strain, P. S., & Cooke, T. P. (1976). An observational investigation of two elementary-age autistic children during free-play. *Psychology in the Schools, 13,* 82–91.

Strain, P. S., Kerr, M. M., & Ragland, E. U. (1979). Effects of peer-mediated social initiations and prompting/reinforcement procedures on the social behavior of autistic children. *Journal of Autism and Developmental Disorders, 9,* 41–54.

Strain, P. S., Shores, R. E., & Timm, M. A. (1977). Effects of peer social initiations on the behavior of withdrawn preschool children. *Journal of Applied Behavior Analysis, 10,* 289–298.

Tremblay, A., Hendrickson, J. M., Strain, P. S., & Shores, R. E. (1980). The activity context of preschool children's social interactions: A comparison of high and low social interactors. *Psychology in the Schools, 17,* 380–385.

Tremblay, A., Strain, P. S., Hendrickson, J. M., & Shores, R. E. (1981). Social interactions of normal preschool children. *Behavior Modification, 5,* 237–253.

Vandell, D. L., & Wilson, K. S. (1982). Social interaction in the first year: Infants' social skills with peers versus mother. In K. H. Rubin & H. S. Ross (Eds.), *Peer relationships and social skills in childhood* (pp. 187–208). New York: Springer-Verlag.

Waldrop, M. F., & Halverson, C. F., Jr. (1975). Intensive and extensive peer behavior: Longitudinal and cross-sectional analyses. *Child Development, 46,* 19–26.

Welkowitz, J., Cariffe, G., & Feldstein, S. (1976). Conversational congruence as a criterion of socialization in children. *Chld Development, 47,* 269–272.

Wellman, H. M., & Lempers, J. D. (1977). The naturalistic communicative abilities of two-year olds. *Child Development, 48,* 1052–1057.

Wiley, P. D. (1983). Development of strategies for coping with peer conflict in children from first through fifth grade. In R. K. Ullmann (Chair), *Assessment of children's social knowledge and attitudes: Coping with peer conflict.* Paper presented at the Annual Meeting of the Association for Behavior Analysis, Milwaukee.

Wing, L., Gould, J., Yeates, S. R., & Brierly, L. M. (1977). Symbolic play in severely mentally retarded and in autistic children. *Journal of Child Psychology and Psychiatry, 18,* 167–178.

4

Children's Friendships

WILLARD W. HARTUP and MICHAEL F. SANCILIO

Children give much time and attention to their friends and remember them for years afterward. Emotionally disturbed children, however, frequently have difficulties in forming and maintaining these relationships. Extreme conditions, including autism, are commonly marked by the complete absence of friends (Rutter, 1970; Rutter & Garmezy, 1983).

The purpose of this chapter is to consider the nature of children's friendships, the reasons for their importance to children, and developmental changes in them. Special attention will be given to individual differences among children and their experience with friends. Pair-to-pair differences in friendships will also be considered, along with certain issues in measuring and classifying these relationships.

WHAT ARE FRIENDSHIPS?

Almost everyone agrees that the essentials of friendship are reciprocity and commitment within a relationship between individuals who see themselves as equals. Friends (a) accept and support one another ("When you tell a friend what you want to do, she doesn't say that's ridiculous"); (b) enjoy one another ("What makes a good friend is that you have lots of fun with them and you can play tricks on them and they don't get angry with you"); (c) confide in one another and share experiences ("You tell them all your secrets and they tell you theirs"); (d) trust one another ("A good friend is someone who won't turn their back on you"); (e) have an intimate and mutual understanding of one another ("A friend is someone you can talk to who sort of has the same ideas as you

WILLARD W. HARTUP and MICHAEL F. SANCILIO • Institute of Child Development, University of Minnesota, Minneapolis, Minnesota 55455.

have but has got different things that they introduce you to as well"). Children themselves describe the satisfactions of friendship in these terms, expressing their notions about friendship mainly in terms of care, help, enjoyment, understanding, affiliation, security, commitment, and sharing (Bigelow & La Gaipa, 1975; Furman & Bierman, 1984; Goodnow & Burns, in press).*

Friendships differ from other attachments. Parents and their children, for example, are usually bound together more passionately and exclusively than friends are, and these relationships are suffused with complementarities—for instance, one individual (the parent) is wise in the ways of the world and the other (the child) is relatively naive. Compliance and control are universal themes in close relationships between children and adults but characterize the relationships between children and their friends much less extensively (Youniss, 1980). Concomitantly, children operate from a position of relative powerlessness when interacting with their parents, but from a stronger and more equal power base when interacting with their friends (Cowan, Drinkard, & MacGavin, 1984).

Lovers, too, have relationships that are different from friendships. To be sure, both kinds of relationships are based on reciprocal expectations and a recognition that the parties involved are "equals." But romantic relationships involve dimensions of passion, exclusiveness, and commitment that friendships ordinarily do not have. Thus, mutuality, intimacy, support, and sharing may be common satisfactions in any relationship that one would describe as "close," but neither children nor adults have difficulty in distinguishing friendships from romantic relationships in terms of affect and exclusivity.

The word *friend* appears in children's vocabularies during the early preschool years (in the third year, approximately), although young children cannot articulate the mutuality and commitment that are the hallmarks of friendship. Indeed, to ask a 4-year-old, "Why is Barry your friend?" is to invite one of the following responses: "Because I like him" or "Because we play." Still, these answers convey a sense of mutual attachment and common interests—themes that continue to be emphasized as children grow older (Youniss, 1980). Thus, even though young children understand friendship mainly in concrete and naive terms, they use the word with an appreciation that reciprocity is its essential feature.

The subsequent development of friendship expectations in children and adolescents seems not to involve the acquisition of new notions but to be a series of transformations and elaborations in the child's understanding of social reciprocity. Mutual understanding, loyalty, and self-disclosure come to be recognized as friendship expectations in preadolescence (Bigelow & La Gaipa, 1975; Furman & Bierman, 1984), but these seem to be transformations of earlier notions about

*The quotations from children's interviews were obtained by Goodnow and Burns (in press) and are used with their kind permission.

reciprocity rather than ideas originating independently that the child then gradually assimilates to the friendship construct.

Observational studies demonstrate that children's interactions with their friends are distinctively different from their interactions with nonfriends. In cooperative settings, friends are more interactive, emotionally expressive, attentive to equity considerations, mutually directive, and vigorous in exploring materials and resources than are nonfriends (Newcomb & Brady, 1982; Newcomb, Brady, & Hartup, 1979). In competitive settings, boys are more assertive with their friends than with nonfriends; differences are less apparent among girls (Berndt, 1981b). Seemingly, then, friendships furnish a basis for competition as well as cooperation—at least among school-aged children. Whether conflicts among friends are more or less intense than conflicts among nonfriends is not known, nor do we know whether friends resolve conflicts in ways that differ from the ways that nonfriends set about resolving them. But the evidence shows that friendships are not necessarily marked by an absence of conflict and contention.

Observational assessment of friendship interaction has not revealed dramatic age differences. The increased intimacy and mutual identification about which children speak more explicitly as they get older (see above) seem to be too subtle to capture in brief behavioral assessments in the laboratory. One investigator (Berndt, 1981a) has shown that fourth-grade friends assist one another and are willing to share rewards more readily than first-grade friends, suggesting that equity considerations are reflected between friends in different ways as children mature. But our knowledge about developmental changes in friendship interaction is not extensive.

WHY ARE FRIENDS IMPORTANT?

Friendships probably serve the same general functions in social and cognitive development as other close relationships. First, they are *contexts* in which certain basic competencies emerge or receive elaboration—e.g., social communication, group entry, and cooperation skills; impulse controls; self-knowledge and self-evaluation; and knowledge about the world. No one has ever established whether childhood friendships contribute directly to the acquisition of these competencies but the adequacy of peer relations in childhood is a strong predictor of mental health status in adulthood (Hartup, 1983).

Second, friendships serve as emotional and cognitive *resources* that enhance individual adaptation, especially in situations that require joint functioning with "coequals" or "peers." Friends are better co-workers than nonfriends (Newcomb & Brady, 1982), an important consideration given that the contributions of two individuals, not one, are needed in many problem-solving situations. The recruitment and utilization of other individuals in problem solving (including delegation, negotiation, and other coactive skills) are increasingly recognized as intelligent behaviors (Goodnow, in press), thus suggesting a special role for friendships in social adaptation. In addition, friendships may buffer or protect the individual from stress, although relatively little is known about this. One investigation indicates that, among boys but not girls, friends assist in the amelioration of anxieties, the resolution of loyalty conflicts, and adaptation to the economic and practical exigencies deriving from divorce (Wallerstein & Kelly, 1980). The extent to which children use their friends for emotional and social support "instead of" or "in addition to" their families is thus an interesting question—unfortunately, a question about which we currently have little information.

Third, childhood friendships are *forerunners* or *precursors* of later relationships. Sullivan (1953) recognized that same-sex friendships during middle childhood are the contexts in which most individuals acquire the capacity for intimacy, and that these relationships have an important bearing on the nature of heterosexual relations that emerge in adolescence. Other possibilities include the notion that the "delicate balance of exchange" worked out between children and their friends (Goodnow & Burns, in press) represents a sort of scaffolding used by the individual to construct relationships with age-mates in adolescence and adulthood. No one assumes that new relationships are mere carbon copies of older ones; moreover, continuities within and across friendships have never been studied. Nevertheless, we can hypothesize that the developmental significance of friendships probably extends to their value as precursors of other relationships as well as to their value in the acquisition of social skills.

These arguments suggest that the child without friends is a child at risk in social and emotional development. Longitudinal evidence is not extensive, however, so that we can't look to empirical evidence to show that friends are childhood prerequisites for successful adaptation in adulthood. The literature shows again and again that children with friends are more socially competent than children without friends, but it is difficult to sort out whether the child's capacity for successfully forming and maintaining friendships is (a) a nonessential "by-product" of more fundamental competencies that predict future adjustment directly or (b) crucial because friendships provide unique and necessary opportunities for the development of certain relevant abilities. Still a third possibility is that friendship experience may not be strictly necessary for healthy adaptation but merely provides an expedient means to that end.

In this chapter, we contend that friends are developmental "advantages" rather than developmental necessities. While children who have friends may generally be better off than children without friends, the "plasticities of childhood" probably permit other relationships or experiences (real or symbolic) to serve the same functions that friendships normally do. Relative to other species, human beings are extremely plastic, meaning that their development is not as restricted by biogenetic programming. In the course of their development, human beings are capable of considerable change and variation in patterns of successful adaptation. Since there is no reason to believe that friendship relations are exceptions to this general principle, it follows that friendships may not be developmental necessities so much as adaptational advantages. That is, these relationships may provide optimal settings for accomplishing various developmental tasks that might also, but with more difficulty, be managed in other ways. Even though friendships appear to be positive forces or protective factors in social development, it may be possible for the individual child to exploit other relationships in order to obtain the same advantages.

But what does the literature tell us about individual differences among children in friendship experience or the socializing consequences of these differences? What do previous studies reveal about pair-to-pair differences in the structure of these relationships, the use of reciprocity rules, the content of the interaction, and their affective nature? Do friendships produce increased similarity between the children involved? Are friendships protective factors in development? What is the friendship experience of autistic children and others whose social adaptation is tenuous? To these questions we now turn our attention.

INDIVIDUAL DIFFERENCES

Children's friendships have been examined in relation to a wide range of conditions. Age and sex differences have been scrutinized, for example, and the friendships of disturbed children have been compared to those of their better adjusted peers.

Ordinarily, the physical and behavioral characteristics associated with friendship formation and maintenance are not regarded as "context-specific," i.e., typical only of the situation in which the attribute is studied. And yet the importance of any variable in social attraction may depend on the social context in which the individual interacts with others (Karweit & Hansell, 1983). The organization of the school environment (where most of the relevant studies have been conducted) can determine which individual characteristics are most directly implicated in friendship relations, at the same time bearing on the ease with which these relationships are formed in the first place. Open classrooms, for example, contain more fluid social hierarchies than traditional classrooms (Hallinan, 1976) and, simultaneously, more students are selected and fewer are neglected as best friends (Epstein, 1983). Further, cooperative classrooms, as contrasted with competitive ones, induce children to believe that their friends like them better (Johnson, Johnson, Johnson, & Anderson, 1976). Important as these results are, most investigators give little attention to setting conditions in considering the relation between individual attributes and children's friendship experiences.

Age. It will probably come as no surprise, but children ordinarily have friends who are the same age as they are. Within classrooms, the correlation between friends' ages is not large, owing to the restricted age ranges that exist in these situations. Within entire schools, however, there is a relatively high concordance between the ages of children and their friends (Kandel, 1978), a state of affairs that is consistent with children's notions that friendships are rooted in equality and equity.

With increasing age, the activities in which friends engage change also. And while equity and reciprocity remain the touchstones of friendship throughout childhood, the behavioral manifestations of these norms change as children grow older. In addition, as noted earlier, intimacy and identity issues become increasingly important in children's friendship expectations during middle childhood and early adolescence.

Sex. Besides chronological age, the characteristic for which children and their friends are most concordant is sex. Cross-sex "best friends" are relatively rare throughout early and middle childhood; even in adolescence, students prefer members of their own sex as best friends, albeit not as exclusively. Epstein (1983), for example, obtained correlations between the sexes of friends approximating .90 between grades 6 and 9, and .70 among 12th-graders.

The friendships of boys and girls differ in several respects: First, boys are members of large friendship networks more commonly than girls; close relationships among girls are more likely to be embedded in smaller groups (Omark, Omark, & Edelman, 1973). Second, girls' friendships are more "intensive" than boys' are, while boys' are more "extensive" than girls' (Waldrop & Halverson, 1975). Sometimes, these differences are thought to derive from sex differences in the games children play; other times, they seem to be linked to differences in the norms that govern social communication (e.g., the stress on autonomy in male–male interaction and the stress on intimacy and interpersonal skills in female–female interaction). Taken together, these studies suggest that sex differences extend to both the size of the friendship networks and the affective intensity of communication within them. (Caution: The size and "intensity" of friendship networks are not necessarily related, and the relevant studies sometimes do not clearly separate them. Consequently, to argue that boys' friendships lack the emotional depth of girls' friendships is to argue on the basis of very slim evidence. On the other hand, it is relatively clear that boys' friendship networks are larger than those of girls.)

Race. Little is known about race differences in the nature of children's friendships. With the approach of adolescence, children increasingly choose same-race individuals as best friends (Singleton & Asher, 1979), although the number of same-race choices among younger children does not depart from chance in many studies (Banks, 1976). To our knowledge, race differences in friendship expectations have not been studied nor have race differences in friendship interaction.

Social Class. Friends resemble one another in social class but, given the relatively homogeneous socioeconomic makeup of most schools, this similarity may be unavoidable. Social attraction, as measured by sociometric tests, varies according to social class (Grossman & Wrighter, 1948), but we do not know whether middle-class children are more likely to have "best friends" than lower-class children—especially with other relevant characteristics, such as IQ, controlled. Nor do we know whether middle- and lower-class friendships (or friendships between children who vary in social class background) differ in any important way.

Competence. Best friends have sometimes been observed to be more similar in IQ than nonfriends, although not in other studies. For example, Roff, Sells, and Golden (1972) found significant correlations (between .22 and .39) between the IQs of best friends, but Challman (1932) did not.

Whether the friendships of bright and dull children differ is not certain, although some extreme differences are relatively clear. For example, gifted children generally exhibit good peer relations, although those with extremely high IQs have sometimes been found to be isolated from their peers (Burks, Jensen, & Terman, 1930; Hollingworth, 1942). At the other end of the distribution, mentally retarded children have relatively few friends, according to assessment in mainstreamed classrooms (Gottlieb, 1975). Cognitive limitations may, to some extent, account for this state of affairs, but the evidence suggests that social skills deficits are also implicated in the poor peer relations of mentally retarded children. Even so, whether friendships among gifted children and friendships among retarded children differ in any qualitative sense from each other, or from the friendships of children with average intelligence, has not been established.

When competence is defined in terms other than IQ, it is apparent that competent children have more friends than less competent children do. This inference can be made on the basis of innumerable sociometric studies that show popular children, as compared to less popular children, to be more friendly, less likely to be inappropriately aggressive, more skillful in entering group activity and sustaining interaction, and so forth (Hartup, 1983).

Again, little is known about differences that may exist between the friendships of more and less competent children, although recent studies indicate some differences in the social networks in which these relationships are embedded. For example, popular (competent) children are more likely to interact in cliquish groups composed of mutual friends than are unpopular children; unpopular children, on the other hand, are more likely to socialize in small groups on the playground and to interact more often with younger and/or unpopular companions than their more popular counterparts (Ladd, 1983).

Criminality. Juvenile delinquents generally have low sociometric status, although studies of popularity have been performed mostly in schools, where delinquent children show little interest—either academic or social (Campbell,

1980). One variable that moderates the relation between delinquency and popularity, however, is socioeconomic status. Among lower-class children, delinquents are sometimes popular and sometimes not, suggesting a class difference in the standards by which criminal behavior is judged. Interestingly, though, popularity differentiates among lower-class children in terms of their criminal prognosis (Roff *et al.*, 1972).

Delinquents turn out to have delinquent friends more commonly than do nondelinquents (Hindelang, 1973; Hirschi, 1969), but these results do not tell us whether delinquents have a greater or lesser number of "best friends" than nondelinquent children. In one instance, delinquency was observed more frequently among children whose attachments to their friends were "weak" than among children whose attachments were "strong" (Hirschi, 1969). Thus, there is the possibility that weak bonding to other children, themselves delinquent, may differentiate children who engage in criminal activity from nondelinquents.

A controversial distinction, sometimes made among juvenile delinquents or children with "conduct disorders," differentiates those who are "socialized" from those who are "un-" or "undersocialized." Undersocialized delinquency is identified with disturbances in interpersonal relationships and a lack of friends—alienation, in a word. Socialized delinquents, on the other hand, have dependable, sustained relationships with others. Different kinds of criminal activity are thought to characterize socialized and undersocialized delinquents, although the specific criminal behaviors identified with each group vary from study to study (Rutter & Giller, 1984). Socialized delinquents are believed to have better prognoses than their undersocialized counterparts, and one follow-up study supports this view (Henn, Bardwell, & Jenkins, 1980). Nevertheless, the importance and meaning of friendship relations in the etiology of delinquency remains controversial. Clearly, the scenario is more complicated than one in which experienced delinquents merely persuade their nondelinquent friends to engage in criminal activity. In many instances, the social relationships of young delinquents are broadly dysfunctional, in ways that go beyond their tendency to choose other delinquents as "best friends."

Behavior Disorders. Children with behavior disorders experience difficulties in relations with other children and, concomitantly, have relatively low sociometric status. For example, among children in a large national sample of individuals referred to child guidance clinics, 30 to 75% (depending on age) were described by their parents as having poor peer relations (Achenbach & Edelbrock, 1981). At all ages, the percentage of clinically referred children with peer difficulties was at least twice as high as the percentage of matched nonreferred children manifesting these problems. Moreover, the children in the clinical sample had significantly fewer friends and less contact with their friends than did children in the nonclinical sample. In other studies, disturbed children have been found to evidence less mature understanding of the reciprocities and intimacies involved in friendships than matched nonclinical samples (Selman,

1980). Finally, emotionally disturbed children have been found to have friendships that are significantly less stable over time than those of nondisturbed comparison groups (Davids & Parenti, 1958), showing yet another way in which the friendship experiences of children with behavior disorders differ from those of children who do not have these difficulties.

Ironically, peer difficulties among autistic children are not often reported because few children with this diagnosis progress far enough to make a consideration of friendship relations relevant (Kanner, Rodriguez, & Ashenden, 1972; Rutter, 1970). Actual friendships, even among those exceptional cases who make significant advances in social adaptation, are rare. More commonly reported is a desire among formerly autistic persons for social connectedness, a desire that these individuals are usually unable to gratify owing to a lack of interpersonal skills (Bemporad, 1979; Rutter, 1970).

As noted, little has been written about the friendships of autistic children other than about those few who have made extraordinary progress. Wing (1983) pointed out that "partnerships between people who are both autistic do occasionally develop, and, more rarely, friendships between an autistic and a nonhandicapped person" (p. 309). In addition, Strain (1984) found that nonhandicapped children in mainstream preschool classrooms sometimes chose "developmentally disabled" classmates as friends, although the presence of autistic children among those chosen as friends was not made entirely clear in these observations. But the paucity of published information on autistic children and their friends obviously reflects the fact that children with autism have deficits in basic areas that affect social interaction and the formation of close relationships with age-mates. In turn, the absence of friendship experience prevents the individual with autism from acquiring and enhancing significant social abilities and skills. Whether one considers the central factor in the development of autism to be a constitutional cognitive deficit or to be a disorder of early social experience, difficulties in friendship relations must be cited as an important concomitant of the condition.

FRIENDSHIP VARIATIONS

Children's friendship relations have rarely been examined qualitatively. We know that some children have fewer friends than others; some seem to have less stable friendships than others; and, sometimes a child's friendships are identified as "strong" or "weak." Rarely, however, are any factors taken into account other than (a) whether the child has friends or not, (b) how many friends the child actually has, and (c) how long the friendship lasts. These measures certainly do not encompass everything about friendships relevant to children's social adaptations. One can imagine that differences in the intensity, exclusivity, and security of these relationships would also account for significant variance in the social and emotional development of the child.

One investigation suggesting that friendship variations may account for significant outcome variance deals with the relation between friendship "integration" and school achievement (Krappman, in press). On the basis of interviews and observations of 6-, 10-, and 12-year-old children, five "types" of children were identified: (a) *intimate friends*—children who have intimate relationships with other children, with whom they pursue negotiated actions and shared interests, either to the exclusion of others or supplemented by other, nonintimate relationships; (b) *partners*—children who move back and forth from social networks to alliances with one or two other children, and who expect involvement with one another but not on an intimate basis; (c) *mates*—children who are members of an extensive social network and who have either high or low social power; (d) *ramblers*—children who oscillate between solitary activities and social participation without establishing enduring relationships and who are either accepted or rejected; (e) *isolates*—children who have very few interactive partners.

These types obviously differentiate among children along more than one dimension; e.g., "intimate friends" and "isolates" differ from one another in terms of both number of associates and the intimacy of their interactions with one another. Nevertheless, these observations are noteworthy because the classification system is based on sociability, exclusivity, acceptance-rejection, and social influence *taken together*, and not just on the number of the children's friends. Illustrating the value of this multidimensional assessment of children's relationships are results showing that friends, partners, and mates (the first three types) are better achievers than ramblers or isolates (the two remaining types). Whether this difference remains when IQ is partialed out is not yet known, but the example is important.

Some 16 years ago, it was the differentiation among mother–child relationships in terms of multidimensional "qualities" that turned out to be a major breakthrough in the study of early attachments and their significance in child development (Ainsworth & Wittig, 1969). Once "secure" relationships could be distinguished from "anxious" or "avoidant" ones on the basis of mother–infant interaction before and after brief separations, the groundwork was laid for showing certain continuities in the mother–child relationship over time and the developmental outcomes to which these relationships contribute (Sroufe & Fleeson, in press). No one has ever tried to assess pair-to-pair variations in children's friendships in this way; there is no well-validated typology distinguishing "secure" friendships from "insecure" ones. And yet friendships that function smoothly might be thought to predict different outcomes from friendships that are chaotic and inconstant.

Clearly, a framework for describing children's friendships is needed. The way to achieve one, however, is not very clear. Cognitive theories suggest one set of dimensions that could be used to describe close relationships (e.g., attributional biases, interpersonal perceptions) while other theories suggest somewhat different bases for description (e.g., affective qualities). Robert Hinde (1979) has delineated eight categories, broadly relevant to close relationships, that include most of the dimensions cited in the various contemporary theories. Ranging from characteristics of specific interactions to more global attributes, these categories may not be equally applicable to every close relationship. Most, however, seem relevant to children and their friends.

Content. This term refers to what the individuals in a relationship do with one another. Content may be specified at many different levels of analysis ranging from broad, functional dimensions (e.g., play, fighting) through more specific activities (e.g., dramatic play, block building, "fooling around") and detailed action sequences (hitting, nurturing). Time-use studies (cf. Medrich, Rosen, Rubin, & Buckley, 1982), for example, demonstrate that American children spend their time with friends engaged mainly in play and "socializing" and that many of these activities involve physically active or "robust" interactions. Among school-aged children, for example, sports accounted for 45% and 26% of the interaction with their friends of boys and girls, respectively, although other types of robust interaction including "general play," "going places," and "socializing" were also commonly mentioned by girls. Other investigators have described friendships in terms of sharing and conflict resolution (Hinde, Titmus, Easton, & Tamplin, 1985; Nelson & Aboud, 1985)—further examples of the content embraced by these relationships.

Although friendships in general have been examined in this manner, pair-to-pair differences among friends have never been systematically described in relation to content. Considerable interest, however, has been evident in content as a means of distinguishing, for example, the social histories of delinquent and nondelinquent children. The most common and obvious observation is that delinquents and their friends engage in criminal activity more frequently than nondelinquents and theirs. Moreover, hierarchies among delinquents may exist according to the kinds of criminal activity engaged in. But little else is known about the content of friendship relations among juvenile delinquents. The friendship interactions of predelinquent children, who are known to have difficulties with peers (Conger & Miller, 1966), would also be of interest, but the matter has been neglected. So, too, we know relatively little about the content of close relationships involving other troubled children.

Diversity. This notion refers to the number of different things the participants in a relationship do together. Do certain boys' relationships encompass only soccer playing and "fooling around," while others, in addition, involve braggadocio, poking fun at girls, *and* homework? Are "school" friendships different from "school and neighborhood" friendships?

Why is diversity important? First, the greater the diversity of interactions, the greater the number of opportunities for interactions of one type to be influenced by those of another type (Hinde & Stevenson-Hinde, in press). Thus, we expect friendships characterized by diversity to have a more general impact on the individual than friendships that are more narrowly focused. Second, diverse relationships furnish a better context than nondiverse ones for the development of self-disclosure and other manifestations of intimacy (Altman & Taylor, 1973). The basic question, then, may not be whether troubled children lack friends but whether or not their friendships are sufficiently diverse to provide a basis for intimate exchange—especially in preadolescence.

Qualities. The affective qualities of relationships may be their most important features. Some friendships, for example, seem suffused with warmth and sensitivity; others are characterized by ambivalence; still others are characterized by sensitivity in one partner and indifference in the other. Friendships are seldom regarded in terms of differences like these, although certain qualities in peer interaction have been studied in relation to sociometric status. Sensitive children, who know how to make appropriate social overtures and who are adept at "group entry" (i.e., who know how to wait for appropriate "openings" and who then insert themselves into a group with references to the ongoing activity rather than with references to themselves), are sought out more frequently as friends than children who are not sensitive (Dodge, Schlundt, Schocken, & Delugach, 1983). Even so, very little is known about qualitative differences in children's friendships and their relevance to the child's adaptation.

The evidence now suggests that insecure attachments to caretakers during the early years are predictive of peer difficulties in the preschool years as well as other adaptational problems (Sroufe & Fleeson, in press). Whether similar consequences also ensue from affectively insecure relationships between children and their friends is a matter of great importance, especially in the etiology of social isolation or conduct disorder. We know that disturbed children are not ascribed a place in the peer group that is as central as the status given to more competent children. But we do not know whether the quality of the close relationships that these children have is, in any way, different from the relationships of other children. One suspects this to be the case.

Patterns in the constituent interactions constituting a relationship may be other important elements to consider. Relationships are different when certain interactions covary (e.g., warmth, demands, and compliance) than when covariation is not the case. First, we use covariations such as these to construct attributional hypotheses; thus, those occurring in the interactions between two individuals carry implications for the manner in which their relationship will be perceived and labeled. Second, the psychological consequences of certain clusters of interactions may be different from other clusterings. For example, the *amount* of stimulation that a mother directs toward her infant does not correlate with the security of the mother–infant attachment although the *contingencies* in the interaction between the mother and the infant do (Bell & Ainsworth, 1972). And still other patterns, such as the relative frequency of positive and negative interactions, may be important in distinguishing certain relationships from other ones. For example, a child who always plays when invited may be regarded as compliant, but one who sometimes refuses and other times insists on playing may be regarded as controlling (Hinde & Stevenson-Hinde, in press).

No one has tried to study the many intricate ways in which children's friendships are patterned. The evidence suggesting that patterns of interaction are important in classifying relationships comes mostly from studies of nonhuman primates (Hinde, 1979). But the importance of these elements in children's friendships may be considerable. We know, for example, that aggressive school-aged children experience more hostile interactions with their contemporaries than nonaggressive children and attribute aggressive intent to them more readily (Dodge, 1980). We do not know, however, whether these attributional biases characterize aggressive children's perceptions of friends and nonfriends equally, and we do not know whether interaction with friends has any special significance as a context for the construction of these biases. Given the amount of time that children spend with their friends, though, the importance of considering these issues is obvious.

Reciprocity and complementarity are also characteristics that differentiate relationships from one another. Some relationships seem to encompass many complementary interactions, i.e., exchanges in which the individuals engage in different but complementary behaviors. Parent–child relationships typically involve numerous complementary interactions, a situation that is well recognized by children as well as by adults (Youniss, 1980). Child–child interactions, on the other hand, are more often reciprocal (i.e., the participants do the same thing or expect the same things of one another). Relationships between children who differ in age are marked by fewer reciprocities and more frequent complementarities than relationships between children who are similar in age (Hartup, 1983). Friendship interactions, however, are believed to be predominately reciprocal.

The reciprocities of friendship extend from conversational exchange (Gottman, 1983) to knowledge about one another (Ladd & Emerson, 1984). Moreover, these reciprocities differentiate between certain kinds of friendship pairs: *mutual friends* (who nominate each other on sociometric tests) perceive themselves as more similar to one another than *unilateral friends* (only one of whom nominates the other).

Some of the instability that marks the friendships of emotionally disturbed children may derive from their failure to understand that these relationships necessitate reciprocal interaction. Indeed, Selman (1980) demonstrated that a sample of "referred" children understood the bilaterality involved in friendship relations less well than a matched sample of nonreferred children. Moreover, a difference in their understanding of these reciprocities remained over the 2 years during which this particular study was carried out. One can speculate, then, that the failure to discriminate among one's close relationships in terms of reciprocity and complementarity may generally characterize disturbed, less mature, and less intelligent persons. Most children are able to adjust their behavior according to the individuals with whom they interact (Shatz & Gelman, 1973); others, however, may not. Careful assessment of the reciprocities and complementarities existing in children's friendships (and how these are understood) should probably figure more centrally in our efforts to evaluate their adaptive success.

Interpersonal perception is the manner in which individuals view one another—the constructs they use to describe one another and the agreement or disagreement in these views. These matters, especially the extent to which two individuals agree in their interpersonal perceptions, contribute to the satisfaction experienced in relationships and how smoothly they function. Diaz and Berndt (1982) compared children's reports about a best friend with the friends' self-reports and found that school-aged children were quite knowledgeable about their friends. And, typically, friends' descriptions of one another are more extensive and cognitively elaborate than descriptions of nonfriends (Livesley & Bromley, 1973).

Friendships vary, however, in the extent to which children see the same things in one another. Ladd and Emerson (1984) determined that mutual friends, as compared to unilateral friends, are (a) more accurate in predicting characteristics common to both partners and (b) more aware of differences between themselves. These results are consistent with the hypothesis that shared knowledge is a basis for mutual attraction and friendship relations, but also with the notion that close relationships increase concordance in interpersonal perception. Whatever the case, it is obvious that unilateral attraction is not accompanied by the same sharing of interpersonal knowledge that mutual attraction is. This means that troubled children, whose attractions to others are frequently not reciprocated, probably fail to experience the concordances in interpersonal perception from which certain friendship satisfactions derive.

Intimacy. Childhood "is marked by the coming of the integrating tendencies which, when they are completely developed, we call love, or to say it another way, by the manifestation of the need for interpersonal intimacy" (Sullivan, 1953, p. 246). Among the earliest manifestations of intimacy in friendship relations is the sharing of secrets. Later, these manifestations extend to empathy, self-disclosure, and altruism.

Clearly evident among older children and adolescents, intimacy expectations differentiate between friendships and acquaintanceships. That is, children do not expect to engage in self-disclosure and empathic responding with their casual acquaintances to the same extent that they do with their friends (Furman & Bierman, 1984). Degree of intimacy is also thought to be one dimension along which the friendships of boys and girls differ (Douvan & Adelson, 1966). In one investigation (Sharabany, Gershoni, & Hofman, 1981) small, though significant, differences in intimacy between same-sex friends were found for girls and boys in the 5th, 7th, 9th, and 11th grades, with overall intimacy levels being similar across the four ages. Only among the oldest children, however, was the intimacy of a friendship with a member of the opposite sex comparable in degree to the intimacy of a friendship with a member of the same sex. For younger subjects, intimacy with opposite-sex friends was much lower than with same-sex friends, although this increased linearly with age—more so among girls than among boys. While not necessarily confirming Sullivan's view that intimacy with same-sex peers is a prerequisite for the development of intimacy with the opposite sex, the former preceded the latter in this (cross-sectional) sample.

Beyond this investigation, intimacy has not been measured effectively in children. In addition to its theoretically crucial role in the development of heterosexual relationships, several issues need to be addressed. First, are young children who interact empathically with their friends and who share secrets with each other especially likely to engage in intimate relationships in preadolescence? Second, does early failure to manifest self-disclosure differentiate children who are at risk for emotional disturbance? Intimacy seems to be entirely beyond the capacities of many disturbed children and adolescents, although it is not clear whether this occurs because of some underlying deficit or because of affective interference. And the literature also suggests that intimacy may be one dimension in children's friendships that affects prognosis among juvenile delinquents (see above). Certainly, there is reason to tackle the measurement issues involved in conducting the relevant studies.

Commitment. A sense of commitment is evident in children's friendships toward the end of middle childhood: A friend is "a person that sticks by you when all the troubles come" (Goodnow & Burns, in press). Nevertheless, this characteristic of friendship interactions is not as clearly manifest among young children as some of the others mentioned. This is not to say that fidelity and working to continue a relationship are unimportant among younger children but, rather, to underscore that our information is too sketchy to conclude very much about the dynamics of commitment in early childhood.

One can argue that the stability of friendships depends, to some extent, on the commitment of individuals to these relationships. Notice that the choice of "best friends" is only moderately stable among 11- to 15-year-olds, with various surveys showing that as many as 50% of children in this age group do *not* choose the same best friend over a 2-week interval (Thompson & Horrocks, 1947). The situation is very different among 16- to 19-year-olds; among older adolescents, the same individuals are chosen between 60 and 90% of the time. Stability of friendship choice, of course, is not the same thing as commitment. Nevertheless, it is unlikely that friendship fluctuations would be as extensive as they are among younger children were commitments more salient in these relationships.

Child–child relations differ from adult–child relations in terms of the conditions that support the commitments of the individuals to one another. Children's relationships with adults are sustained by *exogenous* conditions, including economic and legal sanctions. Children cannot break off their relationships with their parents unilaterally, nor can society intervene in these relationships except under the most extreme conditions of abuse and neglect. Friendships, on the other hand, are supported mostly by *endogenous* conditions and, hence, are more fragile than adult–child relationships. By the end of adolescence, however, parent–child relationships come to rest more squarely on endogenous conditions although, even then, these commitments are not as fragile as friendships are. The dynamics of commitment are obviously complex but are clearly relevant to many important issues in the development and maintenance of friendships.

CONCLUSION

Children with intellectual, emotional, and behavioral disturbances are likely to be unpopular, ineffective in initiating and maintaining good social relations with other children, and unsuccessful in establishing and maintaining friendships. More successful friendship experiences are found among less troubled children, especially those who are intelligent, able, friendly, socially competent, and well socialized. In most instances, these variations reflect a developmental process through which early differences in social competence, usually manifest in family relations, generalize or extend to subsequent social relations—including close relationships with other children (Hartup, 1983).

Friendship experiences contribute, in turn, to individual differences in social adaptation, although this has been difficult to document empirically. We know that good peer relations are developmental forerunners of good adaptations in adulthood, but we do not know exactly what it is that friendships contribute to this end. Circumstantial evidence suggests that friendships serve as contexts for the acquisition of social skills, as cognitive and emotional resources, and as templates in the formation of other relationships. The child without friends, then, is a child at risk in social and emotional development, although it is possible that other relationships can substitute for friendships in certain ways.

Friendship variations are underrecognized in both child development research and clinical practice. Ordinarily, children are differentiated from one another simply in terms of the number and identity of their "best friends" and whether these relationships are more or less enduring. Eight categories were mentioned in this chapter that can be used to assess variations in children's friendship more completely. Which categories require attention depends on the circumstances and the developmental outcomes in which one is interested. We argue that a better understanding of children and their friends—including both typical and atypical children—requires increased attention to the content, affective qualities, reciprocities, intimacy, and commitments marking these relationships. Such qualitative assessment is necessary, first, in establishing the existence of children's friendships (as differentiated from other kinds of relationships), but it is also needed in evaluating the many different variations in the close relationships that children generate with each other. The time has come to establish more clearly the significance of these variations in social and emotional development.

REFERENCES

Achenbach, T. M., & Edelbrock, C. S. (1981). Behavioral problems and competencies reported by parents of normal and disturbed children aged 4 through 16. *Monographs of the Society for Research in Child Development, 46*(1, Whole No. 188).

Ainsworth, M. D. S., & Wittig, B. A. (1969). Attachment and exploratory behavior of one-year-olds in a strange situation. In B. Foss (Ed.), *Determinants of infant behaviour* (Vol. 4, pp. 111–136). New York: Wiley.

Altman, I., & Taylor, D. A. (1973). *Social penetration*. New York: Holt, Rinehart & Winston.

Banks, W. C. (1976). White preference in blacks: A paradigm in search of a phenomenon. *Psychological Bulletin, 83,* 1179–1186.

Bell, S. M., & Ainsworth, M. D. S. (1972). Infant crying and maternal responsiveness. *Child Development, 43,* 1171–1190.

Bemporad, J. R. (1979). Adult recollections of a formerly autistic child. *Journal of Autism and Developmental Disorders, 9,* 179–197.

Berndt, T. J. (1981a). Age changes and changes over time in prosocial intentions and behavior between friends. *Developmental Psychology, 17,* 408–416.

Berndt, T. J. (1981b). Effects of friendship on prosocial intentions and behavior. *Child Development, 52,* 636–643.

Bigelow, B. J., & LaGaipa, J. J. (1975). Children's written descriptions of friendship: A multidimensional analysis. *Developmental Psychology, 11,* 857–858.

Burks, B. S., Jensen, D. W., & Terman, L. M. (1930). *Genetic studies of genius, Vol. 3: The promise of growth*. Stanford, CA: Stanford University Press.

Campbell, A. C. (1980). Friendship as a factor in male and female delinquency. In H. C. Foot, A. J. Chapman, & J. R. Smith (Eds.), *Friendship and social relations in children* (pp. 365–389). Chichester: Wiley.

Challman, R. C. (1932). Factors influencing friendships among preschool children. *Child Development, 3,* 146–158.

Conger, J. J., & Miller, W. C. (1966). *Personality, social class and delinquency*. New York: Wiley.

Cowan, G., Drinkard, J., & MacGavin, L. (1984). The effects of target, age, and gender on use of power strategies. *Journal of Personality and Social Psychology, 47,* 1391–1398.

Davids, A., & Parenti, A. N. (1958). Time orientation and interpersonal relations of emotionally disturbed and normal children. *Journal of Abnormal and Social Psychology, 57,* 299–305.

Diaz, R. M., & Berndt, T. J. (1982). Children's knowledge of best friend: Fact or fancy? *Developmental Psychology, 18,* 787–794.

Dodge, K. A. (1980). Social cognition and children's aggressive behavior. *Child Development, 51,* 162–170.

Dodge, K. A., Schlundt, D. C., Schocken, I., & Delugach, J. D. (1983). Social competence and children's sociometric status: The role of peer group entry strategies. *Merrill-Palmer Quarterly, 29,* 309–336.

Douvan, E., & Adelson, J. (1966). *The adolescent experience.* New York: Wiley.

Epstein, J. L. (1983). Selection of friends in differently organized schools and classrooms. In J. L. Epstein & N. Karweit (Eds.), *Friends in school: Patterns of selection and influence in secondary schools* (pp. 73–92). New York: Academic Press.

Furman, W., & Bierman, K. L. (1984). Children's conceptions of friendship: A multimethod study of developmental changes. *Developmental Psychology, 20,* 925–931.

Goodnow, J. (in press). Some lifelong everyday forms of intelligent behavior: Organizing and reorganizing. In R. Sternberg & R. Wagner (Eds.), *Practical intelligence: Origins of competence in the everyday world.* New York: Cambridge University Press.

Goodnow, J., & Burns, A. (in press). *Home and school: Child's eye view.* Sydney: Allen and Unwin.

Gottlieb, J. (1975). Public, peer and professional attitudes toward mentally retarded persons. In M. J. Begab & S. A. Richardson (Eds.), *The mentally retarded and society: A social science perspective* (pp. 99–126). Baltimore: University Park Press.

Gottman, J. M. (1983). How children become friends. *Monographs of the Society for Research in Child Development, 48*(3, Whole No. 201).

Grossman, B., & Wrighter, J. (1948). The relationship between selection–rejection and intelligence, social status, and personality among sixth-grade children. *Sociometry, 11,* 346–355.

Hallinan, M. T. (1976). Friendship patterns in open and traditional classrooms. *Sociology of Education, 49,* 254–265.

Hartup, W. W. (1983). Peer relations. In E. M. Hetherington (Ed.), P. H. Mussen (Series Ed.), *Handbook of child psychology (Vol. 4): Socialization, personality and social development* (pp. 103–196). New York: Wiley.

Henn, F. A., Bardwell, R., & Jenkins, R. L. (1980). Juvenile delinquents revisited. *Archives of General Psychiatry, 37,* 1160–1163.

Hinde, R. A. (1979). *Towards understanding relationships.* New York: Academic Press.

Hinde, R. A., & Stevenson-Hinde, J. (in press). Relating childhood relationships to individual characteristics. In W. W. Hartup & Z. Rubin (Eds.), *Relationships and development.* Hillsdale, NJ: Erlbaum.

Hinde, R. A., Titmus, G., Easton, D., & Tamplin, A. (1985). Incidence of "friendship" and behavior to strong associates versus non-associates in preschoolers. *Child Development, 56,* 234–245.

Hindelang, M. (1973). Causes of delinquency: A partial replication and extension. *Social Problems, 20,* 471–487.

Hirschi, T. (1969). *Causes of delinquency.* Berkeley: University of California Press.

Hollingworth, L. S. (1942). *Children above 180 I.Q., Stanford-Binet: Origin and development.* Yonkers-on-Hudson, NY: World Book.

Johnson, D. W., Johnson, R. T., Johnson, J., & Anderson, D. (1976). Effects of cooperative versus individualized instruction on student prosocial behavior, attitudes toward learning, and achievement. *Journal of Educational Psychology, 68,* 446–452.

Kandel, D. B. (1978). Similarity in real-life adolescent friendship pairs. *Journal of Personality and Social Psychology, 36,* 306–312.

Kanner, L., Rodriguez, A., & Ashenden, B. (1972). How far can autistic children go in matters of social adaptation? *Journal of Autism and Childhood Schizophrenia, 2,* 9–33.

Karweit, N., & Hansell, S. (1983). School organization and friendship selection. In J. L. Epstein & N. Karweit (Eds.), *Friends in school: Patterns of selection and influence in secondary schools* (pp. 29–38). New York: Academic Press.

Krappman, L. (in press). Peer relations and their possible effects on school achievement. In R. A. Hinde, J. Stevenson-Hinde, & A. N. Perret-Clermont (Eds.), *Social relationships and cognitive development.* London: Oxford University Press.

Ladd, G. W. (1983). Social networks of popular, average, and rejected children in school settings. *Merrill-Palmer Quarterly, 29,* 283–308.

Ladd, G. W., & Emerson, E. S. (1984). Shared knowledge in children's friendships. *Developmental Psychology, 20,* 932–940.

Livesley, W. B., & Bromley, D. B. (1973). *Person perception in childhood and adolescence.* London: Wiley.

Medrich, E. A., Rosen, J., Rubin, V., & Buckley, S. (1982). *The serious business of growing up.* Berkeley: University of California Press.

Nelson, J., & Aboud, F. E. (1985). The resolution of social conflict between friends. *Child Development, 56,* 1009–1017.

Newcomb, A. F., & Brady, J. E. (1982). Mutuality in boys' friendship relations. *Child Development, 53,* 392–395.

Newcomb, A. F., Brady, J. E., & Hartup, W. W. (1979). Friendship and incentive condition as determinants of children's task-oriented social behavior. *Child Development, 50,* 878–881.

Omark, D. R., Omark, M., & Edelman, M. S. (1973). *Formation of dominance hierarchies in young children.* Paper presented at the IXth International Congress of Anthropological and Ethological Sciences, Chicago.

Roff, M., Sells, S. B., & Golden, M. M. (1972). *Social adjustment and personality development in children.* Minneapolis: University of Minnesota Press.

Rutter, M. (1970). Autistic children: Infancy to adulthood. *Seminars in Psychiatry, 2,* 435–450.

Rutter, M., & Garmezy, N. (1983). Developmental psychopathology. In E. M. Hetherington (Ed.), P. H. Mussen (Series Ed.), *Handbook of child psychology, (Vol. 4), Socialization, personality and social development* (pp. 775–911). New York: Wiley.

Rutter, M., & Giller, H. (1984). *Juvenile delinquency: Trends and perspectives.* New York: Guilford Press.

Selman, R. L. (1980). *The growth of interpersonal understanding.* New York: Academic Press.

Sharabany, R., Gershoni, R., & Hofman, J. E. (1981). Girlfriend, boyfriend: Age and sex differences in intimate friendship. *Developmental Psychology, 17,* 800–808.

Shatz, M., & Gelman, R. (1973). The development of communication skills: Modification in the speech of young children as a function of listener. *Monographs of the Society for Research in Child Development, 38* (5, Whole No. 152).

Singleton, L. C., & Asher, S. R. (1979). Racial integration and children's peer preferences: An investigation of developmental and cohort differences. *Child Development, 50,* 936–941.

Sroufe, L. A., & Fleeson, J. (in press). Attachment and the construction of relationships. In W. W. Hartup & Z. Rubin (Eds.), *Relationships and development.* Hillsdale, NJ: Erlbaum.

Strain, P. S. (1984). Social behavior patterns of nonhandicapped and developmentally disabled friend pairs in mainstream schools. *Analysis and Intervention in Developmental Disabilities, 4,* 15–28.

Sullivan, H. S. (1953). *The interpersonal theory of psychiatry.* New York: Norton.

Thompson, G. G., & Horrocks, J. E. (1947). A study of the friendship fluctuations of urban boys and girls. *Journal of Genetic Psychology, 70,* 53–63.

Waldrop, M. F., & Halverson, C. F. (1975). Intensive and extensive peer behavior: Longitudinal and cross-sectional analyses. *Child Development, 46,* 19–26.

Wallerstein, J. S., & Kelly, J. B. (1980). *Surviving the breakup: How children and parents cope with divorce.* New York: Basic Books.

Wing, L. (1983). Social and interpersonal needs. In E. Schopler & G. B. Mesibov (Eds.), *Autism in adolescents and adults* (pp. 337–353). New York: Plenum Press.

Youniss, J. (1980). *Parents and peers in social development: A Sullivan-Piaget perspective.* Chicago: University of Chicago Press.

5

Social Growth in Autism

A Parent's Perspective

CLARA CLAIBORNE PARK

Let me begin with what I might be tempted to emphasize in describing the social behavior of the autistic individual I know best—what I would emphasize, and rightly, if I were a journalist collecting success stories for publicly supported education under PL 94–142. My daughter Jessica, the youngest of my four children, at 25 could easily be presented as a competent adult. Jessy has a part-time job in a college mailroom; she pays taxes. She cleans house, irons, sews, and cooks, responsibly and well. She paints exact, finely rendered, subtly colored acrylics, many of which have been exhibited and sold. She lives at home as a contributing member of her family. Her WAIS IQ 2 years ago was 106 (Verbal: 98, Performance: 116); on the Advanced version of the Raven Progressive Matrices Test, a test of exact observation and logical inference, she scored well above the 95th percentile, higher than all but a tiny fraction of university graduate students (Ellis, 1982). All this being true, why shouldn't I make the claim every parent of a handicapped child dreams of—that she is normal?

Yet you would not have to exchange more than one sentence with her—indeed, you would not have to do more than observe her in a single social interchange at home, at work, or on one of her frequent shopping expeditions—to realize that all of these accomplishments, accomplishments that once seemed in the unreachable realm of miracle, do not add up to the expected sum: a human being fully comprehending of, and thus self-sufficient in, the daily life surrounding her.

For 25 years now, I've been watching social behavior in autism, day by day, hour by hour, often minute by minute. It's examples of that behavior,

CLARA CLAIBORNE PARK • Department of English, Williams College, Williamstown, Massachusetts 01267.

closely observed, that I have to report. A few explanatory hypotheses may creep in from time to time—one doesn't watch without thinking—but these are expendable. I've read many, many books and articles since we first heard the word *autistic,* in 1961, when our daughter was 3, offering explanatory hypotheses ranging from preposterous to likely. But if I have anything to add to what is known already, it comes not out of the literature but out of that minute-by-minute watching, and out of the social interchanges, at first rudimentary, then slowly less and less inadequate, that that close attention made possible. Social behavior in autism, for me, is not a concept, it is a shared experience of growth. If I am to communicate something of that experience, it must be by telling stories, anecdotal and unashamed. They are, I think, true stories; they rely on the notes I still scribble as the event takes place. I do not try to shape them artistically, and I specifically try *not* to shape them according to my preconceptions or my hopes. If I have any advantage over other observers of autism, it must be that for all these years I have been there, morning, noon, and night, experiencing the subject matter of this volume.

We used to wonder, in autism, whether it was the cognitive or the social deficits that were primary—today, perhaps, we see that they are inseparable. But there was never any doubt about which *looked* primary. It was that "autistic aloneness," that "withdrawal" that is not in fact withdrawal from a world experienced but a failure to enter it at all. What the first observers saw—what we ourselves saw in our fourth child—was autism itself, the word Kanner chose for its root meaning, *self*—the individual self-enclosed, apparently impermeable, a walled fortress, the metaphor so obvious and so compelling that Bruno Bettelheim and I, and I am sure many others, arrived at it completely independently. Of course, it is that aloneness that one sees first. In the early months and years the cognitive deficits are not even recognizable, so invisible that for 30 years people could believe there weren't any. The abnormality of that aloneness in a tiny child is so shocking to behold that it not only gave the condition its name but accounted for the psychogenic thrust of the first 30 years of research: How could such a total denial of social interaction be anything but a response to an inadequate or threatening social environment? What one sees first in autism, of course, is not social behavior but its lack.

EARLY YEARS

I saw that at nine months my baby did not respond to the discovery game, peekaboo from behind a diaper, as the other children had, although because she was so pretty and healthy and content I didn't realize the significance of what I was seeing—or not seeing. I saw that she was happiest in her crib, that she'd spend hour upon hour alone there, bouncing up and down and laughing; as the years wore on, though I placed a chair right beside it, and though I once saw her put a leg over the side, she didn't climb out. I saw that she was cheerful by herself and fretted when put with other children "to amuse her." Day by day, I saw the deficits that by now have become familiar in the literature—no reciprocal games, no imitative behavior, no social gestures, no bye-bye, no pointing, not even any reaching or grabbing—no needs, apparently, no desires. Jerome Bruner (1983), reviewing the work of Kenneth Kaye, *The Mental and Social Life of Babies,* has noted how "conventions of interactions develop, if only in games and play, and through them the child begins to develop perspectives on the roles he plays and the complementary roles played by others." And he quotes Kaye: "Language, in fact, does not exist merely for the sake of naming things. Nor does it exist for the sake of propositions about the world. It consists of interpersonal communications about shared and sharable intentions." All this complex growth in language and behavior develops in the interaction between mother and baby; all this had developed in the interaction between me and my normal children, so spontaneously and naturally that I had never thought about it. Now, between this fourth baby and this relaxed, experienced mother, it was not developing at all.

Time passed. She grew; eventually, almost 2, she learned to walk; she even acknowledged a few rudimentary desires. Perhaps now she might want a cookie. If so, we, the parents and siblings who surrounded her, fed her, washed her, cared for her, through whom she looked as through a pane of glass to the wall behind us, became accessible to her perceptions; we were perceived, however, not as people but as tools, as she picked up the hand nearest her and used it, her personal forklift, to pick up what her small, efficient hands would not get for herself.

But the stories from this period have been already told; anyone who wants to fill out the picture of a clinically autistic little girl can find the details in the book I wrote about her (C. C. Park, 1967/1982). Here I need only summarize how she grew, how her repertoire of behaviors slowly expanded as we found ways to activate the hidden cognitive capacities we were slowly discovering: the astonishing ability to discriminate shapes and colors, to categorize, even to count. But matching shapes and colors, assembling ever more complex puzzles, soon cease to seem significant signs of intelligence in a child who can do nothing else. Jessy had "advanced" skills but not the obvious ones: The child who at 2 could elegantly align blocks in parallel lines was at 5 still not toilet-trained (though she could control her bladder so well that she was dry all day), cooperated no better than a rag doll when we dressed her, did not dress herself fully until she was 9-years-old.

All the while, of course, we were working on social responsiveness and cognitive development together, making sure that all teaching was social, as I sat close beside her with our puzzles, snuggled with her under a blanket, crouched with her inside a cardboard box, pushed her on her swing, always from in front so the approach and retreat could model the dynamic of a manageable human relationship. Over the first 4 years the flashes of response became more frequent—the smile and brief eye contact when I went in to her in the mornings, the enjoyment of tickling, of hands-on, intrusive, boisterous play. Indifference was replaced by a kind of attachment; by the time she was 3 she would follow me from room to room. And our house, with three older children, was full of them and their friends; they took her for rides in the wagon; as time went on she would run parallel with them on the grass. Every meal, every activity, was a workshop for social behavior.

SOCIAL DEVELOPMENT AND SPEECH

Lagging far behind even this slow expansion of social responses was speech, the prime instrument of social interchange. The few isolated words she had spoken up to the age of 4½ had no social meaning; she gave no sign of comprehension when we spoke the very same words to her, though a normal child's passive vocabulary, of course, far exceeds the words it actually speaks. Jessy's few words did not include a sound for greeting, or a sound for mother or father, or the names of any of the family; even when at 5 she began to retain the names of people and objects, she did not use them for communication of any kind, least of all of "shared and sharable intentions." She was 6 before she used a word to request something; it was years more before she used a name to call one of us to her or to locate our whereabouts.

It was mysterious, the way she began to learn words when she was 5. We had waited so long; now, suddenly, you could tell her the name of anything, from aardvark to zebra, and she would remember and apply it accurately. But the social incomprehension persisted: Simple, easy words, words like *sister, teacher, friend, I* and *you, him* and *her,* she not only did not pick up spontaneously but found difficult or impossible to learn—and this in a child who at 7 learned at once the names for all the regular polygons. Hexagons and heptagons, of course, are quintessentially unsocial concepts; shapes and numbers are not subject to the bewildering contextual shifts that make ordinary language so different from the comfortable invariancy of mathematics. What normal 11-year-old would say, seeing a friend's new baby, "When I ten, *that* minus one!"? Jessy added verbs only very slowly to her lists of nouns. Verbs are always shifting with the when and what and who of social interchange; for the worst of them, the verb *to be*, Jessy developed the brilliant substitution of *equals*. Outside the exact sciences, words are relative, they take their meanings from the social situations in which they are embedded—friend to you, stranger to me; mother to me, friend to her; I, you, him, her, depending on who is speaking. Jessy was so far from "picking up" these simple social concepts that she was in her mid-teens before we managed to teach her, by the aid of explicit genealogical charts, how to apply correctly such terms as *grandmother, mother, daughter, granddaughter, aunt, cousin*—all of which, of course, can refer to the same identifiable person depending on who is talking, and in relation to whom.

Such an example makes clear that Jessy's cognitive difficulties could not be thought of as a function of a primary autistic isolation. For the adolescent Jessy who needed help to sort out the words for grandmother and granddaughter was by that time a friendly person who had long since learned to recognize her family and friends. The capacity for attachment we had worked so hard to foster in her early years was well established. By the time she was 9 I could already write of her what is true today, that an observer seeing her with someone she knew well might remark the immaturity of her affection but would not think of her as particularly withdrawn (C. C. Park, 1967/1982).

But people she knew well she knew because we, her family and friends, had learned how to talk to her; for the first 6 years of her school experience—a pathetic 2 hours a day, in those days before PL 94–142—she was essentially mute. A good teacher could reach her, talking plainly and well within her developmental level. She could not understand or respond to the rapid speech and social subject matter of normal peers, even normal retarded peers, and what she did not understand she tuned out—just as she had tuned us out for so long. When she was 9, strangers still found her speech unintelligible: largely two- and three-word sentences, and even those mispronounced and syntactically garbled. Outside the family she was at her most autistic. She took no social initiatives, unless you count the rare, sudden hugging of strangers, which we had to discourage. She didn't know how to take such initiatives; she shared none of the interests or concerns of the children she met, was capable of conceiving none of the questions that people ask naturally when they are "getting to know each other." Today, even after all the progress, verbal and social together, she still has little to say to those who do not reach out to meet her on her own turf, to share with her the immediate, concrete concerns of cooking or shopping, or to ask about her "favorite things," which last year included video games (watching, not playing), succeeded this year by rainbows, the constellation Orion, and the rising time of Venus. Though Jessy operates efficiently and well in the predictable routines of her daily life, though she enjoys simple conversations with friends and manages functional interchanges with strangers, the social initiatives still must come from those others who care enough about her to engage her in terms she can understand.

I have said enough to give a sense of where we started and how we progressed, imperceptibly at first, then each month, each year, a little bit faster. I have left out a great deal—it feels like everything—but Jessy's development from 9 to 23 has been described elsewhere (C. C. Park, 1977, 1978, 1982, 1983;

D. Park, 1974; Park & Youderian, 1974). I have summarized enough. Now the stories begin.

MODIFYING BEHAVIOR A CLICK AT A TIME

The first ones come from the years from 13 to 15, when we were discovering, late, the power of behavior modification techniques to help Jessy learn—learn productive behaviors, learn to eliminate or control unproductive ones—by substituting meaningful reinforcers, for Jessy, simple numerical points, for the social incentives that impel normal children to progress.

For so far I have not mentioned the strangest, most crippling feature of Jessy's autism. It had been with her from the beginning—the hidden, withheld quality pervading so much of what she did and didn't do, so that one had to lure, almost trick her into performing even those activities that were fully within her capabilities. As I had lured her into putting rings on a stick when she was 2, completing a five-piece puzzle when she was 3 (and a thousand-piece puzzle when she was 11). Call it inertia, lack of motivation, of drive; anyone who has worked with autistic people can supply hundreds of examples. They won't do even what they *can* do. My first story concerns that refusal to act, that seeming lack of will to do what every child, surely, does "naturally"—to learn, to move forward, to grow. We had lived with it all Jessy's life. I was resigned to coaxing, luring, occasionally forcing. I thought of that inertia as autism's deepest, most fundamental, most massive handicap. If you had told me that the condition I had called "willed weakness" (C. C. Park, 1967/1982) would yield to points, to a behavioral contract, to a golf counter, I would not have believed you.

We began our homemade behavior modification program under the best possible circumstances. Jessy had seen the golf counter on another child, much less severely autistic, who had come to visit. It was everything she liked best: It was mechanical, it was easy to use, it was predictable, it was numerical, it clicked. *She wanted one:*—the first present besides candy she'd ever asked for.

The program had two elements: points for desirable behaviors, leading, if the number agreed on was reached, to a popsicle at the end of the day, and a written contract.* It was important, I think, that Jessy was involved in both, that the process was not entirely imposed from without. It was Jessy who awarded the points or subtracted them for such behaviors as hitting and screaming, even though I was not present. Sometimes she graphed the points, decorative bar-graphs in lovely colors; the day she reached 134, when our goal was only 100, I realized that for mathematical Jessy, the points were their own reward.

*Further details on the program can be found in D. Park (1974) and C. C. Park (1982, 1983).

Equally important, Jessy and I negotiated the contract together. We made of the Sunday contract sessions a social occasion, both actually, as we sat side by side on her bed and talked over the successes and failures of the past week, and theoretically, as I took the opportunity to talk about people's behavior in general. That she enjoyed these sessions was clear; reading was very hard for her and she resisted it, but she loved reading the contract, which I kept easily within her own vocabulary.

One day, after more than a year of behavioral contracts, I set a long-term goal. I had taught Jessy to swim in the usual way, without contract or points, but after a year she still would not go out of her depth, or swim more than the 2 or 3 feet necessary to reach my outstretched arms. If we contracted for 1000 points for swimming the length, I thought, we'd have something to work up to over the next year. What happened? That very night, she walked up to the deep end of the pool, jumped in, and swam the 75-foot length *eight times*.

Another story, less spectacular, but with greater significance for social development:

At this time, as I have said, though Jessy was friendly, even affectionate with people she knew well, we had been unable to persuade her to make the simplest greeting: no hello, no smile, no looking in the eye. On the contract, then, went "Hello" (1 point). Plus a proper name: "Hello, Mrs. Smith" (2 points). Plus eye contact (3 points). Plus a fourth point for doing it all "spontaneously"; in Jessy's words, "without told." Suddenly we began to get reports from school; from Mrs. Smith and Mrs. Jones and the speech therapist whose father had been a London psychoanalyst and who had been working with Jessy for a year: Jessy was so much more *friendly*. "Hello, Mrs. Smith." The click-click-click-click was hardly noticeable. And the new greetings, of course, elicited smiles and delight; Mrs. Smith and Mrs. Jones did not have to be programmed to deliver social reinforcement. Jessy was learning far more than mechanical greeting behavior: She was learning something even more foreign to her—to enjoy praise, since praise and points went together. If Jessy can now say, "I'm proud of myself," and mean it, if she can repeat, "If at first you don't succeed, try, try again," and understand it, it is the result, not of deep therapy that penetrated 14 years of autistic refusal, but of clear behavioral specifications and that little counter.

POINTS AND MOTIVATION

I could scarcely believe how shallow were the roots of that inertia and negativism we had thought to be the core of her condition. The counter opened to me an alternative explanation of this aspect of the autistic handicap, simpler, less poetic than an existential refusal, but closer, I now think, to the facts of our experience. The contract worked because it showed Jessy exactly what to do and gave her a reason for doing it. The counter worked—with this child who could count before she could talk, for whom numbers had always possessed mysterious significance—because it provided, for the first time, a truly significant reward for effort. The tasks of development are hard—hard enough for normal children; for a developmentally disabled child, much harder. What motivates a child to grow? It is a question we never thought we needed to ask—growth is "natural," a child "develops," its potentialities "unfold." The words themselves, in their root meanings, proclaim inevitability. We think about the process only when it fails to occur. But consider a child born, for some still mysterious reason, without the ability to make sense of its environment—with the ability to understand invariant shapes, numbers, routines, rules, but lacking the ability to interpret the constantly shifting, interlocking, mutually dependent appearances that make up the social contexts in which human beings carry on their lives. It isn't IQ; a Down's syndrome child—indeed, a year-old puppy—is far more sensitive to social situations, to body language, to facial expressions, to tones of voice, to disapproval, to praise, *to other people* than autistic Jessy was. Such a chiid will have no *reason* to master those hard developmental tasks. The normal child has strong social reasons to undertake them: to use the toilet like Daddy, to tie its shoes like Katy, to say words, elicit smiles, hugs, approval. Praise encourages it to do what comes naturally even to our cousins the apes, to imitate and join the life around it, to grow independent, not to be a baby any more. A normal baby has social reasons to pay attention to the sounds it hears, to distinguish speech from noise, to imitate those speech sounds and refine them, to notice what effects they produce on those who hear them. Children want to be like other people, and when they fail they are embarrassed or ashamed. But Jessy was immune to emulation or embarrassment. Praise had been meaningless to her, year after year; it came at her from the inexplicable, overwhelming world of what other people think and want. When praised, she had tuned it out, or worse, stopped at once the new behavior that had elicited it. Now, in her 15th year, in another of those reversals of normal processes, she learned to understand and enjoy praise—as a side effect of abstract numbers, of the mechanical reinforcement of a golf counter.

"IS THIS PRAISE?"

My final counter story is the most significant of all in expressing the depth of her social incomprehension, and its range. One Friday, after a year and a half of behavioral contracts, Jessy's teacher called; she had something important to tell me. "Jessy and I have made a decision. Jessy's not going to work for points any more; she's going to work for praise." And Jessy echoed, "Work for praise!" I was surprised at the suddenness of this unilateral decision, yet I understood it. The school had had nothing to do with administering the contract; Jessy had debited and credited herself, with the autistic, rule-governed exactitude that knows no possibility of cheating. But with her astonishing penchant for categorization, she had subdivided the contract, originally consisting of a few simple items, into a proliferating complexity of sub-items and, true to form, was now in danger of occupying herself more with counting clicks than with the behaviors themselves. I had tried to "fade the prompts," to reduce the number of items, but the system was Jessy's and it had taken on an autistic life of its own. Now I was told that Jessy and the teacher had agreed to go cold turkey. I didn't think it would work; I anticipated a hellish weekend and a return to contract security, but I always support the teacher and I said, "Fine."

But it did work. All the behaviors were maintained. Jessy kept on taking out the garbage, setting the table, all the simple, concrete acts that the counter had first rendered possible, then automatic. And of course, with every one, we praised. We smiled, we hugged, we said, "Jessy, that's good, that's wonderful!" And after each instance Jessy, now smiling in open pleasure, chirped, "Is this praise? Is this praise?" The counter had taught her to enjoy praise, she had agreed to work for it, she was 15 years old, and *she didn't even know the meaning of the word.*

Recall that for 9 years she'd known the word *heptagon.* She knew all about squares and primes. But not *this* kind of abstraction—social, relational, taking all its meaning from human interaction. I recalled an earlier lesson the contract had taught, not her, but me: that at first she hadn't any idea what I meant when I included such items as "doing something helpful," "saying something interesting." I'd learned to specify, say six helpful behaviors, to define subjects of conversations that might conceivably be considered interesting. From those specifics Jessy could begin to grasp the social generalization, even, over the years, recognize new examples of the simple social category that hard practice had rendered familiar.

A FULL SCHOOL DAY AT LAST

The counter came into our lives when we needed it most, when Jessy was at last in school full time, learning to read, to write, taking art and later math and typing with normal children. The increased social and cognitive demands of teachers were stressing her capacity for adaptation and tolerance of failure and frustration, both minimized in our home teaching. I have not mentioned the rituals and obsessions that had been part of our lives so long, the sudden mysterious incursions that would turn her usually sunny cheerfulness to shrieking misery. We could handle it at home when she screamed for two hours because someone had turned the wrong light on in the building across the street, or because a cloud had covered the moon, or—the causes were as inexplicable as she was. But school could not be so accommodating. Jessy did not like the bells, but bells there had to be. Nor could she be allowed to scream because she had typed a period instead of a comma, or to hit out in frustration when she was corrected. She was learning in school, and it had to be possible for her to stay there.

We had had to wait until she was 13 before she was accorded a full school day—she who had so much more to learn than other children (C. C. Park, 1977). But once in the regional high school, she remained there until she was 22, learning simple reading and writing, high school accounting and typing, sophisticated artistic techniques, but above all, to control her more bizarre behaviors and obsessions—learning not to scream, not to mumble, learning to cooperate, to take directions, even to accept correction; in short, to get along in a world outside her own home. Without every one of those years of publicly guaranteed education, without the continued efforts of those astonished, often bewildered teachers—let's put it in crude economic terms—Jessy would not be paying taxes today.

REACHING FOR ADULTHOOD

So I will skip those years of accelerating social development, years of small miracles, in which she learned to shop for groceries, to answer the telephone and write down the message, to read a recipe or a note left to tell her of our whereabouts or what to make for supper. I want to talk about the years *since* school, after the cutoff age of 22 when so many people imagine that learning ceases. For Jessy's comprehension has steadily expanded in these years, her language grown more sophisticated, her social perceptions more refined, as she moves toward a new inwardness, a new consciousness of herself as a thinking, feeling being. More stories, then. They will show both progress and problems, together, as they occur in all of us. I will try to sort them into categories, but you'll find they will resist: Speech, comprehension, social awareness are inseparable. Development is a seamless garment. I will try to tell Jessy's stories as much as possible in her own language, with all their syntactical abnormalities, so readers can imagine themselves involved with her in a social interchange, and assess her developmental progress for themselves.

LEARNING ABOUT EMOTIONS

Elsewhere I have written of the eerie feeling we have at times that Jessy is a Martian, a visitor from some pure planet where feelings do not exist (C. C. Park, 1983). This year she asks, "Is it a reason to be sad when old people die?"

A friend has lost his father suddenly; he will therefore not be coming to dinner as expected. We had presented the deaths of grandparents as something to accept without tears—grandfather at 86, depressed and senile, grandmother 92, incapacitated by a stroke. Jessy believed us. How not? In her 25 years, she had picked up no contradictory signals. A normal child would see beneath the apparent acceptance of death to qualify it; our reassurances had unthinkingly assumed that Jessy would recognize that there was sadness there. Yet we should have known; we knew her cheerful interest in funerals as a "good reason" to miss a day of work and still get paid. It was predictable: "I didn't know people get sad when old people die."

Or we watch the news. Most of it is inaccessible to her, too fast, too remote, but a burning building is concrete enough. Someone has been killed. Jessy, cheerful as usual, says what we all think and learn not to say—at what age? 6? 7? "Good thing it didn't happen to us!"

But there is progress. We see a movie. Jessy can follow a film now, if it is simple enough and I am there to provide a running summary; she remembers to this day how the Princess in *Star Wars* was sad when the Death Star destroyed her planet. Another movie is about children lost in the Adirondacks. At a point when they are in grave danger from a murderous tramp who is stalking the little boy with a gun, Jessy surprises me: "I think I am going to cry." Empathy! How long we've waited for it! I tell her they're going to escape, as they fortunately do, and she's all right. Yet two weeks later, on a TV western, the hero, shot by Indians, has an arrow through his shoulder, obviously a serious wound. A railroad track is visible, however, and a train has been mentioned. Jessy has a thing about trains, so: "He will miss the train?" Or in the cartoon presentation of Pinocchio, a story she knows well, she shows interest in the moon rising—she has a thing about the moon lighting up the sky—but walks out on the scene of Pinocchio and Gepetto embracing when Pinocchio becomes a real boy. I recall how, when she was 18, after a psychologist had said she needed to talk about feelings, we tried to provide a vocabulary, only to see her delightedly begin to collect words with similar prefixes—discouraged, disappointed, desperate, depressed, disgruntled, dismayed—her mental energies absorbed in the enterprise of arranging them into hierarchies of severity, her emotions untouched. And I recalled, too, Barbara Caparulo's report (1981) of an autistic young man far less impaired than Jessy, who when asked to characterize how a person in a test photograph felt, replied, "Soft."

FINDING THE RIGHT WORD

Verbal incomprehension and social incomprehension go together. For years we have been trying to convey the important concept of what sort of thing hurts people's feelings. If you scream it hurts their *ears*, but feelings . . . As she watches the Pink Panther (cartoons do not make the demands of film on her comprehension, there is always something to look at and you don't have to follow the story) two blueprints are shown, one for the Panther's modern house and one for a traditional one. That's the one the little man wants, but he doesn't get it. Jessy remarks, "That hurt his feelings."

What *is* the right word to use in those social contexts she is increasingly aware of? "Is it an insult when I scream? Is it hurt your feelings?" It makes me sad, I say; that's not quite the same. Or when she has been reproved because she accused a guest at table of stealing her napkin: " 'Who stole my napkin? ' Is it an insult?" Well, it's almost an insult, it depends on the tone of voice, it depends (I discover as I go along) on the value of the object—"Who stole my money?" is different—*it depends on the context.* "Is it an insult when I say 'I heard you making that noise'?" "Is it an insult when I say someone died?"

How *do* we learn the right words for these slippery social concepts? Nobody teaches us. Jessy had waited patiently to vacuum the room while her father looked over his slides. He'd said he'd be finished in a minute, but then he showed some more. Jessy has grown much, much better at waiting, but a good job of patience is hard to extend when you thought it was finished and then it wasn't. She reports to me, "I told my father he lied. Is that an insult? " It's an insult, all right, but is it a lie? Jessy begins her bizarre, creaky-door noise, banshee crying, once so familiar, now uncommon—because she'd insulted her father, because she'd been corrected, because she'd banged the door and shouted, "Why do you correct me?" and sent herself to her room, because she'd gotten things wrong. Progress? She cares about being corrected now, as she didn't in the long, unsocial, indifferent years when she only shrieked about lights and clouds and moons and gas pumps and bells and gongs and the other phenomena of her autistic world. She didn't care then about the meanings of words, or the niceties of social behavior, or, indeed, whether she could get her shrieking under control, which she does, on this occasion, in less than ten minutes. She really wants to learn, now, to navigate on this mysterious planet of ours, but it's so hard, and it's so hard to help her, and so sad when she fails.

TOWARD SOCIAL SENSITIVITY

For years there was no sensitivity to the needs of others, or their desires. Then—she was in her late teens—it began to appear, with a touching concreteness. "I put nutmeg instead of cinnamon in the pudding because I know you don't like that." Last year she told us she didn't need us to make an Easter egg hunt for her any more—but she made one for us. Another time, two good friends came to visit; by the bed they were to occupy she put two lollipops, two sourballs, two Nabisco wafers, bought with her own money.

"Thinking of others" had been one of our behavioral categories, specified, rewarded. Now it was happening spontaneously. But even thinking of others can be done autistically. Every morning a vitamin C pill with a glass of water appears at my place at breakfast. I *have* to take it, at once, or she will, not scream, certainly, but show her anxiety, refer to it over and over, "bug" me. Initially, helpfully, she located the channel for the evening news when her father came home; now, though she doesn't watch it, she'll be bothered if he switches it on a minute early or turns it off when we have a guest. We remind her of the term we've used for years: *Flexibility Practice*. Even social sensitivity can harden into one of the inflexible patterns that structure the lives of the autistic. Jessy will look for my glasses—she who at 8 could not locate an Easter egg unless it was in plain sight—and find them when I cannot. But if they don't show up, her anxiety triples mine. "Lost, lost, oh lost!"

Some instances of sensitivity are so commonplace as to be imperceptible except to a remembering parent. I notice that she now adjusts her speed to mine when we're walking; she doesn't lag far behind me, as in the long years of her "willed weakness," or stride far ahead, as she did a few years ago. Last month I saw her stroke the cat, not just a prompted, gingerly touch, but properly, starting at the head, with pressure. After 25 years! Slowly the body too learns its language, the language of touch and gesture that Lorna Wing (1972) points out is as foreign to the autistic child as the nuances of speech. But only a year ago Jessy remarked, laughing, "Be sure everybody would jump up and down if I licked somebody in the Arcade!"

TOWARD CONSCIOUSNESS OF SELF AND OTHER

But most encouraging are the increasing signs of explicit consciousness of human relations and her part in them. There is the friendliness, long established now, but rising to consciousness. Jessy is upset about something, probably a missed ritual, and as she's been taught, tries to think about something nice "to take away sadness." What is it? Rainbows? Radio call letters? No. It's "having lunch with Cary," her current home companion. Reinforcers may now be truly social. And Cary's grandfather died last month. "Guess what!" proclaims Jessy proudly. "I cried silently in my mind about her grandfather dying." To cry silently is what erstwhile screamers are encouraged to do—but get that "in my mind"!" This is the fruit of our conversation about our friend's old father. Jessy is not merely learning by rote now imposed canons of behavior; she is groping for the appropriate application.

"Janet"—one of her old companions—"wrote me a note. 'Congratulations for perfect behavior!' That made me proud!" "My father praised me because I didn't carry on about his cold"—colds, and in particular whether she might catch one, being one of her obsessions. Corrections are painful. They are very hard to bear; the screams that once were unleashed only by the infractions of private, idiosyncratic patterns may now occur for social causes. But praise is pleasant; it motivates to control obsessions and screaming overreaction together. Social pleasure, social pain: The familiar human calculus now spurs Jessy too to social learning.

I am reading in the living room; I hear distraught scream-shouting outside. "Mommy! Mommy!" that call I waited so long—ten years, was it?—to hear. When she comes back inside, I tell her I'm not lost; we talk about how to look everywhere before she gets upset, about the bizarre (she knows the word) shrieking that will scare the neighbors. It's good talk, as evidenced next day, when she reverts to it. She points out that she called "Mommy" when she was upset, instead of the "Mom" or "Mother" that she learned last summer was "more mature." "Because," she analyzes correctly, "I was acting like a baby." To know what it is to act like a baby, and to want not to do it? One giant step for humanity. But I don't forget why she was screaming for me in the first place: I had forgotten to eat the candy she had thoughtfully put out for my lunch treat. There it all is: the linking of social comprehension with language, the expanding consciousness of self and other—and the autistic rigidity always lurking beneath.

Here are some things Jessy has said over the past year, raw data, copied directly from sheets I scribbled as she spoke. They speak for themselves.

"I think the reason I misbehaved was because I was missing Janet. I remember I misbehaved a lot at the end of August because I missed my parents."

"If I find a wallet with identification I will call that number and 'I found a wallet' and that person will feel *so relieved*!"

"Sometimes can tell when people are happy even if not smiling because can tell by the face. When people are happy eyes always glow and face shine like sun. And if people are sad face always looks gloomy like clouds. And between happy and sad like partly cloudy."*

And Jessy's memory, always excellent for the concrete, becomes social as well: "Year before that [this] sometimes Joe didn't offer me a chocolate cookie and I didn't say anything and I felt left out but I didn't say anything to Joe because I don't want to hurt his feelings."

Joe is a longtime companion from the special class, now, like her, a graduate. He often walks over to see her and is the nearest she has to a spontaneous peer relationship. Jessy's social life remains very simple. There's Joe, and there are the young people, more than 30 when I last counted, who over the years have served as teachers, therapists, surrogate peers,

*See Park and Youderian (1974) for the elaborate light and weather system of which this social generalization is a reminiscence.

companions,* and whose part in her social learning deserves its own chapter. Only one of these helpers is usually on the scene, but others sometimes come back to visit. More than one friend at a time can present problems. Here Jessy copes with them, not entirely to her own satisfaction:

"I didn't go for the apples because I didn't want to hurt Joe's feelings. I refused Anna's invitation and she said 'Whose loss is that, mine?' I should have accepted the conflict but I wanted to eat lunch with Cary, but I can do that another time. I made a mistake." I make a comment she would have found unintelligible three years ago: "You're getting much more sensitive to other people's feelings." She replies, "Yes, I didn't want to do the same thing to Joe."

SOCIAL BEHAVIOR AND SPEECH

Social behavior and speech are linked inextricably. Thus, proverbs encapsulate social wisdom. Literal-minded Jessy is now paying close attention to these figurative idioms, understanding them, applying them. They please her; invariant, practical, applicable to recurrent situations, they serve to order her world. For instance, I ask can I boil eggs in the water she is heating for rice. "Yes, kill two birds with one stone." Proverbs are very useful for someone who worries obsessively whether the weather will be fair, or where my glasses are. I quoted my grandmother to her: "Sufficient unto the day is the evil thereof." But I like her version better: "Day is sufficient until evil come out." Obviously it surpasses her verbal powers, but not her comprehension, because she not only explained it explicitly as "Don't worry too soon," but herself supplied the equivalent "Don't borrow trouble," and "Don't cross that bridge until you come to it." The bridge isn't easy to handle: "Does it mean go over the bridge or go under?" Prepositions are always tricky. But the meaning is there; when the cat was gone all day ("Lost, oh lost!") and came back at midnight: "Unnecessary sadness! And there wasn't any bridge!" Three months later: The weatherman has predicted sunshine tomorrow, but clouds threaten; Jessy begins to obsess, then remarks, "It would be crossing the bridge too early—I would fall in the water. Last time I crossed the bridge about the clouds." They are useful, these idioms; they have become idioms because they speak to the human condition: "getting off on the wrong foot," "getting up on the wrong side of the bed." So, of the dinner invitation I almost forgot: "If you forgot, then remembered in the middle of the night, then you would get out the wrong side of the bed in the morning." But the application isn't always easy; the subtleties of emotional response are still hard to fathom.

*For more on Jessy's relationship with Joe, and with the companion-therapists, see C. C. Park (1982, 1983).

"Tracy came out of the wrong side of the bed because her father was in bad accident." Now as always, talking is just plain hard: "You can say 'what are you looking for' and 'who are you looking for.' Can you say 'where are you looking for'?"

WHERE IS JESSY NOW?

What, then, is her developmental level? Recently a mother and her 6-year-old visited us. Three-quarters of the things she and her little Jenny did together were right for Jessy too (the rest were too sophisticated). Sharing an enthusiasm for rainbows and four-leaf clovers, and with an adult to mediate the strangeness of a 25-year-old child, the two of them got along very well.

There are other clues to developmental level. In the last three years Jessy has become open to a new avenue of social learning: Reading, which was something strictly functional, practiced at school, just adequate for simple, matter-of-fact, predictable material like cookie recipes, has at last become something we can enjoy together. We can now read stories about people and what they do. We read aloud, to rivet attention through both ear and eye; we take turns, play roles, so Jessy must follow each line and can't tune out. Touchingly, she wants stories about "girls who misbehave." Laura Ingalls Wilder's "Little House" series might have been designed to fill in the gaps for a person without a childhood; not only does Laura misbehave, but she grows, and the books with her, from the simple, concrete language and concerns of a 4-year-old to a young woman. Jessy's more interested in the concrete things she can understand: the long winter when the train couldn't get through and they almost starved, the measles that left sister Mary blind. But we press on and get Laura married before we turn to Beverley Cleary's Ramona series. This is better yet; Ramona is 5 at the start and *really* misbehaves; she has tantrums and lies on her bed and kicks the wall. But Jessy's interest isn't confined to misbehavior; she can still tell you about how Ramona lost her red boot and found a biennial beet, though the high point remains the time Ramona heard about Hänsel and Gretel and baked her rubber doll in the oven and made a mess. And as Ramona grows older and struggles hard to control her temper so people will like her, Jessy's language and social comprehension expand together. Another series, however, doesn't work so well. It's good enough while the girls are 8 and 9, but though we plow ahead, Jessy just can't involve herself in 14-year-old Betsy's wish to be a writer, or her misery when the boy she likes goes skating with her best friend. I attempt once more to explain jealousy to Jessy. Joe used to try to make her jealous, years ago, back when they were together in the special class. He had a list of 100 girl friends, and he'd tell her she wasn't number one any more. It doesn't make any more sense to her now than it did then. She's still in her latency period, such as it is.

She doesn't even masturbate like other people; back when she was 14 she flattened herself prone on her bed and rocked back and forth. The connections made by her autistic mind are equally idiosyncratic; she associated the "rocks" that gave the good feeling with a set of colored rocks someone had given her, drawing rows of rocks whose colors coordinated with her other systems—of lights, of flavors—in ways whose complexities defy interpretation. The drawings lasted only a short time, but she still masturbates by prone rocking, though it's my impression that that has subsided in the last couple of years. But it may be only that she is more successfully keeping it private. If so, that's social progress too.

Let Jessy's own words convey her sense of herself as a sexual being. As you read them, you must supply for yourself the tone: cheerful, detached, matter-of-fact. We have been discussing whether she should answer the door at night when in the house alone; on balance, we agree she shouldn't. "Because there might be criminals and they could rape me. If rape, go to the doctor. If I got raped, call 'I won't be coming in to work because I got raped last night and have to go to the doctor' "—an occasion of interest because, like a funeral, it's an absence from work for which one gets paid. I say she wouldn't have to mention it. "I don't say that because it would be rude. Impolite." Well, it's not exactly that, I say, it's because you don't talk about that part of your body in public places. And Jessy, enlightened, relates it to another such subject: "Like XYZ; that means Examine Your Zipper."

Jessy as a social being? Perhaps the most significant thing I can say is how *nice* she is, how transparent; even in her tactlessness, how totally free of malice; how hard she tries, now, to help, to control herself, to say and do things right. The rest of us have the defects of our virtues; she has the virtues of her defects. It's innocence—there is no other word—and though her social learning will continue to inch forward, her innocence will always be with her, even as she grows more and more responsible and independent.

LOOKING AHEAD

And what of the future? How independent can she be? We used to congratulate ourselves, all those years, on keeping her out of an institution. Now, as we move into our 60s, I see it differently. In 20 years' time we'll be over 80, Jessy in her mid-40s. She already does the routine cleaning, laundry, and yard work in the home she shares with us, and some of the cooking and shopping. Gradually she'll take over more. There's no hurry; she can grow into it slowly and naturally. I've already begun to talk to her about how I used to have to wait for her to catch up when we went for walks, and how as I get older she'll have to wait for me; we like to talk together about things that make her feel adequate and strong. As her parents grow frailer, deafer, more forgetful, I can see no reason why Jessy's strength, her intact senses, her unerring memory shouldn't supplement our failing powers. She already administers one pill; I envisage a typical geriatric array of colored capsules, and Jessy dealing them out, a wee bit tyrannically, to be sure, but more reliably than any nurse. Practical, organized, exact, why shouldn't it be Jessy who keeps *us* out of an institution? That this now seems a perfectly possible future is the measure of her social growth.

One more story. It sums up progress and problems, virtues and defects.

One day not long ago we had guests. With Jessy's friend Cary living with us, it's seven for dinner. But Cary bows out at the last minute to have dinner with her boyfriend. For several days Jessy has felt obsessive anxiety: Everyone must show for dinner; all the places must be taken. It's discouraging, for this is a throwback to a pattern abandoned for 17 years; she hasn't worried about this since she was 8. There's obsessive talk about it at dinner, but she gets it under control. Then to my astonishment she bursts in two hours later while I am watching *King Lear* on television, shrieking, crying over the missing place. It's a bad seizure. I escort her to her room and together we calm her down inside of 10 minutes. And she *appreciates* my help; more, I see her *trying* to get herself under control so I can go back to Shakespeare. Next day she reverts to it, actually makes a generalization about social priorities: "You thought it was more important to cheer me up."

That same day there was a staff party, not in her own office, but in another building. I assumed that as usual I would go with her, but no: "I'm old enough to go by myself." She stayed long enough at the party to say hello to some of the friendly people on the staff and to enjoy the cookies. Then (I was at work, Cary away) she went for a walk, "to see the clear blue sky," and finding herself near the dentist, made an appointment because she'd noticed that her tooth "felt like too much candy." It's all there, continuing problems, continuing progress, defects and virtues. It's the place to end.

REFERENCES

Bruner, J. (1983). State of the child. *New York Review of Books, 30,* 84–89.

Caparulo, B. (1981, July). Development of communicative competence in autism. Proceedings of the 1981 International Conference on Autism. Washington, D.C.: National Society for Children and Adults with Autism, 1981, 232–244.

Ellis, R. (1982). *Cognitive processes in autism: A case study.* Unpublished manuscript. Williams College, Williamstown, MA.

Park, C. C. (1977). Elly and the right to education. *Phi Theta Kappan, 4,* 534–537. (Reprinted in R. E. Schmid, J. Moneypenny, & R. Johnston (Eds.), *Contemporary issues in special education.* New York: McGraw-Hill, 1977.)

Park, C. C. (1978). Review of *Nadia: A case of extraordinary drawing ability in an autistic child* by L. Selfe. *Journal of Autism and Childhood Schizophrenia, 8,* 457–472.

Park, C. C. (1982). *The siege.* (2nd ed. with epilogue and plates). New York: Atlantic-Little, Brown. (Original work published 1967; translated as *Histoire d'Elly,* Paris: Calmann-Lévy, 1972; *Eine Seele lernt leben,* Bern: Scherz, 1973; *Het Beleg,* Baarn: Bosch, 1974; *Belägringen,* Stockholm: Aldus, 1975; "Isolated Elly," Tokyo: Kawade Shobo, 1976; *Et Barn bag faestnings mure,* Denmark: Gyldendal, 1977; *Beleiringen,* Oslo: Gyldendal, 1978; *Ciudadela sitiada,* Mexico: Fondo de Cultura Economica, 1980; *L'Assedio,* Rome: Astrolabio, 1982.)

Park, C. C. (1982). Growth in language: The parents' part. *Topics in Language Disorders,* December, 50–57.

Park, C. C. (1983). Growing out of autism. In E. Schopler & G. Mesibov (Eds.), *Autism in adolescents and adults.* New York: Plenum Press.

Park, D. (1974). Operant conditioning of a speaking autistic child. *Journal of Autism and Childhood Schizophrenia, 4,* 189–191.

Park, D., & Youderian, P. (1974). Light and number: Ordering principles in the world of an autistic child. *Journal of Autism and Childhood Schizophrenia, 4,* 313–323.

Wing, L. (1972). *Autistic children.* New York: Brunner/Mazel.

II

Social Problems of Autistic People

6

An Overview of Social Behavior in Autism

PATRICIA HOWLIN

DEFINITIONS OF SOCIAL SKILLS IN CHILDREN

Over recent years there have been numerous attempts to quantify social behavior and to distinguish children who are socially skilled from those who are not. Many definitions of social competence exist, and although these vary in sophistication, almost all focus on the importance of reinforcement and reciprocity in the development of relationships (Gottman, Gonso, & Rasmussen, 1977; Greenwood, Walker, Todd, & Hops, 1981; Keller & Corlson, 1974; Mueller, 1972).

As well as skill in responding positively to peers, other social and cognitive abilities that are related to successful social development include the child's ability to discriminate and label emotions (Izard, 1971); the ability to communicate accurately and effectively with another person (Gottman, 1977); and the ability to take the role perspective of other individuals and to simultaneously consider both their own and others' points of view (Van Hasselt, Hersen, Whitehill, & Bellack, 1979). In addition, social skills are very much situation-specific. Few, if any, interpersonal behaviors are appropriate in all settings, for social norms vary and are determined by both situational and cultural factors. It is necessary, therefore, to be able to adapt skills effectively according to the requirements of the social context (Bellack & Hersen, 1978).

Thus, although descriptions of social competence differ somewhat from study to study, there is overall agreement that the essence of social behavior consists of the ability to relate to others in a mutually reinforcing and reciprocal fashion and to adapt social skills to the varying demands of interpersonal contexts.

PATRICIA HOWLIN • Institute of Psychiatry, De Crespigny Park, Denmark Hill, London SE5 8AF, England.

The following chapter sets out to explore the methods used to assess social behavior in normal, handicapped, and autistic children. Specific studies of the social behavior of autistic children are then discussed in terms of both their theoretical relevance for our understanding of the nature of autism and their practical relevance for treatment and intervention.

THE ASSESSMENT OF SOCIAL BEHAVIOR

In parallel with studies attempting to define effective social interaction, research methodology has focused on ways of identifying children who are at risk of becoming socially isolated. The two principal methods of assessment that have been used are sociometric techniques and observational measures, although other techniques, such as interviews, self-reports, and social/cognitive tasks, have also been employed.

Sociometric Techniques

The use of sociometric measures to identify socially isolated children has been widely used in studies of peer relationships (Foster & Ritchey, 1979; Van Hasselt *et al.*, 1979). Children may be asked to specify a certain number of children with whom they particularly like, or do not like, to play (Moreno, 1934), or they may be required to rank classmates in terms of their popularity (Hymel & Asher, 1977). Despite the extensive use of sociometric techniques, their long-term reliability and their generalizability to groups other than young, normal preschoolers have still to be established. In addition, correlations with other methods of assessing social behavior, such as teacher ratings or observational measures of frequency of contact, are variable, and predictive validity data are virtually nonexistent. Finally, and most important, sociometric assessment is limited in that it does little to identify the nature of social problems and cannot be used to specify children's assets or deficits. Various other difficulties associated with the use of sociometric assessment are discussed by Foster and Ritchey (1979) and Hymel (1983), and it is suggested that although sociometric techniques may be useful for identifying children at risk of social failure, they need to be accompanied by direct observational data, particularly when used in the context of intervention studies.

Behavioral Observations

Direct observations of children's social interactions have been used both to identify socially incompetent children and to assess the effects of social intervention studies. The data analyzed are generally quantitative in nature, expressing the rate, frequency, or percentage of interactive behaviors, while the observational methods used vary from simple counts of behavior to highly elaborate coding systems. For example, Allen, Hart, Buell, Harris, and Wolf (1964) record only "proximity to" and "interaction with" adults and children by a socially isolated girl. In contrast, Durlak and Mannarino (1977) employ a 19-category coding system in their assessment of children with social problems. More recently, attempts have been made to derive better *qualitative* assessments of children's interactions and, in addition to the frequency of responses, the reciprocity of social contact has been subject to analysis (Greenwood *et al.*, 1981).

Despite the current popularity of observational techniques, Gottman (1977) and Van Hasselt *et al.* (1979) recommend caution in the interpretation of findings since the effects of observer presence, the expectancies of observers and subjects, differences between sampling procedures, reliability decay, observer drift, and many other variables may all influence results.

There are also problems in determining which aspects of social competence should be observed. For example, although variables such as frequency of interaction are assumed to be important in the assessment of competence, they do not necessarily correlate with sociometric status or with improvements following treatment (Gottman, 1977). And, even when more sophisticated measures have been employed, these have not necessarily been adequate to discriminate children already identified as having marked social problems (Foster & Ritchey, 1979). Thus, simply defining and observing particular facets of social behavior does not necessarily guarantee that such behaviors are critical for adaptive social functioning. Given the lack of construct validation in most observational studies, it is impossible to know whether the behavioral constructs evaluated are, in fact, related to social competence, or whether the behaviors rated across different studies are comparable.

The generalizability of findings from observational studies remains questionable and the differential role of specific behaviors in a variety of settings is still to be evaluated. Sampling of a wider range of school populations, in both normal and special educational classes, is needed to establish the representativeness of findings from normal preschool populations (Greenwood *et al.*, 1981). The validity of cross-sectional sampling procedures also requires investigation, since there are indications that cross-sectional findings may agree only poorly with the results of longitudinal studies (Gersten, Langer, Eisenberg, Simcha-Fagan, & McCarthy, 1976).

Foster and Ritchey (1979) discuss a number of additional problems concerning the reliability of observational data and the adequacy of the assessment measures and sampling procedures used. Moreover, there is a more fundamental problem underlying observational studies, which is the assumption that behavior *per se* affects children's status. It is evident that many nonbehavioral variables, such as sex, race, physical attractiveness, weight, academic and athletic ability, and observable handicaps also influence children's acceptance by their peers

(Asher, Oden, & Gottman, 1977; LaGreca, 1981). It is highly likely that both behavioral and nonbehavioral variables interact, not only in their influence on sociometric status but also in the development of socially competent behavior. The relation between the parameters that influence both the development and the perception of socially competent behavior warrants much greater attention if the validity of observational techniques is to be established.

Analogue Tasks

In addition to naturalistic observations of children's behavior, various laboratory simulations of real-life situations (such as role-play tasks) have been used to assess social behaviors and to monitor the effects of social skills training (Beck, Forehand, Wells, & Quante, 1978; Bornstein, Bellack, & Hersen, 1977; Reardon, Hersen, Bellack, & Foley, 1978). Validity studies (Reardon *et al.*, 1978) indicate that ratings of social skills in these situations tend to correlate highly with performance on other laboratory measures. However, the external validity and the test–retest reliability of analogue studies has been criticized by a number of investigators. In particular, the limited validity of role-play tasks with adult populations casts doubt on the usefulness of such measures and the interpretation of such studies must be treated with caution (Bellack, Hersen, & Lamparski, 1979; Kazdin, 1980).

Other Methods of Assessing Social Behavior

In addition to the techniques discussed above, a variety of other methods of assessing children's social competence have been developed. These include *teacher rating scales*, by which teachers are asked to identify the more socially isolated and withdrawn children in their class (Evers & Schwarz, 1973; O'Connor, 1972; Walker & Hops, 1973); *behavioral interviews*, which allow a much wider assessment of social competence as well as difficulties in other areas (Ciminero & Drabman, 1977; Herjanic, Herjanic, Brown & Wheatt, 1975; Rutter & Graham, 1968); *self report inventories,* which are basically designed to measure positive and negative assertiveness (see Reardon *et al.*, 1978); and a variety of *social-cognitive tasks,* which generally involve role taking and assess the individuals' ability to simultaneously consider their own and others' points of view (Duck, Miell, & Gaebler, 1980; Johnson, 1975; Reardon *et al.*, 1978). All these techniques suffer from a number of limitations, and while they may prove useful adjuncts to other methods of assessment, studies of their reliability and validity suggest that they are not acceptable as the sole measure of social competence (see discussions by Foster & Ritchey, 1979; Van Hasselt *et al.*, 1979).

In general, despite the drawbacks discussed above, direct observational methods tend to be the most popular way of assessing social behavior in normal children. In autistic and other handicapped groups, too, observational studies, in both naturalistic and laboratory settings, have proved to be the most widely used means of measuring social competence.

THE ASSESSMENT OF CHILDREN WITH LEARNING HANDICAPS

Given the difficulties of developing adequate measures of social functioning in normal children it is not, perhaps, surprising that assessments of the social problems shown by handicapped children are even more limited. Children with both learning and physical problems are known to be less acceptable to their peers and more socially isolated than normal children (Bruininks, 1978; Bryan, 1974; Siperstein, Bopp, & Bak, 1978). Moreover, their low social status does not improve, even if they are placed with new and different groups of peers (Bryan, 1976).

Because of the high rate of social problems in these populations, attempts have been made to identify factors that contribute to their low acceptance by peers. Even if variables known to affect social acceptance, such as physical attractiveness and athletic or academic ability, are controlled for, problems of peer relations remain. Such findings have led a number of authors to postulate that the processes that interfere with the acquisition of learning skills also interfere with the development of skills that are necessary for successful interpersonal functioning (Bryan, 1974, 1976; Johnson & Mykelbust, 1967; Weiner, 1980). Several studies have attempted to analyze social behavior and social comprehension skills in such children as possible clues to understanding their difficulties in peer relationships. However, these investigations have generally failed to find consistent differences between either the social behaviors or the social perception of skills of normal and handicapped children. In a recent review, LaGreca (1981) examined both the social performance and social comprehension of children with learning handicaps. She found little difference in the frequency of interaction and few differences in the rates of positive social behavior between groups. There was limited evidence that learning-disabled children tended to be involved in more negative interactions with peers; they showed less initiation in peer situations, and they displayed more distracting nonverbal behavior, such as inappropriate head nodding or eye contact. As far as social perception or the understanding and interpretation of social skills were concerned, little or no difference was found, either in children's ability in role-taking tasks or in their comprehension of nonverbal cues. The main area in which learning-disabled children appeared to be at a disadvantage was when they were required to take a more active and assertive communicative role. Unfortunately, the interpretation of all the studies reviewed was complicated by a number of methodological problems. These included the heterogeneity of the subject samples studied, the absence of any uniform definition of learning disabilities, differences in behavioral coding methodology, and the confounding effects of peer status and academic status (LaGreca, 1981). Bryan, Donahue, and Pearl (1981) also suggest that differences in task demands, conversational partners, and sex of subjects may influence the communicative and social competence of learning-disordered children. Systematic evaluation of the social difficulties shown by such children, in both naturalistic and experimental settings, are badly needed if successful attempts are to be made to remediate their problems in developing effective peer relationships.

THE NATURE OF THE SOCIAL DEFICIT IN AUTISM

If studies of peer relations in learning-disabled children are confounded by multiple methodological problems, assessments of autistic children tend to be even less satisfactory. While it is generally agreed that such children do have severe problems in making relationships, descriptions of their social behavior are frequently vague and anecdotal. Thus, the autistic children in an intervention study conducted by Young and Kerr (1979) are described as "having no positive social behaviors," while Strain and Fox (1981) describe their group more positively, although equally imprecisely, as "getting along quite well with peers." Despite the obvious inadequacies of these descriptions, many intervention studies have proceeded in their attempts to "improve" social behaviors on the basis of such assessments.

In general, information about the social handicaps typically exhibited by autistic children has tended to come, not from experimental or intervention studies, but from thorough and detailed clinical accounts of their behavior.

Kanner (1943) suggested that the outstanding characteristic of autistic children was their innate inability to form normal social relationships. Subsequent clinical accounts of autistic children have generally supported Kanner's initial observations (Rutter, 1966, 1978; Wing, 1969), as have comparative studies of autistic and other groups of normal or handicapped children (Bartak, Rutter, & Cox, 1975; Churchill & Bryson, 1972; Hutt & Vaizey, 1966; Sorosky, Ornitz, Brown, & Ritvo, 1968; Wing, 1969).

The nature of the social abnormalities found in autistic children tends to change with age, with the most severe problems being particularly evident in the preschool years (Rutter, 1984). Thus, there is marked delay in the development of specific attachment behaviors and, frequently, a lack of discrimination between parents and other adults. In addition to abnormalities in verbal communication, there are abnormalities in nonverbal interaction. Abnormal eye gaze, for example, is notable, and the initiation of, and responsiveness to, physical contact also tends to be deviant. After the age of 5 years or so, these grosser social abnormalities may become less evident. Nevertheless, many other problems in social functioning persist. In particular, there is a lack of reciprocity and social responsiveness in interactions with other children, a lack of cooperative play, an unusual amount of time spent unoccupied or in ritualistic activities, failure to make personal friendships, a lack of empathy with others' feelings and responses, and, generally, a lack of coordination of social behavior to signify social intention (Lord, 1984; Rutter, 1984). Although such failures in social development are well documented in the clinical literature, there are few empirical investigations of the social abnormalities in autism, or of the specific ways in which social development in autism differs from normal development. Moreover, as is apparent from Table 1, those aspects of social functioning that have been studied tend to be limited to areas that are easily quantifiable, such as the amount of eye gaze or the frequency of contact with peers. Qualitative assessments of the social abnormalities characteristic of autism, or the study of more subtle aspects of social awareness, such as the development of empathy, have received little attention.

The following discussion attempts to provide an overview of recent experimental research of social behavior in autism, and in particular sets out to explore (1) the various aspects of social interaction that have been assessed and the different approaches used in these studies, (2) the interpretation of studies of the social abnormality in autism, and (3) the implication of such studies for treatment and intervention.

Table 1. Studies of Abnormal Social Behaviors in Autistic Children

	Areas of dysfunction investigated
Relationships with adults	Abnormal attachments/lack of differentiation between parents and others
	Abnormalities in social responses
	Recognition of self
	Recognition of emotion in others (analogue only)
	Eye gaze
	Physical withdrawal
	Negativism
Peer relations	Impoverished play
	Lack of cooperative play
	Lack of initiation of contact
	Lack of reciprocity

APPROACHES TO THE ASSESSMENT OF THE SOCIAL HANDICAP IN AUTISM

In general, three principal approaches have been employed in the study of social behavior in autistic children. At the simplest level, analyses have been restricted to the use of quantitative measures such as frequency or duration of peer contact (Romanczyk, Diamant, Goren, Trunell, & Harris, 1975; Strain, Kerr, & Ragland, 1979). However, since frequency counts alone may provide inadequate measures of the highly complex behaviors involved in social interaction (Howlin, 1978; Hutt & Hutt, 1966), more informative, qualitative measures are frequently required (Lord, 1984). Such measures include descriptions both of socially directed actions and of other behaviors that may influence these interactions (McHale, 1983; McHale, Olley, & Marcus, 1981; McHale, Olley, Marcus, & Simeonsson, 1981). Finally, interactive measures are required to analyze the relation between the different types of behavior shown by children during social interchanges and to formulate hypotheses about successful social interactions (Lord, 1984).

Because the nature of the social deficit in autism tends to change with time—with young children showing severe global problems in social development while older children exhibit more specific problems, especially in peer relations—studies of social interaction have tended to reflect these developmental changes.

Thus, studies of young autistic children focus predominantly on abnormalities in their relations with adults, and studies of older children concentrate more on peer interaction.

EARLY DEVELOPMENT

Abnormal Attachment Behaviors

Although abnormalities in the development of specific attachments and the failure to show normal differentiation between parents and others are well documented in the clinical literature, there are no detailed comparative studies of the emergence of attachment behaviors in autistic children. Indeed, until recently there had been few attempts to study attachment behaviors in any systematic fashion. However, in a recent series of studies Sigman and her colleagues (Sigman, Ungerer, Mundy, & Sherman, 1984) have attempted to look in some detail at certain aspects of attachment behavior—notably responsiveness to parents after periods of separation, and parent–child relations during play activities. A group of 18 3- to 5-year-old autistic children were matched with groups of normal and Down's syndrome controls of similar mental age. As a group, autistic children showed more social behaviors toward their mothers than toward strangers, and there were significant increases in the amount of interaction with their mothers after a period of separation. The amount of responsiveness to mothers was related to the amount of symbolic play shown by the children, and among the children who did not respond socially only one manifested symbolic play. Thus, the autistic children clearly showed differential attachments between their parents and strangers, and they were generally no less responsive than the Down's syndrome control children. However, both groups of handicapped children engaged in interaction with their parents significantly less than did normal children.

Other Abnormalities in Social Relationships

In addition to studying the responsiveness of autistic children to their parents, Sigman *et al.* (1984) have investigated a number of other aspects of social communication.

When the social behaviors of autistic, mentally retarded, and normal children were compared, using the Early Social Communication Scales of Seibert and Hogan (1981), the authors found that autistic and matched mentally retarded controls did not differ in the frequency of social responses or social initiations they made. The two groups however, differed significantly in their use of "attention-getting" strategies. Autistic children rarely attempted to share toys or to direct adults' attention, and they were least responsive to the adult's attempts to gain their attention by pointing or looking at objects. The authors conclude that although autistic children were clearly aware of the adult in the social situation, and were as capable as mentally retarded children of using nonverbal acts to initiate or respond to simple social games, they were markedly impaired when references to objects or events were not goal-directed and when the objective of the task was simply to share a focus of visual attention with another person. They appeared to understand the use of other people as agents but failed to show any appreciation that the other person had a perspective that could be shared or directed.

Self-Recognition

A number of psychoanalytic theories of autism have suggested that not only is the autistic child unable to differentiate between familiar and unfamiliar adults but also he is unable to differentiate between self and others (Bettelheim, 1967; Goldfarb, 1961; Mahler, 1955). For instance, the tendency of autistic children to reverse the pronouns *I* and *you* has been quoted as an example of the failure to develop self-identity, although in fact such an interpretation is based on entirely spurious assumptions (Bartak & Rutter, 1974). Ferrari and Matthews (1983) found that autistic children showed self-recognition at a mental age similar to that of other groups of normal or handicapped children. Spiker and Ricks (1983) also found that the failure to show self-recognition was related to linguistic level and mental age, although autistic children did not show normal expressions of pleasure when they did recognize themselves. These results suggest that although some autistic children may fail to show self-recognition, this failure may be due to generalized developmental delay and should not be regarded as evidence for a syndrome-specific deficit. However, there may be differences in the way in which they respond to their self-image.

The Recognition of Emotional Cues in Others

The failure to appreciate or respond to the feelings and emotions expressed by others is common in almost all autistic children, and this lack of empathy frequently prevents the development of friendships in later life (Kanner, Rodriguez, & Ashenden, 1972; Rumsey & Rapoport, 1983; Rutter, 1984).

Although the development of sensitivity to emotional cues has not been directly investigated, there are a number of analogue studies that have attempted to investigate autistic children's perception of people within an experimental context. In a series of experiments, Hobson (1982, 1983, 1984) studied the ability of autistic children to identify emotions from facial expressions and also their sensitivity to bodily features that differentiated between sexes and between adults and children. Autistic children proved to be consistently less competent than controls on all these tasks, although their ability to sort objects according to other criteria was unimpaired. The fact that autistic children are apparently unresponsive to cues of this nature indicates severe limitations in their ability to conceptualize personal relationships.

Sherman, Sigman, Ungerer, and Mundy (1984) also tested the ability of autistic children to differentiate between facial expressions on photographs (Ekman & Friesch, 1978). In comparison with normal controls, autistic children showed no evidence of discriminating between facial expressions, although they were able to discriminate male from female faces. Thus, although they are able to identify certain facial characteristics, they seem unable to interpret those that mark emotionality.

Hobson (1984) has also studied the concept of egocentricism in autistic children. Adopting a Piagetian standpoint (Piaget, 1926; Piaget & Inhelder, 1969), he tested the hypothesis that the capacity to appreciate the viewpoints of others is reflected in the child's ability to recognize points of view in a visuospatial setting. Tasks in which subjects were required to make judgments about different but related views of a three-dimensional scene or object, together with tests of operational thinking, were presented to normal and autistic children. Autistic children were found to be no more implaired in their recognition of visuospatial perspectives than normal children of comparable intellectual levels. They also appeared to perform as well as children with Down's syndrome of similar verbal and mental age. The author concluded that autistic children are not particularly egocentric in their appreciation of visuospatial perspectives, but he suggests, too, that the cognitive functions involved in these tasks are unlikely to have an important bearing on the autistic child's social handicaps.

Obviously, studies such as these are useful in helping to quantify anecdotal reports about certain aspects of the social deficit in autism. However, in that they are restricted to relatively minor facets of social behavior, they can give only limited information about the child's general social development. There are, in addition, problems in generalizing findings from analogue research to clinical situations (Kazdin, 1978, 1980), and adequate normative data are essential if erroneous conclusions are to be avoided.

Gaze Behavior in Autism

Many authors have stressed the importance of early, mutual eye gaze both in the development of attachment and in later communication systems (Argyle & Cooke, 1976; Jaffe, Stern, & Peery, 1973; Robson, 1967). Although autistic children are commonly reported as showing abnormal eye contact, (Rutter, 1978; Wing, 1976; Wolff & Chess, 1964), definitions of what actually constitutes *normal* gaze behavior are notoriously imprecise, and patterns of eye contact change considerably with age. Many normal infants, in the early months of life, will show marked and deliberate gaze avoidance, apparently as a way of terminating contacts with adults (Stern, 1976). Older children, between the ages of 18 months and 5 years, show far less gaze avoidance and may stare long and fixedly at strangers. By school age, however, children tend to show more adult patterns of eye contact in that they are likely to establish eye gaze quite rapidly, initially, but they will also avert their gaze as appropriate to the social setting (Scheman & Lockard, 1979).

The functions of eye gaze in adults have been studied in a large number of investigations and although it is generally agreed that eye contact plays an important role in social interactions, individual differences in amount and duration of gaze behavior are so great, and the variables that affect gaze are so numerous, that Mirenda, Donnelan, and Yoder (1983) conclude that "it is probably safe to say that there is no such thing as normal adult gaze behavior." They also note that the term *eye contact* is probably inappropriate anyway, since most gazing is actually directed at the partner's face and not on small areas such as the eye.

Despite the problems involved in the assessment of gaze behavior, it has been argued (Tinbergen & Tinbergen, 1983) that the avoidance of eye contact is the main deficit in autism, and various theories have been advanced to explain why autistic children exhibit this (Hutt & Ounsted, 1966; Richer & Coss, 1976; Wing, 1978). However, this emphasis on *lack* of normal eye gaze (whatever that means) gives far too simplistic an impression of what is, in fact, a very complex behavior. The experimental inadequacies of many studies of eye contact in autistic children probably also serve to explain the rather conflicting results obtained. Thus, while Richer and Coss (1976) and Castell (1970) report fewer and briefer contacts by autistic children, studies by Churchill and Bryson (1972) and Gardner (1976) failed to find significant differences in the frequency or duration of eye gaze by autistic children. Langdell (1978) found that autistic children spent more time looking at unusual parts of faces than other children. Hermelin and O'Connor (1970) showed that although autistic children tended to look less at human faces than did nonautistic controls, they also looked less at everything and their responsiveness to people was not significantly different from their response to objects. Results from a recent study by Tiegerman and Primavera (1984) suggest that, as with normal children, patterns of eye contact in autistic children change with time and with familiarity of the observer. There are also differences according to the type of interaction analyzed. Mirenda *et al.* (1983) found that although the frequency and duration of eye gaze was comparable in normal and autistic groups of children, the autistic children showed much more variability. They also used more eye contact during monologues while normal children exhibited more in dialogues. Generally, too, older autistic children engaged in more eye contact than their younger counterparts, although this was still idiosyncratic. These findings appear to support the observations of Rutter (1978) and Howlin (1978) that it is deviance in the reciprocal quality of eye contact that distinguishes autistic from normal children and not simply gaze avoidance. It is apparent that in the absence of normative data, theories about the significance of gaze avoidance are premature and probably incorrect. Moreover, it is probably misleading to try to assess eye contact out of context, and assessments of other behaviors involved in social approach and interaction, such as body posture and gestures, facial expression, and voice intonation, are necessary before distinctions can be made about what constitutes abnormalities in eye gaze. It also appears that eye contact may well be related to other maturational factors. Down's syndrome children, for example, also show abnormalities in the use of eye gaze (Sinson & Wetherick, 1981). Early eye contact is often delayed, but when this is established, the frequency and duration of gaze tends to be unduly high (Berger & Cunningham, 1981). This abnormal fixation of eye gaze may, in turn, delay the development of more subtle uses of eye contact and implies impairments in both maturational and psychological processes.

Finally, eye-to-eye gaze should not be considered without reference to the other partner. Gardner (1976), for example, found considerable differences in the behaviors of mothers toward autistic children. With autistic children, mothers terminated mutual facing more frequently than with normal children, but they spent longer time in such contact before terminating it. Tiegerman and Primavera (1984) also found that the experimenter's response affected the amount of looking by the child. When the experimenter began to imitate the autistic child more, eye contact increased. However, since eye contact in normal children is affected by familiarity, this experiment does not make it clear whether it was the actions of the experimenter or increased length of exposure to the setting that was responsible for these changes.

Physical Withdrawal

In parallel with accounts of gaze avoidance in autistic children, there are also many reports of their aloofness and avoidance of physical contact. Tinbergen and Tinbergen (1983) report that "autists [sic] live in an almost continuous state of withdrawal." This withdrawal is considered to be at the very core of the autistic syndrome, and the authors conclude that "distance keeping is their main concern in life". The studies by Richer (1978) and Tinbergen and Tinbergen (1983) have generated a large number of theories on the meaning and role of physical withdrawal in autism. Indeed, even rocking is interpreted as an example of the child's hesitation between social approach and social withdrawal. In the absence of normative data, however, the analysis of these findings is open to considerable criticism. These authors appear to have a predetermined theoretical set that overrides observation. For example, in the analysis of the movements of an autistic girl, the fact that she walked around a stranger who was sitting in her way is cited as an instance of pathological withdrawal (Tinbergen & Tinbergen, 1983). However, since the only other alternatives were for the girl to either walk or trip over the stranger, the conclusions drawn by the authors are questionable.

The physical withdrawal described as typical of autistic children appears to be rather overemphasized in much of the clinical literature. Hutt and Ounsted (1966) for example, found that although autistic children rarely initiated social encounters, once contact with an adult was made they often tolerated a greater degree of proximity and closer physical contact than other children. Castell (1970) found that proximity and approach to adults by both normal and autistic children were very similar, and Churchill and Bryson (1972) also failed to find any significant differences in the amount of physical avoidance shown by normal or autistic children. Even in the studies by Richer (1974, 1976), which particularly emphasized social withdrawal, it was apparent that the children did not avoid contact entirely and up to 30% of their time was spent in social approach behaviors. Strain and Fox (1981) suggest that it may be the high rate of stereotyped behaviors in autistic children that gives the impression of aloofness, rather than an active aversion to physical contact, and Koegel and Covert (1972) found that children's responsiveness to their environment increased if ritualistic behaviors were reduced. Again, contextual variables need to be taken into account if erroneous conclusions about the behaviors of autistic children are to be avoided.

Negativism in Social Interactions

A number of clinical accounts of autistic children have stressed not only their lack of responsiveness but also their negativism in social interactions. Richer and Coss (1974, 1976) suggested that to avoid the risk of increasing negativistic and other autistic behaviors, such as stereotypies, social demands must be kept to a minimum. However, Hutt and Vaizey (1966) found that autistic children made more physical contact as group density in a room was increased. Experimental studies, too, have shown that many assumptions regarding the "negativism" of autistic children are incorrect. Clark and Rutter (1977, 1979, 1981), for example, showed that so-called negativistic behavior was highly dependent on task complexity. If tasks were within the child's level of competence, noncooperative behaviors were not observed. Test performance depended on the intrinsic difficulty of the items presented, not on the child's motivation to succeed. Volkmar and Cohen (1982) also found that the demands of the experimental situation affected the responsiveness of the child. Thus, verbal requests for nonverbal responses tended to be the most effective elicitors of compliance, whereas verbal requests for verbal responses resulted in least compliance.

Studies by Clark and Rutter (1981) and by Volkmar and Cohen (1982) indicate that, contrary to the theories of Richer (1978) and Tinbergen and Tinbergen (1983), higher levels of social intrusiveness by the experimenter result in greater responsiveness on the part of the child. There were no rises in the frequency of stereotyped or other "autistic" behaviors as the level of social demands placed on the child increased, and in fact, Volkmar, Hoder, and Cohen (1985) report significant decreases in such behaviors. These results support an earlier, but related, study by Bartak and Rutter (1973), which indicated that the greater the structure imposed on the autistic child in an educational setting, the greater the responsiveness, in terms of both social and academic attainments.

STUDIES OF OLDER CHILDREN

The Development of Peer Relationships in Normal and Autistic Children

As they grow older, most autistic children begin to form relationships with adults, even if these are not entirely normal in quality. It is in their relations with peers, however, that many gross abnormalities remain. There is a marked absence of cooperative play, as well as very little reciprocity in their relations with other children, and much of their time is spent unoccupied or in stereotyped activities. Few children make personal friendships of any depth (although some older adolescents and adults may develop a network of associates who share similar interests, such as music or railways). Moreover, the lack of empathy with others, as well as leading to inappropriate social behavior, frequently results in increasing isolation as they grow older.

Studies of play and verbal interaction in normal children have indicated a number of variables that differentiate between children who are successful in their interpersonal relations and those who are not. Successful children show more subtlety in their entry into peer groups, employing, sequentially, tactics of waiting and hovering, mimicking the activity enjoyed by the peer group, commenting on the group's activities, and finally, moving progressively closer to the peer group before entering. Tactics that draw attention away from the peer group, such as disruptions, attention getting, and self-reference, tend to be related to negative peer responses (Dodge, Schlundt, Schocken, & Delugach, 1983). Rejected children also tend to spend more time unoccupied or in solitary play behaviors (Ladd, 1983). Many other studies have shown that the use of strategies that involve friendly and positive responses to other children are important in both the initiation and maintenance of interactions (Renshaw & Ascher, 1983). Work with adults by Trower (1980) has shown that successful social interaction involves the effective use of various nonverbal behaviors, such as looking, smiling, gesture, and posture. It is important, too, to vary social behaviors in response to situational changes. Speech tends to be the most important component of social interactions, but it is not the amount of speech that distinguishes socially skilled from unskilled patients, but the way in which speech and nonverbal behaviors are integrated. Greenwood *et al.* (1981) examined various different types of interactive strategies and found a number of age and sex differences in social behaviors. They, too, stress the importance of reciprocity for successful social relationships and found that even at 3 years of age, popular children are highly skilled in obtaining and providing reciprocity in peer interactions. Keane and Congar (1981) have traced changes in social communications over time. Even for very young children between the ages of 1 and 3, skill in being a good listener is crucial for successful social interactions. The ability to take turns in conversation is also apparent at this early age. By the age of 3 years, additional skills that help to sustain interactions emerge. Again, attending skills are important, but the speaker begins to play a more active role in ensuring the attention of the listener. More sophisticated patterns in turn taking emerge, and the reinforcing nature of utterances also becomes important. Between the ages of 6 and 12 years, content becomes an important communication skill and more subtle behaviors such as congruency and speech patterns begin to play an important role.

Studies of nonverbal interactions show that infants begin to initiate these from a very early stage (Becker, 1977; Rheingold & Eckerman, 1975), and the length and frequency of interactions increase with age. As part of normal development, children gradually spend more time interacting with each other, they respond more consistently to peers, and they are able to sustain interactions on particular topics or activities for longer periods (Holmberg, 1980; Keane & Conger, 1981; Mueller & Brenner, 1977). Overall, normal children learn how to be successful onlookers as a first step in social play and social relationships (Doyle, Connolly, & Rivest, 1980; Parten, 1932). Gradually, the number of different types of behaviors exhibited expands, from giving and taking, to imitating simple uses of objects, to joint use of objects and conversations. This expansion in the range of activities allows for longer and more complex interchanges, which, in turn, provide children with greater opportunities to develop successful ways of imitating or responding to their playmates (Holmberg, 1980).

Studies of Social Play in Autistic Children

Many of the studies of play and social behavior of autistic children have depended largely on quantitative measures, such as time spent in social play (Romanczyk *et al.*, 1975). Strain and colleagues (Strain *et al.*, 1979) also measured the number of motor, gestural, and verbal behaviors shown by autistic children in the presence of nonhandicapped peers. Such measures have generally been linked to intervention programs, with the indices of social development being employed as pre- and posttreatment measures of change. These assessments, however, have not generally been made under conditions that are representative of the child's normal environment; neither have they been used to compare the behavior of autistic children with that of normal peers.

Attempts to develop more qualitative measures of the play and social interaction of autistic children have been carried out in a relatively small number of studies. The impoverished play behavior of autistic children and their failure to learn by imitation are well documented clinically, and such deficits are highly likely to limit peer relationships. Ungerer and Sigman (1981) studied a variety of different play behaviors in autistic, retarded, and normal children and, perhaps surprisingly, found that the autistic children displayed a wide range of play behaviors in both unstructured and structured settings. However, whereas functional and symbolic play tended to dominate the play of mentally retarded and normal children, autistic children spent more time in simple manipulation of objects. In particular, the amount of doll-directed play was lower in the autistic than in the other groups, and autistic children showed fewer complex play sequences with toys than did the other children. It was also found that autistic children showed significantly less verbal and nonverbal imitation than mentally retarded or normal controls. Thus, in the absence of imitative or more complex play behaviors, even those autistic children who show more appropriate social responses are unlikely to be able to sustain interactions with normal peers for any length of time.

Martini (1980), for example, assessed the amount and type of contact made by two 8-year-old autistic children in a free-play situation. The children engaged in frequent contacts but these contacts were seldom sustained for longer than a few seconds. However, the study does not explore why these contacts were so brief, nor is it clear whether the autistic children remained at the first stage of "onlooker" or whether they ever went on to attempt more direct forms of interaction.

McHale and her colleagues have attempted to look at more qualitative aspects of children's play and social behavior in a series of studies (McHale, 1983; McHale, Olley, & Marcus, 1981; McHale, Olley, Marcus, & Simeonsson, 1981). They observed autistic children, between 5 and 8 years of age, playing with each other, with a group of nonhandicapped peers, and with their teacher. The autistic children most frequently displayed stereotyped behaviors and solitary play with their autistic classmates and showed more cooperative play with the nonhandicapped children. When nonhandicapped children were introduced into the classroom, autistic children showed increases in the amount of social interaction and decreases in the amount of solitary activity over time. There were no significant changes in the frequency of verbal communication or appropriate play. However, it was found that children spent more time than expected playing in pairs and using gross motor toys, such as tricycles, rather than constructive toys or sensorimotor materials such as spinning tops. There was a great deal of variability in the behavior of the autistic children over the experimental periods but by the end of the trial period the autistic children were spending about 75% of their time in interaction with other children.

In contrast, a study of children's behavior in an exclusively autistic classroom (McHale, Simeonsson, Marcus, & Olley, 1980) indicated that almost 75% of their behavior was asocial, and if social communications were made these were predominantly nonverbal. Although children showed increases in social behavior and communication over time, interactions tended to involve teachers rather than other autistic classmates. There were significant correlations between children's cognitive and social skills as measured by standardized tests and their levels of play and communication, and since most of the children in this group were low functioning, the generalizability of these findings to less handicapped autistic children is unclear. However, it does appear that unless deliberate attempts to foster normal peer contacts are made, the isolation of autistic children is likely to continue.

Lord (1984) has carried out a series of studies examining the social behavior of autistic children in both normal and handicapped groups, using a combination of quantitative, qualitative, and interactive assessments of behavior. The quantitative measures involved included frequency of intervals playing with peers, the number of initiations made by the autistic child, and the number of intervals of continuous interaction in a single activity. More qualitative measures included the absolute distance between children, face-to-face interaction with other children, and the number of intervals spent involved in self-stimulatory behavior or solitary play. Interactive measures included the types of responses and initiations made by each child (e.g., gestural, verbal, positive, negative) and the relationship (for example, imitative or initiative) between the kind of behavior shown by one child and the kind of behavior shown by another. Lord (1984) found that the use of these measures made it possible to discriminate between children according to Wing and Gould's (1979) system of categorizing social deficits. The categories of "aloof," "passive," and "active but odd" proved useful in describing the social behaviors of autistic children and also showed some correspondence with developmental sequences. "Aloof" children could be discriminated from "passive" children on the basis of the frequency of their interactions and their responsiveness to other children's overtures. "Active but odd" children could be discriminated from "passive" or "aloof" children by the number of initiations they made and their ability to make some active contribution to sustaining an interaction. Thus, within the domain of social impairments, Lord proposed a developmental sequence from "aloof" to "passive" in responsiveness, and from "aloof" or "passive" to "active but odd" in rate of initiations. These measures were used to categorize children before treatment and also to make predictions about behavior change.

The results of these studies are fully described by Lord (1984). Briefly, it was found that the introduction of nonhandicapped playmates into the autistic children's classroom resulted in increases in both the amount and quality of play and social behavior. When specially trained peers, who had been taught to prompt and reinforce social behavior, were introduced into the classroom, even greater changes in the autistic children's responsiveness and attempts at initiation were recorded. Nevertheless, social initiations did not generalize to less structured interactions with untrained peers and it tended to be only passive social behaviors, such as responsiveness or attention, that showed generalization. The author noted, too, that individual differences were marked. Although the three categories developed by Wing and Gould (1979) proved useful in distinguishing between children, it was found that children did not remain in the same category over time or across playmates and children tended to move up one category over the course of treatment, i.e., from aloof to passive. These changes in the autistic children's behavior over time, which depended on many variables, including the age, familiarity, and behavior of the interactive partner, suggests that although such systems of categorization are useful, standard settings must be identified if they are to be used reliably for diagnostic or assessment purposes.

The main conclusions to be drawn from the very careful series of studies conducted by Lord and her associates are that, within a structured setting, autistic children can show improvements in social skills. However, improvements tend to center around repetitious, object-oriented interaction. Most of the contacts with normal children involved toy play; changes in interaction were related to increased responsiveness to peers rather than initiation of contacts; the majority of interactions remained of a nonverbal kind and generalization to other settings was extremely limited. Although normal children showed a high degree of similarity, the autistic children were much more variable in their behavior, and it seems that the degree to which autistic children are motivated to interact socially may be an important factor in the successful implementation of such programs.

Although the studies by Lord (1984) are exemplary in many ways, they do not include comparative data from normal children. In a recent study, Van Engeland, Bodnar, and Bolhuis (1984) have used ethological methods to compare the social behavior of groups of autistic and young normal children. They found that quantitative measures of discrete behaviors, even those commonly associated with autism (such as gaze avoidance and motor mannerisms), showed remarkably few differences between groups. Moreover, the frequency of verbal behaviors and social approaches were much the same for autistic and nonautistic subjects. In contrast, however, interactive analysis of the ways in which behavioral systems were organized revealed that the behavior of the autistic children was significantly less cohesive in its organizational structure.

The Interpretation of Studies of Social Behavior

Although direct observational studies of autistic children have yielded valuable information about the nature of their social deficits (Zabel & Zabel, 1982), the interpretation of such data, as the study by Van Engeland *et al.* (1984) indicates, needs to be approached with some caution. Preconceptions about the nature of autism can lead to misinterpretations of even highly reliable measures of behavior. The studies by Tinbergen and Tinbergen (1983) and Richer (1974, 1976), for example, indicate that ethological data can produce invalid conclusions both about the causes of the disorder and about implications for treatment. The correct interpretation of observational data depends on three main requirements:

(1) the analysis of behavioral *systems* rather than discrete behaviors, (2) the analysis of such behaviors within a developmental framework, and (3) the analysis of behaviors according to the specific social context in which they appear.

Restricting analyses to quantitative measures of discrete behaviors may, as indicated above, produce erroneous conclusions. Thus, many behaviors assumed to be highly specific to autism may actually be found almost as often in normal controls (Van Engeland *et al.*, 1984). Qualitative analyses, which investigate behavioral *systems* rather than single behaviors, are required if we are to reach a better understanding of what constitutes both normal and abnormal social functioning.

Since the interpretation of such studies also depends on the child's developmental level, normative data on age-appropriate behaviors are essential. Studies of eye contact, and of the nature of physical and verbal approaches made by normal children during social interactions, have shown that these change considerably over time. What proves to be an acceptable or successful strategy at one age may well be inappropriate at another. Thus, determining what is acceptable social behavior will depend very much on the age (and size) of the autistic child. When placed in a developmental context it is clear that many of the behaviors shown by autistic children cannot be considered as entirely deviant. Gaze avoidance, for example, has frequently been considered as highly specific to the syndrome of autism, and yet developmental studies of normal children suggest that gaze behavior tends to be an indicator of low mental age rather than extreme pathology.

Many other behaviors shown by autistic children are related to mental age. McHale (1983), for example, found that levels of social, symbolic, and communicatory behaviors were positively related to IQ and scores on the Vineland Social Maturity Scale. Ferrari and Matthews (1983) also reported that other aspects of social development, such as the giving of affection and emotional responsiveness, were significantly correlated with mental age.

It is apparent from such findings that autistic children cannot be treated as a homogeneous group and the interpretation of studies of social behavior will depend very much on individual developmental, symbolic, and cognitive levels (Lord, 1984; Sigman *et al.*, 1984). Both Rutter (1984) and Lord (1984) have emphasized the importance of cognitive skills in social processing. Reciprocity in social interactions seems to be the essence of successful relationships and is a skill in which autistic children are particularly lacking. However, whether this should be interpreted as a specifically *social* deficit is unclear. The notion of reciprocity requires complex cognitive sequencing, since the child must learn to attend to social cues, and to interpret and respond to such cues correctly and in a manner that is appropriate to the immediate social context. When the cognitive demands of the situation are limited, either by increased familiarity with the task or by increased structure through training, autistic children appear more socially competent (Lord, 1984). Thus, social behavior with peers cannot be considered without taking into account the cognitive demands of the situation. When an autistic child is placed in a group of normal children, both the social and cognitive requirements placed on him are increased. These cognitive demands may affect the autistic child's behavior just as much as the social demands of the situation, and the reason autistic children generally relate better to adults than to same-age peers may well be that adults, being more predictable and more prepared to structure the situation, make far fewer cognitive demands on the child.

The evaluation of social behavior along a developmental continuum is also important in highlighting the specific deficits of autistic children. Lord (1984), for example, found that although many aspects of the behavior of autistic children, such as attention, imitation, or joint use of objects, could be placed in a developmental sequence, certain deficits of social functioning could not be related simply to developmental delay. In initiating responses, for example, the autistic children fail to make use of very basic social and affective behaviors that are typically observed in normal infants around the age of 7 to 9 months (Rutter, 1980). Such findings suggest that autistic children are not uniformly deviant in their social behaviors; instead, it is the highly variable and uneven development of socially related skills that is so characteristic.

Finally, the interpretation of social behaviors remains highly dependent on the context in which such behaviors are exhibited. Analysis of behaviors such as eye contact, degree of physical proximity, frequency of initiations, or the duration of interactions in social relationships in normal children show that what is appropriate differs according to social context and the behavior of other people involved in the interaction. It is clear, from studies of normal children, that they are highly skilled in adapting to constant shifts and changes in the demands of the social situation. Autistic children, in contrast, although they may show similar rates, overall, of certain social behaviors and may be able to function adequately in a highly structured situation, are not able to adapt to the changing demands of social situations in the same way. Thus, while they may not necessarily lack the essential skills for making social relationships, they do appear to lack the ability to use these flexibly and adaptively.

IMPLICATIONS FOR TREATMENT

Many of the studies of social interaction in autistic children have developed from intervention studies in which the aim was to improve children's social behavior. Because of the problems involved in the assessment of social skills, the majority of studies have restricted themselves to simple counts of behaviors before and after implementation of training programs (Ragland, Kerr, & Strain, 1978; Strain *et al.*, 1979; Tremblay, Strain, Hendrickson, & Shores, 1981; Young

& Kerr, 1979). Although such measures are generally of high reliability, restricting social analyses in this way has tended to lead to overenthusiastic claims for treatment effects. Thus, although many aspects of social behavior may well show improvement following intervention, it is necessary to be aware, as Lord (1984) points out, that even apparently successful treatments do not result in the children becoming normal. They may, with time, show a higher degree of social competence, but difficulties remain in the coordination of social skills, and in their use of language and play, and, most important, they continue to show very little initiation of social contact.

It is also important to be aware of the highly structured and highly staffed nature of the classroom environments involved in these studies, and the generalizability of these findings for children integrated into regular classrooms is highly questionable. Generalization, even in experimental classrooms, may be very limited and the social behaviors learned may be highly specific to particular situations or with particular individuals (Lord, 1984).

Improvements in social behavior do not necessarily affect ratings of peer acceptance (Berler, Gross, & Drabman, 1982), and studies involving the cooperation of normal peers indicate that, even in highly structured settings, there are considerable problems in maintaining the motivation of the normal children over time. Lord (1984) found that after approximately 2 weeks the normal children appeared to have become "exhausted" in their efforts to sustain contact. Sinson and Wetherick (1981), working with more socially responsive Down's syndrome children, found that although normal children made "heroic" efforts to establish contact, they eventually gave up, mainly because of the persistent gaze avoidance of the handicapped group.

In studies of how normal friendships develop, Lewis and Rosenblum (1977) and Hartup (1975) have stressed the importance of reciprocity and positive interaction among individuals who operate at *comparable* levels of complexity. Autistic children are thus doubly handicapped, both by their uneven patterns of development and by their failure to provide the normal child with sufficient reinforcement to maintain interactions. Lord (1984) stresses the importance of providing powerful external incentives in order for normal children to continue to interact with their handicapped peers. However, whether such external reinforcers can ever, ultimately, make up for the lack of reinforcement provided by the autistic children themselves is open to question.

Together with reciprocity, flexibility is probably one of the most important skills necessary for establishing successful social relationships. Teaching autistic children all-purpose behaviors such as eye contact or smiling or verbal greetings will not improve social interactions unless these behaviors are used with appropriate timing, in appropriate contexts. Direct training may be useful in helping the child to develop socially appropriate behaviors, but if such skills are to be effective in the long term, the relationships of these skills to other behaviors and to the interpersonal context in which they occur must be taken into account. As Lord (1984) noted, the ultimate goal is social *interaction*, not the production of isolated behaviors out of context. Given the well-documented problems of autistic children in generalizing newly learned skills to unfamiliar settings, training the child in different types of skills that can be adapted to the demands of a variety of settings may be a more appropriate way of modifying social deficits than teaching specific behaviors that are then expected to generalize.

Finally, in setting up intervention studies, the importance of taking into account the developmental level of the children involved is crucial. The social skills taught must be appropriate to the child's general level of functioning, and normative data on what is appropriate for children of similar developmental stages are vital. It is hardly surprising, for example, that studies to increase eye contact in autistic children have shown very little generalization when the amount of eye contact trained is, in fact, far greater than would be expected of normal children (Mirenda *et al.*, 1983).

SUMMARY

Despite general agreement that the social dysfunction in autism is fundamental to the handicap, investigations to establish the exact nature of the problem are relatively few in number. Many of the early studies of autistic children relied on quantitative measures of behavior, such as duration of eye contact or frequency of interactions, but as they lack comparative data on normal children, the interpretation of results must be treated with caution. Moreover, even comparative studies, using control groups, have produced conflicting results. Some showed autistic children to use significantly lower levels of social behavior; others reported levels that are similar to those of normal children. The limitations of simple, quantitative measures has led to a search for better-developed qualitative and interactional measures (Lord, 1984). From these studies it is clear that, although the frequency of many of the social behaviors shown by autistic children is not necessarily low, there are marked problems in their organization of these behaviors. In particular, the two qualities that appear to be essential for successful peer relations are lacking. These are the ability to relate in a positive and reciprocal way with peers and the ability to adapt interpersonal skills to the ever-changing demands of the social situation.

Assessments of the social deficits shown by autistic children using a developmental framework suggest that many of the problems shown are not syndrome-specific but can be related instead to developmental delays. Not only do these studies indicate the essential need for normative data in any study of abnormal functioning, but they also lend further support to the conclusion of other investigators (Rutter, 1983; Lord, 1984; Sigman *et al.*, 1984) that the social deviance in autistic children cannot be assessed in isolation from other aspects of functioning. It seems likely that the social abnormality in autism stems from a cognitive deficit that affects fine processing of social and emotional cues (Rutter, 1983). Linguistic skills, too, play a crucial role in successful social interactions, and here again autistic children tend to be particularly handicapped. Since social, cognitive, and linguistic development is highly integrated from infancy onward, the social deficits exhibited by autistic children cannot be clearly identified as belonging specifically to any one domain. Thus, in order to develop adequate assessments of the social functioning of autistic children, it is necessary to analyze not only the interaction between social variables but also the ways in which these are related to other aspects of cognitive and linguistic functioning. Cross-sectional and longitudinal studies are needed to identify areas of skill and deficit as precisely as possible and in as many settings as possible. Comparisons with other groups of normal and handicapped children are also required if the social abnormalities that are specific to the syndrome of autism are to be distinguished from those related to more general developmental delays.

REFERENCES

Allen, K., Hart, B., Buell, J., Harris, F., & Wolf, M. (1964). Effects of social reinforcement on isolate behavior of a nursery school child. *Child Development, 35,* 511–518.

Argyle, M., & Cooke, M. (1976). *Gaze and mutual gaze.* Cambridge: Cambridge University Press.

Asher, S., Oden, S., & Gottman, J. (1977). Children's friendships in school settings. In L. G. Lentz (Ed.), *Current topics in early childhood education.* Norwood, NJ: Ablex.

Bartak, L., & Rutter, M. (1973). Special educational treatment of autistic children: A comparative study. I: Design of study and characteristics of units. *Journal of Child Psychology and Psychiatry, 14,* 161–179.

Bartak, L., & Rutter, M. (1974). The use of personal pronouns by autistic children. *Journal of Autism and Childhood Schizophrenia, 4,* 217–222.

Bartak, L., Rutter, M., & Cox, A. (1975). A comparative study of infantile autism and specific developmental receptive language disorder. I. The children. *British Journal of Psychiatry, 126,* 127–145.

Beck, S., Forehand, R., Wells, K., & Quante, A. (1978). *Social skills training with children: An examination of generalization from analogue to natural settings.* Unpublished manuscript, University of Georgia.

Becker, J. (1977). A learning analysis of the development of peer orientated behavior in 9 month old infants. *Developmental Psychology, 13,* 481–491.

Bellack, A., & Hersen, M. (1978). Chronic psychiatric patients: Social skills training. In M. Hersen & A. Bellack (Eds.), *Behavior therapy in the psychiatric setting* (pp. 169–193). Baltimore: Williams and Wilkins.

Bellack, A., Hersen, M., & Lamparski, D. (1979). Role-play tests for assessing social skills: Are they valid? Are they useful? *Journal of Consulting and Clinical Psychology, 47,* 335–342.

Berger, J., & Cunningham, C. (1981). The development of eye contact between mothers and normal versus Down's syndrome infants. *Developmental Psychology, 17,* 678–689.

Berler, E., Gross, A., & Drabman, R. (1982). Social skills training with children: Proceed with caution. *Journal of Applied Behavior Analysis, 15,* 41–53.

Bettelheim, B. (1967). *The empty fortress: Infantile autism and the birth of the self.* New York: Free Press.

Bornstein, M., Bellack, A., & Hersen, M. (1977). Social skills training for unassertive children: A multiple baseline analysis. *Journal of Applied Behavior Analysis, 10,* 183–195.

Bruininks, V. (1978). Actual and perceived peer status of learning disabled students in mainstream programs. *Journal of Special Education, 12,* 51–58.

Bryan, T. (1974). Peer popularity of learning disabled children. *Journal of Learning Disabilities, 7,* 621–625.

Bryan, T. (1976). Peer popularity of learning disabled children: A replication. *Journal of Learning Disabilities, 9,* 307–311.

Bryan, T., Donahue, M., & Pearl, R. (1981). Learning disabled children's communicative competence on referential communicative tasks. *Journal of Pediatric Psychology, 6,* 383–393.

Castell, R. (1970). Physical distance and visual attention as measures of social interaction between child and adult. In S. J. Hutt & C. Hutt (Eds.), *Behaviour studies in psychiatry.* Oxford: Pergamon Press.

Churchill, D. W., & Bryson, C. (1972). Looking and approach behaviour of psychiatric and normal children as a function of adult attention or preoccupation. *Comprehensive Psychiatry, 13,* 171–177.

Ciminero, A., & Drabman, R. (1977). Current developments in the behavioral assessment of children. In B. Lahey & E. Kazdin (Eds.), *Advances in clinical child psychology* (Vol. 1). New York: Plenum Press.

Clark, P., & Rutter, M. (1977). Compliance and resistance in autistic children. *Journal of Autism and Childhood Schizophrenia, 7,* 33–43.

Clark, P., & Rutter, M. (1979). Task difficulty and task performance in autistic children. *Journal of Child Psychology and Psychiatry, 20,* 271–285.

Clark, P., & Rutter, M. (1981). Autistic children's responses to structure and to interpersonal demands. *Journal of Autism and Developmental Disorders, 11,* 201–217.

Dodge, K., Schlundt, D., Shocken, I., & Delugach, J. (1983). Competence and children's sociometric status: The role of peer group entry strategies. *Merrill-Palmer Quarterly, 29,* 309–306.

Doyle, A. B., Connolly, J., & Rivest, L. P. (1980). The effect of playmate familiarity on the social interactions of young children. *Child Development, 51,* 217–223.

Duck, S., Miell, D., & Gaebler, H. (1980). Attraction and communication in children's interactions. In H. Foot, A. Chapman, & R. Smith (Eds.), *Friendship and social relations in children.* London: Wiley.

Durlak, J., & Mannarino, A. (1977). The social skills development program: Description of a school based preventative mental health program for high risk children. *Journal of Clinical Child Psychology, 6,* 48–52.

Ekman, P., & Friesch, V. (1978). *Slides of facial expression.* Palo Alto, CA: Consulting Psychologists Press.

Evers, W., & Schwarz, J. (1973). Modifying social withdrawal in preschoolers: The effects of filmed and teacher praise. *Journal of Abnormal Child Psychology, 1,* 248–256.

Ferrari, M., & Matthews, S. (1983). Self-recognition deficits in autism: Syndrome-specific or general developmental delay. *Journal of Autism and Developmental Disorders, 13,* 317–325.

Foster, S., & Ritchey, W. (1979). Issues in the assessment of social competence in children. *Journal of Applied Behavior Analysis, 12,* 625–638.

Gardner, J. (1976). *Three aspects of childhood autism.* Unpublished doctoral dissertation, University of Leicester.

Gersten, J., Langer, T., Eisenberg, J., Simcha-Fagan, O., & McCarthy, E. (1976). Stability and change in types of behavioral disturbance of children and adolescents. *Journal of Abnormal Child Psychology, 4,* 111–127.

Goldfarb, W. (1961). *Childhood schizophrenia.* Cambridge, MA: Harvard University Press.

Gottman, J. (1977). Towards a definition of social isolation in children. *Child Development, 48,* 513–517.

Gottman, J., Gonso, J., & Rasmussen, B. (1977). Social interaction, social competence, and friendship in children. *Child Development, 46,* 709–718.

Greenwood, C., Walker, H., Todd, N., & Hops, H. (1981). Normative and descriptive analysis of preschool free play social interaction rates. *Journal of Pediatric Psychology, 6,* 343–367.

Hartup, W. (1975). The origins of friendship. In M. Lewis & A. Rosenblum (Eds.), *Friendship and peer relations.* New York: Wiley.

Herjanic, B., Herjanic, M., Brown, F., & Wheatt, T. (1975). Are children reliable reporters? *Journal of Abnormal Child Psychology, 3,* 41–48.

Hermelin, B., & O'Connor, N. (1970). *Psychological experiments with autistic children.* London: Pergamon Press.

Hobson, R. P. (1982, September). *The autistic child's knowledge of persons.* Paper presented at the Symposium on Affective and Social Understanding, Durham, NC.

Hobson, R. P. (1983). The autistic child's recognition of age-related features of people, animals and things. *British Journal of Developmental Psychology, 1,* 343–352.

Hobson, R. P. (1984). Early childhood autism and the question of egocentrism. *Journal of Autism and Developmental Disorders, 14,* 85–104.

Holmberg, M. (1980). The development of social interchange patterns for 12 to 24 months. *Child Development, 51,* 448–456.

Howlin, P. (1978). The assessment of social behavior in autistic children. In M. Rutter & E. Schopler (Eds.), *Autism: A reappraisal of concepts and treatment.* New York: Plenum Press.

Hutt, S. J., & Hutt, C. (1966). *Behaviour studies in psychiatry.* Oxford: Pergamon Press.

Hutt, C., & Ounsted, C. (1966). The biological significance of gaze aversion with particular reference to the syndrome of infantile autism. *Behavioral Science, 11,* 346–356.

Hutt, S., & Vaizey, M. (1966). Differential effects of group density in social behavior. *Nature, 209,* 1371–1375.

Hymel, S. (1983). Preschool children's peer relations: Issues in sociometric assessment. *Merrill Palmer Quarterly, 29,* 237–259.

Hymel, S., & Asher, S. (1977, March). *Assessment and training of isolated children's social skills.* Paper presented at the Meeting of the Society for Research in Child Development, New Orleans.

Izard, C. (1971). *The face of emotion.* New York: Appleton-Century-Crofts.

Jaffe, J., Stern, D., & Peery, J. (1973). Conversational coupling of gaze behavior in prelinguistic human development. *Journal of Psycholinguistic Research, 2,* 321–329.

Johnson, D. (1975). Affective perspective taking and cognitive disposition. *Developmental Psychology, 11,* 869–870.

Johnson, D., & Mykelbust, H. (1967). *Learning disabilities.* New York: Grune and Stratton.

Kanner, L. (1943). Autistic disturbances of affective contact. *Nervous Child, 2,* 217–250.

Kanner, L., Rodriguez, A., & Ashenden, B. (1972). How far can autistic children go in matters of social adaptation? *Journal of Autism and Childhood Schizophrenia, 2,* 9–33.

Kazdin, A. (1978). Evaluating the generality of findings in analogue therapy research. *Journal of Consulting and Clinical Psychology, 46,* 673–686.

Kazdin, A. (1980). Investigating generality of findings from analogue research: A rejoinder. *Journal of Consulting and Clinical Psychology, 48,* 772–773.

Keane, S., & Congar, J. (1981). The implications of communication development for social skills training. *Journal of Pediatric Psychology, 6,* 369–381.

Keller, M., & Carlson, P. (1974). The use of symbolic modelling to promote social skills in preschool children with low levels of social responsiveness. *Child Development, 45,* 912–919.

Koegel, R. L., & Covert, A. (1972). The relationship of self-stimulation to learning in autistic children. *Journal of Applied Behavioral Analysis, 5,* 381–387.

Ladd, G. W. (1983). Social networks of popular, average, and rejected children in school settings. *Merrill Palmer Quarterly, 29,* 283–309.

La Greca, A. (1981). Social behavior and social perception in learning disabled children: A review with implications for social skills training. *Journal of Pediatric Psychology, 6,* 395–416.

Langdell, T. (1978). Recognition of faces: An approach to the study of autism. *Journal of Child Psychology and Psychiatry, 19,* 255–268.

Lewis, M., & Rosenblum, L. (1977). Introduction. In M. Lewis & L. Rosenblum (Eds.), *Friendship and peer relations.* New York: Wiley.

Lord, C. (1984). Development of peer relations in children with autism. In F. Morrison, C. Lord, & D. Keating (Eds.), *Applied developmental psychology* (Vol. 1). New York: Academic Press.

Mahler, M. (1965). An early infantile psychosis. The symbolic and autistic syndrome. *Journal of American Academy of Child Psychiatry, 4,* 554–568.

Martini, M. (1980). Structures of interaction between autistic children. In T. M. Field, S. Goldberg, D. Stern, & A. Sostek (Eds.), *High risk infants and children's adult and peer interaction.* New York: Academic Press.

McHale, S. (1983). Social interactions of autistic and non-handicapped children during free play. *American Journal of Orthopsychiatry, 53,* 81–91.

McHale, S., Olley, J., & Marcus, L. (1981). *Variations across settings in autistic children's play.* Paper presented at the Biannual Meetings of the Society for Research in Child Development, Boston.

McHale, S., Olley, J., Marcus, L., & Simeonsson, R. (1981). Non-handicapped peers as tutors for autistic children. *Exceptional Children, 48,* 263–265.

McHale, S., Simeonsson, R., Marcus, L., & Olley, J. (1980). The social and syntactic quality of autistic children's communications. *Journal of Autism and Developmental Disorders, 10,* 299–314.

Mirenda, P., Donnelan, A., & Yoder, D. (1983). Gaze behavior: A new look at an old problem. *Journal of Autism and Developmental Disorders, 13,* 397–409.

Moreno, J. (1934). *Who shall survive? A new approach to the problem of human interrelations.* Washington, DC: Nervous and Mental Disease Publications.

Mueller, E. (1972). The maintenance of verbal exchanges between young children. *Child Development, 43,* 930–938.

Mueller, E., & Brenner, J. (1977). Origins of social interaction in playgroup toddlers. *Child Development, 48,* 495–506.

O'Connor, R. (1972). Relative efficacy of modeling, shaping and the combined procedures for modification of social withdrawal. *Journal of Abnormal Psychology, 79,* 327–334.

Parten, M. (1932). Social participation among pre-school children. *Journal of Abnormal and Social Psychology, 27,* 243–269.

Piaget, J. (1926). *The language and thought of the child.* (M. Gabain, Trans.). London: Routledge and Kegan Paul.

Piaget, J., & Inhelder, B. (1969). *The psychology of the child.* (H. Weaver, Trans.). London: Routledge and Kegan Paul.

Ragland, E., Kerr, M., & Strain, P. (1978). Effects of social imitations on the behavior of withdrawn autistic children. *Behavior Modification, 2,* 565–578.

Reardon, R., Hersen, M., Bellack, A., & Foley, J. (1978). *Measuring social skill in grade school boys.* Unpublished manuscript, University of Pittsburgh.

Renshaw, P., & Asher, S. (1983). Children's goals and strategies for social interaction. *Merrill-Palmer Quarterly, 29*, 353–374.

Rheingold, H., & Eckerman, C. (1975). General issues in the study of peer relations: Some proposals for clarifying the study of social development. In M. Lewis & L. Rosenblum (Eds.), *Friendships and peer relations*. New York: Wiley.

Richer, J. (1976). The social avoidance behavior of autistic children. *Animal Behavior, 24*, 898–906.

Richer, J. (1978). The partial noncommunication of culture to autistic children—An application of human ethology. In M. Rutter & E. Schopler (Eds.), *Autism: A reappraisal of concepts and treatment*. New York: Plenum Press.

Richer, J., & Coss, R. (1976). Gaze aversion in autistic and normal children. *Acta Psychiatrica Scandinavica, 53*, 193–210.

Robson, K. (1967). The role of eye-to-eye contact in maternal–infant attachment. *Journal of Child Psychology and Psychiatry, 8*, 18–25.

Romanczyk, R., Diamant, C., Goren, E., Trunell, G., & Harris, S. (1975). Increasing isolate and social play in severely disabled children: Intervention and postintervention effectiveness. *Journal of Autism and Childhood Schizophrenia, 5*, 57–70.

Rumsay, J., & Rapoport, J. (1983, August). *Autistic children as adults: Mental and behavioral status*. Paper presented at the meeting of the American Psychological Association, Anchern, CA.

Rutter, M. (1966). Prognosis: Psychotic children in adolescence and early adult life. In J. K. Wing (Ed.), *Early childhood autism: Clinical, educational and social aspects*. London: Pergamon Press.

Rutter, M. (1978). Language disorder and infantile autism. In M. Rutter & E. Schopler (Eds.), *Autism: A reappraisal of concepts and treatment*. New York: Plenum Press.

Rutter, M. (1980). Attachment and the development of social relationships. In M. Rutter (Ed.), *Scientific foundations of developmental psychiatry*. London: Heinemann Medical.

Rutter, M. (1983). Cognitive deficits in the pathogenesis of autism. *Journal of Child Psychology and Psychiatry, 24*, 513–531.

Rutter, M. (1984). Infantile autism and other pervasive developmental disorders. In M. Rutter & L. Hersov (Eds.), *Child and adolescent psychiatry: Modern approaches* (Vol. 2). Oxford: Blackwell Scientific.

Rutter, M., & Graham, P. (1968). The reliability and validity of the psychiatric assessment of the child. I. Interview with the child. *British Journal of Psychiatry, 114*, 563–579.

Scheman, J., & Lockard, J. (1979). Development of gaze aversion in children. *Child Development, 50*, 594–596.

Seibert, J., & Hogan, A. (1981). *Procedures manual for the early social communication scales*. Unpublished manuscript, Mailman Center for Child Development, University of Miami.

Sherman, T., Sigman, M., Ungerer, J., & Mundy, P. (1985). *Knowledge of categories in autistic children*. Manuscript in preparation.

Sigman, M., Ungerer, J., Mundy, P., & Sherman, T. (1984). Cognitive functioning in autistic children. In D. Cohen, A. Donnelan, & R. Paul (Eds.), *Handbook of autism and atypical development*. New York: Wiley.

Sinson, J., & Wetherick, N. (1981). The behaviour of children with Down's syndrome in normal play groups. *Journal of Mental Deficiency Research, 25*, 113–120.

Siperstein, G., Bopp, M., & Bak, J. (1978). Social status of learning disabled children. *Journal of Learning Disabilities, 12*, 11–14.

Sorosky, A., Ornitz, E., Brown, M., & Ritvo, E. (1968). Systematic observations of autistic behavior. *Archives of General Psychiatry, 18*, 437–449.

Spiker, D., & Ricks, M. (1983). Visual self recognition in autistic children: Developmental relationships. *Child Development, 55,* 214–225.

Spiker, D., & Ricks, M. (1985). Developmental relationships in self recognition: A study of 52 autistic children. *Child Development.*

Stern, D. (1976). Mothers and infants at play: The dyadic interaction involving facial, vocal and gaze behaviors. In M. Lewis & L. Rosenblum (Eds.), *The effects of the infant on its caretaker.* New York: Wiley.

Strain, P., & Fox, J. (1981). Peer social initiations and the modification of social withdrawal: A review and future perspective. *Journal of Pediatric Psychology, 6,* 417–433.

Strain, P., Kerr, M., & Ragland, E. (1979). Effects of peer-mediated social initiations and prompting/reinforcement procedures in the social behavior of autistic children. *Journal of Autism and Developmental Disorders, 9,* 41–54.

Tiegerman, E., & Primavera, L. (1984). Imitating the autistic child: Facilitating communicative gaze behavior. *Journal of Autism and Developmental Disorders, 14,* 27–38.

Tinbergen, N., & Tinbergen, E. (1983). *"Autistic" children: New hope for a cure.* London: Allen and Unwin.

Tremblay, A., Strain, P., Hendrickson, J., & Shores, S. (1981). Social interactions in normal preschool children. *Behavior Modification, 5,* 237–253.

Trower, P. (1980). Situational analysis of the components and processes of behavior of socially skilled and unskilled patients. *Journal of Consulting and Clinical Psychology, 48,* 327–339.

Ungerer, J., & Sigman, M. (1981). Symbolic play and language comprehension in autistic children. *Journal of the American Academy of Child Psychiatry, 20,* 318–337.

Van Engeland, H., Bodnar, F., & Bolhuis, G. (1984). Some qualitative aspects of the social behavior of autistic children: An ethological approach. *Journal of Child Psychology and Psychiatry.*

Van Hasselt, V., Hersen, M., Whitehill, M., & Bellack, A. (1979). Social skill assessment and training for children: An evaluative review. *Behaviour Research and Therapy, 17,* 413–437.

Volkmar, F., & Cohen, D. (1982). A hierarchical analysis of patterns of noncompliance in autistic and behavior-disturbed children. *Journal of Autism and Developmental Disorders, 12,* 35–42.

Volkmar, F., Hoder, E., & Cohen, D. (in press). A naturalistic study of autistic children: I. Effects of treatment structure on behavior. *Journal of Child Psychology and Psychiatry.*

Volkmar, F., Hoder, E., & Cohen, D. (in press). A naturalistic study of autistic children: II. Compliance in relationship to task demands. *Journal of Child Psychology and Psychiatry.*

Walker, H., & Hops, M. (1973). The use of group and individual reinforcement contingencies in the modification of social withdrawal. In L. Hamerlynck, L. Hardy, & E. Mash (Eds.), *Behavior change: Methodological concepts and practice.* Champaign, IL: Research Press.

Weiner, J. (1980). A theoretical model of the acquisition of peer relationships of learning disabled children. *Journal of Learning Disorders, 13,* 42–53.

Wing, L. (1969). The handicaps of autistic children: A comparative study. *Journal of Child Psychology and Psychiatry, 10,* 1–40.

Wing, L. (1976). *Early childhood autism* (2nd ed.). London: Pergamon Press.

Wing, L. (1978). Social behavioral and cognitive characteristics: An epidemiological approach. In M. Rutter & E. Schopler (Eds.), *Autism: A reappraisal of concepts and treatment.* New York: Plenum Press.

Wing, L., & Gould, J. (1979). Severe impairments of social interaction and associated abnormalities in children: Epidemiology and classification. *Journal of Autism and Developmental Disorders, 9,* 11–29.

Wolff, S., & Chess, S. (1964). A behavioral study of schizophrenic children. *Acta Psychiatrica Scandinav., 40,* 438–466.

7

Communication as a Social Problem in Autism

DEBORAH G. GARFIN and CATHERINE LORD

When Leo Kanner (1943) first described the syndrome of autism, the primary deficit was assumed to be social. That is, autistic children were described as having a basic inability to relate to other people. While there has been debate in the ensuing years regarding which additional characteristics should be included in the definition of autism (see American Psychiatric Association, 1980; Rutter, 1978a), all conceptualizations of autism have included language and communication deficits. The purpose of this chapter is to discuss the relationship between communication and social problems in autism. In particular, we will focus upon the aspects of communication that bear most directly on social functioning. In addition, elements of social development that affect the learning and use of communication skills by persons with autism will be considered.

For purposes of this discussion, the term *communication* is used to refer to both verbal and nonverbal giving and receiving of information between two or more individuals. Production and comprehension of both nonverbal communication and formal language will be considered separately since special problems exist in each domain for the person with autism. In addition to describing the communication problems of autistic children, suggestions will be made for teaching specific skills and manipulating the environment in order to promote social development and increase independent functioning in social situations, particularly with peers. Although the ability to relate to adults often improves as autistic children develop, peer interactions generally remain severely impaired

DEBORAH G. GARFIN • Department of Psychology, North Texas State University, Denton, Texas 76203. CATHERINE LORD • Department of Psychology, Glenrose Hospital, Edmonton, Alberta T5G 0B7, Canada.

(Rutter, 1978b; Wing, 1976). Our assumption is that much of this difficulty with peers is due to problems in communication.

Strategies for remediation with autistic persons must take into account the effect of their communication deficits on social interaction. Some suggestions will be based on research that has documented their effectiveness. Others will be presented on the basis of their logical and face validity since the research base for psychoeducational interventions has only recently begun to be developed. The hope is that with increased understanding of the handicaps of autistic individuals, interventions will take into account the real communication needs of these children in social contexts rather than merely focusing on methods and content of language.

RELATIONSHIP BETWEEN COMMUNICATION AND SOCIAL RELATIONS

Communication is one type of social behavior. For communication to take place, some sort of mutual reciprocity is required such that there must be a give-and-take of information between people. While this statement sounds obvious from a social perspective, the critical elements in communication lie in what the interactors perceive as the message given and received, not the actual form of the message. This transfer of information, at least in part, is goal-directed. The goals of communication are determined by the needs of the participants. Because these needs and goals most often involve other people, communication cannot be considered in a vacuum but must be understood within social contexts (Bransford & Nitsch, 1978; Bruner, 1975).

For example, two 6-year-old boys are playing with some blocks. The children are sitting next to each other on the floor, each building his own structure. One child decides he wants a block in the other boy's pile and asks him for the block, offering one of his own in exchange. In order for this social-communicative interaction to have occurred successfully, there first had to be a need—that is, a reason for the interaction to take place. In this case, the child who initiated the interaction wanted a block. Subsequent behavior was then directed at realizing this goal. A good deal of social awareness was also necessary to successfully attain the goal. There was probably an understanding of (1) possession (e.g., the blocks in the pile nearest each boy "belonged" to him, (2) the social norm specifying the need to request the block rather than grab it, and (3) the likelihood that a "trade" would increase the chances of compliance.

As will be discussed throughout this chapter, autistic children have major deficits in basic aspects of both social and communication skills. Especially in young children with autism, there may be far less intrinsic motivation to interact with or please other people, particularly other children or unfamiliar adults

(Wing, 1976). This is not to claim that throughout development *all* autistic persons remain uninterested in social interaction for its own sake. However, it is important to realize that typical assumptions about young children's inherent feelings and reciprocal pleasure in sociability (e.g., that a baby will enjoy smiling at us over her mother's shoulder, that a preschooler will sit down and be quiet just because that is what the other children are doing and because that is what the teacher has requested) cannot be made automatically for children with autism.

In addition, the usual external motivations for developing and/or using social skills may be only minimally present in children with autism. For example, a child who is not interested in building would have less need to request a block from another child than would a child fascinated by building. Training initiation skills in an autistic child cannot be appropriately carried out in the absence of a social context that is meaningful *to that child*. We need to ensure that the child has a reason to initiate.

One practical implication of these statements is that teachers or parents must take care that social skills programs are a generally positive experience for the autistic child, as well as a context for acquiring specific behaviors. The goal is for the child to come to associate the pleasure of social experiences with being around other people. For example, the goal of teaching a child to greet his sister by looking at her face and saying her name assumes that the child has some motivation other than pleasing his mother for interacting with his siblings. If interactions with his sister are generally positive, this may well be the case. If not, it seems more appropriate to work first on setting up positive, potentially motivating experiences with her and then to concentrate on specific initiating behaviors. In contrast to the above, consider a child who learns that he will receive a poker chip whenever he greets an aggressive classmate if his teacher is holding a certain clipboard. In this case, the poker chip rather than the consequences of a social initiation is the reinforcer. Additionally, the fact that this aggressive classmate is someone the child would much rather avoid than seek out is ignored. In planning a successful social intervention, it is critical to take into account what is *socially* motivating to the particular child with whom we are working.

WHAT CHILDREN COMMUNICATE ABOUT

In line with the above emphasis, it may be helpful to first consider the kinds of things children communicate about. Generally, when nonhandicapped children are together, they are playing. During early childhood, this "play" most often revolves around some sort of object use (Rubin, Fein, & Vandenberg, 1983). For example, children might engage in an exchange of toys, imitate the use of a tool, and/or use objects in some sort of joint or mutual manner (e.g., playing with a ball and bat) (Holmberg, 1980). Much of this play in young children is imaginative. It often consists of enacting everyday activities such as preparing and eating meals or going to work, school, or the doctor (Rubin, 1977).

One of the reasons autistic children interact so poorly with peers may be that their play skills are so limited. They may not know how to use familiar objects and toys, and even when they do, autistic children may choose to attend to perceptual aspects of objects rather than use them in a symbolic or constructive fashion. Thus, teaching autistic children how to play and use materials appropriately may be one step in the direction of giving them something to communicate about with their peers (Lord, 1984a). In addition, encouraging or even systematically reinforcing types of play that have particularly good potential for being interactive may also be necessary (Romanczyk, Diament, Goren, Trunell, & Harris, 1975).

On the other hand, it is important to realize that certain types of play are most often defined by language. For example, two children are each playing with a set of trains and tracks. One child silently places the tracks in a row and then moves a train up and down them. In contrast, the other child talks to himself, "All aboard. Gonna be late. Better hurry or you'll miss the train. We're off to St. Louis," as he places the trains and tracks. While the physical content of the two boys' play is virtually identical, the language of the second boy allows us to know what he is imagining. With the first child, it is difficult to tell what he is thinking. From the perspective of a potential playmate, the language of the latter child makes this play more interesting and his ideas much more accessible than having to rely on the physical context or nonverbal cues provided by the first child.

In fact, while language (especially verbal language) is increasingly incorporated into play as nonhandicapped children develop (Holmberg, 1980), speech is of critical importance in the success of interactions between preschoolers as well (Mueller, 1972). Mueller found that not only the presence of a verbal initiation but the ease with which the verbalization was understood predicted the likelihood of a response from another child. Thus, autistic children are handicapped in terms of both limited play skills and limited language skills that might facilitate play.

COMPREHENSION

This section will address the comprehension difficulties experienced by autistic children as well as relate these problems to the ability to engage in social interactions. While nonverbal and verbal comprehension deficits will be considered separately, it should be noted that even autistic children who are quite verbal frequently have trouble interpreting nonverbal communication (Hobson, 1984).

Nonverbal Comprehension

Often it is readily apparent that autistic children do not understand what is said to them. A less obvious but perhaps no less handicapping deficit is the difficulty many autistic children have in comprehending nonverbal communication. Nonverbal cues such as gestures, facial expressions, and voice intonations are comprehended by nonautistic children at a very early age (Schaffer, Hepburn, & Collis, 1983). Even infants are responsive to a stern voice, a smile, a wave of the hand. Normally developing children not only notice these nonverbal communications but frequently are able to interpret and respond to them appropriately. For example, a toddler might be eating some raisins, notice her little brother looking at the raisins longingly, realize that he would like some, and offer to share the snack with him.

In contrast, autistic children are usually quite poor at responding appropriately to nonverbal communications, including gestures, facial expressions, and voice intonations (Ricks & Wing, 1976). However, it is not always clear exactly where the difficulty exists. That is, does the autistic child have problems (a) picking up relevant cues (e.g., is he attending to the color of the person's eyes rather than the emotion the eyes are communicating), (b) interpreting the nonverbal information (e.g., realizing that by raising his eyebrows his mother is "commenting" on his noisiness), and/or (c) knowing the appropriate responses to make given the nonverbal input and social context (such as passing the butter on to the next person after taking some)? Clearly, these abilities have major social implications, especially given that nonverbal cues are often the primary source of information concerning the affect and attitudes of the speaker (Argyle, 1972). Brief consideration of some research data will help clarify these issues.

In a study of the recognition of faces, autistic children were found to attend to the lower half of the faces more often and the upper half of faces less often than did other children (Langdell, 1978). This finding suggests that even the initial information that autistic children receive from nonverbal cues may differ from that attended to by normally developing children.

In another study, Hobson (1984) had autistic and mentally retarded children and nonhandicapped children (ages 5–9 years) match pictures of either objects or expressions with corresponding gestures, vocalizations, or contexts. None of the children had difficulty matching objects with their relevant characteristics. However, the autistic children had more difficulty than the other two groups when matching faces depicting affect with corresponding gestures, vocalizations, and contexts. In addition, the autistic children had difficulty matching gestures, vocalizations, and contexts with pictures depicting people who differed on the basis of age and sex. It seems probable that the autistic children *could* see the differences between facial expressions or between age- and sex-appropriate characteristics but that they did not realize the importance of these features in this task. In a second study by the same author, autistic and nonautistic children sorted photos that differed in terms of emotion portrayed (happy, nonhappy), sex, and type of hat worn (floppy or wooly hat). About two-thirds of both groups sorted the photographs on the basis of sex. However, the next preference by the nonautistic children was for emotional expression, while the autistic children focused on the hats.

Those who live and work with autistic children also report major problems in picking up cues from others regarding affect and attitude (see Park, Chapter 5, this volume). Even those children with high verbal skills often have difficulties interpreting information that is abstract and socially determined. Perhaps one reason why socially relevant information is so difficult to comprehend is that the interpreter has to take into account large amounts of information at one time and apply fairly sophisticated rules that are relatively specific to context (Hermelin & O'Connor, 1970). For example, consider the pieces of information the child needs to integrate in order to interpret raised eyebrows. Depending upon what else the face is doing, the raised eyebrows might represent fear, surprise, or anticipation. Depending on the context, the intention of the communicator may be not to indicate any of these emotions but rather to tease the other person by expressing an emotion obviously inappropriate to the situation. Thus, not only an understanding of the features of nonverbal behaviors that require attention but also the social context in which the interaction is occurring is necessary to interpret affect and attitude.

An additional problem for the autistic child arises from the difficulties in social perspective taking. In fact, this is another example of the importance of context. Usually after a nonhandicapped person notices and interprets a nonverbal cue (e.g., a sigh along with a look at her watch indicating that she is anxious to leave), he is able to figure out why the other person feels this way (e.g., the conversation has been going on a long time). For the autistic person, however, even if the cue is noted and interpreted correctly, the reason for the person's emotion may not be correctly understood. In part, this comes from a difficulty in taking the perspective of the other person. This often occurs because interests and concerns of the person with autism can be vastly different from those of other people. The nonautistic person may understand that topics such as the weather, sports, politics, and current events are likely to be of interest to most people. In contrast, the autistic person may not realize that lengthy conversations about bus schedules, elevators, and clocks are unlikely to be of extreme interest to most people. Thus, even if immediate social nonverbal cues are perceived and correctly interpreted, the autistic person may not know why he or she is being given these messages. If what has gone wrong is not clear to the autistic person, knowing how to remedy the situation is equally difficult.

In helping autistic children develop nonverbal comprehension skills, it is important to assess where the deficits exist: Is the problem one of not attending to potential sources of information, not knowing how to interpret information, and/or not knowing how to respond? This assessment will determine, in part, where an intervention is to be targeted. One child might be attending to relevant nonverbal cues but not interpreting them accurately. Another child might realize that he has angered a peer and even understand why, but might not know what to do to remedy the situation. Consider an autistic 12-year-old who had a very poor concept of "personal space." He would stand very close to other people and would put his head close to theirs when conversing. While this child was aware of the fact that both peers and adults constantly tried to move farther away from him, he did not understand *why* they moved away and thus he responded by moving in closer again. The boy was given a simple explanation of what was happening (i.e., "People don't like it when you stand too close to them, so they move away") and then was taught to stand one step away from people. This procedure was slightly effective. However, in the end, a social perspective-taking task made the greatest difference in his behavior. During a role-playing session, a peer was instructed to stand very close to the autistic adolescent and to continue to approach him whenever an attempt was made to increase the distance between them. This made the adolescent very uncomfortable. When he was helped to realize how other people felt, the problem was rectified by his attending to what was now a more meaningful cue (i.e., when people move away from you, it means you are standing too close to them) and using a concrete strategy (i.e., measuring interpersonal distance in steps rather than by his own comfort level).

Those who interact with autistic children can facilitate nonverbal comprehension by overemphasizing and exaggerating these nonverbal cues. Selecting a limited repertoire of cues that can be repeated frequently and across different situations will also increase the likelihood of the autistic child's learning their meaning. Peers can be instructed to use similar strategies. Finally, prompts, actual demonstrations, and role playing can be invaluable in communicating with autistic children. Imitation can be a very natural component of play and in one sense is the foundation for turn-taking behavior.

Verbal Comprehension

Unlike most normally developing children, the young autistic child often appears to be uninterested and unresponsive to the speech of others (Bartak, Rutter, & Cox, 1975; Ricks & Wing, 1976). Educators in autism programs know that much of this apparent lack of interest is the result of the child's not understanding what is being said (Lord & Baker, 1977). The content of language and the context in which it is said are factors that severely limit the autistic child's verbal comprehension.

The content of the autistic child's receptive language is deficient in quantitative and qualitative ways. Receptive vocabulary is typically much lower than one would expect given the nonverbal skills of the child (Lockyer & Rutter, 1970). Even when individual words are understood, autistic children have particular difficulty understanding words ordered to make sentences (Lord, 1984b). In fact, in one study, 8- to 14-year-old children with autism who had an average nonverbal mental age of 5 1/2 years and average receptive vocabulary scores of 4 1/2 years generally followed simple directions ("put the big apple on the chair") less well than normally developing 2-year-olds (Lord & Allen, 1979).

One social implication of this discrepancy is that interactions with nonautistic peers may be hampered by difficulty in finding a good "match" in terms of verbal and nonverbal skills and interests. Even a mentally retarded peer who is not autistic is likely to be more competent at communication than the autistic child and thus may place too high language demands on him. The confusion of interacting with a child who has discrepant levels of verbal and nonverbal skills is exacerbated by the fact that many autistic children are echolalic (Bartak *et al.*, 1975). Delayed echolalia, especially when used in appropriate situations, can give the listener the impression that an autistic child is far more sophisticated linguistically than he or she really is. This impression can lead to overexpectations, often unconscious, for what the autistic child can understand.

Language comprehension deficits of autistic children may also be described qualitatively. These deficits include difficulties in comprehending language denoting abstract concepts such as space, time, and emotion. Relational terms such as prepositions and pronouns are also very difficult for autistic children to comprehend. Again, these deficits often represent gaps in comprehension; a child might understand concrete words such as *trapezoid* or *conveyer belt* but not understand when someone says, "It's mine" or "Put it in the box."

To complicate matters even more, the context in which verbal language is presented to the child can reduce comprehension even further. Even when vocabulary within the child's repertoire is used, comprehension may decrease as a function of one or more of the following: (a) amount of language presented (i.e., number of words), (b) number of different ideas presented (e.g., multiple commands), (c) overall stimulation from the environment (e.g., noise), and (d) learning-dependent context cues (e.g., who says it, where it is said). These factors also serve to reduce comprehension in nonautistic children, but for them, positive use of nonverbal cues and social context may compensate (Lord & O'Neill, 1983).

These qualitative and quantitative verbal comprehension deficits have profound effects on the autistic child's ability to relate to peers. Even higher-functioning verbal children with autism may have a very difficult time interacting with nonhandicapped peers due to subtle but significant comprehension deficits involving the failure to understand colloquial expressions, humor, and more abstract concepts and ideas. Lack of effective strategies for letting others know when they are confused or do not understand what has been said further exacerbates these problems. Although there has not been systematic study of autistic children's ability to assess their own comprehension, it is known that young normal and retarded children have poor metacognitive abilities—that is, understanding of their own thinking (Campione & Brown, 1977; Flavell & Wellman, 1977). Thus, effective communication with peers may be limited not only by general developmental delays and poor social awareness but also by minimal metacognitive abilities.

Teaching autistic children strategies for dealing with confusing situations seems as important as teaching comprehension skills directly. Some children acquire strategies on their own. The child who exclaims, "I don't understand!" or "I'm so confused!" elicits reactions from the speaker that may help him increase his comprehension. For example, the speaker might repeat what has been said, perhaps more slowly, rephrase a comment, reduce language demands by simplifying the language (e.g., shortening sentences) or adding nonverbal cues such as demonstrations and/or visual cues. Peers interacting with autistic children need to be sensitive to signs of confusion and to be aware of ways of improving comprehension.

There is further motivation for modifying the autistic child's language environment. Autistic children who become overwhelmed in language-filled situations frequently engage in negative behaviors (Schopler, 1976). Previous assumptions regarding the high degree of noncompliance associated with autism have been shown to be invalid. Often, "noncompliance" disappears when tasks are designed to fit the developmental level of the child (Clark & Rutter, 1977; Volkmar, Chapter 9, this volume). Thus, what may be initially assumed to be noncompliance is in fact the child indicating that he does not understand what is expected of him.

Further indirect evidence for the effect of language environment on the behavior of autistic children was obtained from a series of studies in which dyads of autistic and nonhandicapped peers interacted (Lord, 1984a). When playing with the nonhandicapped playmates, autistic children showed few self-stimulatory and unusual behaviors. After the first few sessions, they were remarkably responsive in positive ways to the initiations of the nonhandicapped children. At least in part, the autistic children's appropriate behavior seemed to be a function of the low cognitive demands and the familiarity of the situation. The play sessions were short (15 minutes) and occurred daily for several weeks within a familiar environment. In contrast to his behavior in a typical "teaching" situation with an adult, the autistic child was able to control the interactions by turning or walking away when he began to feel overwhelmed. This meant that interactions were often quite brief, but they gradually became longer, especially for the higher-functioning children. A variety of toys were available to the children, but there was no "task" to complete and verbal communication was not necessary in order for the children to relate socially. Although all of the children in the studies could speak, little verbal interaction occurred and what did was usually supplemented with gestures from the nonhandicapped children. Verbal initiations by the nonhandicapped peers that were clear requests for specific behaviors were more likely to elicit a response from the autistic children than were nonspecific "conversational" comments. Thus, appropriate social behavior with age-mates can occur even in severely retarded autistic children in situations where the children are not overwhelmed by intense language or cognitive demands. This finding argues for designing social skill interventions, at least for younger and/or lower-functioning children, in such a way that verbal demands are minimized to ensure positive, low-intensity experiences.

PRODUCTION

Verbal Production

The productive language of autistic children has received much attention. Their language is described as being both delayed and deviant (Bartak *et al.*, 1975; Cantwell, Baker, & Rutter, 1978). That is, in some ways the children have been found to follow normal sequences of language development but at far older ages than normally expected (Tager-Flusberg, 1981), while in other ways the children have been found to follow sequences that cannot be easily fit into normal patterns (see Howlin, 1984). Delays in productive language are of particular significance because, like the acquisition of receptive skills, expressive language development often lags behind the development of other cognitive skills (Bartak *et al.*, 1975). These discrepancies can be confusing to those who work with autistic children. Indeed, this frequently noted scatter of skills makes it very important to assess carefully all aspects of developmental functioning. An autistic 4-year-old may have age-appropriate perceptual and fine motor skills even though his speech is less sophisticated than most normally developing toddlers.

Deviant language production is perhaps the feature that most clearly differentiates autistic children from language-handicapped (dysphasic) children (Bartak *et al.*, 1975). Deviant production refers to the content as well as the use of language. With respect to content, autistic children are more likely to reverse the pronouns *you* and *I*, engage in echolalic speech, and produce stereotyped or metaphorical language than are dysphasic children. These behaviors can be bewildering to other children as well as adults. In a way, the mute child draws less attention to him/herself than the child with unusual language. Additionally, the child with some nonmeaningful speech is often judged as having more knowledge of productive as well as receptive language than he really has.

When compared to language-handicapped, nonautistic children with normal nonverbal intelligence, autistic children are less likely to talk spontaneously and are more likely to choose peculiar topics of conversation. Autistic children also less readily use the language they have and are less successful in communicating their thoughts, feelings, and needs (Tager-Flusberg, 1981). For example, even among children who have developed some productive language, there is relatively little spontaneous initiation of communication (Cantwell *et al.*, 1978) (e.g., asking a question without a prompt). Thus, the autistic child is doubly handicapped by delays in language acquisition as well as by difficulties in using the language he or she has. Consider the following example:

Jack calls his friend Fran up on the telephone and asks her whether or not she would like to come over for dinner. Fran accepts, and the two then agree on a time. Fran thanks Jack and both say good-bye.

The above communication reflects a successful social interaction. While the interaction appears relatively brief, the skills necessary to engage in such an interaction are numerous and complex. However, there is a relatively large degree of structure inherent within this type of interaction. That is, the phone conversation has a clear beginning and end, and the driving force of the interaction is goal-directed (e.g., extending an invitation and receiving a response). As such, this type of interaction is within the abilities of at least some higher-functioning, verbal autistic youngsters. Autistic children would have much more difficulty with an interaction type that was less structured and more open-ended (e.g., a conversation with a seatmate during a bus ride). Thus, in teaching communication skills to children and adults with autism, some attention might be paid to the types of interactions in which the autistic person is most likely to engage. Setting up situations that provide a high degree of structure and organization might provide more predictability for the person with autism and help the interaction seem more positive than trying to teach social skills in less structured contexts.

Even within a relatively simple structure, there are components that would present major problems to the person with autism. For example, someone has to begin the interchange. Social initiation has consistently been reported as being of great difficulty for autistic children. As discussed earlier, one strategy that may be effective in increasing the chance of initiation is to ensure that there is maximum motivation to interact. Thus, there is more motivation for an autistic child to ask for a desired toy than to say, "Hello, nice to meet you," to a stranger.

Taking the issue of motivation a step further, consider why Jack might want Fran to come over for dinner. Why ask Fran, in particular, and not a stranger on the street? Perhaps Jack was recently over to Fran's for dinner and wants to reciprocate. Perhaps Jack has found out that Fran's dog ran away and wants to cheer her up. These possibilities require that Jack have some understanding of social conventions, sensitivity to another person's perspective (e.g., feelings and attitudes), and/or awareness of human behavior. These are all areas of great deficit for the person with autism. Because motivations may differ greatly from person (autistic or not) to person, helping an autistic person link his communications to his intentions has to be done on an individual basis. On the other hand, sometimes the complexity of trying to anticipate all possible social situations is so great that providing the person with autism with concrete guidelines (e.g., such as teaching the boy to stand one step away from others or teaching the phrase "I'm interested in . . ., are you?" as a way to begin conversations) may be necessary as well.

Other socially determined components of the interaction include use of social amenities and word choice—again, aspects of communication that are pragmatic. In the above conversation, Fran accepts the invitation and thanks Jack. The thank-you was not an essential part of the communication in the sense that without the amenity the purpose or goal of the interchange would still be attained. However, Fran's thank-you communicated to Jack that she appreciated the invitation and that she felt positive about the interchange. Of course, the way in which the thank-you was said would also be significant. Intonation of voice would provide information as to whether Fran was excited, apprehensive, or perhaps ambivalent about the event.

Intentional versus Nonintentional Communication

An interesting distinction has been made by Hermelin and O'Connor (1985) between intentional and nonintentional communication (what they refer to as voluntary/propositional and spontaneous/unlearned communication, respectively). Intentional communication refers to a deliberate and voluntary attempt to convey information; for example, a child asks for some food, points to a toy she desires, or pushes away work she does not want to do.

In contrast, nonintentional communication refers to information that is transmitted without deliberate or conscious awareness. These productions are spontaneous and presumably unlearned, and they generally reflect emotional states (Hermelin & O'Connor, 1985). Some examples of nonintentional communication include the startle response (involuntary raising of arms when startled), a smile in response to a pleasant stimulus, or the voice intonation of a tense and anxious speaker.

Fortunately, what is transmitted nonintentionally by persons without autism is usually consistent with information conveyed intentionally. For example, a child who approaches a peer and says, "Want to play?" may (a) establish eye contact, (b) increase proximity to the other child, (c) extend a toy to his friend, and perhaps (d) smile. While the initial request may have occurred as a result of some deliberation, it is likely that other components of the social-communicative interaction (e.g., making eye contact, smiling) were produced automatically and nonintentionally.

In contrast, there often seem to be discrepancies between what is communicated intentionally and nonintentionally by autistic children. Voice intonation may not match the content of what is said. Nonverbal body language may have little to do with how the autistic child actually feels in a given situation. For example, the child's body may be turned away from the person with whom he or she is interacting. However, for these children, "normal" unlearned, innate behaviors may simply not be a part of their internal "wiring." Rather than reflecting some sort of negative affect toward the other person, these behaviors may not be reflecting anything at all concerning attitude or affect toward the situation but may simply be a very basic lack of social skill or knowledge on the part of the autistic person. Assumptions made about nonintentional productions by nonautistic children may not apply to autistic children. Those who interact with autistic children frequently note how formal and effortful their communicative attempts appear (Mesibov, Chapter 13; Park, Chapter 5, this volume). Communication is a type of social interaction, and given this, it is crucial that we help the autistic individual maximize the ease and effectiveness of their communications as well as acquire the basic methods to do so.

One social implication that arises from this communication problem is that the autistic child is likely to be misunderstood by peers. Nonintentionally transmitted information may be given more credence than information that is produced intentionally. As Hermelin and O'Connor (1985) suggest, productions that are presumed to be spontaneous and nondeliberate may be perceived as less amenable to deception. Direct social skills training should take into account the possibility that learning a normally spontaneous behavior such as smiling or making eye contact may, for a child with autism, be as difficult as, if not more difficult than, learning how to ask for help.

For example, an autistic although quite verbal young adult spoke in a very loud and rough voice that sounded rather aggressive. This aggressive quality of his speech did not reflect how the young man actually felt about what he was saying. However, unless someone knew him, his communications were very frequently misinterpreted. In this instance the young man might be instructed to lower his voice and told, "People don't like to hear loud voices, it frightens them." However, this type of change is not easy to make, just as it is very difficult for a nonhandicapped person to change automatic aspects of communication such as the speed or loudness of speech.

Once the child has acquired the skill, an additional problem becomes one of how to develop the behavior into something that appears spontaneous rather than formal and deliberate (e.g., a smile that seems "painted on" or forced). The only guidelines we have for facilitating this process are those derived from our understanding of normal learning. Two of these principles included overlearning and modeling. For example, learning how to read becomes an automatic process as the reader repeatedly practices decoding words (LaBerge & Samuels, 1977). Clearly, autistic children need frequent and continual practice in using social-communicative skills. As discussed earlier, this practice needs to occur in an environment in which *they* perceive social interactions as potentially positive.

Besides opportunities to practice, autistic children need frequent and concrete examples of appropriate social-communicative behavior that they can then imitate. Even normal children learn how to interact with other children by being around their peers. If an autistic child seldom sees normally developing children, it is unrealistic to expect him or her to learn age-appropriate social behavior from interactions with adults.

Nonverbal Production

Nonverbal communication plays an important role in setting up and maintaining social interactions. Consider the necessary prerequisites for the interaction described earlier between the two boys with the blocks. First, there had to be some awareness of another person. Then, there had to be some motivation to initiate an interaction. An initiation then occurred that had to be followed by a response in order for the interaction to proceed. Much of this process occurs nonverbally regardless of the participants' verbal abilities.

For example, eye contact denotes an interest and awareness of another person. By definition, this is mutual behavior and, when absent, reduces the likelihood of further interaction. Kubicek (1980), in her study of mother–infant interaction involving a nonhandicapped infant and his autistic twin, found that when the nonautistic infant would establish eye contact with the mother, the mother would be most likely to initiate a social game (e.g., playing peekaboo). In contrast, the mother's interaction with the autistic infant generally consisted of an attempt by the mother to establish eye contact, a behavior by the infant that effectively avoided the mother, followed by repeated attempts by the mother to attain eye contact. Social interaction is very difficult (impossible?) when some sort of mutuality is absent. Some communication of interest on the part of the child was necessary before the mother could move on to more complicated and interactive social exchange (e.g., play).

Similarly, it seems reasonable to assume that these same problems would occur during attempted interactions between autistic children and other nonhandicapped children (nonautistic children). Without some indication of interest on the part of the autistic child, it would be unlikely that a peer would be willing to engage in any sort of interactive play. In a study of peer social interaction, Sinson and Wetherick (1981) found that Down's syndrome children were much less interactive in normal play groups than in their special nursery. The authors suggest that social initiations on the part of the normal peers may have been discouraged by the Down's syndrome children's unintentional refusals to look at them as they approached. In fact, one aspect of peer-training regimes (i.e., where playmates have been taught how to play with autistic children) that seems critical is preparing the nonhandicapped child for his partner's initial lack of response. Several peer-coaching programs have included role-play and demonstration sessions where this possibility is experienced (Lord, 1984a; Strain, Kerr, & Ragland, 1979). Various ways the nonhandicapped child can handle this situation can then be rehearsed. The point can also be discussed that the autistic child's nonverbal communication of avoidance may be more due to his deficient social skills than to a real lack of interest.

Another form of nonverbal communication is gesture. Atwood (1984, cited in Hermelin & O'Connor, 1984) conducted an observational study in which the spontaneous use of gesture during meal- and playtimes was recorded. There were qualitative differences in the use of gesture by autistic, Down's syndrome, and nonhandicapped children matched for mental age. Nonhandicapped and Down's syndrome children used a wider range of gestures in these settings as compared to autistic children. Specifically, in these situations, the autistic children used gestures mainly as attempts to terminate the interaction (e.g., gestures indicating "go away" or "be quiet"). In contrast, children in the other two groups also included other types of instrumental gestures (e.g., "come here," "sit down") as well as gestures indicating how they were feeling.

In interpreting these findings, it is important to distinguish between knowledge and use. The autistic children in Atwood's study may have known how to use other types of gestures. However, in the settings in which the children were studied, there may not have been any reason or motivation for the autistic children to have used any other gestures than ones attempting to terminate interaction (e.g., perhaps mealtimes were particularly difficult for the autistic children).

Again, we return to the importance of social context. While the use of gesture can be an important tool for communication, it is not sufficient for us merely to teach these skills in a rote manner. Developing the skill to physically form the gesture may be necessary for spontaneous production, but it is far from sufficient. In fact, in one study, autistic children were found to be as capable of producing gestures on demand as children with only language delays (Bartak *et al.*, 1975). Yet in spontaneous conversation, the autistic children showed far less *use* of gesture than did language-delayed children. The motivation that must be present to elicit a communicative gesture needs to be considered. Clearly, in situations that are unpleasant for the child, it would be appropriate to work on gestures directed at terminating interaction. On the other hand, if the teaching goal was to develop skill at communicating through gesture such verbalizations as "come here," "give it to me," or "hello," we need to be sure that the child is in a context that naturally elicits these meanings. For example, if the teaching goal was for the autistic child to learn to use a gesture indicating "give it to me," one might set up a situation such that the autistic child was paired with a peer who had something desired by the child with autism (e.g., miniature cars to line up in a row). Initially, *any* attempt by the autistic child to indicate that he wanted a car would be reinforced by the peer by giving him a car. Gradually, a more sophisticated request could be shaped and prompts faded.

SUMMARY AND CONCLUSIONS

In this chapter, we have considered the role of communication in the social behavior of autistic persons. Clearly, this represents a reciprocal relationship. Just as communication problems affect the autistic person's ability to engage in social interactions, so do social deficits influence communicative behavior. In designing interventions for persons with autism, we must therefore address *both* areas of functioning.

The role of motivation was a theme that appeared frequently throughout this chapter. Autistic persons must have a *need* to communicate and interact socially in order for such behavior to occur. Regardless of how much we teach specific skills (e.g., how to ask another child to play), these skills will not be *used* unless there is a reason to use them (e.g., playing with peers is enjoyable). This means that we have to carefully set up social experiences for autistic children so that they are rewarding and pleasurable. For example, a child with very limited language skills is *not* going to enjoy a social experience in which high language demands are placed on him. When nonautistic persons (adults or peers) are included in these experiences, we can promote positive social interaction by helping them understand the autistic person's social and communicative limitations (e.g., avoiding eye contact may not imply lack of social interest).

Certainly, motivation to interact socially is not sufficient. Social and communicative skills training is critical. In order to engage in successful social interactions, autistic persons often need training in picking up relevant cues from others and interpreting these cues (both elements of comprehension). However, sensitivity to appropriate social cues and knowledge of what the cues mean must be followed by knowledge of what appropriate responses are necessary (an element of production). As discussed throughout the chapter, both nonverbal and verbal components of language comprehension and production play important roles in social behavior. In addition, the importance of developing appropriate play skills was discussed.

In summary, we have tried to emphasize the interdependence of social and communicative functioning in autistic persons. Deficits in both areas make it critical that those working with the autistic be particularly sensitive to the impact of the social environment on communicative behavior as well as the manner in which communication demands may effect social functioning. Suggestions were presented for facilitating skills development in autistic persons as well as modifying the environment in ways to maximize the utilization of these skills.

REFERENCES

American Psychiatric Association (1980). *Diagnostic and statistical manual of mental disorders* (3rd ed.). Washington, DC: Author.

Argyle, M. (1975). *Bodily communication*. London: Methuen.

Bartak, L., Rutter, M., & Cox, A. (1975). A comparative study of infantile autism and specific developmental receptive language disorder: I. The children. *British Journal of Psychiatry, 126*, 127–145.

Bransford, J. D., & Nitsch, K. E. (1978). Coming to understand things we could not previously understand. In J. K. Kavanagh & W. Strange (Eds.), *Speech and language in the laboratory, school, and clinic* (pp. 267–307). Cambridge, MA: M.I.T. Press.

Bruner, J. S. (1975). From communication to language—Psychological perspective. *Cognition, 3*, 255–289.

Campione, J. C., & Brown, A. L. (1977). Memory and metamemory development in educable retarded children. In R. V. Kail & J. W. Hagen (Eds.), *Perspectives on the development of memory and cognition* (pp. 367–406). Hillsdale, NJ: Erlbaum.

Cantwell, D., Baker, L., & Rutter, M. (1978). A comparative study of infantile autism and specific developmental receptive language disorder: IV. Analysis of syntax and language function. *Journal of Child Psychology and Psychiatry, 19*, 351–362.

Clark, P., & Rutter, M. (1977). Compliance and resistance in autistic children. *Journal of Autism and Childhood Schizophrenia, 1*, 33–48.

Flavell, J. H., & Wellman, H. M. (1977). Metamemory. In R. V. Kail & J. W. Hagen (Eds.), *Perspectives on the development of memory and cognition* (pp. 3–33). Hillsdale, NJ: Erlbaum.

Hermelin, B., & O'Connor, N. (1970). *Psychological experiments with autistic children*. New York: Pergamon Press.

Hermelin, B., & O'Connor, N. (1985). Logico-affective states and nonverbal language. In E. Schopler & G. Mesibov (Eds.), *Communication problems in autism*. New York: Plenum Press.

Hobson, R. P. (1984). The autistic child's recognition of age-related features of people, animals and things. *British Journal of Developmental Psychology, 1*, 343–352.

Holmberg, M. C. (1980). The development of social interchange patterns from 12 to 42 months. *Child Development, 51*, 448–456.

Howlin, P. (1984). The acquisition of grammatical morphemes in autistic children: A replication of the findings of Bartolucci et al., 1980. *Journal of Autism and Developmental Disorders, 14*, 126–138.

Kanner, L. (1943). Autistic disturbances of affective contact. *Nervous Child, 2,* 217–250.

Kubicek, L. F. (1980). Organization in two mother–infant interactions involving a normal infant and his fraternal twin who was later diagnosed as autistic. In T. M. Field, S. Goldberg, D. Stern, & A. M. Sostek (Eds.), *High risk infants and children: Adult and peer interactions* (pp. 99–112). New York: Academic Press.

LaBerge, D., & Samuels, S. J. (Eds.). (1977). *Basic processes in reading: Perception and comprehension.* Hillsdale, NJ: Erlbaum.

Langdell, T. (1978). Recognition of faces: An approach to the study of autism. *Journal of Child Psychology and Psychiatry, 19,* 255–268.

Lockyer, L., & Rutter, M. (1970). A five to fifteen-year follow-up study of infantile psychosis: IV. Patterns of cognitive ability. *British Journal of Social and Clinical Psychology, 9,* 152–163.

Lord, C. (1974, April). Variations in the acquisition of negation. In *Paper and Reports on Child Language Development No. 8* (pp. 78–86). Committee on Linguistics, Stanford University.

Lord, C. (1984a). The development of peer relations in children with autism. In F. J. Morrison, C. Lord, & D. P. Keating (Eds.), *Advances in applied developmental psychology* (pp. 165–229). New York: Academic Press.

Lord, C. (1984b). Language comprehension and cognitive disorder in autism. In L. Siegel & F. J. Morrison (Eds.), *Cognitive development in atypical children* (pp. 67–82). New York: Springer-Verlag.

Lord, C., & Allen, J. A. (1979). *Comprehension of simple sentences in autistic children.* Paper presented at the Midwest Psychological Association, Chicago.

Lord, C., & Baker, A. (1977). Communicating with autistic children. *Journal of Pediatric Psychology, 2,* 181–186.

Lord, C., & O'Neill, P. J. (1983). Language and communication needs of adolescents with autism. In E. Schopler & G. B. Mesibov (Eds.), *Autism in adolescents and adults* (pp. 57–77). New York: Plenum Press.

Mueller, E. (1972). The maintenance of verbal exchanges between young children. *Child Development, 43,* 930–938.

Ricks, D. M., & Wing, L. (1976). Language, communication and use of symbols. In L. Wing (Ed.), *Early childhood autism* (pp. 93–134). Oxford, England: Pergamon Press.

Romanczyk, R. G., Diamant, C., Goren, E. R., Trunell, G. & Harris, S. L. (1975). Increasing isolate and social play in severely disturbed children: Intervention and postintervention effectiveness. *Journal of Autism and Childhood Schizophrenia, 5,* 57–70.

Rubin, K. H. (1977). Play behaviors of young children. *Young Children, 32,* 16–24.

Rubin, K. H., Fein, G. G., & Vandenberg, B. (1983). Play. In P. H. Mussen (Ed.) & E. M. Hetherington (Vol. Ed.), *Handbook of child psychology* (Vol. 3, pp. 693–774). New York: Wiley.

Rutter, M. (1978a). Diagnosis and definition. In M. Rutter & E. Schopler (Eds.), *Autism: A reappraisal of concepts and treatment* (pp. 1–25). New York: Plenum Press.

Rutter, M. (1978b). Developmental issues and prognosis. In M. Rutter & E. Schopler (Eds.), *Autism: A reappraisal of concepts and treatment* (pp. 497–505). New York: Plenum Press.

Schaffer, H. R., Hepburn, A., & Collis, G. M. (1983). Verbal and non-verbal aspects of mothers' directives. *Journal of Child Language, 10,* 337–355.

Schopler, E. (1976). Towards reducing behavior problems in autistic children. In L. Wing (Ed.), *Early childhood autism* (pp. 221–246). London: Pergamon Press.

Sinson, J. C., & Wetherick, M. E. (1981). The behavior of children with Down's syndrome in normal play groups. *Journal of Mental Deficiency Research, 25,* 113–120.

Strain, P. S., Kerr, M. M., & Ragland, E. U. (1979). Effects of peer-mediated social initiations and prompting/reinforcement procedures on the social behavior of autistic children. *Journal of Autism and Developmental Disorders, 9,* 41–54.

Tager-Flusberg, H. (1981). On the nature of linguistic functioning in early infantile autism. *Journal of Autism and Developmental Disorders, 11,* 45–56.

Wing, L. (1976). Diagnosis, clinical description, and prognosis. In L. Wing (Ed.), *Early childhood autism* (pp. 15–64). London: Pergamon Press.

8

Cognitive Impairments Affecting Social Behavior in Autism

AMITTA SHAH and LORNA WING

The nature of the association between the social and the cognitive impairments found in autistic people has been, and still is, the subject of debate. (For recent reviews of the argument, see Rutter, 1983; Fein, Pennington, Markowitz, Braverman, & Waterhouse, 1984.) In the past, various kinds of cognitive dysfunctions have each been put forward as the primary underlying handicap. Some more recent formulations suggest that impairment of the capacity to engage in reciprocal social interaction is the basic deficit. A third view is that both the cognitive and social problems are the result of some other, more fundamental, but as yet undefined impairment. Although considerable advances have been made in analyzing both these aspects of autism, there is insufficient evidence to show which of the hypotheses mentioned above is correct. In any case, it is difficult to disentangle cause and effect in view of the apparent interdependence of the two systems in the development of the normal child, as illustrated schematically in Figure 1.

In this chapter, therefore, we do not argue for any one theoretical view. Instead, our aim is to discuss the impairments in the context of recent advances in understanding the underlying aspects of social and cognitive functions. Relevant studies will be considered under three headings: first, the association between general cognitive ability and social behavior; second, impairments of specific social skills; and third, specific cognitive impairments found in autism and their relation to social behavior.

AMITTA SHAH and LORNA WING • Medical Research Council Social Psychiatry Unit, Institute of Psychiatry, De Crespigny Park, Denmark Hill, London SE5 8AF, England.

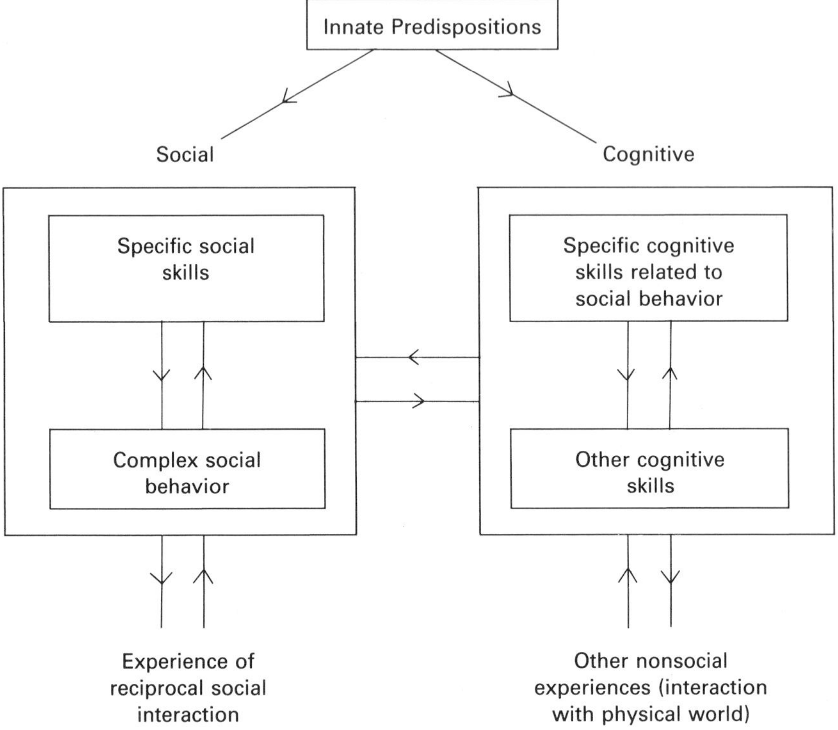

FIGURE 1. The relations between social and cognitive development.

GENERAL COGNITIVE ABILITY AND SOCIAL BEHAVIOR

Various studies have shown that there is an association between the level of general intellectual functioning and the severity of the autistic syndrome. The lower the level of performance on standardized intelligence tests, the more severe are the manifestations of the autistic pattern of behavior likely to be (Bartak & Rutter, 1976; DeMyer *et al.*, 1974; Wing & Gould, 1979). Wing and Gould (1979) carried out an epidemiological study of children with autism and autisticlike conditions. They found that the children's levels of ability as measured on visuospatial skills were distributed along a continuum of severity ranging from profoundly retarded to normal. This continuum was reflected in the clinical features, in verbal and nonverbal communication, and in practical skills relevant to social adaptation and independence, such as self-help and occupation. The severity of the social impairment was as closely related to general cognitive level as were the other aspects of the autistic picture.

The study mentioned above also included nonautistic severely retarded children. It was found that the prevalence of social impairment among all children in the population studied who had IQs below 50 steadily increased with decreasing intelligence levels, varying from 40% in the moderately retarded to 80% among those with profound mental retardation.

From the results of the same study, Wing (1981a) noted that impairment of social interaction varied in its manifestations, and that the qualitative differences were significantly associated with overall intelligence. At the lower end of the scale of ability were the (rather rare) children who were completely aloof and indifferent to others and who really could be described as "treating people like objects." These were the most severely affected in all areas and had no skills apart from physical mobility. At the other extreme were those who were very aware of the social environment and who wanted to make contact with other people, and to be socially accepted. Their social and cognitive problems were far more subtle and would be missed on brief acquaintance. They were shown in the naive and one-sided approaches made to others and a tendency to talk on and on about a limited range of special interests. This small group were the least intellectually handicapped, and though they tested in the mildly retarded, the normal, or occasionally even the superior range of IQ, poor gross motor coordination was quite common. In between these extremes there were children with varying degrees of social impairment, including those who passively accepted, and quite enjoyed, social approaches made by others, but who rarely or never initiated approaches themselves. These tended to have limited skills on verbal tests, but their nonverbal ability (especially as shown on visuospatial tests) was better and ranged from a moderately retarded level to above average.

Other workers have also reported an association, in autistic people, between general level of intelligence and problems affecting social skills. DeMyer (1976), in a study investigating intellectual disabilities of autistic children, found a significant relationship among IQ, social relatedness, socially adaptive behavior, and communicative speech. Bartak and Rutter (1976) compared two groups of autistic children, one with nonverbal IQs of 70 or above, the other below this level. The latter showed the more severe social impairment. Rutter (1970) and Lotter (1974) found, in follow-up studies, that overall IQ in childhood was predictive of eventual level of social functioning in autistic adults. Newson, Dawson, and Everard (1984), in a study of the more able autistic people, reported a positive relationship between higher levels of intelligence and better outcome in terms of achievement of independent living and lessening of autistic features in adult life.

The patterns of scores on scales for assessing intelligence are of interest. The majority of autistic people have higher overall scores on performance tests than on verbal tests. However, some have equal scores on both, while in others, verbal scores are better. Whatever the overall pattern, there are characteristic strengths and weaknesses shown within each scale. On the verbal scale, they have most problems with tests requiring comprehension of abstract concepts and the application of common sense and learned knowledge to hypothetical social situations. They do better on tests relying on rote memory and the formation of simple concepts. On the performance scale, most autistic people obtain their best scores on tests requiring visuospatial skills (for example, block design) but tend to have particular problems on tasks requiring the attribution of meaning. It is tempting to assume that the aloof, usually nontalking autistic person would have a higher performance score, while the person who has repetitive speech, makes active but odd social approaches, and is clumsy in motor function would do best on the verbal tests. While there is a tendency for this to be true, in practice there are too many exceptions to accept the different patterns as explanations of the different types of abnormal social interaction (Wing, 1981b; Wolff & Barlow, 1979).

Although there is an association between overall intelligence level and degree of social impairment, other evidence suggests that there cannot be direct cause and effect in either direction. First, a substantial proportion of children with severe or profound mental retardation do not show the type of social impairment characteristic of the autistic spectrum of disorders. Second, as already mentioned, social impairment can occur in people who perform at a normal or superior level on standardized intelligence tests.

One hypothesis (Damasio & Maurer, 1978; Wing, 1981a) that might account for these clinical facts is that a particular area or function of the brain is responsible for the skills necessary for normal social interaction. This area may, rather rarely, be specifically impaired without any other part of the brain being affected. Then the individual concerned would be autistic but high functioning. Much more often, as a result of a more generalized cause of brain pathology, the specific area is affected together with other aspects of brain function, resulting in autism combined with mental retardation. Impairment of various brain functions that leaves the specific area intact would produce a person who was mentally retarded but not autistic. This formulation fits with the fact that conditions likely to cause gross brain damage, such as maternal rubella or encephalitis in the early years, are much more common among severely retarded autistic people than among the higher-functioning group (Wing, 1976; Wing & Gould, 1979). Epileptic fits are also more common among the more severely impaired group (Bartak & Rutter, 1976; Rutter, 1970). A clinical illustration of the possible interrelationship involving social impairment, IQ, and brain dysfunction is provided by the triplets studied by Burgoine and Wing (1983). These 17-year-old boys fitted the picture of a variant of autism known as Asperger's syndrome (Asperger, 1944; Wing, 1981b). Despite the fact that they were monozygous, the severity of the autistic behavior, the degree of social impairment, and the level of IQ differed among all three, and each of these variables was correlated with the severity of the perinatal problems each had experienced.

However, this hypothesis does not explain the differences in the qualitative manifestations of social impairment that tend to be found at different levels of overall ability. Bartak and Rutter (1976) suggested that autism in those with nonverbal IQs in the normal range may be qualitatively different from the condition seen in mentally retarded people. Other workers have speculated that the mildly retarded or normally intelligent people who were passive or odd in social interaction as children, but never aloof, are different in kind from those who had the classic indifference to people in the early years. Asperger (1944), who described the former group, believed that the condition was different from Kanner's autism, and the term *Asperger's syndrome* is sometimes used as a separate diagnostic label. The problem in accepting any of these hypotheses is that, in any individual, the quality of social interaction may vary from one situation to another. Sometimes, with increasing age, the clinical picture changes from that of one group to another. Thus, some children with good visuospatial skills are aloof early on but, with the passing years, become passive, or active but odd in social interaction, and indistinguishable from Asperger's syndrome (Wing, 1981b).

Another possible explanation is that the specific underlying handicap in all autistic children, whatever their level of intelligence, is the same, but the more able children develop the cognitive capacity to learn the mechanics of socially appropriate behavior, thus compensating for their handicaps to some extent. This accords with the clinical observation that participation in and tolerance of social interaction, when it occurs, tends to increase with age and is assisted by carefully managed exposure to social situations. However, the persistence of subtle problems affecting social behavior suggests that the improvement is only surface deep and applies only to those routines of social interaction that can be learned by rote.

Various authors have hypothesized that intelligent autistic children may learn appropriate behaviors in a different way from nonautistic children. Ricks and Wing (1975), in their descriptions of communicative impairments in autism, discussed how autistic children who make progress have to learn the rules of nonverbal behavior by rote "instead of developing these skills naturally as part of the process of maturation" (p. 201). "They have to learn by rote both the meaning of and the way to use non-verbal social cues and this is a long slow process which is never completed" (p. 204). Hermelin (1983) has suggested that, when the innate system of social interaction is missing, the learning of verbal and nonverbal skills may proceed by a different route from that followed when the system has been spontaneously generated. She likens the autistic child's language acquisition to the normal person's learning of a second language. Prizant (1983), too, discusses the similarities in strategies of language acquisition in autistic children and those of older normal children learning a second language. One tendency that is shared by both is to repeat utterances that are beyond their processing capacities, and this allows the child to use "extracts" of the language without being able to create any novel utterances. The bright verbal autistic child's reliance on stereotyped phrases has often been noted (see, for example, Ricks & Wing, 1975).

SPECIFIC SOCIAL IMPAIRMENTS

An analysis of the specific social behaviors that are abnormal in autism suggests that "social impairment" consists of difficulties in the spontaneous use of the systems of nonverbal and verbal communication that make for effective reciprocal social interchange. Such systems come into play automatically in normal social interaction, usually without conscious awareness, but their absence or impairment makes the autistic person appear very odd to other people.

One of the most characteristic abnormalities of social behavior in autism is that of eye gaze. It is well documented that young classically autistic children show marked visual avoidance (Bartak, Rutter, & Cox, 1975; Kanner, 1943; Wing, 1976). With increasing maturity, eye contact tends to occur more often, but its timing is abnormal. Argyle and Cook (1976) have summarized the development of eye contact in normal infants and stress the important part that it plays from a very young age in interpersonal communication and in establishing relationships. Rheingold (1961) and Stern (1974) have noted that the patterns of making and breaking eye contact start as early as the third month and remain consistent throughout life. Thus, mutual eye gaze develops very early in infancy and is one of the first forms of reciprocal communication for the normal infant. The autistic person, by contrast, if he uses eye gaze at all, is not able to use it appropriately for communication. The tendency is to look too closely and too long into the eyes of the other person sometimes, and not to look at all at other times, rather than synchronizing the mutual making and breaking of eye contact (Mirenda, Donnellan, & Yoder, 1983).

It has been noted (Bartak *et al.*, 1975; Ricks & Wing, 1975) that autistic children rarely use gesture as a substitute for speech, unlike children who are deaf or have developmental receptive speech disorders. There have been attempts to teach autistic children manual sign languages, but with very rare exceptions only minimal success has been reported with a few simple and obvious signs. Those children who learn a number of signs tend to copy them when prompted but show limited or no spontaneous use of them. Attwood (1984) made a comprehensive study of the gesturing behavior of autistic children in both experimental and natural settings. He found that, compared to Down's syndrome children and normal 4-year-olds, autistic children gestured less frequently, and, when they did so, they used only pointing or instrumental gestures, such as those required to obtain physical needs. There was a developmental sequence in the complexity of these gestures, and the more intelligent autistic children were able to produce instrumental gestures on demand as effectively as the control children. However, none of the autistic children used the types of expressive gestures with which the normal and Down's syndrome subjects in the study showed emotions in a social context, such as touching another person to express sympathy or shaking a fist in mock (or real) anger. Autistic people do show emotions, though these tend to be extreme, such as rage, terror, or misery, but their physical means of expression are idiosyncratic and do not appear to subserve social communication of these feelings. For example, one child known to the present authors quivers her hand in front of her face when very angry or very happy. The only way her parents (but no one else) can tell the difference is in subtle variations in the squealing noise she makes at the same time.

Difficulty in using the normal range of facial expressions has been described. Langdell (1981) reported that autistic children were much less successful than normal children in looking "happy" or "sad" either on command or by imitating another adult. No experimental studies of spontaneous facial expressions in autistic people have been reported in the literature, but clinical observations (for example, Ricks & Wing, 1975) suggest that, as with bodily gestures, most autistic people do show the extreme emotions on their faces, but otherwise facial expression is not effectively used for communicating emotional states.

The language of autistic children, even of those who develop large vocabularies and good grammar, shows characteristic impairments (Bartak *et al.*, 1975; Ricks & Wing, 1975; Churchill, 1978). These include a tendency to have restricted and repetitive "one-way conversations" about their topic of interest, a lack of use of colloquial speech, a lack of appreciation of subtle humor in language, and a tendency to take things literally. Intonation is absent or abnormal in pattern. Detailed linguistic analyses of the spontaneous speech of verbal autistic children have shown that their phonology and syntactic development are delayed but not deviant compared with normal controls matched on mental age (Bartolucci & Pierce, 1977; Boucher, 1976; Waterhouse & Fein, 1975). Various authors (Cromer, 1981; Frith, 1982; Tager-Flusberg, 1981) have discussed how the characteristic problems in autism can be seen as pragmatic rather than linguistic deficits. Pragmatics refers to the comprehension and use of language within a context rather than its precise and literal interpretation. Tager-Flusberg (1981) has also reported that, in verbal autistic children, there is a close relationship between pragmatic development and social functioning, which are both unrelated to grammatical ability. In normal children, by contrast, pragmatic development is closely related to level of grammar. The high-functioning verbal autistic children do not have difficulty in mastering the mechanics of language, but they do not use language to communicate reciprocally with other people.

It appears, from the studies of the various aspects of social interaction and communication described above, that, at least for those autistic people without additional handicaps, the problem is not an absence of the physical mechanisms of gesture, facial expression, and speech, but a failure to use them correctly in social situations or as aids for effective communication. It might be suggested that this is due to unwillingness or lack of interest, but those closely acquainted with autistic people who are not very severely mentally retarded can observe their attempts to interact, which fail because of the inability to apply the basic skills appropriately. Autistic people with sufficient language to tell of their own experiences describe the distress they feel when they make one mistake after another when trying to fit into a social setting.

Recently, there has been much interest in the origins of reciprocal communication and social behavior in normal infants. Results of the studies emphasize the importance of temporal organization of those aspects of the infant's behavior that are specifically adapted for social interaction. The main evidence comes from observations of the preverbal communication of human infants, which show how early it is possible to detect signs that mother and child can share meanings. Condon and Sanden (1974) reported that infants moved synchronously with adult speech in the first days of life. Schaffer (1974) and Trevarthen (1974) described similar temporal rhythmic synchrony in the mouth and limb movements shown by infants under 12 weeks of age during interactions with their mothers. Bateson (1975) and Schaffer, Collis, and Parsons (1977) found that the turn-taking pattern characteristic of adult vocal interchange is also evident at preverbal levels. Jaffe, Stern, and Peery (1973) have suggested that there may be regularities in the temporal patterning of mother–infant gazing that are similar to those found in adult verbal conversation. From evidence of these early interaction patterns, many authors (Newson & Newson, 1975; Schaffer, 1979; Trevarthen, 1974) have suggested that the infant is innately preadapted to participate in two-way social interchange.

One further study in this area must be mentioned since the findings raise questions concerning the relevance of these early patterns of synchronized behavior for normal social interaction in later life and for the abnormalities found in autism. Jones (1977) compared mother–child communication patterns in infants with Down's syndrome and in normal infants. The Down's syndrome infants failed to show the precise timing in turntaking shown by normal infants. Yet, Down's syndrome children, in general, are able to engage in social interaction appropriate for their mental age (Attwood, 1984; Wing & Gould, 1979). However, it is possible that the development of such behaviors is delayed rather than absent in Down's syndrome infants, especially in the light of evidence that some aspects of social behaviors, such as outward expression of emotion, develop late in Down's syndrome children (Emde, Katz, & Thorpe, 1978).

There are no studies of mother–child interaction patterns in autistic infants. However, there is some evidence that preverbal vocalizations of autistic children aged between 3 and 5 years are significantly different from those of normal preverbal children. Ricks (1975) found that, while normal children aged 8 months and retarded nonautistic (including Down's syndrome) children aged between 5 and 8 years, who were not yet talking shared a common vocal "language" of intoned sounds, which could be understood by any mother, each autistic child had his or her own idiosyncratic vocalizations, which could be understood only by the child's own mother. Ricks (1975) also found that recordings of preverbal vocalizations of autistic children aged 3 to 5 years did not show the conversational inflections found in the preverbal babble of normal children.

Thus, many of the more subtle social and communication skills in which autistic children show abnormalities appear to be well established in normal infants at a very early stage in life, and are very possibly innate. Early theories suggesting that the social interaction problems in autism are due to the child's conscious and deliberate emotional withdrawal now seem most likely to be incorrect. A more acceptable explanation is that autistic children lack the neurological organization necessary for the development of normal social skills. The problem is to define in more detail the precise nature of these abilities, which are so varied and complex in their manifestations.

SPECIFIC COGNITIVE IMPAIRMENTS

In the field of normal child development there is an increasing interest in identifying specific cognitive skills that might directly underlie social interaction. This area of function has been termed *social cognition,* which Shantz (1975) defines as "the child's intuitive or logical representation of others, that is, how he characterizes others and makes inferences about their covert, inner psychological experiences." (p. 250).

Baron-Cohen (1983) investigated autistic children's conception of another person's mind and their ability to attribute mental states to other people. He found that the majority of the autistic children, unlike mental-age-matched Down's syndrome children and normal 4-year-old children, were not able to understand that another person had been deceived. This was tested by setting up a situation that required the subjects to discriminate between, on the one hand, the actual location of an object and, on the other, the place where a story character mistakenly believed that object to be. The autistic children chose the real position of the object when asked where the character thought it was. Another experiment in the series (Baron-Cohen, 1984) suggests that autistic children are able to attribute physical causality to objects but are specifically impaired in attributing mental states to people that have to be inferred from their actions in picture stories.

Hobson (1983a) investigated the ability of autistic children to attribute emotional states to people by using contextual cues of sounds, gestures, or actions. He found that the autistic children, compared to nonautistic retarded children matched on age and nonverbal IQ, showed significant impairment in the ability to link the context to the picture face depicting the appropriate emotional expression. The control condition showed that they had no problem with interpreting cues in a similar task using objects. However, it is hard to be sure that the tasks involving emotional expressions and those involving inanimate objects were truly equivalent in level of difficulty. Hobson (1983b), in a card-sorting task, also found that autistic children were less able than control children to differentiate between young and old people, and puppy dogs and adult dogs. Yet normal children at very young ages are known to respond differentially to children and adults. Findings regarding autistic children's ability to differentiate gender are mixed. Although Hobson (1983a) reported that autistic children were less able than control children to differentiate between males and females, Abelson (1981), in a more direct investigation of the problem, found that this ability was related to their mental age and the more able autistic children were able to distinguish gender perfectly. The discrepancy illustrates the problem inherent in this research of equating task difficulty across studies. The present authors' clinical experience suggests that the problem may not be one of differentiating between males and females on the basis of external appearance, but of understanding the implications of gender in everyday life.

The studies discussed above point to the possibility that autistic people have specific deficits in cognitive abilities underlying person perception and reciprocal social interaction. The question whether these deficits in social cognition are the underlying cause of the abnormalities of social behavior and interpersonal relationships remains open. The reverse causal relationship is also a possibility. As already touched upon (see Figure 1), participation in normal social interaction may be essential for the development of the child's ability to conceptualize and attribute various states to other people. As discussed by Shantz (1975), the normal child's ability to differentiate between people on various physical characteristics, and to understand what other people see, feel, think, and intend, develops gradually between the ages of 3 and 10 years. It is interesting to note here that Hobson (1984) found that autistic children were able to infer another person's visual perspective as well as were normal children of comparable ability on tests of operational thinking. However, this sort of "role taking" is less likely to be dependent upon experience of normal social interaction because it is more a visuospatial than a social skill.

Another major area of research comprises attempts to specify the underlying cognitive abnormalities affecting processing of all kinds of information. Such impairments may be associated with the problems of understanding and timing social interaction. Although the precise deficit has not yet been pinpointed, it is possible to speculate about the general nature of the cognitive abnormality on the basis of research findings.

Hermelin, O'Connor, and Frith (summarized in Hermelin & Frith, 1971; Hermelin & O'Connor, 1970) have established that autistic people have a cognitive deficit at a central level affecting the ability to encode stimuli meaningfully by using rules and structures inherent in the stimuli. Their conclusions are drawn from experiments in which normal, autistic, and mentally handicapped children matched for mental age were required to recall verbal and nonverbal material presented either as random strings or as structured patterns. Unlike the control groups, autistic children benefited significantly less from structure. For example, they did not remember meaningful sentences much better than nonsensical strings of words. Similarly, with nonverbal material, they failed to abstract the rules governing the patterns to be replicated. These authors have suggested that the central problem is that of extracting rules or key features that normal people use to reduce information when the information to be retained exceeds the immediate memory span. The autistic person tends to rely on an extended form of the uncoded immediate memory system. They have very good short-term memories for information that depends on distinct item retention rather than on the abstraction of meaning.

A tendency to disregard meaning has also been demonstrated in a spatial rather than a sequential cognitive task (Shah & Frith, 1983). On an embedded-figures task, in which success depended on not being distracted by the meaning of the context in which the crucial figure was embedded, autistic children performed significantly better than mental-age-matched normal children and mental- and chronological-age-matched mentally retarded nonautistic children.

A study investigating the reading ability of "hyperlexic" autistic children (Frith & Snowling, 1983) has demonstrated a similar failure to take meaningful context into account. Autistic, dyslexic, and normal children matched for reading age were compared on various reading tasks. Autistic children's reading comprehension scores were generally found to be lower than their reading accuracy scores. By analyzing this deficiency, the authors were able to trace the comprehension deficiency to a specific difficulty in using semantic (meaningful) context when there were no syntactic cues available.

These studies concerning specific abnormalities in cognitive processing provide some evidence that the autistic person tends to ignore overall meaning in context when interpreting information, regardless of whether the input is sequential or spatial. Frith (1983) has suggested that the failure to take meaningful context into account may be a central deficit that accounts for the cognitive and the social impairments. Awareness of the total context is considered especially important for effective social interaction.

This type of theory was adumbrated by Rimland (1965), who suggested that the autistic child's basic problem may be an inability to integrate new stimuli with remembered past experience. He hypothesized that the autistic child stores and recalls memories of events as unintegrated fragments.

Ricks and Wing (1975) discussed such deficits in relation to the autistic person's difficulty in developing "inner language." They suggested that autistic people are not able to use their store of concepts (coded as symbols) in order to develop ideas about the world; more able autistic people can form simple concepts but have problems with complex abstractions based on a multiplicity of concepts derived from different categories of experience.

The hypotheses concerning the use of context to derive meaning can be made more specific by relating them to models of normal cognitive processes. In the last decade, cognitive psychologists have increasingly acknowledged the role of context, meaning, and past experience in the interpretation of information. Various theories have been proposed (Neisser, 1976; Norman & Rumelhart, 1975; Palmer, 1975) that emphasize the constant interplay between external sensory information and internal conceptual structures. A central element of these theories is the idea of *schemas*. This term was used by Bartlett as early as 1932 when he described memory as an active, constructive phenomenon rather than a passive process. Other cognitive psychologists have extended this formulation and have also tended to use it interchangeably with other similar concepts such as scripts, frames, or prototypes. Fiske and Linville (1980) define schemas as "cognitive structures of organized prior knowledge, abstracted from experience with specific instances." Thus, "schemas" refer to structures or systems that represent the knowledge accumulated by the person. These structures are not static or discrete but are constantly modified by experience and are also overlapping. The schemas are based on abstractions from the organization and reorganization of instances, and thus are qualitatively different from the original collections of raw data. Knowledge is not regarded as a "copy" of sensations but as a matter of active construction. Various models have been put forward to explain how the schemas interact with external sensory information during perception. It is beyond the scope of this chapter to discuss these in any detail. In simple terms, what many of the models suggest (e.g., Friedman, 1979; Neisser, 1976; Palmer, 1975) is that, during perception, an appropriate frame or schema is evoked and its context is used to guide subsequent processing. Under normal circumstances, the appropriate frame or frames are active, so that a lot of the perception of the global properties of the stimulus occurs automatically. This is especially true for familiar or expected environments or events. When preexisting schemas are not sufficient for recognition or categorization, there is a more interactive process involving the internal schema (or context), the global aspects of the stimulus (external context that provides the overall meaning), and the constituent details of the stimuli. If there is a context-related cognitive deficit in autism, it could operate at any of the levels of processing specified above.

The findings regarding the autistic child's tendency to ignore meaningful perceptual contexts suggests that, during perception, the appropriate internal schemas are not activated sufficiently to allow interpretation based on the global aspects of environment/events—so that perception is based on the detailed cues provided in the stimulus itself. Preliminary findings from our ongoing research on visuospatial skills suggest that autistic children have an advantage in performing spatial tasks that require the subject to ignore the overall perceptual context and, instead, work on the individual units that constitute the whole. The commonly reported ability of many autistic children to notice minute details and to react to very small changes in their surroundings would be explained by this deficit. In contrast, the normal tendency to interpret information within the wider context allows the nonautistic person to ignore or disregard small differences that occur within a meaningful pattern.

The other possibility is that the deficit relates to the internal context directly. The autistic child may have a problem in constantly modifying and updating the schemas through experience and so cannot build up a coherent cognitive map of the world and its possibilities. Additionally, or perhaps alternatively, there may be a problem in using the available schemas in a flexible and interactive way with the information that is actually currently available.

The difficulties that the verbal autistic children have in using and comprehending meanings according to the context in which they are used may be due to problems either in building up the internal context or in using it. An experiment by Tager-Flusberg (1981) suggests that the latter may be more relevant. She investigated strategy use in sentence comprehension and found that autistic children did not use their existing conceptual knowledge about probable relational aspects of the environment to the same extent as normal children.

A recent study by Gould (1984) showed that autistic children's performance on a standardized test of symbolic play was significantly better than the level of development shown in their spontaneous play. Some children could demonstrate that they understood the function of miniature objects and could arrange a related set of them in appropriate ways with no difficulty, but they never engaged in any spontaneous imaginative activities. This is another example of autistic children failing to use the formal knowledge they possess. It is a particularly significant one, since the inner world of the imagination is built up initially through copying and then elaborating on other people's actions. It can be hypothesized that play of this kind is associated with the development of social empathy and social skills.

It appears from these studies that the problem in autism is that of not *using* available knowledge rather than not *having* the knowledge. This is analogous to the findings, mentioned earlier, that autistic people, unless multiply handicapped, have the physical mechanisms for communication but do not use them to communicate. There is a marked contrast with nonautistic retarded people who have poor cognitive and physical skills but use them to communicate and socialize to the best of their ability. As emphasized previously, the problem in autism is not the lack of desire to interact, but lack of the ability to apply existing skills.

SPECULATIONS

From the available evidence it seems that there may be a significant and important association between the social and the cognitive impairments in autism, and that the latter include both general and specific aspects. But relationships among all the factors that might underlie the overt behavior are complex, and, as yet, the studies that have been carried out have not yielded any definite answers. The pursuit of the essence of the social impairment has, so far, resembled the hunting of the Snark in Lewis Carroll's poem—when you think you have it in your grasp, it turns out to be something else (Carroll, 1876/1976). Hence, this final section has been entitled "Speculations" rather than "Conclusions."

What is certain is that the basic autistic impairment must be related to normal child development. The latter field is rapidly growing and changing, so it is not surprising that theories concerning autism are still in a fluid state. Some recent work on normal infants suggests that a surprising range of skills related to social behavior exists at a very early age. For example, Dunkeld (1973) and Meltzoff and Moore (1977) have found that normal babies can imitate other people's mouth movements and other movements of the face and hands virtually from birth. Bower and Wishart (1979) reported that 8- to 10-week-old babies produced different kinds of smiles in different situations. The same authors have proposed that normal babies first perceive abstract qualities of the environment (such as a general idea of "humanness") and only later focus on specific sensory stimuli (such as the detailed characteristics of individual faces). Ricks (1979) investigated the first meaningful words produced by normal infants and concluded that these are applied to categories of experience rather than specific objects. The basis of the categories may be quite obscure to adults.

The hypotheses developed by these workers reverse previous notions concerning the timing and sequence of the relevant aspects of normal development, suggesting a progression from the abstract, or global, to the concrete and specific, rather than vice versa. These ideas have considerable relevance to autism. Possibly, autistic infants have little or no original capacity for abstraction, and perceive only specific stimuli, thus deviating from the normal developmental path from the outset. This could account for their lack of recognition of "humanness," their social impairment, their fascination with simple sensory stimuli, and their peculiar cognitive style.

Exploration of these ideas would necessitate the early identification of infants whose behavior differed from the norm in relevant areas, and subsequent long-term follow-up. This type of work poses considerable logistic problems, but the discovery of early markers of autism would be of inestimable value for both theory and practice.

REFERENCES

Abelson, A. G. (1981). The development of gender identity in the autistic child. *Child: Care, Health and Development, 7,* 347–356.

Argyle, M., & Cook, M. (1976). *Gaze and mutual gaze.* London: Cambridge University Press.

Asperger, H. (1944). Die "autistischen Psychopathen" im Kindesalter. *Archiv für Psychiatrie und Nervenkrankheiten, 117,* 76–136.

Attwood, A. (1984). The gestures of autistic children. Unpublished doctoral dissertation, University of London.

Baron-Cohen, S. (1983, December). *The autistic child's "theory of mind."* Paper accompanying poster display at the BPS Conference, London.

Baron-Cohen, S. (1984, May). *The autistic child's ability to attribute mental states and physical causality.* Paper presented at the BPS Postgraduate Conference, Nottingham.

Bartak, L., & Rutter, M. (1976). Differences between mentally retarded and normally intelligent autistic children. *Journal of Autism and Childhood Schizophrenia, 6,* 109–119.

Bartak, L., Rutter, M., & Cox, A. (1975). A comparative study of infantile autism and specific developmental receptive language disorders: The children. *British Journal of Psychiatry, 126,* 127–145.

Bartlett, F. C. (1932). *Remembering: A study in experimental and social psychology,* London: Cambridge University Press.

Bartolucci, G., & Pierce, S. J. (1977). A preliminary comparison of phonological development in autistic, normal and mentally retarded subjects. *British Journal of Disorders of Communication, 12,* 137–147.

Bateson, M. C. (1975). Mother–infant exchanges: The epigenesis of conversation interaction. *Annals of the New York Academy of Sciences, 263,* 101–113.

Boucher, J. (1976). Articulation in early childhood autism. *Journal of Autism and Childhood Schizophrenia, 6,* 297–302.

Bower, T., & Wishart, J. (1979). Towards a unitary theory of development. In E. Toman (Ed.), *Origins of the infant's social responsiveness.* Hillsdale, NJ: Erlbaum.

Burgoine, E., & Wing, L. (1983). Identical triplets with Asperger's syndrome. *British Journal of Psychiatry, 143,* 261–265.

Carroll, L. (1976). *The hunting of the snark: An agony in eight fits.* London: Folio Society. (Original work published 1876.)

Churchill, D. W. (1978). *Language of autistic children.* Washington, DC: Winston.

Condon, W. S., & Sanden, L. W. (1974). Neonate movement is synchronized with adult speech: Interactional participation and language acquisition. *Science, 183,* 99–101.

Cromer, R. F. (1981). Developmental language disorders: Cognitive processes, semantics, pragmatics, phonology, and syntax. *Journal of Autism and Developmental Disorders, 11,* 57–73.

Damasio, A. R., & Maurer, R. G. (1978). A neurological model for childhood autism. *Archives of Neurology, 35,* 777–786.

DeMyer, M. (1976). Motor, perceptual-motor and intellectual disabilities of autistic children. In L. Wing (Ed.), *Early childhood autism* (2nd ed., pp. 169–196). Oxford: Pergamon Press.

DeMyer, M., Barton, S., Alpern, G., Kimberlin, C., Allen, J., Yang, E., & Steele, R. (1974). The measured intelligence of autistic children. *Journal of Autism and Childhood Schizophrenia, 4,* 42–60.

Dunkeld, J. (1973). *The development of imitation in infancy.* Unpublished doctoral dissertation, University of Edinburgh.

Emde, R. N., Katz, E. L., & Thorpe, J. K. (1978). Emotional expression in infancy: II. Early deviations in Down's syndrome. In M. Lewis & L. Rosenblum (Eds.), *The development of affect* (pp. 351–359). New York: Plenum Press.

Fein, D., Pennington, B., Markowitz, P., Braverman, M., & Waterhouse, L. (1984). Towards a neuropsychological model of infantile autism: Are the social deficits primary? *Journal of American Academy of Child Psychiatry.*

Fiske, S. T., & Linville, P. W. (1980). What does the schema concept buy us? *Personality and Social Psychology Bulletin, 6,* 543–557.

Friedman, A. (1979). Framing pictures: The role of knowledge in automotized encoding and memory for gist. *Journal of Experimental Psychology: General, 108,* 316–355.

Frith, U. (1982). Psychological abnormalities in early childhood psychoses. In J. Wing & L. Wing (Eds.), *Handbook of psychiatry* (Vol. 3). London: Cambridge University Press.

Frith, U. (1983, August). *Autism: Social and cognitive deficits.* Paper accompanying poster presentation at the 7th Biennial Meeting of the International Society for the Study of Behavioural Development, Munich, Germany.

Frith, U., & Snowling, M. (1983). Reading for meaning and reading for sound in autistic and dyslexic children. *British Journal of Developmental Psychology, 1,* 329–342.

Gould, J. (1984). The Lowe and Costello Symbolic Play Test in socially impaired children. *Journal of Autism and Developmental Disorders.*

Hermelin, B. (1983). Thoughts and feelings. *Australian Autism Review, 1,* 10–19.

Hermelin, B., & Frith, U. (1971). Psychological studies of childhood autism. Can autistic children make sense of what they see and hear? *Journal of Special Education, 5,* 1107–1117.

Hermelin, B., & O'Connor, N. (1970). *Psychological experiments with autistic children.* Oxford: Pergamon Press.

Hobson, R. P. (1983a). *Origins of the personal relation, and the unique case of autism.* Paper presented to the Association for Child Psychology and Psychiatry.

Hobson, R. P. (1983b). The autistic child's recognition of age-related features of people, animals, and things. *British Journal of Developmental Psychology, 1,* 343–352.

Hobson, R. P. (1984). Early childhood autism and the question of egocentrism. *Journal of Autism and Developmental Disorders, 14,* 85–106.

Jaffe, J., Stern, D. N., & Peery, J. C. (1973). "Conversational" coupling of gaze behavior in prelinguistic human development. *Journal of Psycholinguistic Research, 2,* 321–330.

Jones, O. H. M. (1977). Mother–child communication with prelinguistic Down's syndrome and normal infants. In H. R. Schaffer (Ed.), *Studies in mother–infant interaction.* London: Academic Press.

Kanner, L. (1943). Autistic disturbances of affective contact. *Nervous Child, 2,* 217–250.

Langdell, T. (1981). *Face perception: An approach to the study of autism.* Unpublished doctoral dissertation, University of London.

Lotter, V. (1974). Social adjustment and placement of autistic children in Middlesex: A follow-up study. *Journal of Autism and Childhood Schizophrenia, 4,* 11–32.

Meltzoff, A., & Moore, M. K. (1977). Imitation of facial and manual gestures. *Science, 198,* 75–80.

Mirenda, P. L., Donnellan, A., & Yoder, D. E. (1983). Gaze behavior: A new look at an old problem. *Journal of Autism and Developmental Disorders, 13,* 397–409.

Neisser, U. (1976). *Cognition and reality.* San Francisco: Freeman.

Newson, E., Dawson, M., & Everard, P. (1984). *The natural history of able autistic people: Their management and functioning in social context* (Report to DHSS). Child Development Research Unit, The University of Nottingham.

Newson, S., & Newson, E. (1975). Intersubjectivity and the transmission of culture: On the social origins of symbolic functioning: *Bulletin of the British Psychological Society, 28,* 437–446.

Norman, D. A., & Rumelhart, D. E. (1975). Memory and knowledge. In D. A. Norman & D. E. Rumelhart (Eds.), *Explorations in cognition*. San Francisco: Freeman.

Palmer, S. E. (1975). Visual perception and world knowledge: Notes on a model of sensory-cognitive interaction. In D. A. Norman & D. E. Rumelhart (Eds.), *Explorations in cognition*. San Francisco: Freeman.

Prizant, B. M. (1983). Language acquisition and communicative behavior in autism: Toward an understanding of the "whole" of it. *Journal of Speech and Hearing Disorders, 48*, 296–307.

Rheingold, H. L. (1961). The effect of environmental stimulation upon social and exploratory behaviours. In B. M. Foss (Ed.), *Determinants of infant behaviour* (Vol. 1). London: Methuen.

Ricks, D. M. (1975). Vocal communication in pre-verbal normal and autistic children. In N. O'Connor (Ed.), *Language, cognitive deficits and retardation*. London: Butterworths.

Ricks, D. M. (1979). Making sense of experience to make sensible sounds. In M. Bullowa (Ed.), *Before speech: The beginning of interpersonal communication*. London: Cambridge University Press.

Ricks, D. M., & Wing, L. (1975). Language, communication, and the use of symbols in normal and autistic children. *Journal of Autism and Childhood Schizophrenia, 5*, 191–221.

Rimland, B. (1965). *Infantile autism. The syndrome and its implications for a neural theory of behaviour*. London: Methuen.

Rutter, M. (1970). Autistic children: Infancy to adulthood. *Seminars in Psychiatry, 2*, 435–450.

Rutter, M. (1983). Cognitive deficits in the pathogenesis of autism. *Journal of Child Psychology and Psychiatry, 24*, 513–531.

Schaffer, H. R. (1974). Early social behaviour and the study of reciprocity. *Bulletin of the British Psychological Society, 27*, 209.

Schaffer, H. (1979). Acquiring the concept of the dialogue. In M. H. Bornstein & W. Kessen (Eds.), *Psychological development from infancy: Image to intention*. Hillsdale, NJ: Erlbaum.

Schaffer, H. R., Collis, G. M., & Parsons, G. (1977). Vocal interchange and visual regard in verbal and pre-verbal children. In H. R. Schaffer (Ed.), *Studies in mother–infant interaction*. London: Academic Press.

Shah, A., & Frith, U. (1983). An islet of ability in autistic children: A research note. *Journal of Child Psychology and Psychiatry, 24*, 613–620.

Shantz, C. V. (1975). The development of social cognition. In E. M. Hetherington (Ed.), *Review of child development research* (Vol. 5). Chicago: University of Chicago Press.

Stern, D. N. (1974). Mother and infant at play: The dyadic interaction involving facial, vocal and gaze behavior. In M. Lewis & L. A. Rosenblum (Eds.), *The effect of the infant on its caregiver*. New York: Wiley.

Tager-Flusberg, H. (1981). Sentence comprehension in autistic children. *Applied Psycholinguistics, 2*, 5–24.

Trevarthen, C. (1974). Conversations with a two-month old. *New Scientist, 62*, 230–235.

Waterhouse, L., & Fein, D. (1975, December). *Language behaviour in autistic and schizophrenic children*. Paper presented at the Linguistic Society of America, San Francisco.

Wing, L. (1976). Epidemiology and theories of aetiology. In L. Wing, (Ed.), *Early childhood autism* (2nd ed). Oxford: Pergamon Press.

Wing, L. (1981a). Language, social, and cognitive impairments in autism and severe mental retardation. *Journal of Autism and Developmental Disorders, 11*, 31–44.

Wing, L. (1981b). Asperger's syndrome: A clinical account. *Psychological Medicine, 11*, 115–129.

Wing, L., & Gould, J. (1979). Severe impairments of social interaction and associated abnormalities in children: Epidemiology and classification. *Journal of Autism and Developmental Disorders, 9*, 11–29.

Wolff, S., & Barlow, A. (1979). Schizoid personality in childhood: A comparative study of schizoid, autistic and normal children. *Journal of Child Psychology and Psychiatry, 20*, 29–46.

9

Compliance, Noncompliance, and Negativism

FRED R. VOLKMAR

ISSUES IN THE DEFINITION OF COMPLIANCE, NONCOMPLIANCE, AND "NEGATIVISM"

The disposition to comply with the requests of others typically appears early in life. It emerges without extensive training in a responsive social environment (Stayton, Hogan, & Ainsworth, 1971) and appears to develop in the context of the infant's preferential interest in social interaction, imitation, and social-communicative transactions. As infants begin to integrate sensorimotor schemas, they develop the ability to selectively attend and to develop synchronous patterns of interaction with their caregivers. The earliest forms of compliance probably arise as infants begin to differentially regulate their gaze in response to adults. These social-communicative transactions appear to be important prerequisites for language development (Bruner, 1975). The infant is an important participant in this process as he or she begins to organize experience and action. As infants enter the second year of life, their increasing differentiation and autonomy also give rise to the capacity to oppose the will of others. This process is an important developmental phenomenon that implies increasing cognitive sophistication, ability, and continued social engagement. Compliance and other prosocial and self-regulatory behaviors become increasingly differentiated over the course of development (Kopp, 1982).

During certain developmental periods, e.g., in the toddler and adolescent, noncompliance to the requests or demands of adults are commonly viewed by parents as preferential modes of activity, although this impression is contradicted

FRED R. VOLKMAR • Child Study Center, Yale University, New Haven, Connecticut 06510.

by the few studies available (e.g., Minton, Kagan, & Levine, 1971; Rutter, Graham, Chadwick, & Yule, 1976; Stayton *et al.*, 1971). Among handicapped children the perception of willful, intentional noncompliance (or negativism) is also common. For example, autistic and other pervasively impaired children are often viewed as "negativistic." To the extent that this phenomenon exists it presents an important obstacle to treatment. If handicapped children are, indeed, unusually "negativistic," it is even more difficult to provide them with the educational interventions that may improve long-term outcome. In considering the issue of noncompliance or "negativism" in handicapped children, it is important to consider the ways such behaviors may be operationally defined as well as the important perspective that research on normally developing children provides in understanding such behavior.

The definition of compliance would, at first glance, appear to be a straightforward matter. Unfortunately, this is not so, and the variety of definitions used to define compliance and noncompliance or "negativism" have complicated our understanding of the phenomenon and the interpretation of research studies. Definitions have varied both in their degree of sophistication and parsimony. Some investigators have used rather broad definitions that focus on naturally occurring behaviors, often social in nature, e.g., avoidance of eye contact or gaze aversion (Hutt & Ounsted, 1966), while others have emphasized performance on specific cognitive tasks the child had previously mastered (Cowan, Hoddinott, & Wright, 1965).

Compliant responses could most simply be defined as correct responses to a request, while noncompliant responses could be most simply defined as failure to respond or incorrect responses to a request. Negativism might then be described as willful noncompliance. Obviously there are important considerations involved in considering the meaning of compliance or noncompliance for any given individual. If a response is not in a child's behavioral repertoire or if she or he can not understand the specific request, the failure to produce the requested response might be described, behaviorally, as noncompliant, but such noncompliance is neither particularly interesting nor surprising and obviously should not be used to label the child as noncompliant. For example, if a normal toddler were asked to ride a bicycle, it is extremely improbable that he or she would be able to do so, and if most adults were asked, in grammatically correct Latin, to perform some activity, they would also be unable to comply with the request. Accordingly, a strict definition of compliance would include the proviso that the requested response is within the child's behavioral repertoire. Furthermore, this example also clarifies another important issue in understanding compliance since the toddler would probably not be able either to perceive or verbally reflect on his or her inability to perform the requested activity, while the adult might well ask for clarification. This "metacognitive" ability to reflect on one's inability to understand or comply with a request and to ask for clarification is a developmental phenomenon and typically does not emerge until school age in the normally developing child (Beal & Flavell, 1982). In handicapped, developmentally delayed populations this ability may often not be present, especially when the child's expressive language skills are limited or absent, and this suggests the need for even greater parsimony and experimental rigor in defining noncompliance and "negativism" in this population. As a practical matter the child's developmental level and motivational hierarchy must be considered in understanding compliant and noncompliant behaviors. Given the typical inability of handicapped children to reflect on their own behavior and cognitive processes, attributions of willful noncompliance or "negativism" must be carefully made.

The term *negativism* has also been variously defined in both clinical and research literature. For example, in adults with major psychiatric disorders (e.g., schizophrenia) it refers to resistance and ambivalence, while in children and in disabled populations it has more commonly referred to willful noncompliance. Many clinical studies (e.g., Bettelheim, 1967) have described handicapped, especially autistic, children as negativistic. Though differences in definition and experimental procedure have complicated the interpretation of research studies, they have, at best, lent only mixed support to this concept. Negativism is most strictly defined as deliberate noncompliance; i.e., the child is capable of performing a requested activity, realizes that a request has been made, but chooses not to comply with it. Various attempts to define "negativistic" responses have been made (Wallace, 1975). Unfortunately, the usual experimental paradigms employed to study such behaviors—i.e., a child is examined in a strange room by a strange examiner making unfamiliar requests—might be expected to increase the likelihood that children would not comply with requests. For example, Jose and Cohen (1980) found that novel teachers were more likely than familiar ones to elicit such behaviors. Clark and Rutter (1977) have suggested that it would be best to move from a restricted definition of "negativism" as deliberately incorrect responses to a broader one emphasizing the child's lack of involvement and poor motivation. Certainly the notion that a child deliberately responds incorrectly suggests a remarkable degree of task and social involvement, which is not typically seen in severely impaired children. Accordingly, the term *noncompliant* appears to be more parsimoniously applied in situations in which a child, known to be task-competent, fails to produce a response upon request. The term *negativism* would then be reserved for those instances in which it can be demonstrated that a child *deliberately* refuses to comply.

PERSPECTIVES FROM CHILD DEVELOPMENT RESEARCH

A consideration of compliance, noncompliance, and "negativism" in the normally developing child is helpful in understanding the behavior of exceptional children. At birth infants are social creatures. The roots of compliance and other prosocial behaviors can be traced to early infancy with the development of an interest in others. Infants, preferring human faces over other visual stimuli, are capable of distinguishing facial expressions of emotion, and begin to vocalize when spoken to. As the infant learns to coordinate existing sensorimotor schemas, the ability to perform voluntary motor activities emerges. The use of gaze aversion and head turning provides the infant with a measure of control over his own experience (Rheingold, 1961). As the infant gains more control and differentiation over his or her activities, a sense of voluntary control begins to emerge (Kopp, 1982). The earliest examples of compliance include the child's differential responsiveness to social and linguistic signals even before the acquisition of receptive speech; e.g., very young children will typically direct their gaze in accordance with the directions of caregivers (Chapman, 1981). The roots of compliance have been the subjects of theoretical debate for many years (Freud, 1915/1965; Sears, 1960). The development of the capacity to comply with various parental requests and the incorporation of internal standards is a complex phenomenon depending on cognitive and social factors (Kopp, 1982) and has long been recognized as an important landmark in development (Gesell & Amatruda, 1945). Given the widespread impression of parents and clinicians that young children are often noncompliant, it is surprising that the available research literature suggests that this may not, in fact, be the case.

In a study of 25 infants from 9 to 12 months of age Stayton *et al.* (1971) observed that the earliest manifestations of compliance emerged independent of parental efforts. The early disposition toward compliance was related to maternal responsiveness, though not to the frequency with which requests were made. In that study a few of the brighter 1-year-olds also exhibited some evidence of "internalized controls," i.e., could self-inhibit activity. A similar study of 2-year-olds, observed in their homes (Minton *et al.*, 1971) suggested that while mothers differed in their levels of intrusiveness and control, children were generally compliant. The frequency and form in which mothers make requests of toddlers are significantly related to the child's compliance, as is the child's developmental level; typically mothers augment verbal requests with gestures that may attract the child's attention to an activity (Chapman, 1981). Mothers' impressions that toddlers are noncompliant may then reflect their success in using extralexical cues in guiding the child's attention in the face of the child inability to comprehend the lexical content of the mother's instruction. The importance of lexical content to the child increases as the child progresses developmentally; for example, fluent and nonfluent, young, normally developing children have been observed to respond differentially to distorted commands, with fluent youngsters relying on syntactical elements compared to nonfluent subjects, who were more likely to rely on familiar semantic elements (Wetstone & Friedlander, 1973). The important contributions of environmental setting are suggested by the differences in the nature of demands made of nursery school students when home and school environments are compared (Tizard, Hughes, Pinkerton, & Carmichael, 1982).

The response of younger children to ambiguous or contradictory requests also suggests the importance of developmental factors in understanding compliance. In a series of studies Volkmar and Siegel (1982) found that a large group of 1- to 3-1/2-year-old subjects responded appropriately to a simple request to either approach or stay away from an experimenter when such requests were presented either with speech or with facial expression and gestures. However, when requests were contradictory, e.g., when the experimenter visually indicated that the child should approach but said, "Stay away," in a cold tone of voice, subjects were more likely to rely on the auditory aspect of the message to derive meaning. The pattern of the subjects' responses to the differing messages formed a cumulative, unidimensional, or Guttman scale suggesting the importance of developmental factors in determining the child's response. The ability to reflect on ambiguous requests is also a developmental phenomenon. Beal and Flavell (1982) observed the responses of a group of kindergarten-age subjects to tasks involving inadequate instructions; subjects as a group were unable to reflect on the inadequate nature of the instructions even when the ambiguous nature of the instruction was emphasized. Similar developmental changes have been observed in the development of helping, self-regulatory, and other prosocial behaviors (Kopp, 1982; Ladd, Lange, & Stremmel, 1983).

In summary, the normally developing child appears to be predisposed to comply with adult requests. Parents' impressions of "negativism" in 2- and 3-year-old children may reflect the real, though infrequent, episodes of true negativism. However, attributions of "negativism" in other instances may result when parents are unable to gain the child's attention to tasks or when the child is both incapable of compliance and unable to reflect on this inability. The ability of the child to comply is closely associated with the nature and saliency of the request and the child's developmental level. Instances in which children partially comply with adult requests may be viewed by parents as negativistic but from the child's perspective may be adaptive attempts to comply. These important developmental perspectives are useful in considering the clinical issues raised by the noncompliant child.

CLINICAL ISSUES

Oppositional Syndromes

At times, in otherwise normally developing children, oppositional or negativistic behavior may become extreme and sufficiently problematic that parents seek professional help in managing the child. Epidemiological studies indicate that up to one-fifth of the school population may exhibit pronounced degrees of noncompliance (Greene, Langer, Herson, Eisenberg, & McCarthy, 1973; Werry & Quay, 1971), and such children are seen in a significant proportion of children referred for evaluation (Gilpin & Worland, 1976). Boys appear to be more commonly affected than girls (Werry & Quay, 1971) and racial and ethnic differences also may exist (Comer, 1976). The family backgrounds of such children may be remarkable for parents who are overly concerned with issues of control (Levy, 1955).

Differences in parental styles of interaction appear to be important determinants of such behaviors. The parents of noncompliant children may be more intrusive and disruptive (Peed, Roberts, & Forehand, 1977) and may be more commanding and controlling than other parents (Forehand, 1977). Careful analysis of the underlying parental patterns of responsiveness (e.g., Wahler, 1969) often reveals inappropriate reinforcement for noncompliant, attention-seeking behaviors. In a careful observational study of compliance in a natural setting Lytton and Zwiner (1975) observed a large sample of 2-1/2-year-old boys. A sequential analysis of their naturalistic data revealed that compliance varied as a function of parental action and command. Physical control and negative actions were more likely to produce noncompliance, while positive actions were more commonly associated with compliance.

The current *Diagnostic and Statistical Manual* (DSM-III; American Psychiatric Association, 1980) includes a category for *oppositional disorder*. This term replaces the earlier term *passive aggressive personality disorder* and is defined by pervasive opposition to authority, opposition even in the face of self-interest, unwillingness to respond to reasonable persuasion, etc. Such disorders, in DSM-III, are differentiated from conduct disorders, schizophrenia, and pervasive developmental disorders. Oppositional disorder is assumed to be relatively chronic and to seriously interfere with school performance. While this "disorder" appears to be a common presenting complaint for many parents of otherwise normally developing children, fundamental questions about the validity of this diagnostic concept remain. Issues of prevalence, definition, the association with maladaptive parental style, and similar questions remain to be addressed. The usefulness of this diagnostic category in handicapped populations has not yet been systematically assessed. Though children with conduct disorders and autism are commonly viewed as oppositional or "negativistic," such individuals are specifically not included in the oppositional disorder category.

Autism and Related Conditions

Clinicians have often reported pathological degrees of "negativism" among handicapped, and especially autistic, children. In Kanner's original (1943) report of 11 cases of autism he mentioned the difficulties children had in complying with some tasks, e.g., portions of intelligence tests. Notions of negativism may be traced to Kanner's early description of this behavior and his impression of the need for preservation of sameness in his sample: "Everything that is brought to the child from the outside, everything that changes his external or even internal environment, represents a dreaded intrusion" (Kanner, 1943, p. 36; Prior & MacMillan, 1973). His initial impression that such children were not mentally retarded reflected his attribution of poor performance to unwillingness to cooperate with testing procedures rather than to inability. Kanner's impression that autistic children were of normal intelligence was based on their performance on selected parts of IQ tests and on the unusual islets of ability that such children sometimes exhibit. As longitudinal data became available, this notion was not supported by subsequent research, which has amply documented the persistent intellectual deficits of autistic children (Lockyer & Rutter, 1969). In addition, autistic children's cooperation and responsiveness are increased when test items more appropriate to their intellectual level are employed (Alpern, 1967). Thus, the poor performance of autistic individuals appears not to be simply a function of "negativism."

Clinical reports of "negativism" in autistic individuals commonly appeared in the decades subsequent to Kanner's initial description (Bettelheim, 1967; Boatman & Szurek, 1960; Ekstein, Bryant, & Friedman, 1958; Zaslow & Breger, 1969). These clinical impressions focused on the clinicians' experience of the withdrawal, active isolation, resistance, and poor cooperation typically experienced in the course of psychotherapeutic work with such children. These impressions arose in the context of psychogenic views of the pathogenesis of the disorder; the impressions of negativism were often seen as attempts by the child to adapt to a pathological environment. Subsequent research has, of course, cast considerable doubt on psychogenic theories of etiology so that most investigators currently favor biological, rather than psychogenic, notions of causation (DeMyer, Hingtgen, & Jackson, 1981). Practically, the impression of willful noncompliance arises when a child who has previously emitted an appropriate response to a request fails to do so on command, stops before completing a requested activity, or exhibits selective failures to respond. The frequent use of stereotyped, self-stimulatory behaviors in response to requests and demands is also often perceived as an aspect of "negativism" in this population. As with autistic echolalia (Fay, 1969), such behaviors can be understood within either an adaptive or a deficit theoretical model, e.g., as a compensatory mechanism within the context of the interaction. Studies of the response of children to their environment suggest important extrinsic determinants of the child's behavior.

The issue of treatment "structure" in facilitating adaptive behavior is an important one. While some theoretical conceptions of the disorder (e.g., Tinbergen & Tinbergen, 1972) argue for the importance of a less demanding, unstructured treatment approach, experimental work suggests that autistic individuals function most appropriately in structured situations. Schopler, Brehm, Kinsbourne, and Reichler (1971) observed that autistic children responded more favorably to a structured versus an unstructured treatment approach. Bartak and Rutter (1973a, 1973b) observed that more highly structured, i.e., more task-oriented, special education programs generally were associated with better outcomes than were less structured ones. Gaze and social behavior vary as a function of adult attention and preoccupation (Churchill & Bryson, 1972). Clark and Rutter (1981) observed that a group of autistic children responded positively to interpersonal and task-oriented demands. These studies suggest that autistic individuals behave most appropriately when exposed to predictable, highly contingent, and structured environments. In part, earlier clinical impressions of "negativism" in this population may therefore have been a function of the less structured, psychotherapeutic approaches employed in early therapeutic interventions.

RESEARCH STUDIES

As mentioned previously, a variety of factors have complicated the interpretation of research studies. Differences in definition, subject population, experimental methods, and other factors have made comparisons across studies difficult. Definitions have ranged from "less-than-chance" performance on an object-sorting task (Cowan *et al.*, 1965), to a failure to produce an appropriate response, known to be in the child's behavioral repertoire, on command (Morrison, Miller, & Mejia, 1971), to broader definitions encompassing avoidance of eye contact, social withdrawal, etc. (see Wallace, 1975, for a discussion). While some investigators have argued that "negativism" is a central feature of the behavior of autistic individuals (Sroufe, Steucher, & Stutzer, 1973), experimental studies, employing strict definitions of the concept, have not consistently supported this concept.

Important contributions of the effects of experimental procedures *per se* have often not been considered in interpreting research studies. For example, handicapped children may be more likely to exhibit noncompliance in an experimental setting as a result of such extraneous factors as novelty of the setting or requests. Jose and Cohen (1980), in an experimental study of negativism in autistic and emotionally disturbed children, found that novel teachers were more likely to elicit aloofness from autistic subjects. Important questions of the ecological validity of observational data have typically not been addressed (Lytton, 1973).

In an interesting study of compliance and resistance in autistic children, Cowan *et al.* (1965) examined the performance of subjects in an object-sorting task in which instructions and task complexity were invariant. The subjects' performance was significantly below chance levels; i.e.,subjects appeared to be responding at levels below that expected if they were randomly responding, though some subjects were noted to become more compliant over time. This result appeared to convincingly demonstrate the existence of "negativism," strictly defined. However, Clark and Rutter (1977) were unable to replicate this result. In their study the developmental level of the subjects (i.e., the presence of some language) was significantly related to performance, and subjects either could do the task (and did so) or performed at chance levels. With an even more complicated discrimination task, subjects exhibited more errors but failed to exhibit negativism. While these results, in part, might have reflected differences in samples, they suggested that deliberate avoidance of correct responses was not typical. In a subsequent study of task difficulty and task performance in autistic children, Clark and Rutter (1979) observed that the distribution and types of errors made by the subjects on the Board Form of the Raven Progressive Matrices were a function of the intrinsic difficulty of the items rather than "negativism" on the part of subjects; i.e., the child's intellectual level predicted success or failure rather than a lack of subject cooperation.

Another approach has focused on particular patterns of noncompliance or "negativism" in autistic individuals. Unique patterns of noncompliance have been observed in such children (Jose & Cohen, 1980); as compared to emotionally and cognitively disturbed youngsters, autistic individuals were more likely to engage in self-stimulation, look around the room, and make errors. Wallace (1975) studied negativism in autistic, behavior-disturbed, and normal children aged 5 to 12. Subjects were presented with two tasks in each of three conditions (verbal requests for verbal responses, verbal requests for nonverbal responses, and nonverbal requests for nonverbal responses); each subject had previously demonstrated task competence and was repeatedly asked to comply with the experimental request. The responses of subjects were rated along a continuum of negativism as either correct, reversals, incomplete, substitute, or refusals. Normal children uniformly were correct. While there were no significant differences between groups in overall "negativism" scores, there were significant differences among the conditions. The autistic subjects were similar to the behavior-disturbed group except in respect to verbal requests for verbal responses, where there were much more negative reactions. The imitation task (nonverbal requests for nonverbal responses) elicited less "negativism" than did verbal requests for nonverbal responses.

Volkmar and Cohen (1982) reanalyzed Wallace's (1975) data by dichotomizing subjects as either compliant or noncompliant on the basis of the frequency with which subjects were correct. Scalogram analysis of the resulting data revealed that the individual children's responses formed a cumulative, unidimensional, or Guttman scale. This suggests that patterns of noncompliance were rule-governed and that a developmental progression in the ability of subjects to comply to the differing requests might be involved. The ability to examine individual differences in patterns of compliance is of interest since previous reports (e.g., Clark & Rutter, 1981) had noted differences in individual styles of responding. Volkmar and Cohen (1982) refrained from equating noncompliance with negativism given the regularity in the subjects' performance.

In a subsequent study (Volkmar, Hoder, & Cohen, 1985) observational data on the frequency of compliance to staff requests and of other behaviors were collected in a naturalistic setting. Nineteen autistic individuals were observed in their familiar residential environment while they interacted with familiar caregivers making familiar requests. Subjects were observed on ten separate occasions in each of three settings, which varied in staff child ratio (either 1:1, 1:2, or 1:4) using a time-sample procedure. The frequencies of compliance, partial compliance, noncompliance, stereotypy, vocalization, echolalia, and self-injurious behaviors were obtained. The ecological validity of these data is especially important since it allows a detailed examination of patterns of compliance and noncompliance in relationship to other behaviors. Subjects were compliant to requests in approximately 75% of instances in which a request was made of them. This result was true regardless of setting. Subjects responded incorrectly less than 10% of the time. Noncompliance was related to other behaviors (e.g., looking away from staff and task, stereotypy). When the data were dichotomized the pattern of compliance/noncompliance replicated the earlier (Volkmar & Cohen, 1982) report of a unidimensional, cumulative hierarchy. This result is presented in Table 1. Each subject is represented by a row of the table. Subjects who were correct two-thirds, or more, of the time in response to a particular request type were defined as compliant (+), while subjects who exhibited correct responses in more than one-third of the instances in which a request was made of them were defined as noncompliant (−). Subjects are arrayed such that the +'s form a stairway from bottom left to top right of the table. Subjects were most likely to comply with verbal requests for action and least likely, overall, to respond correctly to verbal requests for verbal responses. The subject who is represented by the top row of the table was uniformly noncompliant while the five subjects represented by the bottom five rows were uniformly compliant to the different types of requests. Arrayed between these extremes are the remainder of the sample, who were rated as noncompliant to at least one type of request. This stairway structure perfectly represents the responses of all but two children. When evaluated by Scalogram analysis, the data in this table meet the criteria for a Guttman scale. The correlation between the subject's rank on the scale and IQ (r_s = .56, $p < .01$) suggests the importance of developmental level in determining scale position and compliance. These data suggest that when observed in a familiar setting with familiar staff members making familiar demands, autistic individuals were typically compliant. Furthermore, noncompliance was a function of the type of request made to the subject and could be systematically related to other aspects of the child's behavior such as gaze (Mirenda, Donnellan, & Yoder, 1983).

Table 1. Scaling of Compliance[a]

Subject no.	Request: Response:	V V	V V+NV	NV NV	V NV
16		−	−	−	−
2		−	−	−	+
4		−	−	+	−
6		−	−	+	+
10		−	−	+	+
17		−	−	+	+
19		−	−	+	+
12		−	−	+	+
8		−	+	+	−
11		−	+	+	+
14		−	+	+	+
9		−	+	+	+
18		−	+	+	+
7		−	+	+	+
1		+	+	+	+
3		+	+	+	+
13		+	+	+	+
15		+	+	+	+
5		+	+	+	+

Note: Adapted from Volkmer, F. R., Hoder, E. L., & Cohen, D. J. (1985). "Compliance, 'negativism,' and the effect of treatment structure on behavior in autism: A naturalistic, behavioral study." By permission of Pergamon Press.
[a]V = verbal, NV = nonverbal, + = compliant (≥ 67% correct), − = noncompliant (<33% correct).

In a subsequent study (Volkmar, Ali, & Cohen, 1985) 26 autistic individuals in a day treatment program were given a series of ambiguous, contradictory, or impossible requests. In the ambiguous request series subjects were asked to choose from among four dinosaurs that were colored blue, orange, green, and brown. After establishing that the subjects knew the colors of the dinosaurs, the experimenter asked on six occasions for dinosaurs of a color not present—e.g., "Hand me the red one." Except for the two subjects with the highest intellectual level, subjects uniformly attempted to comply with the experimenter's request by selecting the colors closest to the color names, e.g., orange for red. The two subjects with the highest IQs uniformly stated, "I can't do it" or "It's not there." Similarly, in response to ambiguous or contradictory requests, subjects typically attempted to comply. The observations that teacher verbalizations increase response rates (Hughes, Worley, & Neel, 1983) and that treatment procedures that facilitate task completion increase autistic children's motivation to persist (Koegel & Egel, 1979) also suggest the importance of extrinsic factors in determining compliance.

With the exception of Cowan's original study, subsequent investigations have generally failed to confirm the clinical impression of widespread "negativism" in autistic children. Rather, the performance of subjects in response to task demands seems more predictably related to task difficulty, novelty of the situation and examiner, treatment structure, and similar factors. In addition, the observed hierarchies in patterns of compliance highlight the importance of developmental factors.

INTERVENTION STRATEGIES

In normally developing children the ability to reflect on one's behavior and capacities is an important cognitive landmark. This ability does not typically appear until school age; studies of the responses of younger children to ambiguous or contradictory communications (e.g., Beal & Flavell, 1982) suggest its importance for allowing the child to monitor the nature of requests made by others. This "metacognitive" ability allows the normally developing child to ask for clarification or communicate his or her inability to comply. Typically autistic individuals do not appear to exhibit this ability; i.e., they are not able, when confronted with a difficult or complicated request, to verbally reflect their incapacity to the other participant in the transaction. This inability further complicates the attribution of willful noncompliance or "negativism" to autistic individuals and has important implications for designing intervention programs.

In either handicapped or nonhandicapped populations, a first step in the management of the apparently noncompliant child must be a careful analysis of the child's behavior within the context of the child's developmental level and environment. Misattributions of "negativism" may be more likely to occur when parents or teachers have inappropriate expectations of the child, when the meaning and context of the behavior are not fully appreciated, or when children are observed in relatively unstructured settings. In addition, the interpersonal "style" of the parent or teacher may be related to noncompliance (Clark & Rutter, 1981). Mistaken impressions of noncompliance may be more common in children with unusual islets of ability and may account, in part, for the widespread clinical impression of "negativism" among autistic children. The term *noncompliant* should be reserved to describe those children who characteristically fail to comply with familiar requests that are known to be within the child's behavior repertoire. The term *negativistic* should be used only when it can be reasonably demonstrated that the child understands the request and *intentionally* fails to comply; the term *noncompliant* is more parsimonious and more behaviorally descriptive. By carefully analyzing the nature and context of noncompliant behaviors, a variety of techniques may be used to facilitate compliance and to increase appropriate responding.

Psychotherapeutic techniques in which underlying issues of autonomy, control, and self-esteem may be addressed may be helpful in nonhandicapped populations (Gilpin, 1976). However, the particular cognitive and linguistic deficits exhibited by autistic individuals complicate the use of such intervention strategies. Accordingly, behavioral techniques have more commonly been employed in the treatment of autistic and other developmentally handicapped individuals (Roberts, Hatzenbuehler, & Bean, 1981). Most studies of intervention employ such behavioral techniques, though the relative efficacy of different techniques is difficult to establish since many studies confound the differential effects of social and other types of reinforcement, resulting improvement may not generalize to other situations, and small numbers of individuals or specific behaviors are typically studied.

Clearly, parents and other caregivers should be a part of any assessment and intervention process to facilitate consistency of the intervention program and generalizability of the resulting behavior change. Time-out procedures and differential attentiveness on the part of parents may be used to facilitate compliance, and the value of parental reinforcement may increase as a result (Wahler, 1969; Hobbs, Forehand, & Murray, 1978). Bean and Roberts (1981) studied the response of 24 clinic-referred noncompliant preschoolers to several time-out release contingencies; compliance significantly increased as a result of time-out. The duration of the time-out period (Hobbs *et al.*, 1978) and of the contingencies for temporal release (Hobbs & Forehand, 1975) should be carefully considered in designing an intervention program.

To the extent that noncompliance results from inconsistent contingencies in parental or caretaker behavior, such behavior can be modified; detailed guides to parent training have now appeared (Forehand & McMahon, 1981). A careful behavioral analysis may reveal that self-stimulatory or other maladaptive behaviors may seriously interfere with performance and may merit special attention (Risley, 1968). Noncompliant responses have commonly been related to such behaviors (Jose & Cohen, 1980; Volkmar, Hoder, & Cohen, 1985). Accordingly, to facilitate compliance such behaviors may be important targets of intervention in handicapped populations (Koegel & Covert, 1972). The ecological context of the behavior is also an important consideration. Compliance to requests appears to be a function of the "structure" within the child's treatment environment; i.e., autistic and other handicapped individuals are most likely to comply in highly structured, contingent settings (Schopler *et al.*, 1971). In less structured settings maladaptive behaviors increase and compliance to adult requests may be more variable (Volkmar, Hoder, & Cohen, 1985). Effects of interpersonal variables, e.g., the adult's style of interaction, should also be considered in designing intervention strategies (Clark & Rutter, 1981; Hughes *et al.*, 1983).

The question of motivational effects on compliance has been the topic of debate. Handicapped, especially autistic, children are commonly viewed as poorly motivated, though as Clark and Rutter (1979) have pointed out, it is not particularly helpful to invoke motivational explanations for performance deficits when motivation covaries with task demands. However, since motivation to persist in an activity appears to be a function of success/failure experience (Koegel & Egel, 1979), careful consideration of the child's abilities must be part of the intervention program. Variation in tasks may increase the child's interest and task engagement and may facilitate compliance (Dunlap & Koegel, 1980). If developmentally inappropriate requests are frequent, handicapped individuals may be even less likely to comply with other, more appropriate, requests. For example, Laura H., a 10-year-old, relatively high-functioning autistic girl, was enrolled in a special education program and was referred for evaluation because both her parents and the school believed her to be unusually "negativistic" and difficult to manage. A careful developmental assessment revealed marked scatter in her cognitive abilities. Her educational program emphasized cognitive skills that were not appropriate to her developmental level, was somewhat inconsistent, and was not highly structured. Laura had few success experiences, and both parents and teachers appeared to inadvertently reinforce noncompliance. When parents and teachers became more aware of her abilities, a more appropriate educational program was instituted and a time-out procedure was employed both at school and at home. As a result she became markedly more compliant and improved behaviorally.

SUMMARY

Insights from basic child developmental research and issues in the definition of compliance, noncompliance, and negativism raise several important theoretical questions in regard to understanding noncompliance in handicapped populations. Although noncompliance is a common reason for clinical referral and may be an important issue in designing treatment programs, available research suggests that extrinsic and developmental factors may be more important determinants of a child's compliance than had previously been thought. Even in normally developing children who are widely regarded as oppositional or negativistic (e.g., the toddler), compliance to reasonable adult requests seems to be the norm. Given the developmental levels that many handicapped children attain, noncompliance would appear to be the exception rather than the norm if a developmental perspective (Zigler, 1969) is employed in conceptualizing such behaviors. Perceptions of noncompliance may be related to misattributions on the part of caregivers, unrealistic expectations, and the inability of the child to reflect on his or her own incapacity. The need for a developmental perspective is suggested by an appreciation of the complex processes of self-regulation and autonomy that arise normally in the course of development. To the extent that noncompliant or "negativistic" behaviors characterize the child's behavior in a familiar setting with familiar caregivers, such behaviors can be viewed more realistically as the target for appropriate behavioral interventions. A variety of techniques may be used to facilitate compliance. By attempting to view the behavior of handicapped children within the context of their developmental level and within an adaptive framework it is possible to achieve a better understanding of the meaning of a child's behavior.

ACKNOWLEDGMENTS

The author gratefully acknowledges the support of the William T. Grant Foundation, MHCRC Grant 30929, CCRC Grant RR00125, NICHD Grant HD-03008, NIMH Grant MH00418, and Mr. Leonard Berger. The author thanks Donald J. Cohen, Alberta E. Siegel, and Rhea Paul for their careful critique of an earlier version of this chapter.

REFERENCES

Alpern, G. D. (1967). Measurement of "untestable" autistic children. *Journal of Abnormal Psychology, 72,* 478–486.

American Psychiatric Association. (1980). *Diagnostic and statistical manual of mental disorders* (3rd ed.). Washington, DC: Author.

Bartak, L., & Rutter, M. (1973a). Special educational therapy and autistic children: A comparative study. I. Design of the study and administration of units. *Journal of Child Psychology and Psychiatry, 14,* 161–179.

Bartak, L., & Rutter, M. (1973b). Special educational therapy and autistic children: A comparative study. II. Follow-up findings and implications for services. *Journal of Child Psychology and Psychiatry, 14,* 241–270.

Beal, C. R., & Flavell, J. H. (1982). Effects of increasing the salience of message ambiguities on kindergartners' evaluations of communicative success and message adequacy. *Developmental Psychology, 18,* 43–48.

Bean, A. W., & Roberts, M. W. (1981). The effect of time-out release contingencies on changes in child noncompliance. *Journal of Abnormal Child Psychology, 9,* 95–105.

Bettelheim, B. (1967). *The empty fortress.* New York: Free Press.

Boatman, M., & Szurek, S. A. (1960). A clinical study of childhood schizophrenia. In D. Jackson (Ed.), *The etiology of schizophrenia.* New York: Basic Books.

Bruner, J. (1975). From communication to language—A psychological perspective. *Condition, 3,* 255–287.

Chapman, R. S. (1981). Cognitive development and language comprehension in 10- to 21-month olds. In R. E. Stark (Ed.), *Language behavior in infancy and early childhood.* New York: Elsevier.

Churchill, D., & Bryson, C. Q. (1972). Looking and approach behavior of psychotic and normal children as a function of adult attention or preoccupation. *Comparative Psychiatry, 13,* 171–177.

Clark, P., & Rutter, M. (1977). Compliance and resistance in autistic children. *Journal of Autism and Childhood Schizophrenia, 7,* 33–48.

Clark, P., & Rutter, M. (1979). Task difficulty and task performance in autistic children. *Journal of Child Psychology and Psychiatry, 20,* 217–285.

Clark, P., & Rutter, M. (1981). Autistic children's responses to structure and to interpersonal demands. *Journal of Autism and Developmental Disorders, 11,* 201–217.

Comer, J. P. (1976). The oppositional child: Is the black child at greater risk? In E. J. Anthony & D. C. Gilpin (Eds.), *Three faces of childhood.* New York: Spectrum.

Cowan, P. A., Hoddinott, B. A., & Wright, B. A. (1965). Compliance and resistance in the conditioning of autistic children. *Child Development, 36,* 913–923.

DeMyer, M. K., Hingtgen, J. N., & Jackson, R. K. (1981). Infantile autism reviewed: A decade of research. *Schizophrenia Bulletin, 7,* 388–451.

Dunlap, G., & Koegel, R. (1980). Motivating autistic children through stimulus variation. *Journal of Applied Behavior Analysis, 13,* 619–627.

Ekstein, R., Bryant, K., & Friedman, S. W. (1958). Childhood schizophrenia and allied conditions. In L. Bellak (Ed.), *Schizophrenia.* New York: Logos Press.

Fay, W. (1969). On the basis of autistic echolalia. *Journal of Communication Disorders, 2,* 38–47.

Forehand, R. (1977). Child noncompliance to parent commands: Behavioral analysis and treatment. In M. Hersen, R. M. Eisler, & P. M. Miller (Eds.), *Progress in behavior modification* (Vol. 5). New York: Academic Press.

Forehand, R. L., & McMahon, R. J. (1981). *Helping the noncompliant child: A clinician's guide to parent training.* New York: Guilford Press.

Freud, S. (1965). *Introductory lectures on psychoanalysis.* Reprinted in *The complete psychological works of Sigmund Freud* (Vol. 15). London: Hogarth Press. (Original work published 1915)

Gesel, A. L., & Amatruda, C. S. (1945). *The embryology of behavior: The beginnings of the human mind.* New York: Harper.

Gilpin, D. C. (1976). Psychotherapy of the oppositional child. In E. J. Anthony & D. C. Gilpin (Eds.), *Three faces of childhood.* New York: Spectrum.

Gilpin, D. C., & Worland, J. (1976). Symptomatic oppositionality as seen in the clinic. In E. J. Anthony & D. C. Gilpin (Eds.), *Three faces of childhood.* New York: Spectrum.

Greene, E. L., Langer, T. S., Herson, J. H., Jameson, J. D., Eisenberg, J. G., & McCarthy, E. D. (1973). Some methods for evaluating behavioral variation in children 6 to 18. *Journal of the American Academy of Child Psychiatry, 12,* 531–545.

Hobbs, S. A., & Forehand, R. (1975). Effects of various durations from time-out on children's deviant behavior. *Journal of Behavior Therapy and Experimental Psychiatry, 6,* 256–257.

Hobbs, S. A., Forehand, R., & Murray, R. G. (1978). Effects of various durations of timeout on the noncompliance behavior of children. *Behavior Therapy, 9,* 652–656.

Hughes, V., Worley, M. R., & Neel, R. S. (1983). Teacher verbalizations and task performance with autistic children. *Journal of Autism and Developmental Disorders, 13,* 305–316.

Hutt, C., & Ounsted, C. (1966). The biological significance of gaze aversion with particular reference to the syndrome of infantile autism. *Behavioral Science, 11,* 346–356.

Jose, P. E., & Cohen, D. J. (1980). The effect of unfamiliar tasks and teachers on autistic children's negativism. *Journal of the American Academy of Child Psychiatry, 19,* 78–89.

Kanner, L. (1943). Autistic disturbances of affective contact. *Nervous Child, 2,* 227–250.

Koegel, R. L., & Covert, A. (1972). The relationship of self-stimulation to learning in autistic children. *Journal of Applied Behavior Analysis, 5,* 381–387.

Koegel, R. L., & Egel, A. L. (1979). Motivating autistic children. *Journal of Abnormal Psychology, 88,* 418–426.

Kopp, C. B. (1982). Antecedents of self-regulation: A developmental perspective. *Developmental Psychology, 18,* 199–214.

Ladd, G. W., Lange, G., & Stremmel, A. (1983). Personal and situational influences on children's helping behavior: Factors that mediate compliant helping. *Child Development, 54,* 488–501.

Levy, D. M. (1955). Oppositional syndromes and oppositional behavior. In P. Hoch & J. Zubin (Eds.), *Psychopathology of childhood.* New York: Grune and Stratton.

Lockyer, L., & Rutter, M. (1969). A five to fifteen year follow-up study of infantile psychosis—III. Psychological aspects. *British Journal of Psychiatry, 115,* 865–882.

Lytton, H. (1973). Three approaches to the study of parent–child interaction: Ethological, interview, and experimental. *Journal of Child Psychology and Psychiatry, 14,* 1–17.

Lytton, H., & Zwiner, W. (1975). Compliance and its controlling stimuli in a natural setting. *Developmental Psychology, 11,* 769–779.

Minton, C., Kagan, J., & Levine, J. A. (1971). Maternal control and obedience in the two year old. *Child Development, 42,* 873–894.

Mirenda, P. L., Donnellan, A. M., & Yoder, D. E. (1983). Gaze behavior: A new look at an old problem. *Journal of Autism and Developmental Disorders, 13,* 397–409.

Morrison, D., Miller, D., & Mejia, B. (1971). Effects of adult verbal requests on the behavior of autistic children. *American Journal of Mental Deficiency, 75,* 510–518.

Peed, S., Roberts, M., & Forehand, R. (1977). Evaluation of the effectiveness of standardized training program in altering the interaction of mothers and their noncompliant children. *Behavior Modification, 1,* 323–350.

Prior, M., & MacMillan, M. B. (1973). Maintenance of sameness in children with Kanner's syndrome. *Journal of Autism and Childhood Schizophrenia, 3,* 154–167.

Rheingold, H. L. (1961). The effects of environmental stimulation upon social and exploratory behavior in the human infant. In B. M. Foss (Ed.), *Determinants of infant behavior.* London: Methuen.

Risley, T. R. (1967). The effects and side effects of punishing the autistic behaviors of a deviant child. *Journal of Applied Behavior Analysis, 1,* 21–34.

Roberts, M. W., Hatzenbuehler, L. C., & Bean, A. W. (1981). The effects of differential attention and time out on child noncompliance. *Behavior Therapy, 12,* 93–99.

Rutter, M., Graham, P., Chadwick, O. F. D., & Yule, W. (1976). Adolescent turmoil: Fact or fiction? *Journal of Child Psychology and Psychiatry, 17,* 35–56.

Schopler, E., Brehm, S. S., Kinsbourne, J., & Reichler, R. J. (1971). Effect of treatment structure on development in autistic children. *Archives of General Psychiatry, 24,* 415–421.

Sears, R. R. (1960). The growth of conscience. In I. Iscoe & H. Stevenson (Eds.), *Personality development in children.* Austin: University of Texas Press.

Sroufe, L. A., Steucher, H. U., & Stutzer, W. (1973). The functional significance of autistic behaviors for the psychotic child. *Journal of Abnormal Child Psychology, 1,* 225–240.

Stayton, D. J., Hogan, R., & Ainsworth, M. D. S. (1971). Infant obedience and maternal behaviors: The origins of socialization reconsidered. *Child Development, 42,* 1057–1069.

Tinbergen, E. A., & Tinbergen, N. (1972). Early childhood autism: An ethological approach. In *Advances in Ethology, Journal of Comparative Ethology* (Supplement No. 10). Berlin: Paul Perry.

Tizard, B., Hughes, M., Pinkerton, G., & Carmichael, H. (1982). Adult's cognitive demands at home and at nursery school. *Journal of Child Psychology and Psychiatry, 23,* 106–116.

Volkmar, F. R., & Siegel, A. E. (1982). Responses to consistent and discrepant social communications. In R. S. Feldman (Ed.), *Development of nonverbal behavior in children.* New York: Springer-Verlag.

Volkmar, F. R., & Cohen, D. J. (1982). A hierarchical analysis of patterns of noncompliance in autistic and behavior-disturbed children. *Journal of Autism and Developmental Disorders, 12,* 35–42.

Volkmar, F. R., Ali, R., & Cohen, D. J. (1985). *An experimental analysis of compliance in autistic children.* Paper presented at biennial meeting of the Society for Research in Child Development, Toronto, April 1985.

Volkmar, F. R., Hoder, E. L., & Cohen, D. J. (1985). Compliance, "negativism," and the effect of treatment structure on behavior in autism: A naturalistic behavioral study. *Journal of Child Psychology and Psychiatry,* in press.

Wahler, R. G. (1969). Oppositional children: A quest for parental reinforcement control. *Journal of Applied Behavior Analysis, 2,* 159–170.

Wallace, B. (1975). Negativism in verbal and nonverbal responses of autistic children. *Journal of Abnormal Psychology, 84,* 138–143.

Werry, J. S., & Quay, H. C. (1971). The prevalence of behavior symptoms in younger elementary school children. *American Journal of Orthopsychiatry, 41,* 136–148.

Wetstone, H. S., & Friedlander, B. A. (1973). The effect of word order on young children's responses to simple questions and commands. *Child Development, 44,* 734–740.

Zaslow, R. W., & Breger, L. A. (1969). A psychogenic theory of the etiology of infantile autism and implications for treatment. In L. Breger (Ed.), *Clinical cognitive psychology.* New York: Prentice-Hall.

Ziegler, E. (1969). Developmental versus difference theories of mental retardation and the problem of motivation. *American Journal of Mental Deficiency, 73,* 536–549.

III

Major Issues and Theoretical Perspectives

10

Mainstreaming Handicapped Children in Public School Settings

Challenges and Limitations

SUSAN M. McHALE and WENDY C. GAMBLE

In this chapter we describe the foundations of the movement to educate handicapped children with nonhandicapped children in regular school classrooms, and we review the research literature relevant to mainstreamed school programs. Because little information relevant to the mainstreaming of autistic children is available, we focus on handicapped populations in general but discuss some of the specific issues that may arise when autistic children are placed in regular school classrooms. The chapter concludes with an examination of strategies for implementing successful integrated programs for handicapped and nonhandicapped children.

THE FOUNDATIONS OF MAINSTREAMED SCHOOL PROGRAMS

The move to educate autistic and other handicapped children in mainstreamed school environments is part of a national and international effort (Hegarty, Pocklington, & Lucas, 1982) to integrate handicapped persons into the everyday life and activities of society. In the United States this social movement was formalized with the passage of Public Law 94–142, the Education for All Handicapped Children Act of 1975, which mandates that all handicapped children be educated in the *least restrictive environment* that is appropriate to their needs. The least restrictive principle is the basis for integrating handicapped and

SUSAN M. McHALE and WENDY C. GAMBLE • College of Human Development, Pennsylvania State University, University Park, Pennsylvania 16802.

nonhandicapped children in public school settings and is explicated in the *Federal Register* Rules and Regulations as follows:

> (1) That to the maximum extent appropriate, handicapped children, including children in public or private institutions or other care facilities, are educated with children who are not handicapped, and
> (2) That special classes, separate schooling, or other removal of handicapped children from the regular educational environment occurs only when the nature or severity of the handicap is such that education in regular classes with the use of supplementary aids and services cannot be achieved satisfactorily. (Quoted in Turnbull, Leonard, & Turnbull, 1981, p. 27)

With the passage of this law have come major changes in educational programs throughout this country. Indeed, the mandate has been described as an event of major significance in the history of education (e.g., Brodinsky, 1979; Lance, 1976), and the reform it embodies as one of the more "daring challenges" to face educators as well as the public at large (Brodinsky, 1979, p. 239). The foundations of the Education for All Handicapped Children Act include educational, legislative, and philosophical arguments (e.g., Abeson, 1981; Bricker, 1978; Gottlieb, 1981).

First, special education classrooms did not prove to be more effective than regular classrooms in educating handicapped children (see Dunn, 1968), and therefore there seemed to be no reason for placing children in segregated settings. Second, legal reforms in the 1960s and 1970s ensured that all children had the right to be educated, even those severely handicapped children whose training was difficult and expensive. Third, the segregation of handicapped children was thought to stigmatize these children. Placing disabled youngsters in regular classrooms, in contrast, was expected to enhance their acceptance by nonhandicapped individuals.

Although the arguments for mainstreamed education are compelling, the degree to which such programs have accomplished their goals is less clear (Gottlieb, 1981). We will discuss the success of the mainstreaming movement shortly. First, however, we will describe how the least restrictive principle actually has been interpreted in establishing educational programs in public school settings.

MAINSTREAM SCHOOL PROGRAMS

The least restrictive educational environment is one in which handicapped children are educated with children who are not handicapped. In practice, such integration occurs on several levels. In the Warnock Report, a document that provided the impetus toward mainstreamed education in Great Britain, three forms of integration are identified: locational, social, and functional mainstreaming. Locational integration involves children being taught in the same school, moving special education classes to the same parts of the school building as regular classes, or placing handicapped children in the same classroom as their nonhandicapped peers. Social integration refers to handicapped and nonhandicapped children's joint participation in nonacademic activities, such as eating lunch, attending assemblies, or sharing recess times. Functional integration—probably the ultimate goal of the advocates of the least restrictive environment principle—occurs only when disabled children are involved on either a full-time or a part-time basis in regular classrooms and school activities (including academic activities) to a similar extent as their nonhandicapped classmates (Hegarty *et al.*, 1982). In the case of autistic children, the population of primary interest here, integration efforts generally center around locational and sometimes social integration, as we will see in a later part of this chapter.

Other schemas classify mainstreamed school programs solely in terms of the extent of contact between handicapped and nonhandicapped children, regardless of the form or context in which integration occurs. For instance, Cruickshank identifies a continuum of placements ranging from the least to the most normalized settings: "residential settings, special schools in public school systems, special classes in public schools, resource rooms, tutorial programs, itinerant teachers, regular class placement" (Cruickshank, 1977, p. 5).

In short, no one kind of mainstreamed school program exists for children with different handicapping conditions. Rather, when the best interests of children are being served, children are placed in regular school environments to the extent that they can function successfully in those settings. The underlying principle, however, seems to be that the best environment for a child is the most integrated situation with which he or she can cope.

In actuality, the mandate for the least restrictive appropriate education in public schools usually is taken to mean that most mildly retarded children will be educated in regular classrooms and provided with additional aid through the use of resource rooms or teachers, and that most severely and profoundly retarded children will be educated in public schools, though within special classrooms (Gottlieb & Leyser, n.d.). Alternatives to these strategies, however, have appeared in the literature and will be considered later in this chapter. First, however, we will present some of the criticisms that have been leveled against the practice of integrating handicapped and nonhandicapped children since the late 1970s when the mandates of PL 94–142 first were implemented.

THE EFFICACY OF MAINSTREAM SCHOOL PROGRAMS: PROBLEMS AND SUCCESSES

Almost a decade has passed since the Education for All Handicapped Children was signed into law, and since that time educators, scientists, and parents have been debating the question of how successful mainstream programs have been. A number of writers have addressed this issue and have used empirical data (e.g., Gottlieb, 1981; Meyers, MacMillan, & Yoshida, 1980), conceptual arguments (e.g., Cruickshank, 1977; Mesibov, 1976; Sabatino, 1981; Turnbull *et al.*, 1981), and clinical anecdotes (e.g., Silverman, 1979) in support of their positions. Upon reviewing this literature, probably the most accurate answer to the question of whether mainstreaming is successful is that it depends upon the characteristics of a specific child, the nature of a given program, and the way in which one defines success. This general conclusion holds both for the population of handicapped children at large and for autistic children in particular.

One of the most compelling arguments against the normalization movement has been that individual factors—specifically, the needs of individual children—have not been taken into account. That is, several writers (e.g., Gottlieb, 1981; Mesibov, 1976; Sabatino, 1981) have argued that although the intent of PL 94–142 was to provide a handicapped child with an *appropriate* education in the least restrictive environment, the major emphasis simply has been to place all handicapped children into contact with nonhandicapped children. As Gottlieb (1981) notes: "from a practical perspective, mainstreaming has focused almost exclusively on administrative and process issues. The content of the educational program to which EMR children should be exposed while they are in the mainstream and the specialized methods that may be required to deliver the content have seldom been a major consideration either in the professional literature or in legal degrees" (p. 116).

When individual children's needs in particular classroom placements are not taken into account, the least restrictive environment can be the most restrictive of the child's development (Cruickshank, 1977). "A child placed in a so-called least restrictive situation who is unable to achieve, who lacks an understanding teacher, who does not have appropriate learning materials, who is faced with tasks he cannot manage, whose failure results in negative comments by his classmates, and whose parents reflect frustration to him when he is home, is indeed being restricted on all sides" (Cruickshank, 1977, p. 194).

In short, "normal" environments have been romanticized (Hegarty *et al.*, 1982) when, in fact, they may be appropriate for most handicapped children only under certain conditions. Researchers and educators who work with autistic children, for example, have placed particular emphasis on attending to the individual needs and strengths of a given child when developing educational and therapeutic programs (e.g., Lansing & Schopler, 1978). We will elaborate at a later point in this chapter on some of the social considerations that need to be taken into account in designing programs for both autistic children and populations of handicapped children in general.

Taking into account the limitations inherent in the first mainstreamed school programs established under PL 94–142, what outcomes have these programs achieved thus far? Given the goals originally set for the integration of handicapped and nonhandicapped children—namely, the cognitive and social development of exceptional children and attitude changes in nonhandicapped peers and teachers—how successful have programs been to date? In discussing the outcomes of integration attempts, we first will review data on handicapped populations in general, and then focus on studies of autistic children.

Several reviews of the effects of mainstreamed programs on handicapped children have been published recently (e.g., Corman & Gottlieb, 1978; Kaufman & Alberto, 1977; Meyers, MacMillan, & Yoshida, 1980). Unfortunately for those who are attempting to make decisions about the utility of mainstreamed programs, the methodological limitations of efficacy studies cited in these research reviews are so extensive that it is simply impossible to decide at this time whether mainstreaming programs work. The limitations of these studies include inadequate or biased sampling, inappropriate or unreliable outcome measures, and a lack of attention to instructional techniques or classroom ethos used in different programs (Kaufman & Alberto, 1977; Meyers *et al.*, 1980). These studies also are limited in that they tend to be atheoretical and fail to consider the processes through which particular outcomes may or may not be achieved (Jones, Gottlieb, Guskin, & Yoshida, 1978), and they do not assess the consequences of mainstreamed programs—for both handicapped and nonhandicapped children—using other than short-term longitudinal designs. For the benefit of future research in this area, Jones *et al.* (1978) have discussed many of the limitations of mainstream program efficacy studies and proposed guidelines for the evaluation of such programs that are in keeping with the guidelines set by PL 94–142.

The Effects of Integrating Handicapped Children

Given the problems with this literature, it is not surprising that findings about the success of mainstreaming are inconsistent and ambiguous. Like the earlier studies conducted between the 1930s and 1960s, several recent studies conducted in the mid- to late-1970s reveal no clear-cut benefits in regard to academic achievement for children who are either mainstreamed or educated in special classes (e.g., Budoff & Gottlieb, 1976; O'Leary & Schneider, 1977). Other studies reveal positive gains for children in integrated programs (Ipsa & Matz, 1978) (though no control group was employed) and advantages to integrated as compared with segregated handicapped children (Rodee, 1971; Walker, 1972, cited in Gottlieb, 1981), whereas still other studies reveal poor academic outcomes for EMR children who are educated in integrated settings (Meyers *et al.*, 1980).

In regard to handicapped children's socioemotional functioning, the results of recent studies also are equivocal. Studies of preschoolers in highly structured integrated settings reveal gains in social interaction and play (e.g., Apolloni,

Cooke, & Cooke, 1977; Fredericks *et al.*, 1978). Studies of school-aged handicapped children's social behavior suggest that integrated children's social behavior is the same as (e.g., Pastor & Swap, 1978), or better than, that of segregated children (e.g., Gampel, Gottlieb, & Harrison, 1974; Gottlieb, Gampel, & Budoff, 1975). In keeping with these results, Budoff and Gottlieb (1976) report that integrated mildly handicapped children like school better than do segregated children. Children with lower IQs who are physically handicapped, however, may prefer special classrooms. Finally, in studies of handicapped children's self-concepts, differences, when they are found, tend to favor mainstreamed children (e.g., Carroll, 1967), though other studies reveal no group differences (e.g., Budoff & Gottlieb, 1976).

In contrast to these positive results, studies of handicapped children's acceptance by nonhandicapped peers reveal somewhat negative outcomes. That is, contrary to the expectations that underlie the move toward mainstreaming, children who have contact with handicapped peers in their classrooms view these peers as negatively as, or more negatively than, they do handicapped peers in special classrooms (e.g., Goodman, Gottlieb, & Harrison, 1972; Gottlieb, Cohen, & Goldstein, 1974). In addition, handicapped children are not as well accepted as nonhandicapped children regardless of their placement. Further analyses of this issue reveal that the amount of contact between disabled and nondisabled youngsters and the context of the children's contact may make a difference (Corman & Gottlieb, 1978). When we discuss some of the strategies that have been adopted to overcome problems that arise when handicapped children are placed in regular classrooms, we will see that the issue of handicapped children's relationships with peers has been one of fundamental concern (e.g., Gresham, 1982; Guralnick, 1978; Hoben, 1980).

The Integration of Autistic and Nonhandicapped Children

Thus far our review of the issues and consequences of mainstream school programs has focused on mentally and physically disabled children in general. Only a few studies have addressed the effects of mainstreaming autistic children. While there is encouraging evidence documenting the feasibility of educating groups of autistic children in special classrooms and even of integrating some of these handicapped youngsters into regular classrooms, many school systems exclude autistic children from regular school programs (Halpern, 1970).

One notable exception is North Carolina's statewide system of classroom programs for autistic children and adolescents established under the auspices of Division TEACCH. The parent training approach developed at Division TEACCH, in which parents are taught to assume the role of cotherapists for their autistic children, allows for these disabled children to be reared in the context of their families and, as such, reflects the philosophy behind the least restrictive principle. When the TEACCH program began in 1966, this approach represented a dramatic shift from previous treatments for autistic children, which tended to involve "removal of the child from the [supposedly] damaging impact of the parental home to placement in residential care" (Marcus, Lansing, Andrews, & Schopler, 1978, p. 625). At present, in addition to this parent component, the TEACCH program also includes 32 classrooms for autistic children and adolescents that are located in public schools (Mesibov & Schopler, 1981). These classrooms are self-contained to provide for an individualized instructional program for each child, but in addition, children can participate in the specific regular classroom programs that are appropriate to their needs. The self-contained classrooms also serve as resource rooms for other children in the schools, thus providing a benefit to other students as well as giving the autistic children exposure to nonautistic children within the context of their own classroom (Reichler & Schopler, 1976).

Evaluations of the TEACCH parent program and classrooms have revealed positive consequences for autistic children, their families, and the nondisabled children with whom they have contact at school (McHale, 1983; McHale & Simeonsson, 1980; Schopler, Mesibov, DeVellis, & Short, 1981). Educating autistic children in different kinds of mainstreamed environments is clearly a viable strategy; however, this endeavor presents professionals with some formidable challenges. In this section of the chapter we review some special considerations that pertain to mainstreaming autistic children and then discuss the results of several empirical studies that have assessed the effectiveness of mainstreamed programs for these youngsters.

Mainstreaming autistic children involves both the generic issues related to integrating handicapped children in general and issues related to autism in particular. Autistic children are handicapped and share with other handicapped children a diagnosis, a label, and the fact that they are in need of special services. As is the case with other handicapped children, mainstreaming may prove to be beneficial for autistic children (e.g., because of exposure to appropriate role models and the "nonautistic" curriculum taught in regular classrooms) or detrimental (because of peer rejection, less teacher attention, inappropriate teaching methods and materials, and negative teacher and/or community attitudes). However, autistic children also have unique characteristics. In designing classroom programs for autistic children, educators are confronted with numerous problems that often do not exist, certainly in classrooms for nondisabled children, but even in establishing programs to educate children with other disabling conditions.

The specific characteristics of autistic children have been noted in other chapters. We review them briefly here, however, focusing particularly on those features that are relevant in determining the educational needs of these children (Bartak & Pickering, 1976; Fredericks, Buckley, Baldwin, Moore, & Stemel-Campbell, 1983; Lansing & Schopler, 1978).

1. Delays or problems in language development. Mutism, echolalic speech, and deficits in receptive and expressive speech even after language has developed, are common in autistic children. Such characteristics mean that the usual instructional techniques of regular classroom environments will be inappropriate. These deficits also mean that nonhandicapped peers will experience difficulties in engaging in social interaction and play with autistic children.

2. A general failure to develop social relationships. This characteristic may include a failure to respond to teacher requests, to make eye contact with teacher or peers, to initiate play with peers or form friendships, and to show affection. Taken together, these attributes may be one basis for autistic children's social rejection by nonhandicapped peers or for negative attitudes expressed by regular classroom teachers.

3. Inappropriate and/or ritualistic and repetitive behaviors. These may include such behaviors as standing up in the middle of an activity and walking around or out of the room, manipulation of fingers or rhythmic stereotypic activities with objects, and self-injurious behaviors. Again, such behaviors lessen the chances of positive social interactions with nonhandicapped peers and increase the chances of social rejection. In addition, they interfere with teachers' attempts to instill cognitive gains and increase the likelihood of teacher–child interactions that involve disciplinary actions.

4. Isolated areas of high-level functioning (e.g., visual-spatial skills) in children who otherwise show marked retardation in other areas of functioning. For teachers and children who interact with autistic children, the presence of certain skills in combination with these children's generally good gross motor skills and "intelligent physiognomies" (Kanner, 1943) may lead to higher expectations for these children's performance in areas in which the children display marked deficiencies. When autistic children fail to meet those expectations, more negative attitudes in regular classroom teachers and peers may result. On the other hand, given the importance of physical activity in the play and social interaction of young children and the role of physical attractiveness in peer popularity and acceptance, autistic children may have some advantage over other handicapped children in regard to peer attitudes, at least in the early grades.

5. Apparent deficits in responding to environmental stimuli, including a tendency to respond only to visual or auditory cues (overselectivity). This attribute, again, means that regular classroom instructional strategies and materials may be inappropriate for teaching autistic children.

As this inventory of potential deficit areas indicates, there is tremendous variation in the types and severity of autism: variations that the single label "autistic" obscures. As we saw in the case of the general population of handicapped children, educational programs for autistic children must be chosen with the needs and strengths of the individual child in mind. To date, research on autistic children in integrated classroom settings has not dealt explicitly with this issue. Some work shows that the effects of integration may be positive, mostly in terms of fostering appropriate social behavior in the classroom and acceptance of nonhandicapped peers. Although autistic children are rarely placed in regular school classrooms for their academic work, some studies have investigated potential means through which this might be feasible. We discuss cognitive and social acquisitions by autistic children in integrated environments in the following pages.

Fostering Cognitive Growth in Integrated Settings. In terms of fostering autistic children's cognitive growth, working in a highly structured one-to-one setting has been shown to be an effective technique for teaching autistic children a variety of skills (Lansing & Schopler, 1978). When discussing mainstreaming, however, two problems arise in using this procedure. First, what is taught during one-to-one training sessions frequently does not involve those prerequisite skills that are necessary for learning in groups. Second, implementing this approach in a public school system is cost-prohibitive. Recent investigations, however, suggest some viable means for overcoming the disadvantages of one-to-one instruction in relation to integrating autistic children into regular school classrooms for academic work.

In relation to the first issue, it is clear that if autistic children are to succeed in classroom environments, they will need to learn how to behave and how to learn in groups. Koegel and Rincover (1974) have developed a strategy for teaching autistic children such skills. These investigators, using behavior modification techniques, taught eight autistic children in one-to-one (child-to-teacher) preliminary sessions some basic skills necessary in the classroom, such as sitting quietly, imitation or echoing word sounds when prompted, or responding to the teacher's requests. Performance of these skills in two groups, with ratios of eight children to one teacher and two children to one teacher, then were assessed while the one-to-one training sessions were continued throughout the time the children were being observed in the larger groups.

The initial findings revealed that the classroom skills taught in the one-to-one sessions were not exhibited consistently in the larger group of eight children or even in groups of two children with one teacher. When an alternative procedure was introduced, however (one that involved gradually reducing the schedule of reinforcement for appropriate responding in the one-to-one sessions and gradually increasing the group size), appropriate classroom behaviors were observed. The results of this study suggest that training children in basic classroom skills prior to creating groups for academic instruction, while more beneficial than simply bringing these children together and expecting changes, was still ineffective. Teaching classroom skills in one-to-one sessions while successively thinning the schedule of reinforcers and increasing the size of the group, however, was a technique that facilitated appropriate classroom behavior.

Another study of relevance here involved training a 5-year-old autistic child, using operant techniques, to display appropriate behavior in a regular classroom in an effort to create an effective mainstreamed program (Russo &

Koegel, 1977). In this study, a therapist initially was present in the classroom, dispensing tokens (that later could be exchanged for food rewards) for appropriate classroom and social responses. During this treatment phase it was observed that the child's self-stimulatory behavior declined while the number of social behaviors and expected classroom responses increased. Between the 14th and 15th weeks of the program, the kindergarten teacher was trained in behavioral techniques; also during this time the density of token reinforcers was reduced. By the 16th week, the regular classroom teacher successfully took over treatment and the distribution of tokens, and the levels of appropriate school behaviors were maintained.

At the end of the kindergarten year, the child was graduated to the first grade. Upon her entry into first grade, behavioral assessments indicated that the child's social behaviors had decreased, while her self-stimulatory behaviors had increased since kindergarten. Retreatment by the therapist and training of the first grade teacher again proved effective: Improvements in the child's behaviors were observed and maintained. These researchers report that no further problems occurred during the first grade, and that the child successfully completed her second- and third-grade years, even though she had different teachers who had not been trained in the behavioral techniques.

In sum, integration of autistic children into classes with nonhandicapped children, though necessitating considerable effort on the part of therapists and teachers alike, does seem possible. The generalizability of these results (the effectiveness of this type of program for other autistic children), however, remains to be determined. Even if such procedures do prove effective, the question of cost and time effectiveness eventually must be considered. Although children can function adequately in classrooms without retreatments or teacher training, the initial intensive involvement of both therapists and teachers still may prove to be prohibitive in instigating this type of program. One potential means of reducing the direct involvement of teachers and therapists, however, would be to involve other persons in the child's social environment. Various investigators have recognized the utility of educating parents of autistic children to facilitate maintenance of appropriate behavior as well as to provide additional training for their children (Lovaas, Koegel, Simmons, & Long, 1973; Marcus *et al.*, 1978).

In addition, within the classroom, peers may play a significant role in ensuring that autistic children have successful classroom experiences. Nonhandicapped classmates may be directly involved in fostering academic-like skills in autistic children by becoming models or tutors for their handicapped peers. Three studies have shown, for instance, that nonhandicapped peer models can improve autistic children's speech and language (Coleman & Stedman, 1974) and foster their learning on receptive labeling tasks (Charlop, Schreibman, & Tyran, 1983) and discrimination tasks (Egel, Richman, & Koegel, 1981). Caution must be exercised in drawing conclusions about the efficacy of this technique, in part, because of the small number of children studied (five children in all across the two investigations). Nonetheless, the findings are encouraging.

The effectiveness of using children as tutors has been demonstrated with learning-disabled and socially disadvantaged youth (e.g., Cloward, 1972; Gartner, Kohler, & Riesman, 1971), and recently, evidence has emerged to suggest that nonhandicapped children also may be able to tutor autistic children. Two projects have demonstrated that peer tutors were effective in increasing positive social behaviors (Strain, Kerr, & Ragland, 1979) (an area of competence we will discuss later in greater detail) and in reducing off-task and increasing on-task behaviors in a task involving color and pattern matching (McHale, Olley, Marcus, & Simeonsson, 1981). Once again, the preliminary nature of this research must be stressed. In the Strain *et al.* work, the increase in positive behaviors did not generalize to a different setting. McHale *et al.*, however, noted that at least one form of generalization occurred. That is, the autistic children were able to use "cognitive" skills they had acquired through teachers' instruction in a different setting, i.e., with their peers.

Fostering Social Gains in Autistic Children in Integrated Settings. Peers also may be effective behavior change agents in meeting a second important goal of integrated classroom programs, that is, instilling appropriate social behavior in these children. Several of the TEACCH classrooms described earlier, for instance, regularly provide for contact between autistic children and children from regular school classrooms (see McHale & Boone, 1980). The mechanisms through which peers may promote appropriate social behavior in autistic children include social reinforcement, modeling, and possibly the egalitarian and playful context of peer interaction (McHale, 1983). A number of studies have examined the effects on autistic children of interacting with nonhandicapped peers (e.g., Lord, 1984; McHale, 1983; Strain *et al.*, 1979), and the results of these studies may be considered as evidence of the efficacy of "mainstreaming" for promoting appropriate social behavior in autistic children.

A major difficulty in teaching autistic children is that they do not show an intrinsic interest in learning, and the extrinsic contingencies normally effective in a classroom setting—such as a smile, a pat on the back, verbal praise, or showing disappointment—are generally ineffective in promoting desired behavior changes (Ferster, 1961; Lovaas, Schaeffer, & Simmons, 1965). Many treatment programs have relied on primary reinforcers, such as giving or withholding food, as a means of motivating these children. The problem, however, as noted by a number of investigators (Ferster, 1967; Koegel & Rincover, 1977; Lovaas & Newson, 1976) is that such extrinsic reinforcers are artificial, in that they do not occur in the child's natural environment (i.e., the classroom). Gains made in training settings disappear or behaviors that are extinguished in the training settings reappear unless reinforcers remain constant across these settings. Obviously, the continued use of pretzels, raisins, and candy in the classroom is cumbersome and restrictive. The establishment of secondary or conditioned reinforcers, where social events between autistic children and their teachers and peers maintain previously learned behaviors and enhance further learning, is a necessary step toward mainstreaming.

One technique that has been used to overcome this problem involves pairing primary and secondary reinforcers (saying "good job" while offering edibles), and eventually eliminating the primary contingencies. An alternative method is to gradually introduce natural consequences (at least in the latter stages of training) (Fredericks *et al.*, 1983). Using these methods, students learn what consequences will operate in other contexts.

Beyond these operant paradigms, the reinforcement value of social stimuli has particular significance with regard to the role of observational learning or modeling in autistic children's development. A large number of studies have examined the role peers can play in the development, maintenance, and modification of nonhandicapped children's behavioral patterns, especially their function as reinforcing agents (Hartup, 1970). In keeping with these findings, researchers became interested in the potential of nonhandicapped peers as agents of behavior change for handicapped children, and in several recent investigations nonhandicapped peers have served as the primary agents of change in educational or therapeutic programs for children with a number of different types of handicapping conditions (Guralnick, 1978).

The utility of employing reinforcement or modeling techniques with autistic children initially was doubted, however, as these youngsters tend to be unresponsive to social stimuli, and mere togetherness of autistic and nonhandicapped children, it was thought, would not be sufficient to produce positive behavior changes (e.g., Strain & Cooke, 1976). Furthermore, assessments of observational learning of low-functioning autistic children with adult models showed that only a small portion of the adult-modeled responses are learned by these children (Metz, 1965; Varni, Lovaas, Koegel, & Everett, 1979), although the dissimilarity of model characteristics such as age or gender may have directly affected the probability of the model being imitated (Varni *et al.*, 1979).

Despite these concerns, several investigators recently have demonstrated the effectiveness of using peers in structured and unstructured interactions with autistic children in increasing positive social and communication behaviors (Lord, 1984; McHale, 1983; Ragland, Kerr, & Strain, 1978; Strain *et al.*, 1979). In the studies by Strain and his colleagues (Ragland *et al.*, 1978; Strain *et al.*, 1978), peers were trained explicitly to direct social interactions toward autistic children or use prompting and social reinforcement with these children. Both techniques were effective in increasing autistic children's rate of positive social behavior, though no generalization (to no-treatment play sessions) was observed.

Investigations by Lord (1984) and McHale (1983) more closely approximated the environment of the regular school classroom. In Lord's (1984) investigation, autistic children were grouped in triads (with two nonhandicapped peers) for special play sessions. Although the nonhandicapped children were given a minimum of instruction on how to interact with the autistic children, increases in the children's social behavior as well as generalizations to play with autistic classmates were observed. Further analyses revealed that same-age nonhandicapped peers were more effective in eliciting social behavior from the autistic children than were younger children.

McHale (1983) observed a special class of six low-functioning autistic children during 30-minute play sessions with six same-aged nonhandicapped children. Different groups of nonhandicapped youngsters came to the autistic children's classroom each day for a week to play and were given a minimum of instruction about how to interact with the children. (They were told that it was their job to teach the autistic children to play.) Over 10 week of observations, social behavior by the autistic children increased and solitary behavior decreased.

Variations in the samples included in these studies enable at least a preliminary consideration of the question of whether such positive benefits may not be possible for all autistic children or all nonhandicapped peers. Individual child characteristics, such as the child's language abilities, degree of social isolation, frequency of self-stimulatory behaviors, as well as the classroom environment and the nonhandicapped model's attitudes or feelings about interacting with the handicapped child, all may influence the success of modeling and reinforcement techniques. However, these investigations have demonstrated that both high-functioning (Egel *et al.*, 1981) and low-functioning (Lord, 1984) autistic children will be responsive to behaviors of same-aged normal and autistic peers, and to a lesser extent, children younger than themselves. In addition, it is important to recognize that two of these studies found that peers served as effective behavior change agents without being trained to do so (Lord, 1984; McHale, 1983). Thus, although we find that autistic children generally may be unresponsive to social stimuli unless otherwise trained, they appear to be receptive to another form of social stimuli—that is, social stimuli and social reinforcers for peers.

Fostering Nonhandicapped Peers' Positive Attitudes toward Autistic Children. In addition to the effects of mainstreaming on autistic children, nonhandicapped peers also may respond positively to integration experiences. For instance, a public school in Tallahassee, Florida (Campbell, Scaturro, & Lickson, 1983), recently instituted a program designed to encourage nonhandicapped students to play a part in the education of their autistic peers. A peer tutoring program was formed, and interested students volunteered to participate. Although the information on the effects of their experiences as peer tutors is primarily anecdotal, it appears as though the tutors felt very positive about involvement, especially in their roles as advocates and their ability to change the attitudes of their peers toward the autistic children.

These findings are in keeping with another study of nonhandicapped peers' attitudes toward autistic children (McHale & Simeonsson, 1980). In this study, school-age children's attitudes toward and understanding of autistic children were assessed before and after a week of daily half-hour play sessions with same-aged autistic peers. Results revealed that the children's attitudes were highly favorable on both occasions and that children's understanding of the autistic children's abilities and disabilities increased over the week of contact. Further analyses revealed that children's initial understanding of autistic children was correlated with the frequency with which the children attempted to communicate (in verbal and nonverbal ways) with the autistic youngsters.

These findings are inconsistent with the results of research discussed earlier on children's attitudes toward handicapped peers. It may be that autistic children are accepted more readily than other handicapped children because of their gross motor skills, which are important in the play interactions of school-age children and their general physical attractiveness, an attribute shown to be of importance in many studies of peer popularity.

Another basis may be in the way attitudes were measured in these studies. Many attitude studies employ sociometric techniques that implicitly or explicitly require children to rate their handicapped peers *relative to* their nonhandicapped peers. In contrast, in the latter studies of children's attitudes toward autistic peers, youngsters simply were asked about their feelings toward the autistic children. We would argue that fostering *positive* attitudes toward handicapped children—not fostering *the same* attitudes as are displayed toward nonhandicapped peers—is the most appropriate goal for mainstreamed school programs.

Finally, and perhaps most important, the context in which mainstreaming occurred in the two studies described here may have been responsible for the children's positive attitudes. In both programs children were recruited to "help" the autistic children. In a context in which altruistic behavior is expected of nonhandicapped children and in which they can feel good about successful interactions they may have with their handicapped peers, the deviant and often frustrating behaviors that autistic (or other disabled) children often display may become less important.

In sum, these studies demonstrate that when integration occurs under certain conditions, children will express positive attitudes toward disabled peers. Given that fostering such positive attitudes is one important goal of PL 94–142, we would argue that mainstreaming should take place specifically in those contexts in which accepting attitudes on the parts of nonhandicapped youngsters will arise. Moving children from special to regular classrooms does not, in itself, lead to the outcomes intended by PL 94–142 and those desired by parents and professionals. The goals of integration will be met only if specific strategies are developed to achieve particular desirable outcomes such as academic and social growth in disabled children and acceptance and understanding of handicapping conditions in nondisabled youngsters. In the final section of this chapter we review some important considerations for implementing mainstreamed programs, and describe attempts to overcome some of the difficulties that arise in integrating handicapped and nonhandicapped children.

STRATEGIES TO ENHANCE THE EFFECTIVENESS OF MAINSTREAM PROGRAMS

Until recently, in many school districts mainstreaming has meant that "special educators are more involved with placing children in the least restrictive environment than with educating them [and their handicapped peers] in the least restrictive environment" (Gottlieb, 1981, p. 122). Lately, however, a number of articles have appeared in the literature that have outlined effective strategies for implementing integrated classroom programs. These writings have stressed (1) the importance of preparation for all involved—administrators, teachers, and handicapped and nonhandicapped children alike—prior to the implementation of the program (Hegarty *et al.*, 1982; Simpson & Edwards, 1980); (2) the importance of flexibility in establishing different contexts for integration (Gottlieb, 1981; Mesibov, 1976); and (3) the importance of working actively to promote positive contact between handicapped and nonhandicapped children (Gresham, 1982; Guralnick, 1978; Hoben, 1980; Snyder, Apolloni, & Cooke, 1977).

At the highest level, school administrators must be helped to understand the needs of teachers in mainstreamed classrooms and the demands that will be placed upon them so that they may effectively support teachers in their endeavors to provide an appropriate education for all children in the mainstreamed environment (Cruickshank, 1977; Hegarty *et al.*, 1982). This support should be effective but also practical—such as reducing class size or providing days off for teachers attending special in-service training programs (Powers, 1983). Teachers report that they require instruction and assistance in dealing with children who display severe academic deficits and problematic classroom behavior (Meyers *et al.*, 1980), and it is up to school administrators to provide the necessary resources if integrated programs are to work.

In fact, the importance of preparing regular classroom teachers for mainstreaming is paramount. Many writers, for instance, have stressed the necessity of establishing rapport between special and regular education teachers (Simpson & Edwards, 1980) and fostering in teachers supportive attitudes toward integrated programs (Larrivee, 1981; Powers, 1983; Schopler & Olley, 1980). This may mean including regular classroom teachers in decision making and program development relevant to the special child's placement, providing training for regular classroom teachers regarding strategies for working with special children (e.g., Dunlap, Koegel, & Egel, 1979), and establishing opportunities for support, consultation, and feedback from resource personnel subsequent to a child's placement (Simpson & Edwards, 1980). As many researchers and educators have noted, handicapped children will not be able to make academic and social gains simply by being placed in regular classrooms; appropriate curricula and instructional strategies also must be implemented and this requires extensive training of the teachers involved.

One of the most significant roles of the regular classroom teacher is structuring the classroom program to promote the social integration of handicapped and nonhandicapped children. Observations of children in mainstreamed classrooms have shown repeatedly that simply placing handicapped and nonhandicapped children in proximity to one another will not result in positive interactions between the two groups (e.g., Allen, Benning, & Drummond, 1972; Devoney, Guralnick, & Rubin, 1974). Guralnick (1978) describes two approaches for facilitating children's interaction. The first focuses on curricular or programmatic characteristics and the second on training handicapped children in social behaviors and activities so that they will be able to behave appropriately once they join the regular group. An additional strategy that seems important is to prepare *nonhandicapped* children so that they will be more willing and able to become involved in positive ways with their disabled peers.

Curricular or programmatic approaches to fostering social integration include, most importantly, a careful choice of the context or activities in which integration occurs. Involving a small number of disabled and nondisabled children in special projects or recreational activities (Aloia, Beaver, & Pettus, 1978; Ballard, Corman, Gottlieb, & Kaufman, 1977; Chennault, 1967; Johnson, Johnson, DeWeerdt, Lyons, & Zaidman, 1983; Lilly, 1971; McDaniel, 1970; Rucker & Vincenzo, 1970; Stainbeck, Stainbeck, & Jaben, 1981) is one effective strategy for fostering social interaction and positive attitudes of nonhandicapped children toward disabled peers. The development of such activities for use with severely handicapped and nonhandicapped students is described by Brown *et al.*, (1979). An alternative approach is to design activities in which nonhandicapped children are given a special invitation to become involved in activities with handicapped children in the capacity of teacher helpers (e.g., McHale, 1983; Poorman, 1980). Other programmatic considerations for fostering social integration include the nature of the classroom's physical layout and equipment (Hoben, 1980; Twardosz, Cataldo, & Risley, 1974), and encouragement and reinforcement by teachers (Fredericks *et al.*, 1978; Guralnick, 1978; Hegarty *et al.*, 1982; Hoben, 1980).

To promote handicapped children's acceptance in the regular classroom and to enable them to profit from their instruction in that context, these children also must be prepared for their mainstream program. For instance, giving students experience with materials used in the regular classroom and with instructional styles employed (e.g., amounts and forms of teacher attention and feedback) may aid in the children's adjustment (Simpson & Edwards, 1980). In addition, disabled children may be provided with training in social skills through modeling, reinforcement, role playing, and coaching techniques so that their behavior is more in keeping with the expectations of nondisabled peers (Gresham, 1982; Russo & Koegel, 1977; Snyder *et al.*, 1977).

Handicapped children are not the only ones who need to be prepared for mainstreamed classrooms. Unless professionals attend to the attitudes and potential reactions of nondisabled youngsters, one of the primary goals of the mainstreaming movement, promoting positive societal attitudes toward individuals who are handicapped, cannot be achieved. Investigators have described several attempts to promote positive attitudes toward handicapped children (e.g., Gottlieb, 1981; Schroeder, 1978; Westervelt & McKinney, 1980). Components these programs seem to have in common are that children are provided with an understanding of a specific handicapping condition and the limitations it imposes on a child, but also, that they are given opportunities to appreciate what they have in common with a disabled peer regardless of the nature or extent of his or her handicapping condition. Like teachers, parents, and other family members, children need to be taught that a handicapping condition is one, but not necessarily the most important, characteristic of a child.

Finally, in addition to those who are directly involved in mainstreamed school classrooms, some researchers have noted the importance of educating parents about this process (Hegarty *et al.*, 1982; Simpson & Edwards, 1980; van Breukelen, 1980). Providing parents with information about the program in which their child will be involved and giving parents the opportunity to meet with the regular classroom teacher may encourage parents to act as partners in the educational process, a strategy that ultimately will be of benefit to the child.

CONCLUSIONS

This review of research on mainstreaming handicapped children suggests that the potential advantages of mainstreamed school programs can be achieved only when programs are designed with the strengths and needs of individual children in mind and when special care is taken to prepare all those involved with the child's educational experiences. If mainstreaming is to be an educational strategy and not just a classroom placement, educational administrators, teachers, and researchers will need to work toward developing programs that will be effective for particular children. This promises to be a costly endeavor, however, in terms of time, energy, and monetary resources. As yet, it does not appear that mainstreaming programs, as they currently are implemented, have had detrimental effects on children's social and academic functioning; neither, however, have the original goals of mainstreamed school programs been met with unequivocal success. The mandate of PL 94–142, to educate handicapped children in the least restrictive environment, represents a formidable challenge, and indeed, it would be simpleminded to expect that the task will be easy.

REFERENCES

Abeson, A. (1980). The implementation of PL 94–142: From infancy forward. *Journal of Special Education, 15,* 33–38.

Allen, K., Benning, P., & Drummond, T. (1972). Integration of normal and handicapped children in a behavior modification preschool: A case study. In G. Semb (Ed.), *Behavioral analysis and education.* Lawrence, Kansas: University of Kansas Press.

Aloia, G., Beaver, R., & Pettus, W. (1978). Increasing initial interactions among integrated EMR students and their nonretarded peers in a game-playing situation. *American Journal of Mental Deficiency, 82,* 573–579.

Apolloni, T., Cooke, S., & Cooke, T. (1977). Establishing a normal peer as a behavioral model for developmentally disabled toddlers. *Perceptual and Motor Skills, 44,* 231–241.

Ballard, M., Corman, L., Gottlieb, J., & Kaufman, M. A. (1977). Improving the social status of mainstreamed retarded children. *Journal of Educational Psychology, 69,* 605–611.

Bartak, L., & Pickering, C. (1976). Aims and methods of teaching. In M. P. Everand (Ed.), *Some approaches to teaching autistic children.* Oxford: Pergamon Press.

Bricker, D. (1978). A rationale for the integration of handicapped and nonhandicapped preschool children. In M. Guralnick (Ed.), *Early intervention and the integration of handicapped and nonhandicapped children.* Baltimore: University Park Press.

Brodinsky, B. (1979). Something happened: Education in the seventies. *Phi Delta Kappan, 61,* 238–241.

Brown, L., Branston, M., Baumgart, D., Vincent, L., Falvey, M., & Schroeder, J. (1979). Utilizing characteristics of a variety of current and subsequent least restrictive environments as factors in the development of curricular content for severely handicapped students. *AAESPH Review, 4,* 407–424.

Budoff, M., & Gottlieb, J. (1976). Special class students mainstreamed: A study of an aptitude (learning potential) x treatment interaction. *American Journal of Mental Deficiency, 81,* 1–11.

Campbell, A., Scaturro, J., & Lickson, J. (1983). Peer tutors help autistic children enter the mainstream. *Teaching Exceptional Children, 15,* 64–69.

Carroll, A. (1967). The effects of segregated and partially integrated school programs on self-concept and academic achievement of educable mental retardates. *Exceptional Children, 34,* 93–99.

Charlop, M., Schreibman, Li, & Tryan, A. (1983). Learning through observation: The effects of peer modeling on acquisition and generalization in autistic children. *Journal of Abnormal Child Psychology, 11,* 355–366.

Chennault, J. (1967). Improving the social acceptance of unpopular mentally retarded pupils in special classes. *American Journal of Mental Deficiency, 72,* 455–458.

Cloward, R., (1972). Studies in tutoring. *Journal of Experimental Education, 36,* 14–25.

Coleman, S. L., & Stedman, J. M. (1974). Use of a peer model in language training in an echolalic child. *Journal of Behavior Therapy and Experimental Psychiatry, 5,* 275–279.

Corman, L., & Gottlieb, J. (1978). Mainstreaming mentally retarded children: A review of research. In N. R. Ellis (Ed.), *International review of research in mental retardation* (Vol. 9). New York: Academic Press.

Cruickshank, W., (1977). Least restrictive placement: Administrative wishful thinking. *Journal of Learning Disabilities, 10*, 193–194.

Devoney, C., Guralnick, M., & Rubin, H. (1974). Integrating handicapped and nonhandicapped preschool children: Effects on social play. *Childhood Education, 50*, 360–364.

Dunlap, G., Koegel, R., & Egel, A. (1979). Autistic children in school. *Exceptional Children, 45*, 552–558.

Dunn, L. (1968). Special education for the mildly retarded: Is much of it justifiable? *Exceptional Children, 35*, 5–22.

Egel, A. L., Richman, G. S., & Koegel, R. L. (1981). Normal peer models and autistic children's learning. *Journal of Applied Behavior Analysis, 14*, 3–12.

Ferster, C. (1961). Positive reinforcement and behavioral deficits in autistic children. *Child Development, 32*, 437–456.

Ferster, C. (1967). Arbitrary and natural reinforcement. *Psychological Record, 17*, 341–347.

Fredericks, H., Baldwin, V., Grove, D., Moore, W., Riggs, C., & Lyons, G. (1978). Integrating the moderately and severely handicapped preschool child into a normal day care setting. In M. Guralnick (Ed.), *Early intervention and the integration of handicapped and nonhandicapped children*. Baltimore: University Park Press.

Fredericks, H., Buckley, J., Baldwin, V., Moore, W., & Stemel-Campbell, K. (1983). The educational needs of the autistic adolescent. In E. Schopler & G. Mesibov (Eds.), *Autism in adolescents and adults*. New York: Plenum Press.

Gampel, D., Gottlieb, T., & Harrison, R. (1974). A comparison of the classroom behaviors of special class EMR, integrated EMR, low IQ and nonretarded children. *American Journal of Mental Deficiency, 79*, 16–21.

Gartner, A., Kohler, M., & Riesman, F. (1971). *Children teach children*. New York: Harper & Row.

Goodman, H., Gottlieb, J., & Harrison, R. (1972). Social acceptance of EMR's integrated into a non-graded elementary school. *American Journal of Mental Deficiency, 76*, 412–417.

Gottlieb, J. (1981). Mainstreaming: Fulfilling the promise? *American Journal of Mental Deficiency, 86*, 115–126.

Gottlieb, J., Cohen, L., & Goldstein, L. (1974). Social contact and personal adjustment as variables relating to attitudes toward EMR children. *Training School Bulletin, 71*, 9–16.

Gottlieb, J., Gampel, D., & Budoff, M. (1975). Classroom behavior of retarded children before and after reintegration into regular classes. *Journal of Special Education, 9*, 307–315.

Gottlieb, J., & Leyser, Y. (n.d.). *Friendship between mentally retarded and non-retarded children*. Unpublished manuscript, Northern Illinois University.

Gresham, G. (1982). Misguided mainstreaming: The case for social skills training with handicapped children. *Exceptional Children, 48*, 422–433.

Guralnick, M. (1978). Integrated preschools as educational and therapeutic environments: Concepts design and analyses. In M. Guralnick (Ed.), *Early intervention and the integration of handicapped and nonhandicapped children*. Baltimore: University Park Press.

Halpern, W. I. (1970). The schooling of autistic children: Preliminary findings. *American Journal of Orthopsychiatry, 40*, 665–671.

Hartup, W. W. (1970). Peer interaction and social organization. In P. Mussen (Ed.), *Carmichael's manual of child psychology* (Vol. 2). New York: Wiley.

Hegarty, S., Pocklington, K., & Lucas, D. (1982). *Educating pupils with special needs in the ordinary school*. Windsor, Berkshire: NFER-Nelson.

Hoben, M. (1980). Toward integration in the mainstream. *Exceptional Children, 47*, 100–105.

Ipsa, J., & Matz, R. (1978). Integrating handicapped preschool children within a cognitively oriented curriculum. In M. Guralnick (Ed.), *Early intervention and the integration of handicapped and nonhandicapped children*. Baltimore: University Park Press.

Johnson, R., Johnson, D., DeWeerdt, N., Lyons, V., & Zaidman, B. (1983). Integrating several adaptively handicapped seventh grade students into constructive relationships with nonhandicapped peers in science class. *American Journal of Mental Deficiency, 6,* 611–618.

Jones, R., Gottlieb, J., Guskin, S., & Yoshida, R. (1978). Evaluating mainstreaming programs: Models, caveats, considerations, and guidelines. *Exceptional Children, 44,* 588–603.

Kanner, L. (1943). Autistic disturbances of affective contact. *Nervous Child, 2,* 217.

Kaufman, M., & Alberto, P. (1977). Research on efficacy of special education for the mentally retarded. In N. R. Ellis (Ed.), *International review of research in mental retardation* (Vol. 8). New York: Academic Press.

Koegel, R. L., & Rincover, A. (1974). Treatment of psychotic children in a classroom environment: I. Learning in a large group. *Journal of Applied Behavior Analysis, 7,* 45–59.

Lance, W. (1976). Who are all the children? *Exceptional Children, 43,* 66–77.

Lansing, M., & Schopler, E. (1978). Individualized education: A public school model. In M. Rutter & E. Schopler (Eds.), *Autism: A reappraisal of concepts and treatment.* New York: Plenum Press.

Larrivee, B. (1981). Effect of inservice training intensity on teachers' attitudes toward mainstreaming. *Exceptional Children, 48,* 34–39.

Lilly, M. (1971). Improving social acceptance of low sociometric states, low achieving students. *Exceptional Children, 37,* 341–347.

Lord, C. (1984). Peer interaction of autistic children. In F. J. Morrison, C. Lord, & D. Keating (Eds.), *Advances in applied developmental psychology.* New York: Academic Press.

Lovaas, O. I., Koegel, R. L., Simmons, J. Q., & Long, J. (1973). Some generalizations and follow-up measures on autistic children in behavior therapy. *Journal of Applied Behavior Analysis, 6,* 131–166.

Lovaas, O. I., & Newson, C. D. (1976). Behavior modification with psychotic children. In H. Leitenberg (Ed.), *Handbook of behavior modification and behavior therapy.* Englewood Cliffs, NJ: Prentice-Hall.

Lovaas, O., Schaeffer, B., & Simmons, J. (1965). Building social behavior in autistic children by use of electric shock. *Journal of Experimental Research and Personality, 1,* 99–109.

Marcus, L. M., Lansing, M., Andrews, C., & Schopler, E. (1978). Improvement of teaching effectiveness in parents of autistic children. *Journal of the American Academy of Child Psychiatry, 17,* 625–639.

McDaniel, C. (1970). Participation in extracurricular activities, social acceptance, and social rejection among educable mentally retarded students. *Education and Training of the Mentally Retarded, 5,* 4–14.

McHale, S. (1983). Changes in autistic children's social behavior as a function of interaction with nonhandicapped children. *American Journal of Orthopsychiatry, 53,* 81–91.

McHale, S., & Boone, W. (1980). Play between autistic and nonhandicapped children: An innovative approach to mainstreaming. *Pointer, 24,* 28–33.

McHale, S., Olley, J., Marcus, L., & Simeonsson, R. (1981). Nonhandicapped peers as tutors for autistic children. *Exceptional Children, 48,* 263–264.

McHale, S., & Simeonsson, R. (1980). Effects of interaction on nonhandicapped children's attitudes toward autistic children. *American Journal of Mental Deficiency, 85,* 18–24.

Mesibov, G. (1976). Implications of the normalization principle for psychotic children. *Journal of Autism and Childhood Schizophrenia, 6,* 359–364.

Mesibov, G., & Schopler, E. (1981, March). Community-based programs for autistic adolescents. In A. Cain (Chair), *Community programs for the treatment of severely disturbed adolescents.* Paper presented at the meeting of the American Orthopsychiatric Association, New York.

Metz, J. R. (1965). Conditioning generalized imitation in autistic children. *Journal of Experimental Child Psychology, 2,* 389–399.

Meyers, D., MacMillan, E., & Yoshida, R. (1980). Regular class education of EMR students from efficacy to mainstreaming: A review of issues and research. In J. Gottlieb (Ed.), *Educating mentally retarded persons in the mainstream.* Baltimore: University Park Press.

O'Leary, S., & Schneider, M. (1977). Special class placement for conduct problem children. *Exceptional Children, 44,* 24–30.

Pastor, D., & Swap, S. (1978). An ecological study of emotionally disturbed preschoolers in special and regular classes. *Exceptional Children, 45,* 213–215.

Poorman, C. (1980). Mainstreaming in reverse with a special friend. *Teaching Exceptional Children, 12,* 136–142.

Powers, D. (1983). Mainstreaming and the inservice education of teachers. *Exceptional Children, 49,* 432–439.

Ragland, E., Kerr, M., & Strain, P. (1978). Effects of peer social initiations on the behavior of withdrawn autistic. *Behavior Modification, 2,* 565–578.

Reichler, R., & Schopler, E. (1976). Developmental therapy: A program model for providing individual services in the community. In E. Schopler & R. Reichler (Eds.), *Psychopathology and child development.* New York: Plenum Press.

Rincover, A., & Koegel, R. L. (1977). Research on the education of autistic children: Recent advances and future directions. In B. B. Lahey & A. E. Kazdin (Eds.), *Advances in clinical child psychology* (Vol. 1). New York: Plenum Press.

Rodee, M. (1971). *A study to evaluate the resource teacher concept when used with high level educable retardates at a primary level.* Unpublished doctoral dissertation, University of Iowa.

Rucker, C., & Vincenzo, F. (1970). Mainstreaming social acceptance gains made by mentally retarded children. *Exceptional Children, 36,* 679–680.

Russo, D. C., & Koegel, R. L. (1977). A method for integrating an autistic child into a normal public school classroom. *Journal of Applied Behavior Analysis, 10,* 579–590.

Rutter, M., & Bartak, L. (1973). Special educational treatment of autistic children: A comprehensive study. II. Follow-up findings and implications for services. *Journal of Child Psychology and Psychiatry, 14,* 241–270.

Sabatino, D. (1981). Are appropriate educational programs operationally achievable under mandated promises of PL 94–142? *Journal of Special Education, 15*(1), 9–23.

Schopler, E., & Bristol, M. B. (1980). Autistic children in public schools. Reston, VA: ERIC Clearinghouse on Handicapped and Gifted Children.

Schopler, E., & Mesibov, G. (Eds.). (1984). *The effects of autism on the family.* New York: Plenum Press.

Schopler, E.,Mesibov, G., DeVellis, R., & Short, A. (1981). A treatment outcome for autistic children and their families. In P. Mittler (Ed.), *Frontiers of knowledge in mental retardation: Proceedings of the Fifth Congress of IASSMC, Vol. I. Social, educational, and behavioral aspects* (pp. 293–301). Baltimore: University Park Press.

Schopler, E., & Olley, J. G. (1980). Comprehensive educational services for autistic children: The TEACCH Model. In C. R. Reynolds & T. B. Gutkin (Eds.), *Handbook of school psychology.* New York: Wiley.

Schroeder, C. (1978, August). *The psychologist's role in PL 94–142: Consultation strategies with peer groups of handicapped children.* Paper presented as part of the symposium Pediatric Psychology: School as a Mental Health Provider, American Psychological Association, Eighty-sixth annual convention, Toronto Canada.

Silverman, M. (1979). Beyond the mainstream: The special needs of the chronic child patient. *American Journal of Orthopsychiatry, 49,* 62–68.

Simpson, R., & Edwards, L. (1980). Mainstreaming behavior disordered students: A perspective. *Journal of Research and Developmental in Education, 13,* 58–73.

Stainbeck, W., Stainbeck, T., & Jaben, T. (1981). Providing opportunities for interaction between severely handicapped and nonhandicapped students. *Teaching Exceptional Children, 13,* 72–75.

Strain, P. (1977). An experimental analysis of peer social initiations on the behavior of withdrawn preschool children: Some training and generalization effects. *Journal of Abnormal Child Psychology, 5,* 445–456.

Strain, P., & Cooke, T. (1976). An observational investigation of two elementary-age autistic children during free play. *Psychology in the Schools, 13,* 82–91.

Strain, P., Kerr, M., & Ragland, E. (1979). Effects of peer-mediated social initiations and prompting/reinforcement on the social behavior of autistic children. *Journal of Autism and Developmental Disorders, 9,* 41–54.

Snyder, L. Apolloni, T., & Cooke, T. (1977). Integrated settings at the early childhood level: The role of nonretarded peers. *Exceptional Children, 43,* 262–269.

Turnbull, A., Leonard, J. E., & Turnbull, R. (1981). Defensible analyses of PL 94–142: A response. *Journal of Special Education, 15*(1), 25–32.

Twardosz, S., Cataldo, J., & Risley, T. (1974). An open environment design for infant and toddler day care. *Journal of Applied Behavior Analysis, 7,* 529–546.

van Breukelen, P. (1980, September). *Our vision on the problem of whether children with autistic behavior should be taught in a situation with normal children or with other handicapped children.* Paper presented at the conference of the National Society for Autistic Children, Warwick University.

Varni, J. W. Lovaas, O. I., Koegel, R. L., & Everett, N. L. (1979). An analysis of observational learning in autistic and normal children. *Journal of Abnormal Child Psychology, 7,* 31–43.

Westervelt, V., & McKinney, J. (1980). Effects of a film on nonhandicapped children's attitudes toward handicapped children. *Exceptional Children, 46,* 294–296.

11

Behavioral Approaches to Social Skill Development in Autism

Strengths, Misapplications, and Alternatives

ANNE M. DONNELLAN and BEVERLY A. KILMAN

The social interaction deficit in autism was early recognized as pathognomonic to the disorder, with Kanner noting that the children appeared to have "come into the world without innate ability to form the usual, biologically affective contact with people . . ." (Kanner, 1943, p. 43). Now, after decades of debate regarding the preeminence of the linguistic versus the cognitive deficit in autism (Rutter, 1982a), impairment in the ability to develop and maintain adequate social relationships is again being addressed as central to autism (Hermelin, 1982; Rutter, 1985, 1982b). Hermelin particularly stresses the difficulty that these individuals have in understanding and utilizing nonverbal communicative information and suggests that this difficulty may account, at least in part, for the inability to understand thoughts and feelings—their own or those of others. She further suggests that, since many persons with autism have learned to develop linguistic ability through various external interventions, they may be able to learn this nonverbal language as though they were developing a foreign language.

Practitioners anxious to assist individuals with autism to utilize verbal and nonverbal information for social interaction will find the task easier said than done. Unfortunately, according to Groden (1982), there are few guidelines available to assist in the process. Even for children without the problems associated with autism, there are "very few intervention procedures for children deficient in social interaction behaviors and skills" (Greenwood, Walker, & Hops, 1977). Yet there is evidence that social behaviors are amenable to reinforcement and

ANNE M. DONNELLAN • School of Education, University of Wisconsin-Madison, Madison, Wisconsin 53706. BEVERLY A. KILMAN • San Diego Regional Center for the Developmentally Disabled, San Diego, California 92123.

other forms of intervention. Several early studies utilized contingent attention and other social reinforcers to increase social behaviors such as infant smiling (Brackbill, 1958); cooperation (Azrin & Lindsley, 1956); promptness, cleanliness, and nonaggressive behavior (Phillips, 1968); and peer interaction (Kirby & Toler, 1970). Other investigators noted that environmental manipulations such as the utilization of certain kinds of games and play materials can have a positive influence on social interactions of normal preschoolers (Hartup, 1970; Qulitch & Risley, 1973). And, it has been shown that socially withdrawn children can acquire some social behaviors when these are modeled for them (Bandura, Ross, & Ross, 1961; Rogers-Warren & Baer, 1976) as well as when the modeling is combined with instruction and social reinforcement (Cooke & Apolloni, 1976).

Similar interventions have been used with developmentally disabled children with some success. Peer social interaction was increased in two severely retarded withdrawn children by using adult reinforcement and food (Whitman, Mercurio, & Caponigri, 1970) and by the use of shaping procedures and pairing high and low interacting dyads (Morris & Dolker, 1974). Task arrangement and other environmental manipulations have been used to increase interactions of children and adolescents considered retarded (Keilitz, Tucker, & Horner, 1973; Mithaug & Wolfe, 1976), and nonhandicapped peers have been found to be particularly helpful in promoting more appropriate social interactions at least among withdrawn behaviorally disordered preschoolers (Strain, 1977; Strain, Shores, & Timm, 1977). In addition, Liberman and his colleagues (Liberman, King, Derisi, & McCann, 1976) have used personal effectiveness training successfully with persons labeled chronic schizophrenic. And Goldstein, Sprafkin, and Gershow (1984), McGinnis and Goldstein (1984), Spivack and Shure (1974), and others have developed useful social skills training models for students labeled emotionally disturbed.

Attempts to develop social interaction behaviors in individuals with autism have been fewer, but there have been some limited successes here as well. One of the earliest was a study by Lovaas, Schaffer, and Simmons (1965) that used electric shock to reduce self-stimulatory and other "bizarre" behaviors. As the adults became paired with shock reduction, affection and other social behaviors increased toward the adults. Over the years, of course, less intrusive procedures have been found to adequately manage problem behaviors (see LaVigna & Donnellan, in press, for a review), and such extreme interventions are no longer justified. Much of the most successful work in developing social behaviors in autistic children has, in fact, utilized fairly indirect intervention. Strain and Shores (1977), in a review of the behavioral studies aimed at increasing peer interactions, found that the use of extrinsic reinforcers typically interrupted the interactions. Strain's later work as well as that of McHale (1983) has utilized peer confederates successfully to assist the autistic children to develop social skills and play behaviors. McHale (1983) suggests that play behaviors can better be taught to these children by their nonhandicapped peers who are given even minimal instruction than by trained adults. Moreover, whereas earlier efforts had produced little generalization (Strain, Kerr, & Ragland, 1979; Strain, Shores, & Kerr, 1976), their recent work suggests that generalization does occur if the children have access to developmentally integrated settings (Strain, 1983). This finding is compatible with others (e.g., Donnellan, Anderson, & Mesaros, 1984; Mesaros, 1984) indicating that heterogeneous environments (that is, environments in which the majority of the individuals do not have the social deficits associated with autism) are more likely to support positive social behaviors on the part of the persons with autism.

It appears, then, that though social interaction and communication deficits are central to the problem of autism, it is reasonable to assume that these deficits can be ameliorated. Several investigators, in particular behavioral psychologists, have systematically demonstrated that these individuals can develop some ability to socially interact in appropriate ways. Yet it cannot be denied that the social deficits of autism remain even in those cases where there is considerable improvement in cognitive and linguistic ability (Rutter, 1982a; Wing & Gould, 1979). Fortunately, there are enough reports of individuals who do improve socially to reject any notions that these skills are less amenable to remediation than cognitive or linguistic skills.

Another possible concern might be that the technology available is inadequate or inappropriate for promoting social development. Although, as indicated earlier, much of the success reported has been based on behavioral principles, the results from applying extrinsic contingencies are insufficient. The assumption that the technology is faulty is, however, almost as dangerous as assuming that the social problems of autism are not amenable to systematic intervention. A less dangerous assumption (Donnellan, 1984) is the one that forms the basis for this chapter. To paraphrase Chesterton, the position taken here is: "It is not that behavioral technology has been tried and found wanting but that it has not been sufficiently or appropriately tried." That is, techniques developed through applied behavioral analysis have an important role to play in the development of social interaction and communication for individuals with autism. That role will not be realized until it is put in its proper context. That context is similar to the role that behavioral technology ought to play as an essential part of a triad in any curriculum development strategy. Thus, in this chapter the role that behavioral psychology can play in social skill development for persons with autism will first be presented in the context of general curriculum development issues. The characteristics of applied behavioral methodology as it is traditionally utilized will then be described in terms of how these characteristics might enhance or inhibit the development of social interaction skills for individuals challenged by the problems of autism. Some results of misapplication of this methodology will be addressed along with a description of an ongoing program that attempts to integrate behavioral, developmental, and functional curriculum information to assist individuals with autism to become socially competent.

THE CURRICULUM DEVELOPMENT TRIAD

Among special educators a notion has developed over the past decade that there are at least three different and, in fact, competing approaches to classroom program development: the behavioral (e.g., Lovaas, 1981), the functional (e.g., Brown *et al.*, 1979), and the developmental approaches (e.g., Wood, 1975). Viewing these three approaches to program development as competitive has resulted in an overstating of each in turn. In fact, each has an essential role to play as part of a curriculum development triad, and neglect of any one results in a lack of balance.

CONTRIBUTIONS OF BEHAVIORAL, FUNCTIONAL, AND DEVELOPMENTAL APPROACHES

Behavioral. The unique contribution of the behavioral approach to the education of children with autism has been reported elsewhere (e.g., Koegel, Rincover, & Egel, 1982). It tells us "how" to organize the task, the stimuli, and the contingencies to maximize learning. It is the technology most frequently employed and serves well. Because of the importance of this technology to effective programming of social skill development in autism, the role of the behavioral approach will be discussed in detail later in this chapter.

Functional. Just as behavioral technology provides the answers to "how" to teach, the functional approach provides the "what" or the content taught. The question always first asked: "What does this person need to know?" can best be answered by obtaining an inventory of the skills required of a person to succeed in a variety of current and subsequent environments (e.g., Brown *et al.*, 1979). This method ensures that the individual's time will not be wasted on meaningless tasks (Donnellan, 1980), that in fact the tasks learned are appropriate to the age, family setting, and community patterns of the learner. This is particularly important for individuals with autism who often have significant problems with generalization (e.g., Donnellan & Mirenda, 1983) and with overselectivity (Schreibman, Koegel, & Craig, 1977). The "least dangerous assumption" is that having been taught to respond in the presence of a particular set of stimuli, they are unlikely to spontaneously generalize to a different stimulus or situation. Thus, it is critical that the skills, tasks, cues, consequences, etc., chosen be referenced against the requirements of the environments in which they will ultimately need to function (Brown, Nietupski, & Hamre-Nietupski, 1976). The functional approach provides a variety of strategies for developing curricula that teach chronological-age-appropriate functional skills in natural environments in response to natural cues and consequences.

Developmental. The question "What does the person know now?" must be a companion to the "need to know" question. Teaching material already within the individual's repertoire or material well beyond one's present ability needs to be adapted to the learner (Baumgart *et al.*, 1982; Yoder, 1980). To avoid repetitive teaching and to provide the relevant adaptations requires an assessment of what the person "knows now" and what the probable relationship of this knowledge is to the task to be taught. The body of knowledge that is best suited to this complex issues is the developmental one (Bruner, 1975; Inhelder & Piaget, 1958; Piaget, 1960; Schopler, Reichler, & Lansing, 1980). The developmental approach provides a forum for discovering what the child already knows, it provides a framework for viewing the proximity of that knowledge to the knowledge needed, and finally, it gives some guidelines to the manner in which that material is learned by other children without handicaps.

The importance of assessing the developmental readiness and developmental abilities of the child with autism as the first step in educational planning has been well demonstrated in many successful programs (e.g., Schopler *et al.*, 1980). With this information about the child one is prepared to find the spot where the child's abilities fit along the developmental continuum for a particular skill. Again using information about normal development, it is also possible to determine the number of developmental steps between where the child is and where the child needs to be, and, further, it is possible to determine the approximate sequence of the usual intervention steps to "break down" the task (Schopler *et al.*, 1980). The individual may then be provided with experiences that allow him/her to move along the developmental path.

PROBLEMS WITH IGNORING BEHAVIORAL, FUNCTIONAL, OR DEVELOPMENTAL APPROACHES

With information from all three approaches, a concrete curriculum can be developed to teach something of importance in the natural environment to the individual, with the minimum task adaptation required for success using the most efficient technology available. When any one part is overlooked, or if only one approach is applied, the program loses impact, usefulness, or relevance.

Behavioral. First, there is the case of the application of behavioral technology without reference to either developmental or functional relevance. In part, this phenomenon results from the fact that behaviorism itself is essentially content-free and does not dictate what is to be taught. At best, this allows a powerful technology to be applied regardless of the task. At worst, it can be applied arbitrarily to teach irrelevant subject matter or even to eliminate behavior without regard to the function of that behavior (Donnellan, Mirenda, Mesaros, & Fassbender, 1984; LaVigna & Donnellan, in press; Carr, 1985). As noted, this chapter will later address the behavioral technology issues at length.

Functional. In programs that apply only this approach, one finds "functional" curriculum strategies that are nonfunctional for a particular individual. If the task is appropriate but the staff does not have technical competency, the only technology offered may be repeated practice without reference to the strengths and weaknesses of that methodology (see Donnellan, Mesaros, & Anderson, 1984). Or, by ignoring crucial developmental information, one may attempt to teach a task well beyond the student's conceptual knowledge (see Prizant, 1982). For example, a student with little understanding of cause-and-effect relationships is repeatedly prompted through "table wiping" when a developmentally appropriate adaptation (Baumgart *et al.*, 1982) would make repeated practice unnecessary and might even encourage generalization and spontaneity (Donnellan & Mirenda, 1983; Mirenda & Donnellan, in press, a).

Developmental. On the other hand, there are any number of examples of curriculum strategies that rely primarily on developmental checklists. The misuse of the developmental approach leads to serious curriculum distortions; this same student might never get an opportunity to wipe a table because he is developmentally "not ready" (see Brown *et al.*, 1979, for a review of this issue). Having been assessed and found to have a mental age of 8 months, he might be taught to pull a string to bring a loop closer to him because that is a skill expected of babies at a similar developmental level. Such a misapplication of developmental information has been resoundingly and appropriately criticized elsewhere (Brown *et al.*, 1979; Donnellan, 1984) but continues in practice to the detriment of students with severe handicaps such as autism. Developmental experiences must be cast in age-appropriate context for at least two reasons. First, as noted earlier, the generalization problems of this population make it dangerous to assume that they will transfer their learning across widely differing stimulus situations. Second, having individuals perform developmentally relevant but chronologically age-inappropriate actions, such as having a teenager complete a preschool age puzzle, runs the risk of devaluing and stigmatizing the individual (Wolfensberger, 1972). For a full discussion of the developmental approach, see Schopler *et al.* (1980).

INTEGRATION OF APPROACHES

A "low inference" curriculum approach (Donnellan, 1984) that chooses developmentally relevant tasks and sound technology to teach those tasks with natural materials, settings, and instructional arrangements reflecting the ultimate functioning needs of the individual is critical (Brown *et al.*, 1976; Donnellan, 1980). The curriculum thus developed will be one that will teach something of developmental relevance and of importance within a natural, age-appropriate context with the minimum of task adaptations required for success and using the most efficient technology available.

AN INTEGRATED SOCIAL SKILLS CURRICULUM

Nowhere is the need for strategies that integrate the behavioral, functional, and developmental approaches more critical than in the area of a social skills curriculum. We will begin our discussion of such strategies by addressing in detail the strengths and limitations of the behavioral methodology as it is typically applied to social skills training. This methodology merits special attention in any discussion of social skills programming for at least three reasons. First, properly applied, the behavioral technology has been shown to contribute much to the welfare of students with autism (see Koegel *et al.*, 1982). Second, there is no area of development more needful and worthy of an effective technology. Those few successful interventions that systematically address social skill development have been based on behavioral principles, and there is every reason to believe that these can be expanded and improved upon. Third, the misapplication of the technology can be harmful as it can promote the teaching of irrelevant skills and/or be used to eliminate supposedly aberrant behaviors from an already limited behavioral repertoire. Social skills development best illustrates the necessity of matching methodology with content and process to maximize the potential for success and avoid the dangers of misapplied technology. The following section will address the strengths and limitations of the behavioral approach to social skill development in students with the problems associated with autism.

BEHAVIORAL APPROACHES—STRENGTHS

Perhaps the single greatest strength of the behavioral approach has been described by Carr (1985): "The strength and promise of behaviorism lies in its commitment to empiricism and not on its reliance on any specific set of treatment procedures. This generic notion of behaviorism paves the way for a consideration of concepts and data derived from a variety of sources. . . ." It is this adherence to empiricism and eschewing of any theoretical model (Keller & Schoenfeld, 1950; Skinner, 1950) that allowed early applied behaviorists to assert and to demonstrate that students with autism could learn (Ferster, 1961; Ferster & DeMyer, 1962; Lovaas, 1977), despite the generally pessimistic attitudes about education of the handicapped in the 1960s. The inherent characteristics of the behavioral model make it well suited to the education of those individuals with autism who apparently have limited ability to learn from more abstract, more subtle, and less structured approaches. These characteristics include the following:

Specificity of Responses. The empiricism of the behavioral model requires that the response be defined in observable and measurable terms. For students with autism who have limited response repertoires, it is particularly important that educational efforts be predicated upon clearly defined goals and objectives that specify the present level of functioning as well as anticipated postintervention functioning. Thus, a social skill under consideration might be "comfort with proximity of others," which could be clearly and objectively defined in terms of both topography and frequency for a given student.

Accountability. Students with severe handicaps such as autism have much to learn in a short time. It is, therefore, essential that their school time be used efficiently and productively. The very specificity of the behavioral approach allows for objective and reliable evaluation of educational efforts and a consequent opportunity to devise and revise strategies that are reasonably successful within the time available.

Flexibility. As noted by Carr (1985), the behavioral methodology can be systematically applied using data that are generated by nonbehaviorists. Currently, for example, many behaviorally oriented researchers and educators are applying information generated by psycholinguists and others looking at pragmatic aspects of language and communication (Carr, 1983; Donnellan, Mirenda, *et al.*, 1984; Duchan, 1982). From its earliest application (Thorndike, 1913), behaviorism has been ruled by the law of effect rather than adherence to authority. In an area as poorly understood as social skill development, such flexibility and openness is essential.

Powerful, Effective, and Varied Teaching Technology. Behavioral methodology has been shown to be effective in teaching students with autism and other severely handicapping conditions a wide variety of skills. In particular, the techniques of shaping (Gold and Associates, 1978), incidental teaching (see Carr, 1983, for a review), and time delay (Snell & Gast, 1981) appear to have particular applicability for social skill development.

There is also a body of literature concerned with covert manipulation that shows considerable promise for social skill development. Cautela and Baron (1977) describe "covert conditioning" as a set of imagery-based procedures that alter response frequency by the manipulation of consequences (p. 356). According to Groden (1982), the covert literature includes a number of procedures that involve the use of imagery to modify behaviors that are overt as well as covert. These include desensitization (Wolpe, 1958), implosive therapy (Stampfl & Levis, 1967), covert control (Homme, 1965), hypnosis (Barber, 1969), and cognitive behavior modification strategies (Meichenbaum, 1973). These procedures have been used in a wide variety of situations that potentially have significance for individuals with autism (see Mirenda, in press, for a review of this literature); however, they have seldom been utilized with the autistic learner population. In one of the few investigations of the use of covert procedures with persons with autism, Groden (1982) successfully used imagery to covertly reinforce the social initiation behavior of three children. Others have hesitated to apply covert techniques to this population because of their well-documented limitations in imagination. However, Groden argues persuasively that covert procedures hold great promise for individuals with autism if the procedures are suitably modified to the developmental level of the individual. She further argues:

> There are also a number of advantages in using covert procedures. They are efficient; there are no instruments or tokens to dispense; normal classroom programming is not interrupted; imagery allows for many more trials; environments can be created in imagery and therefore behaviors can be rehearsed in a private setting and changes can take place in the school, home or the community; and imagery procedures can eventually be used as self control since the individual can learn to produce scenes on his own. (p. 15)

It is hoped that future research will build on the success of Groden's work to apply covert behavioral procedures to the social needs of individuals with autism.

Powerful, Effective, and Varied Nonaversive Technology. Many of the behavior problems of persons with autism are problems primarily because of deficits in the area of social interaction. That is, the problem often lies not in the behavior but in the fact that the person does not know the appropriate social rules relative to the behavior. Often, then, the issue is not one of eliminating the behavior but of bringing the behavior under more appropriate stimulus control or of reducing it to a socially appropriate level. Masturbation and excessive question asking are two such behaviors that often cause difficulties for students with autism and those who live or work with them. An effective social skills training program incorporating functional and developmental as well as behavioral information can remediate some of the social deficits that contribute to these difficult situations. Such a program is described later in this chapter. However, the results of such social skills programs are typically not rapid, and socially inappropriate behaviors often have serious consequences for individuals and for entire programs. Some straightforward, nonaversive behavioral interventions have been shown to be extremely effective in dealing with such problems (e.g., Donnellan & LaVigna, in press; see LaVigna & Donnellan, in press, for a comprehensive review of nonaversive procedures for managing behavior). Such procedures can bring even the most serious of problem behaviors under appropriate control (e.g., Donnellan, LaVigna, Zambito, & Thevdt, 1985) while longitudinal social skill development programs are taking effect.

BEHAVIORAL APPROACHES—MISAPPLICATIONS

Rigid Stimulus Control and Artificiality

Behavioral technology as applied to the teaching of students with autism has relied heavily on the use of the discrete trial format (Donnellan-Walsh, Gossage, LaVigna, Schuler, & Traphagen, 1976; Koegel, Russo, & Rincover,

1977). This teaching format, or some variation thereon, has contributed greatly to the ability of persons with autism to become more independent and productive citizens (see Koegel *et al.*, 1982) and has much to contribute to more effective teaching of individuals with autism. It has been argued, however, that the very success of the discrete trial format may have kept the practitioner from asking important questions about content, context, and spontaneity (see Donnellan, Mesaros, *et al.*, 1984) and may actually contribute to some of the generalization problems often found in autism (Donnellan & Mirenda, 1983; Koegel & Rincover, 1977; Stokes & Baer, 1977). At a minimum, excessive reliance on repeated practice and the artificiality typically associated with the discrete trial format can cause teachers and others to be inappropriately optimistic about their success in teaching social interaction skills. The all too common situation in which a child and a teacher sit in an isolated setting and the child repeatedly responds "Fine" to the teacher's cue "How are you?" may teach the behavior but still be meaningless in terms of educational validity (Voeltz & Evans, 1983). It should be noted, of course, that whereas the technology is essentially content-free, the artificiality is not inherent in the procedure. Nonetheless, the widespread misuse of the technology requires that these problems be addressed directly and that researchers and practitioners rethink the applicability of discrete trial techniques to social development of persons with autism (see Donnellan, Mesaros, *et al.*, 1984, for a review).

Teacher-Directed Activities/Maintenance of Child as Responder

Whether or not a teacher is utilizing the discrete trial, there is a tendency in behaviorally oriented programs to rely heavily on teacher-directed activities (Donnellan, Mesaros, *et al.*, 1984). In part, this is due to a legitimate concern that the child learn to respond in the presence of appropriate instructional cues (Donnellan-Walsh *et al.*, 1976). For some activities, this is probably a reasonable approach; however, social interaction cues are variable and by definition social. Given the pervasive nature of the social interaction problems in autism, this emphasis on the child as a mere responder is a potential hindrance to social skill development. Recently, for example, Mirenda and Donnellan (in press, b) studied the social interaction ability of two groups of subjects labeled retarded or autistic when the adult cointeractant used a facilitative versus a directive style of interaction. When given an opportunity to do other than merely respond to adult questions, every one of the subjects used that opportunity appropriately, albeit with difficulty. All attempted to expand on topics, to change topics, and to initiate new topics. Although keeping the student in a responder mode is hardly limited to behaviorally oriented practitioners (Cusick, 1973), the emphasis on response and cue specificity is particularly apparent in the behavioral literature. In social interaction programs, teachers and other practitioners might do well to expand their methodological repertoire to include behavioral techniques that encourage spontaneity—such as shaping, incidental teaching, and time delay, noted earlier, which allow for and encourage spontaneity.

Emphasis on Consequence Strategies and Artificial Reinforcers

The behavioral literature provides many useful strategies for analyzing behavior and remediating excesses and deficits (e.g., Goldiamond, 1974). Nonetheless, there is an unfortunate tendency in applied programs dealing with autistic students to rely heavily on the relationship between behavior and its imposed consequence and, indeed, on sequences that are highly artificial. Where the issue is social development, this tendency can have fairly ludicrous results. Carr (1980), for example, notes the problems inherent in "reinforcing" communicative attempts with arbitrary reinforcers that are not meaningfully related to the response, such as giving a child candy for correctly requesting a sock. And as noted earlier, Strain and Shores (1977) reported that attempts to apply artificial contingencies to reinforce social interaction between children interfered with the ongoing interaction. As social interaction and communication are imbedded in context, they cannot meaningfully be divorced from that context. Fortunately, many recent studies have begun to address context in analyzing the communicative attempts of persons with autism and other severe handicaps (Frankel, 1982; Prizant, 1978; Schuler, 1980; Schuler & Goetz, 1981). This area of behavioral research, which puts far less emphasis on artificial consequence strategies, appears to hold promise for the social interaction development.

Utilization of Punishers

The use of punishment for managing aberrant behavior without reference to context or to the possible communicative function of that behavior is a strategy of particular concern to those addressing the social interaction needs of this population. Mesaros (1983) reviewed behavioral interventions with autism in seven major journals and found that in 27 behavior reduction interventions, 23 used punishment without assessment of the potential communicative function of the behavior. In addition to the ethical and legal questions involved in the use of punishment (LaVigna & Donnellan, in press; Martin, 1975), there is a growing awareness that many apparently aberrant behaviors, even severe injurious behavior (SIB), may serve communicative functions (Carr, 1983; Durand, 1982; Iwata,

Dorsey, Slifer, Bauman, & Richman, 1982) and that elimination should not be undertaken before a careful analysis. Donnellan, Mirenda, *et al.* (1984) present one model for analyzing the functions of behavior, and several authors have suggested replacement strategies in lieu of behavior reduction or elimination (e.g., Repp & Deitz, 1974; Russo, Cataldo, & Cushing, 1981). The recent behavioral literature reflects a tendency to reach beyond the limits of classical behaviorism and make use of information from developmental psychology, linguistics, and pragmatics to understand rather than merely to manage problem behaviors. Nonetheless, all too many articles still are published that rely on punishers to eliminate behaviors without a functional analysis of the behaviors (e.g., Friman, Cook, & Finney, 1984).

DEVELOPMENTAL, FUNCTIONAL, AND BEHAVIORAL CONSIDERATIONS IN DEVELOPING SOCIAL SKILLS CURRICULA

Developmental Considerations

The developmental approach provides the guidelines for the San Diego Social Skills Program (Kilman, 1981; Kilman & Negri-Shoultz, in press) and suggests some of the answers to the following questions: (1) What do these young people know? (2) What do most children know that allows them to interact and socialize? (3) What sequence do children usually follow in acquiring these skills? Formal and informal testing, developmental checklists, and analysis of videotapes of the interactions of these youths contribute answers to the first question. The developmental literature and observations of normally social and communicative children suggest the answers to questions (2) and (3). Language and social interaction are imbedded in context and learned through action. It is necessary to create experiences for learners with autism that allow them to discover those subtle rules of social interaction that appear to come naturally to others. This is done in part by providing an "augmented natural environment."

The "Augmented Natural Environment." Children with autism are provided "good enough" parenting (Winnicott, 1958) and presumably a "normal" environment (see Donnellan, 1985, for a review of this literature). The natural environment that ordinarily provides the opportunity to discover recurrent patterns, to appreciate sequence, to "de-center," to understand the uniqueness of others, and to become socially skilled and communicatively competent hypothesis-making human beings is insufficient in autism. Hermelin's (1982) second language analogy is apt here. Learning to speak a second language as an adolescent or an adult is a much different task from acquiring language as an infant and a young child. Similarly, learning social and communicative competence is much more complex if one has autism, and the task requires an augmented natural environment that highlights the rules and patterns an autistic person ordinarily might miss. The developmental literature provides the normal learning patterns; the autism literature and observation provides a basis for amplification to compensate for the deficits in autism. Of special importance is an understanding that people with autism experience the following:

1. Difficulty responding to novel stimuli presented in the auditory mode (Courchesne, Kilman, Galambos, & Lincoln, 1984), which requires clarity of cues and greater use of nonverbal, experiential information.
2. Difficulty detecting and attending to events of moderate or low impact, which requires greater intensity of presentation.
3. Problems with sequence and cause/effect relationships, which requires highlighting of relationship information.

Functional Considerations

It is necessary to state exactly what it is we wish to be learned. Formal and informal ecological inventories of the schools, homes, and potential non-handicapped peer groups provided formation for the San Diego project in the development of long-range goals (see Ford *et al.*, 1980, for an example of a strategy for inventorying recreation/leisure environments). This information is essential to the utilization of skills in integrated and heterogeneous environments. Functional analysis also provides a data base from which to recast developmental activities into ones that are chronologically age-appropriate. For example, one would carefully assess the ability of the potential learner to initiate spontaneous turn-taking in conversation. The child language literature can be reviewed to find what activities usually accompany and presumably support the further development of this skill (Bruner, 1975). The "normal" activity of peekaboo, for example, might be suggested and then recast in an activity which contains similar ritualized turn-taking playfulness but which is also chronologically age-appropriate: for example, a game of catch. Ball games including throw and catch are seen as appropriate in our culture for individuals from the first year of life until "the old-timers" game on the Fourth of July.

Analysis of the strengths and deficits of an individual in a variety of environments is required for the development of goals and objectives as well as of games and activities that will make socially required behavior patterns explicit for individuals with autism. Such activities can be utilized to highlight recurrent patterns, to emphasize cause and effect, to clarify sequence, and to otherwise address the many cognitive/linguistic impairments associated with autism in the context of chronologically age-appropriate and functional skill development.

Behavioral Considerations

A social skills program must call upon the most advanced technology to deliver the program; the behavioral literature provides an empirically based, reliable, and measurable system for this purpose. The behavioral literature assists the staff in the San Diego project in clarification of long-range goals and objectives, in redesigning tasks to meet these objectives, and in selection of appropriate interventions to shape and enhance learning.

Developing Long-Range Goals and Objectives. On the basis of the developmental and functional information, eight goals or target behaviors were developed for the group. These, in turn, could be stated as measurable objectives for individual members in keeping with the empirical underpinnings of behaviorism. The eight goals of the group are (1) comfort with the proximity of other individuals, (2) imitation of interactions, (3) cooperation or shared action, (4) turn taking in games and social interaction, (5) initiation of action, first in play and then in conversation, (6) asking for help, for social contact, and for information, (7) negotiation for space, for choice of activity with regard and appreciation for differing expectations and needs of the other, and (8) alertness to the social context and to the behavior that such a context requires.

Task Analysis and Environmental Manipulation in Designing Activities to Meet Goals and Objectives. The developmental assessment and functional analysis provide information with respect to what facts are needed by the individual to succeed in social interactions. In the group, this information is presented by way of games and activities that allow members to "discover" and use the facts. The behavioral literature provides essential information on task analysis (e.g., Gold and Associates, 1978), ecological analysis (e.g., Rogers-Warren & Warren, 1977), within-stimulus prompts (e.g., Schreibman, 1975), and other techniques for designing, analyzing, and restructuring activities that will allow for such discovery. In the San Diego project, this information was utilized to define the characteristics of activities to meet the goals and objectives. These characteristics and some examples of activities follow.

Characteristics of Tasks to Support Social Development

1. The task must be chronologically age-appropriate and developmentally relevant. A functional analysis of a preadolescent's after-school recreation program may indicate that board or card games are popular among his peers. The developmental information on the youngster may indicate that he has very poor understanding of means–ends relationships required to play the game. For a 12-year-old, however, it must be emphasized that the simpler preschool games would likely be stigmatizing. Thus, chronologically age-appropriate games such

as Yatzee and War may mean nothing to him except as some ritualized form of perpetual motion. Most individuals with autism need to have cause and effect emphasized; therefore, it seems reasonable that their activities should have a clear end point. The rules of the games could be adapted (see Mirenda & Donnellan, in press, for a discussion of adaptations) and/or games could be chosen in which the effect is clearer. The card game Concentration is one that emphasizes visual spatial memory and also allows for spatial representation of the end point. Both characteristics are likely to make it a good activity for many of these young people with autism.

2. The task must ensure proximity. Many individuals with autism keep a significant distance between themselves and others. Social behavior or at least person-to-person contact is more likely to occur with close proximity. If the task forces close proximity, the possibilities for producing a behavior to which the environment can respond is increased. Activities such as the game of Twister can pull group members into close proximity. Moreover, functional analysis of a task can include fairly precise measurement of socially acceptable patterns of proximity under given stimulus conditions, and this can be used to differentially reinforce or shape appropriate approximations.

3. The task must require more than one person to be involved. One-person activities are not social and require little communicative competence. Yet many individuals with autism appear to prefer activities for one. One adolescent in the group stated that it was easier to play ball alone. In the "augmented environment" the task analysis often includes redefining or remodeling an activity so that it cannot be performed individually. For example, many building activities can be done alone. In the San Diego group, either the activity is chosen that requires two or more people or the environment is manipulated to require more than one. If necessary, the materials are distributed about the room so that the person with the wood does not also have the hammer, still another has the nails, and another the saw. Requesting equipment, assistance, etc., from peers then is required if the task is to be completed.

4. The task should emphasize the uniqueness of individuals. Skilled communication requires more than asking for and keeping "the ball" going in discourse; it also requires the ability to explain things and to appreciate the needs of the listener in presenting that explanation. This is extremely difficult for most persons with autism (see Hermelin, 1982). The task then must be designed in order to make the other person's needs apparent. The environment/activity is rearranged so that successful completion requires such information to be exchanged. An example of this principle may be seen in the very popular activities of making tacos or passing out varieties of juice available. The rule is that one may not pour one's own juice or make one's own taco. If the individual wishes the taco to be made in the favored way, this information must be made quite clear to the cooking partner. Extra cheese, but no tomatoes, must be explained

in some way. Further, it is necessary to pay attention to other persons so that their tacos have no lettuce but plenty of meat (or whatever they wish) if disappointment, ridicule, anger, or some other negative response from the other is to be avoided.

Other opportunities to compare attributes and opinions occur in the structured discussions, in activities involving comparison of pets, number of family members, or hobby preference, or, at an even simpler level, in lotto games using group members' pictures or in games requiring comparison of eye color.

5. The task itself must make clear an orderly sequence of steps involved from initiation to completion. If the sequence is clear enough, information about time, order, and cause–effect relationships can be discovered. In particular, as noted earlier, cause–effect phenomena are highlighted with an obvious display. The completion of tasks is highlighted with an end point that prevents the perseveration seen so often in autism. Persons with autism frequently miss relationships and frequently fail to appreciate the goal of an activity. To make a goal salient and the steps that lead to the goal clear, the activity must stop itself. For example, an easy, valued teenage activity is making popcorn. Popcorn, once popped, is transformed, cannot be repopped, and becomes edible. If a within-stimulus cue such as an air popper with a transparent top is used, the process of the transformation can be witnessed. Any food preparation activity will, of course, have a nonrecurring, final end point in the eating.

Role of the Group Leader or Teacher

Preparing the Environment.

Obviously, the group leader must draw on developmental, functional, and behavioral information to creatively design or rework activities that meet all of the above criteria. Almost any activity, however, can be recast with these criteria in mind to make optimal use of the time spent. The role of the group leader or teacher in this model is, first and foremost, to use available information to prepare the environment to ensure success in the interaction/activity for the students. The session that is well planned appears to any casual observer to be simply a group of young people having a nice time interacting together, with the professional(s) sitting in and occasionally participating. Thus, the curriculum or activity carries the information, the context, and the impetus for activity.

Behavioral Techniques Utilized by the Group Leader.

The role that the leader performs may be unobtrusive, but it consists of a number of carefully planned elements, the technology for which comes from behavioral psychology. In addition to designing the tasks that promote social-communicative growth, initiation, spontaneity, and generalization, as well as monitoring individual growth in these areas, the leader utilizes a variety of interventions to enhance and expand such growth. Some of these are listed below.

Social Reinforcement, Incidental Teaching, and Shaping Techniques. The group leader at all times provides the individuals with autism his/her attention, respect, approval, and naturally occurring chronological-age-appropriate social reinforcers. Incidental teaching is stressed (Carr, 1985), with the leader actively listening for any verbal or nonverbal communicative act and returning it with the appropriate social response. The goal is to increase the number of behaviors available; thus, wherever possible, existing behaviors are supported and shaped (Martin & Pear, 1983). If behaviors occur that seem impossible to shape or redirect into prosocial behaviors, these are treated with nonaversive strategies (LaVigna & Donnellan, in press). Wherever possible, the situation or activity provides the management of the behavior (see Donnellan & Mirenda *et al.*, 1984, for a discussion of such ecological manipulations). For example, providing an activity interesting enough to bring the member to it avoids the need to demand attendance, to stop self-stimulating behavior, or to require someone to pay attention.

Shifting Reinforcement to Group Members. At the same time as he/she is supporting communication attempts, the group leader works toward a shift of the focus of the communication away from the leader and toward the other members. In early sessions, a diagram of the interaction will probably resemble a star with all of the communication arrows coming from and going to the leader. It is the leader's responsibility to shift this pattern to a circular one in which most of the interactions occur between members. The shift toward the peers as both the target and the reinforcing agent is facilitated by ensuring that any primary reinforcers that are an outgrowth of an activity (for example, the popped corn) are given out by the group members. It is further supported by prompting the autistic individuals to provide social reinforcers to their peers.

Prompts. These interventions (Donnellan-Walsh *et al.*, 1976; Koegel *et al.*, 1977) are used but are faded as quickly as possible. The prompts used are varied each time they are presented to avoid fostering prompt dependency and, as noted earlier, to incorporate "within-stimulus prompts" (Schreibman, 1975) as often as possible. The goal is to have the major portion of the information come from the experience of interaction with the task and with peers, not from the prompt. Since the prompt does not carry the information, but only "nudges" to action, variation or inconsistency of prompt does not seem to produce confusion (see LaVigna & Donnellan, in press; Woods, in press, for a discussion of the placement of prompts versus correction procedures for individuals with autism).

Coaching. One specialized form of prompt used to ensure that appropriate interactions are performed and completed is "coaching from the sidelines." In this procedure, the leader moves through a social interaction with the young person. Ordinarily, this involves a leader-coach at each end of the interaction. This technique is especially useful in sustaining discourse over several turns.

When a child is at an impasse, he might be asked, "What would you like to do about this?" This has been a valuable tool to assist individual members in learning to deal with problem behaviors from peers. For example, one young woman was bothered by repeated hair pulling, which the young men in the group began as a means of interaction, teasing, and gaining her attention. The leader did not stop the behavior, but through coaching, the young woman was able to handle this behavior herself within two sessions. The leader said nothing to the hair pullers, but rather asked the young women if she liked having her hair pulled. When she said no, he asked her to help him think what a person could do to stop someone from doing this. Then he helped her rehearse her response. He continued to help her say, "Please stop that," until she initiated this herself in a timely manner. In a very short period of time, the behavior was taken care of and the young woman had a skill that she used in other situations without coaching.

Dramatic Modeling. Modeling is a major component in social learning (Bandura, 1969) and is a major tool of any group leader. However, because people with autism tend not to notice subtle occurrences, dramatic modeling replaces the usual modeling. Patterns of behavior are heightened in this way with somewhat larger-than-life demonstrations and increased volume for emphasis. For example, greeting behaviors and good-bye behaviors are modeled dramatically until imitation occurs. Once the members are initiating appropriate greetings and leave taking, the leaders respond in a warm but natural manner. Again, following Hermelin (1982), this exaggerated modeling is similar to the way in which one simplifies and emphasizes key points in the teaching of a second language. Each new activity is also modeled by the two leaders. The leaders model methods of handling unacceptable behavior for the group members. Continuous incidental teaching is done similarly with just a slight increase in "volume" or change in emphasis.

Errorless Learning and Information Feedback. In the San Diego group, members receive verbal feedback from the group leader plus feedback from the successful completion of the task itself utilizing the principles of errorless learning (Terrace, 1963). As a result of the gradual increase in the difficulty of the task, group members constantly have an opportunity to see themselves in a succeeding position. A number of activities are presented over time with gradual variations that increase the complexity and produce satisfaction. For example, simple building tasks beginning with large blocks, moving to Tinker Toys, and finally proceeding to the building of functional objects offer immediate experience of competency for latency age and preteenagers. It also provides a skill competence that can become the context for social exchange. The leaders accompany this experiential success with verbal positive feedback: "That turned out very well." Negative feedback is of a neutral, informational nature, "You're holding all the popcorn." Criticism is never used. Where necessary, questions replace any negative comments or corrections: "Do you all want him to keep all the popcorn to himself?" "How could you let him know that?"

Use of these techniques, and meeting once weekly for a series of eight to ten meetings repeated approximately quarterly throughout the year over several years, has produced significant growth in social communicative competence, development of enduring friendships (more than three years), and initiation of social contacts (invitations to parties, brunches, and picnics, weekend get-togethers, and trips to recreational sites) in the San Diego group. The members have made it clear in verbal and written reports that they enjoy the group and that it is important to them. The individuals with autism now take responsibility for seeing to it that the groups continue by calling or writing letters if there is a delay in the beginning of a new series of eight sessions. One young man said to the other members, "If I ever have a kid with autism, I'm bringing him right here."

CONCLUSION

The evidence from San Diego and from other social groups around the country indicates that autistic individuals have a desire and some capacity for positive social contact. Their efforts may be "heavily accented" but they are showing ability to learn the language of social interaction. The need for attention to the social development of persons with autism can no longer be ignored or replaced with "behavior management." Social skill curricula utilizing developmental information and functional assessment constitute a critical need. Helping people with autism learn to do what is "natural" for most of us will require more thought and planning and must employ a more sophisticated use of behavioral strategies than were ordinarily applied in the past. However, there is clear evidence that these individuals have a potential for substantial gains that makes such an undertaking well worth the effort and planning involved. The bonus to the workers is the opportunity to work with people who are able to produce, respond, communicate, and even laugh a little. This is a rich reward.

REFERENCES

Azrin, N. H., & Lindsley, O. R. (1956). The reinforcement of cooperation between children. *Journal of Abnormal Psychology, 52,* 100–102.

Bandura, A. (1969). *Principles of behavior modification.* New York: Holt, Rinehart & Winston.

Bandura, A., Ross, D., & Ross, S. A. (1961). Transmission of aggression through imitation of aggressive models. *Journal of Abnormal and Social Psychology, 64,* 575–582.

Barber, T. X. (1969). *Hypnosis, a scientific approach.* New York: Reinhold.

Baumgart, D., Brown, L., Pumpian, K., Nisbet, J., Ford, A., Sweet, M., Messina, R., & Schroeder, J. (1982). Principle of partial participation and individualized adaptations in educational programs for severely handicapped students. *Journal of the Association for the Severely Handicapped, 7*(2), 17–27.

Brackbill, Y. (1958). Extinction of the smiling response in infants as a function of reinforcement schedule. *Child Development, 29,* 115–124.

Brown, L., Branston, M. B., Hamre-Nietupski, S., Pumpian, I., Certo, N., & Gruenewald, L. (1979). A strategy for developing chronological age appropriate and functional curricular content for severly handicapped adolescents and young adults. *Journal of Special Education, 13,* 81–90.

Brown, L., Nietupski, J., & Hamre-Nietupski, S. (1976). The criterion of ultimate functioning and public school services for severely handicapped students. In M. A. Thomas (Ed.), *Hey, don't forget about me: Education's investment in the severely, profoundly and multiply handicapped* (pp. 2–15). Reston, VA: Council for Exceptional Children.

Bruner, J. (1975). The ontogenesis of speech acts. *Journal of Child Language, 2,* 1–9.

Carr, E. G. (1980). Generalization of treatment effects following educational intervention with autistic children and youth. In B. Wilcox & A. Thompson (Eds.), *Critical issues in educating autistic children and youth* (pp. 118–134). Washington, DC: U.S. Department of Education, Office of Special Education.

Carr, E. G. (1983). *Application of pragmatics to conceptualization and treatment of severe behavior problems in children.* Paper presented at the Annual Convention of the American Psychological Association, Anaheim, CA.

Carr, E. G. (1985). Behavioral approaches to language and communication. In E. Schopler & G. Mesibov (Eds.), *Current issues in autism: III. Communication problems in autism.* New York: Plenum Press.

Cautela, J. R., & Baron, M. G. (1977). Covert conditioning: A theoretical analysis. *Behavior Modification, 1,* 351–368.

Cooke, F. P., & Apolloni, T. (1976). Developing positive social-emotional behaviors: A study of training and generalization effects. *Journal of Applied Behavior Analysis, 9,* 65–78.

Courchesne, E., Kilman, B. A., Galambos, R., & Lincoln, A. J. (1984). Autism: Processing of novel and auditory information assessed by event-related brain potentials. *Electroencephalography and Clinical Neurophysiology, 59,* 238–248.

Cusick, P. (1973). *Inside high school.* New York: Holt, Rinehart & Winston.

Donnellan, A. M. (1980). An educational perspective of autism: Implications for curriculum development and personnel development. In B. Wilcox & A. Thompson (Eds.), *Critical issues in educating autistic children and youth* (pp. 53–88). Washington, DC: U.S. Department of Education, Office of Special Education.

Donnellan, A. M. (1984). The criterion of the least dangerous assumption. *Behavior Disorders, 9,* 141–150.

Donnellan, A. M. (Ed.). (1985). *Classic readings in autism.* New York: Teachers College Press.

Donnellan, A. M., Anderson, J. L., & Mesaros, R. A. (1984). An observational study of stereotypic behavior and proximity related to the occurrence of autistic child/family member interactions. *Journal of Autism and Developmental Disorders, 14*, 205–210.

Donnellan, A. M., & LaVigna, G. W. (in press). Non-aversive control of socially stigmatizing behaviors. *Pointer.*

Donnellan, A. M., LaVigna, G. W., Zambito, J., & Thevdt, J. (1985). A time limited intensive intervention strategy to avoid institutionalization. *Journal of the Association for Persons with Severe Handicaps, 10*(3), 123–131.

Donnellan, A. M., Mesaros, R. A., & Anderson, J. L. (1984). Teaching students with autism in natural environments: What educators need from researchers. *Journal of Special Education, 18*, 505–522.

Donnellan, A. M., & Mirenda, P. L. (1983). A model for analyzing instructional components to facilitate generalization for severely handicapped students. *Journal of Special Education, 17,* 317–331.

Donnellan, A. M., Mirenda, P. L., Mesaros, R. A., & Fassbender, L. L. (1984). A strategy for analyzing the communicative functions of behavior. *Journal of the Association for Persons with Severe Handicaps, 11,* 201–212.

Donnellan-Walsh, A., Gossage, L. D., LaVigna, G. W., Schuler, A. L., & Traphagen, J. D. (1976). *Teaching makes a difference.* Santa Barbara, CA: Santa Barbara County Schools.

Duchan, J. F. (1982). Recent advances in language assessment: The pragmatics revolution. In R. Naremore (Ed.), *Recent advances in language sciences.* San Diego: College Hill Press.

Durand, V. M. (1982). Analysis and intervention of self-injurious behavior. *Journal of the Association for the Severely Handicapped, 7,* 44–53.

Ferster, C. B. (1961). Positive reinforcement and behavioral deficits of autistic children. *Child Development, 32,* 437–456.

Ferster, C. B., & DeMyer, M. K. (1962). A method for the experimental analysis of the behavior of autistic children. *American Journal of Orthopsychiatry, 32,* 89–98.

Ford, A., Brown, L., Pumpian, I., Baumgart, D., Nisbet, J., Schroeder, J., & Loomis, R. (1980). Strategies for developing individualized recreation/leisure plans for adolescent and young adult severely handicapped students. In L. Brown, M. Falvey, I. Pumpian, D. Baumgart, J. Nisbet, A. Ford, J. Shcroder, & R. Loomis (Eds.), *Curricular strategies for teaching severely handicapped students functional skills in school and nonschool environments* (Vol. 10). Madison, WI: University of Wisconsin-Madison and Madison Metropolitan School District.

Frankel, R. M. (1982). Autism for all practical purposes: A micro-interactional view. *Topics in Language Disorders, 3,* 33–42.

Friman, P. C., Cook, J. W., & Finney, J. W. (1984). Effects of punishment on the self-stimulatory behavior of an autistic child. *Analysis and Intervention in Developmental Disabilities, 4,* 36–46.

Gold, M., & Associates (1978). *Try another way training manual.* Sacramento: California Project.

Goldiamond, I. (1974). Toward a constructional approach to social problems. *Behaviorism, 2,* 1–84.

Goldstein, A., Sprafkin, R. P., & Gershow, N. J. (1984). *Skillstreaming the adolescent.* Champaign, IL: Research Press.

Greenwood, C. R., Walker, H. M., & Hops, H. (1977). Issues in social interaction/withdrawal assessment. *Exceptional Children, 43,* 490–499.

Groden, J. (1982). *The use of imagery procedures to increase initiations of verbal behavior among autistic children and adolescents: A multiple baseline analysis.* Unpublished doctoral dissertation, Boston College.

Hartup, W. (1970). Peer interaction and social organization. In P. Mussen (Ed.), *Manual of child psychology* (3rd ed.). New York: Wiley.

Hermelin, B. (1982). Thoughts and feelings. *Australian Autism Review, 1,* 10–19.

Homme, L. (1965). Perspectives in psychology XXIVL: Control of coverants, the operants of the mind. *Psychological Record, 15,* 501–511.

Inhelder, B., & Piaget, J. (1958). *The growth of logical thinking from childhood to adolescence.* New York: Basic Books.

Iwata, B. A., Dorsey, M. F., Slifer, K. J., Bauman, K. E., & Richman, G. S. (1982). Toward a functional analysis of self-injury. *Analysis and Intervention in Developmental Disabilities, 2,* 3–20.

Kanner, L. (1943). Autistic disturbances of affective contact. *Nervous Child, 2,* 273–280. (Reprinted in A. Donnellan (Ed.). (1985). *Classic readings in autism.* New York: Teachers College Press).

Keilitz, I., Tucker, D. J., & Horner, R. D. (1973). Increasing mentally retarded adolescents' verbalizations about current events. *Journal of Applied Behavior Analysis, 6,* 621–630.

Keller, F. S., & Schoenfeld, W. N. (1950). *Principles of psychology.* New York: Appleton-Century-Crofts.

Kilman, B. (1981). Developing social skills. In D. Park (Ed.), *Proceedings of the 1981 International Conference on Autism* (pp. 318–327). Washington, DC: National Society for Autistic Children.

Kilman, B., & Negri-Shoultz, N. (in press). Developing educational programs for working with "near normal" people with autism. In D. J. Cohen & A. M. Donnellan (Eds.), *Handbook of autism and disorders of atypical development.* New York: Wiley.

Kirby, F. D., & Toler, H. C. (1970). Modification of pre-school isolate behavior: A case study. *Journal of Applied Behavior Analysis, 3,* 309–314.

Koegel, R. L., & Rincover, A. (1977). Research on the difference between generalization and maintenance in extra-therapy responding. *Journal of Applied Behavior Analysis, 10,* 1–6.

Koegel, R. L., Rincover, A., & Egel, A. L. (Eds.). (1982). *Educating and understanding autistic children.* San Diego: College Hill Press.

Koegel, R. L., Russo, D. C., & Rincover, A. (1977). Assessing and training teachers in the generalized use of behavior modification with autistic children. *Journal of Applied Behavior Analysis, 10,* 197–205.

LaVigna, G. W., & Donnellan, A. M. (in press). *Alternatives to punishment: Non-aversive strategies for solving behavior problems.* New York: Irvington Press.

Liberman, R. P., King, L. W., Derisi, W. J., & McCann, M. (1976). *Personal effectiveness.* Champaign, IL: Research Press.

Lovaas, O. I. (1977). *The autistic child: Language development through behavior modification.* New York: Irvington Press.

Lovaas, O. (1981). *Teaching developmentally disabled children.* Baltimore: University Park Press.

Lovaas, O. I., Schaffer, B., & Simmons, J. Q. (1965). Building social behavior in autistic children by use of electric shock. *Journal of Experimental Research in Personality, 1,* 99–109.

Martin, R. (1975). *Legal challenges to behavior modification: Trends in schools, corrections, and mental health.* Champaign, IL: Research Press.

Martin, G., & Pear, J. (1983). *Behavior modification: What it is and how to do it.* Englewood Cliffs, NJ: Prentice-Hall.

McGinnis, E., & Goldstein, A. (1984). *Skill streaming the elementary school child.* Champaign, IL: Research Press.

McHale, S. M. (1983). The effects of repeated interaction on promoting play and communication between autistic and non-handicapped children. *American Journal of Orthopsychiatry, 53,* 1.

Meichenbaum, D. (1973). Cognitive factors in behavior modification: Modifying what clients say to themselves. In C. M. Franks & G. T. Wilson (Eds.), *Annual review of behavior therapy, theory, and practice.* New York: Brunner Mazel.

Mesaros, R. A. (1983). *A review of the issues and literature regarding positive programming and contingency management procedures for use with autistic children.* Unpublished manuscript, University of Wisconsin-Madison.

Mesaros, R. A. (1984). *Behavioral differences among autistic students in homogeneous and heterogeneous classroom grouping arrangements.* Unpublished doctoral dissertation, University of Wisconsin-Madison.

Mirenda, P. (in press). Covert conditioning. In G. W. LaVigna & A. M. Donnellan, *Alternatives to punishment: Non-aversive strategies for solving behavior problems.* New York: Irvington Press.

Mirenda, P., & Donnellan, A. M. (in press, a). Utilizing developmental, ecological and behavioral strategies in curriculum planning. In D. J. Cohen & A. M. Donnellan (Eds.), *Handbook of autism and disorders of atypical development.* New York: Wiley.

Mirenda, P. L., & Donnellan, A. M. (in press, b). The effects of adult interaction styles on conversational behavior in adolescents with handicaps. *Language, Speech, and Hearing Services in Schools.*

Mithaug, D. E., & Wolfe, M. S. (1976). Employing task arrangements and verbal contingencies to promote verbalizations between retarded children. *Journal of Applied Behavior Analysis, 9,* 301–314.

Morris, R. J., & Dolker, M. (1974). Developing cooperative play in socially withdrawn retarded children. *Mental Retardation, 12,* 24–27.

Phillips, E. L. (1968). Achievement place: Token reinforcement procedures in a home style rehabilitation setting for "pre-delinquent" boys. *Journal of Applied Behavior Analysis, 1,* 213–223.

Piaget, J. (1960). The definition of states of development. In J. Tanner & B. Inhelder (Eds.), *Discussions on child development* (pp. 116–135). New York: International Universities Press.

Prizant, B. M. (1978). *An analysis of the functions of immediate echolalia in autistic children.* Unpublished doctoral dissertation, State University of New York, Buffalo.

Prizant, B. M. (1982). Speech-language pathologists and autistic children: What is our role? (Part I). *ASHA, 24.*

Qulitch, H. R., & Risley, T. R. (1973). The effects of play materials on social play. *Journal of Applied Behavior Analysis, 6,* 573–578.

Repp, A. C., & Deitz, S. M. (1974). Reducing aggressive and self-injurious behavior of institutionalized retarded children through reinforcement of other behaviors. *Journal of Applied Behavior Analysis, 7,* 313–315.

Rogers-Warren, A. R., & Baer, D. M. (1976). Correspondence between saying and doing: Teaching children to share and praise. *Journal of Applied Behavior Analysis, 9,* 335–354.

Rogers-Warren, A., & Warren, S. F. (1977). *Ecological perspectives in behavior analysis.* Baltimore: University Park Press.

Russo, D.C., Cataldo, M. F., & Cushing, P. J. (1981). Compliance training and behavioral covariation in the treatment of multiple behavior problems. *Journal of Applied Behavior Analysis, 14,* 209–222.

Rutter, M. (1982a). Cognitive deficits in the pathogenesis of autism. *Journal of Child Psychology and Psychiatry, 24,* 513–531.

Rutter, M. (1982b). New directions in childhood psychotherapy. In S. I. Harrison & J. F. McDermott, Jr. (Eds.), *Deviations in development* (Vol. 2, pp. 979–1017). New York: International Universities Press.

Rutter, M. (1985). Introduction. In A. M. Donnellan (Ed.), *Classic readings in autism.* New York: Teachers College Press.

Schopler, E., Reichler, R. J., & Lansing, M. (1980). Teaching strategies for parents and professionals. In E. Schopler & J. Reichler (Eds.), *Individualized assessment and treatment for autistic and developmentally disabled children* (Vol. 2). Baltimore: University Park Press.

Schreibman, L. (1975). Effects of within stimulus and extra stimulus prompting on discrimination learning in autistic children. *Journal of Applied Behavior Analysis, 8,* 99–112.

Schreibman, L., Koegel, R. L., & Craig, M. S. (1977). Reducing stimulus overselectivity in autistic children. *Journal of Abnormal Child Psychology, 5,* 425–436.

Schuler, A. L. (1980). Teaching functional language. In B. Wilcox & A. Thompson (Eds.), *Critical issues in educating autistic children and youth* (pp. 154–178). Washington, DC: U.S. Department of Education.

Schuler, A. L., & Goetz, C. (1981). The assessment of severe language disabilities: Communicative and cognitive considerations. *Analysis and Intervention in Developmental Disabilities, 1,* 333–346.

Skinner, B. F. (1950). Are theories of learning necessary? *Psychological Review, 57,* 193–216.

Snell, M. E., & Gast, D. L. (1981). Applying time delay procedures to the instruction of the severely handicapped. *Journal of the Association for the Severely Handicapped, 6,* 3–14.

Spivack, G., & Shure, M. B. (1974). *Social adjustment of young children: A cognitive approach to solving real-life problems.* San Francisco: Jossey-Bass.

Stampfl, T. G., & Levis, D. J. (1967). Essentials of implosive therapy: A learning theory-based psychodynamic behavioral therapy. *Journal of Abnormal Psychology, 72,* 496–503.

Stokes, T. F., & Baer, D. (1977). Toward an implicit technology of generalization. *Journal of Applied Behavior Analysis, 10,* 349–367.

Strain, P. (1977). An experimental analysis of peer social initiations on the behavior of withdrawn preschool children: Some training and generalization effects. *Journal of Abnormal Child Psychology, 5,* 445–455.

Strain, P. (1983). Generalization of autistic children's social behavior change: Effects of developmentally integrated and segregated settings. *Analysis and Intervention in Developmental Disabilities, 3,* 23–34.

Strain, P. S., Kerr, M. M., & Ragland, E. (1979). Effects of peer-mediated social initiations and prompting/reinforcement procedures on the social behavior of autistic children. *Journal of Autism and Developmental Disorders, 9,* 41–53.

Strain, P. S., & Shores, R. E. (1977). Social reciprocity: A review of research and educational implications. *Exceptional Children, 43,* 526–530.

Strain, P. S., Shores, R. E., & Kerr, M. M. (1976). An experimental analysis of "spillover" effects on the social interaction of behaviorally handicapped preschool children. *Journal of Applied Behavior Analysis, 9,* 31–40.

Strain, P. S., Shores, R. E., & Timm, M. A. (1977). Effects of peer social initiations on the behavior of withdrawn preschool children. *Journal of Applied Behavior Analysis, 10,* 289–298.

Terrace, H. S. (1963). Discrimination learning with and without errors. *Journal of Experimental Analysis of Behavior, 6,* 1–27.

Thorndike, E. L. (1913). *The psychology of learning: II. Educational psychology.* New York: Teachers College Press.

Voeltz, L. M., & Evans, I. M. (1983). Educational validity: Procedures to evaluate outcomes in programs for severely handicapped learners. *Journal of the Association for the Severely Handicapped, 8,* 3–15.

Whitman, T. L., Mercurio, J. R., & Caponigri, V. (1970). Development of social responses in two severely retarded children. *Journal of Applied Behavior Analysis, 3,* 133–138.

Wing, L., & Gould, J. (1979). Severe impairments of social interaction and associated abnormalities in children: Epidemiology and classification. *Journal of Autism and Developmental Disorders, 9,* 11–29.

Winnicott, D. W. (1958). *Collected papers.* New York: Basic Books.

Wolfensberger, W. (1972). *The principle of normalization in human services.* Toronto: National Institute on Mental Retardation.

Wolpe, J. (1958). *Psychotherapy by reciprocal inhibition.* Stanford, CA: Stanford University Press.

Wood, M. M. (Ed.). (1975). *Developmental theory.* Baltimore: University Park Press.

Woods, T. (in press). The technology of instruction: A behavior analytic approach. In D. J. Cohen & A. M. Donnellan (Eds.), *Handbook of autism and disorders of atypical development.* New York: Wiley.

Yoder, D. (1980). Augmentative communication systems for severely speech handicapped children. In D. Bucher (Ed.), *Language development and intervention with the exceptional child* (pp. 24–38). New York: Jossey-Bass.

12

A Developmental Model for Facilitating the Social Behavior of Autistic Children

GERALDINE DAWSON and LARRY GALPERT

INTRODUCTION

In Kanner's (1943) original description of autistic children, as well as in the current DSM–III criteria for diagnosis of early infantile autism, the inability to relate normally to other people is given as a fundamental characteristic of this disorder. Yet, as Rutter (1983) has pointed out, "until very recently, the social abnormalities of autistic children have been the least studied of all the features of the syndrome, in spite of the fact that it is they that give rise to the name of the syndrome, autism" (p. 524). Instead, research has focused on the cognitive and language characteristics of autistic children. This research has not only led to a better understanding of the nature of their cognitive and linguistic deficits, it has also been the basis for a variety of therapeutic strategies, particularly language interventions, aimed at remediating them. It is encouraging, in light of this focus on language intervention, that many autistic children who have been exposed to intensive therapeutic and educational experiences have achieved quite adequate linguistic skills by adolescence. Their remaining difficulties lie within the social, rather than the strictly linguistic, realm. Thus, although these adolescents may be able to formulate and express complex ideas, their social use of language and their general ability to comprehend and adapt to subtle social cues remain serious problems.

GERALDINE DAWSON • Department of Psychology, University of Washington, Seattle, Washington 98195. LARRY GALPERT • Department of Psychology, University of North Carolina, Chapel Hill, North Carolina 27514.

Partly because of the recognition that language intervention alone cannot remedy the social deficits of autistic people and partly as a result of the continued search by scientists for the fundamental deficits in autism, investigators recently have begun to view the social behavior of autistic children as an area of research and as a direct focus of intervention. Fortunately, the research literature on the early development of affect and social behavior in normal infants is rapidly expanding. The empirical findings and theoretical formulations generated by this emphasis allow us to construct developmental models for disorders characterized by basic abnormalities in social functioning such as those seen in early infantile autism.

The purposes of this chapter are to provide a framework for a developmental model of autism and to suggest some implications of such an approach for designing therapies for autistic children. We begin by providing a brief survey of recent research on the early social development of normal infants. The social deficits found in autism and their influences on development are then discussed. Next, we outline the features of a developmental approach to the treatment of autistic children. An example of such a treatment strategy follows. Finally, we discuss the limitations and some possible criticisms of such a therapeutic approach with autistic children.

The basic tenets of the model presented here are founded on theories of normal infant development, as well as on current research on the early development of affect, patterns of social interaction, and social cognition. Briefly, these tenets are as follows: First, many aspects of social and affective development appear generally to proceed in an orderly, sequential manner. Sroufe (1979) has suggested that affective and social development may be viewed as progressing through a series of hierarchical stages analogous to Piaget's stages of cognitive development. Although Sroufe's stage theory is still speculative, the notion that many aspects of early affective and social behavior emerge in a fairly reliable sequence is not (Lewis & Rosenblum, 1978). Similar to cognitive and linguistic development, early social and affective capacities are prerequisite for subsequent development; earlier-developing competencies provide a basis for later, related competencies. Second, it is clear that the young infant has numerous sensorimotor competencies that prime the infant to be socially responsive and thus are critical for social and emotional growth. The deficits of autistic children appear to involve these basic social competencies required for the establishment of normal patterns of social interaction. Third, most theories of early development (e.g., Sroufe, 1979) argue for the inseparability of affective, social, and cognitive development. These systems appear to develop in a mutually supportive, interlocking manner. The implication for autistic children is that their basic affective and social deficits are likely to have significant impact on their cognitive development, and vice versa. Moreover, as the relationships among these developmental domains become specified, it may be possible to describe and predict how the autistic child's particular impairments in one domain are related to impairments in other domains. Another implication of this integrative view of development is that arguments for the primacy of affective versus cognitive impairments in the pathogenesis of autism may no longer be meaningful. As will be evident later, it appears that the behavioral deficits that characterize autism cannot be considered purely cognitive. Rather, the behaviors in which autistic children are impaired serve both socioemotional *and* cognitive functions. A fourth premise of a developmental approach is the recognition of the parent–child relationship as a two-way, interactive system. The success of early social interactions relies on infants' behavioral propensities that permit them to provide feedback to their parents, as well as on the parents' ability to respond to their infants' initiations (Lamb & Easterbrooks, 1981). In the case of autism, the young child may neither initiate social interactions (for example, babbling and smiling) nor provide contingent feedback to his or her parents (for example, eye contact and soothability). Although the specific effects these deficiencies have on parental behavior are unknown, they will undoubtedly influence the parent's sense of efficacy and may lead to increases or decreases in parental attempts to provide infant stimulation (Brazelton, 1982).

The problem of how to provide optimal social experiences for the autistic child is a difficult one. Some suggestions based on a developmental model for facilitating early social behavior will be made later in this chapter. The primary characteristics of such a therapeutic approach may be outlined as follows: First, as deficiencies in early social interactions are a basic feature of autism, they should be a direct focus of intervention. Second, therapeutic strategies to facilitate their social development should take into account each child's specific developmental limitations. An evaluation of each child's competencies in the social and affective realms will determine the focus of intervention. Social experiences that are appropriate for the child's developmental level—that is, at or slightly above the child's current capacities—are thought to be optimally stimulating of future development. Third, facilitation of early social competencies is expected to lead to improvements in cognitive and affective realms, and to pave the way for later communicative development (for example, use of communicative language).

EARLY SOCIAL DEVELOPMENT IN NORMAL INFANTS

Perception of Social Stimuli

An extensive literature exists on the early development of infants' perception of other persons. Studies suggest that the neonate has certain visual attentional strategies that lead to a preference for social rather than nonsocial stimuli. These include a tendency to seek out and respond to both movement (Haith, 1966; Wickelgren, 1969) and contour density (Karmel, Hoffman, & Fegy, 1974; Kessen, Haith, & Salapatek, 1970). By 1 to 3 months of age, infants prefer actual faces to representations of faces (Dirks & Gibson, 1977; Lewis, 1969; McCall & Kagan, 1967; Polak, Emde, & Spitz, 1964; Wilcox, 1969), animate to inanimate faces (Carpenter, 1974; Field, 1979; Haith, Bergman, & Moore, 1977; Piaget, 1952; Sherrod, 1979), and regularly arranged faces to scrambled or altered faces (Caron, Caron, Caldwell, & Weiss, 1973; Kagan, Henler, Hen-Tov, Levine, & Lewis, 1966). These studies suggest that a cognitive schema for faces emerges fairly early as a result of visual attentional strategies that make people salient in the infant's environment.

By approximately 3 months of age, infants make more complex visual discriminations among social stimuli. For example, they recognize specific persons (Bernard & Ramey, 1977; Cohen, 1974; Sherrod, 1979) and discriminate among various facial expressions (Field, Woodson, Greenberg, & Cohen, 1982; Oster, 1981). Voices also attract the attention of young infants, and do so more effectively than other sounds (Church, 1970; Hutt, Lenard, & Precht, 1969). Moreover, by 2 to 4 months of age, an infant expects mother's face to accompany mother's voice, a finding that suggests complex intermodal coordinations have been made (Spelke, 1976; Spelke & Cortelyou, 1981). Thus, it appears that very young infants possess numerous perceptual capacities that help them appreciate and interpret social stimuli.

Early Patterns of Social Interaction

In addition to having a capacity to perceptually organize the social world, infants quickly establish a variety of patterns of interacting with other people. They both respond to and initiate social interactions from birth. Young infants express themselves through, gaze, motor activity, facial expression, and vocalizations.

Gaze Patterns

So central is the role of gaze in early patterns of interaction that Rheingold (1961) has suggested that visual, not physical, contact is the basis of human sociability. By 3 months of age, gaze patterns form a kind of "dialogic" exchange between parent and infant. Typically, short cycles of attending to the parent and withdrawing or turning away underlie sustained period of interaction. The infant does not stare continuously but alternately gazes at and away from the mother's face. As the mother responds to the ebb and flow of the infant's gaze, the two partners create a rhythmic pattern of mutual approach and withdrawal (Stern, 1974).

A major function of gaze is to allow infants control over the amount of stimulation they receive (Brazelton, 1982; Brazelton, Koslowski, & Main, 1974). Looking away typically results in a reduction of parental stimulation (Stern, 1971). Thus, the young infant's gaze allows the parent to be sensitive to the infant's attentional capacities and need for withdrawal.

The idea that mother–infant gaze patterns are an early form of dialogue is supported by observations that the temporal patterns of mother–infant gaze are similar to those of adult verbal conversations (Jaffe, Stern, & Peery, 1973). Stern (1974) argues for continuity between early gaze patterns and the later gaze patterns that become coordinated with speech (Kendon, 1967). Thus, infant gaze appears to serve both as a signal indicating readiness to engage in interaction, as it does in later verbal interactions, and as a means for a controlling perception and arousal (Stern, 1977).

Another gaze pattern is prolonged mutual gaze, which parents usually interpret as "loving" (Stern, 1974, p. 209). Robson (1967) views this eye-to-eye contact as critical for mother–infant bonding and as a primary elicitor of maternal responses to the infant. Mothers often interpret their young infants' sustained gaze to be sign of recognition and acknowledgment. A failure to engage in eye-to-eye contact, such as by a blind infant, is often experienced by the mother as a rebuff (Fraiberg, 1974). The gaze patterns of mother and infant are thus crucial for the mother as well as for the infant's own development.

Vocalizations

Vocalizations also play an important role in early interactions. Rosenthal (1982) found that, as early as 3 days of age, the infant is more likely to start vocalizing in the presence of maternal vocalization than in its absence. Moreover, it has been demonstrated that newborns prefer their mothers' voices over those of other mothers (DeCasper & Fifer, 1980). As has been found in studies of 2- to 4-month-old infants (Anderson, Vietze, & Dokecki, 1977; Freedle & Lewis, 1977; Stern, Jaffe, Beebe, & Bennet, 1975), the patterns of vocal exchange between mother and neonate are both simultaneous and alternating (Rosenthal, 1982), although the former predominates. Both patterns of exchange are viewed by various investigators as precursors of later verbal communication (Freedle, & Lewis, 1977; Rosenthal, 1982). This notion is supported by the observation that, even when the infant fails to vocalize following mother's utterance, mothers pause as if to anticipate a response (Stern, 1977). Thus, the infant at a very early age is exposed to interactions that have the form of conversations.

Affect

By about 3 months of age, infants express emotions in response to specific events. Sroufe (1979) describes three basic affective systems: pleasure/joy, wariness/fear, and rage/anger. According to Sroufe, the first emotions within each of these systems are apparent by 3 to 4 months. By 4 to 6 months, the infant demonstrates differential affective responses to the affective expressions of others (Oster, 1981). The infant's affective expressions are important elicitors of parental responses and thus play a key role in the development of early social interaction. Lamb (1981) has postulated that one of the earliest predictable and salient sequences of interaction between parent and infant is the "distress–relief" sequence. He further suggests that contingent responding by the parent to the infant's distress allows the infant to form social expectations, that is, to learn that distress predictably brings relief and, moreover, that a person is responsible for this positive experience.

Imitation

Imitation is among the most important and widely studied patterns of parent–infant interaction. Recent studies have shown that neonates can imitate facial expressions, as well as finger and hand movements, shortly after birth (Abravenel & Sigafoos, 1984; Field et al., 1982; Meltzoff & Moore, 1977). Although there is considerable controversy over whether this early imitation is reflexive or intentional, the phenomenon itself suggests that neonates have some form of body representational system. Studies of 2- to 3-month-old infants also report instances of facial and body imitation; however, much more common is the observation of mothers imitating their infants' expressions, often in an exaggerated form (Papousek & Papousek, 1977; Trevarthen, 1977). Imitation becomes more systematic by 4 to 6 months, at which time the infant imitates familiar vocalizations and a variety of other familiar acts, such as waving and banging (Stern, Jaffe, Beebe, & Bennet, 1975; Uzgiris, 1972).

Most of the research on infant imitation has stressed the cognitive function of imitation, in particular its role in the development of symbolic thought (Piaget, 1962). However, several investigators (Bower, 1977; Uzgiris, 1981a, 1981b) argue that imitation equally serves a social function. As a communicative act, imitation serves the function of shared mutuality, the significant element being the connection or congruence experienced by both partners rather than the content of the act itself. Uzgiris (1981b) states that both mothers and infants find an imitative response to be salient and interesting. Mothers often pay special attention to infant behaviors that match their own while ignoring others and infants smile in response to their mothers' imitations (Papousek & Papousek, 1977).

These smiles underscore the social nature of imitation. Uzgiris (1981b) makes the point that "an instance of imitation can epitomize the presence of mutuality; to do something that has just been done by the other is to know something not only about the act but also about the similarity between oneself and the other" (p. 151).

Reciprocity and Intentionality

To become fully social, the infant's interactions must acquire reciprocity and intentionality. The early dialogues between mother and infant are not truly reciprocal since it is primarily the mother's responsibility to sustain the interaction by synchronizing her responses to the infant's behaviors (Garvey, 1977; Schaffer, 1977). However, her responses affect the infant in such a way that a cycle of mutual influence emerges, forming the beginnings of reciprocal interaction (Tronick, Als, & Adamson, 1979). A classic example of this process has been described by Kaye and Wells (1980). In their observation of mother–infant feeding, they noted that when neonates paused between bursts of sucking, mothers tended to jiggle them. At first, the infants' cycles of bursts and pauses were independent of the mother's jiggling. However, as the mothers continued to jiggle during their infants' pauses, the infants' sucking eventually became responsive to the jiggling. That is, after jiggling, the chances that the baby would resume sucking increased. Thus, mothers' responses to their infants' natural cycles of behavior eventually led to the creation of a reciprocal exchange. Later, as infants come to differentiate and adopt the various roles in social play, a more fully developed sense of reciprocity emerges.

The roots of intentionality lie in the infant's perception of itself as an effective social agent. The parent's sensitive, contingent responding to the infant's behavior allows the infant a sense of control over the social environment. In this way, infants develop expectations of other people as well as what Schaffer (1977) calls an "effectance motive," that is, a confidence that their behavior can produce consequences. For this motive to develop, parents' responses must be contingent, predictable, and repetitive (Lamb, 1981). Furthermore, the infant must be able to perceive contingent relationships. Experimental evidence (Rovée-Collier & Lipsitt, 1981) suggests that they do so by about 3 months of age.

Social behavior is facilitated rather than directly taught by the parent. Facilitation occurs in the context of natural parent–infant interactions and social play. Parents use a number of interactive strategies to maximize social growth (Schaffer, 1977). To begin with, they are sensitive to the state and attentional focus of their infant. After gaining the infant's attention, parents time their own actions to be responsive to the infant's spontaneous behavior. Moreover, their actions are simplified and exaggerated (Schaffer, 1977). Two things are required of the infant for this facilitative process to work. First, the infant must provide the parents with behavioral cues, such as signs of interest and pleasure, that guide and modulate the parents' actions. Second, the infant must be receptive to the stimulation provided; that is, he or she must have the perceptual capacity to make sense of the social stimuli. In the next section, we discuss the autistic child's impairments in these fundamental competencies and their implications for development.

SOCIAL DEFICITS OF AUTISTIC CHILDREN

The characteristic impairments of autism involve the early expressive and receptive capacities that are the foundation of social interaction. In contrast to the wealth of studies of early social and affective development in normal infants, relatively few systematic studies of social behavior in autism exist. What we currently know about the social deficits of autistic children rests primarily on clinical descriptions, although some epidemiological and experimental studies also exist (e.g., Hermelin & O'Connor, 1970; Hutt & Hutt, 1970; Wing, 1981). Descriptive studies of the social behavior of autistic children and their caretakers in natural, interactive contexts are relatively few. In this section, the primary social deficits of autistic children, that is, those that characterize the syndrome and appear to exist from its onset, are described. These deficits are most characteristic of young (that is, below 5 years) autistic children since some aspects of social behavior typically improve in later childhood.

Gaze Patterns

Of the deviant social behaviors shown by young autistic children, abnormal eye-to-eye gaze has received the most attention by investigators. Considerable evidence confirms that autistic children use gaze abnormally (Castell, 1970; Hutt & Vaizey, 1966; O'Connor & Hermelin, 1967). However, the nature and cause of abnormal gaze patterns are unresolved questions. Some investigators claim that autistic children selectively avoid social contact, including eye contact, because of the anxiety such encounters precipitate (Richer, 1978; Tinbergen & Tinbergen, 1972) or because of the heightened state of arousal that accompanies eye-to-eye contact (Hutt & Ounsted, 1970). Other investigators argue that "poor eye contact can be seen as arising from the absence of any mechanism for understanding the environment" (Wing, 1978, p. 41). Experimental studies concerning this issue offer conflicting and ambiguous results (e.g., Clark & Rutter, 1981; Hermelin & O'Connor, 1970; Hutt & Ounsted, 1970; Mirenda, Donnellan, & Yoder, 1983; Richer, 1978). Resolution awaits careful observation of autistic children in natural social interactions. Whether autistic children actively avoid or simply fail to attend to faces, it seems clear that they use gaze in an abnormal way (Rutter, 1978; Mirenda *et al.*, 1983). The subjective impression of those interacting with a young autistic child is one of decreased eye contact and social aloofness.

A finding that has been consistently reported in the research literature is that the *amount* of eye contact and social responsiveness exhibited by autistic children is related to the *complexity* of the social stimuli or encounter. For example, Ferrara and Hill (1980) found that autistic children both manipulated and looked at social toys more than nonsocial toys only when they were both of low complexity. In addition, autistic children showed a preference for manipulating toys of low complexity, while normal children preferred those of high complexity. Similarly, Hermelin and O'Connor (1963) found that the complexity of a social encounter affected autistic children's social responsiveness. They reported that autistic children did not differ from mentally retarded children in their approaches and responses to people as long as the contacts were simple and nonverbal. When the autistic children were spoken to, their social responsiveness decreased. This study suggests that social withdrawal is, at least in part, a function of the autistic child's ability to make sense of social interactions. Complexity must be defined *relative* to a given child's cognitive abilities. Dawson and Adams (1984) found that the autistic child's social responsiveness and eye contact significantly increased when an experimenter presented an imitation task that was appropriate for the child's developmental level, as previously assessed on a scale of imitation development. Thus, the autistic child's withdrawal in response to novel, complex stimuli appears to be related to the child's level of cognitive development.

Vocalizations

We know very little about the early vocalizations of autistic children. Parents often report that their autistic child did not babble as a young infant. Clinicians are commonly faced with an autistic child of preschool age who exhibits little or no prelinguistic babbling. Ricks (1979) compared the early vocalizations of 3- to 5-year-old autistic and mentally retarded children and of normal infants. Parents of normal infants found it easy to understand the message (for example, request, frustrated) conveyed by the vocalizations of their own and other normal children but had difficulty interpreting those of an autistic child. The parents of normal infants also had difficulty distinguishing their own infant's vocalization from those of other infants. In contrast, parents of autistic children could interpret their own child's vocalization as well as those of the normal infants. Moreover, the parents of autistic children selected their own child with ease. Ricks's study suggests that when vocalizations are present in autistic children, they are both atypical and idiosyncratic.

Affect

The early affective expressions of autistic children have not been systematically studied. Parents often report that, as an infant, their autistic child was exceptionally "good" and undemanding. Such accounts may reflect the autistic infant's impairments in expressing the typical emotions that command attention from the parent. Clinical observations suggest that, by preschool age, autistic children do exhibit emotional reactions to specific events, including pleasure, wariness, and rage. However, more highly developed emotions, such as shame, affection, and guilt (usually evident by 2 to 3 years in normal children), are lacking. As Sroufe (1979) points out, these more sophisticated emotions are tied to increasing levels of self-awareness and to role differentiation. Interestingly, several studies (Dawson & McKissick, 1984; Ferrari & Matthews, 1983; Neuman & Hill, 1978) have found that autistic children do not have a specific impairment in visual self-recognition; however, they respond differently to their mirror images than do normal children. In particular, autistic children's failure to exhibit the self-conscious or coy reactions that most infants do (Amsterdam, 1972; Dixon, 1957; Lewis & Brooks-Gunn, 1979) suggests that some aspect of self-awareness is lacking.

Autistic children also have difficulty discriminating among, and comprehending, facial expressions. This characteristic appears to persist into adulthood, as reported in case studies by Bemporad (1979) and Rutter (1983). A lack of empathic responses by autistic children is often noted. Empathy requires that the child be able to adopt the perspective of another person. Althogh Hobson (1984) found that autistic children were no more impaired than normal or retarded children (of similar mental age) in visuospatial perspective taking, Dawson and Fernald (1985) found that autistic children had difficulty in conceptual and affective perspective taking, the latter being more difficult for them. Furthermore, these investigators found that the children's level of perspective-taking ability was correlated with their level of social skills.

Imitation

As noted earlier, mutual imitation is one of the early forms of communication between infant and parent. Numerous studies have documented autistic children's lack of spontaneous gestural imitation and their specific impairments on tasks requiring motor imitation, relative to certain other sensorimotor tasks (Curcio, 1978; Dawson & Adams, 1984; DeMyer *et al.*, 1972; Hammes & Langdell, 1981; Ricks & Wing, 1975; Wing, 1981). Using the Uzgiris-Hunt Developmental Scales (Uzgiris & Hunt, 1975), Dawson and Adams (1984) assessed imitation and object permanence in a group of 15 4- to 6-year-old autistic children. Most of the children were found to have well-developed object permanence skills. In contrast, half of the children were functioning at the level of normal 1- to 4-month-old infants in their imitative ability, and only 3 of the 15 children had imitation skills commensurate with their object permanence skills. Moreover, the children's ability to imitate, but not to solve object permanence tasks, was correlated with other aspects of their social behavior, including levels of social responsiveness, free play, and language. A relationship between imitation ability and social relatedness was also reported by Wing and Gould (1979). DeMyer (1976) and Dawson (Dawson & Adams, 1984) consider the autistic child's problems in motor imitation to be one of the primary obstacles in establishing and learning from social relationships.

Need for Predictability

Autistic children appear to need a high degree of predictability and consistency in their environments (Rutter, 1978). Clinically, we know that these children do not adapt well to changes in their environments and seem to function best in highly structured, routine settings (Schopler, Brehm, Kinsbourne, & Reichler, 1971). Ferrara and Hill (1980) reported that, in an experimental play situation, autistic children's behavior became "seriously disorganized" when they were not able to predict the sequence of events; conversely, their responsiveness to the environment increased when the timing of the events was predictable. Normal children of similar mental age were able to adapt to the unpredictable sequences. This need for a high degree of predictability is likely to interfere with autistic children's social development. Although parents do tend to provide contingent, predictable responses to their children's behavior, the degree of predictability in naturally occurring interactions may not be sufficient for the autistic child to benefit from it.

IMPLICATONS OF EARLY SOCIAL DEFICITS FOR DEVELOPMENT

The early deficits of autistic children will have a number of immediate effects on their social environment and experiences. Social stimuli may not be particularly salient or meaningful; thus, the child's access to social experiences may be limited. Deficient expressive capacities, such as gaze, vocalizations, and facial expressions, make it difficult for others to provide contingent and appropriate feedback (Als, 1982). Impairments in perceiving contingent relationships, as well as a failure to imitate body movements and facial expressions, place them at a further disadvantage.

The failure to establish early social relationships will also have three major secondary consequences. Reciprocity, a basic feature of social interaction, may fail to develop. As Rutter (1983) has recently pointed out, "More than anything else it is the reciprocity of social interchange that is missing in autism" (p. 525). Thus, even when autistic individuals are motivated to seek out friendships and social experiences, their attempts to do so lack sensitivity to others and thus appear awkward and inflexible. Their social behavior is deficient in the very features that characterize early mother–infant interactions: namely, synchronization, mutuality, and reciprocity. This is later reflected in the autistic individual's use of language, which shows an enduring impairment in its pragmatic aspects even when the formal elements have been mastered. At first, the child may not use language in a communicative manner. Later, when attempts to communicate are made, the child usually has difficulty adjusting his or her language to the needs of the listener and fails to recognize that communication involves turn taking. Thus, even the higher-functioning autistic adolescent tends to use a formal, rigid style, speaks for long periods of time without allowing for a response from the listener, and fails to consider whether the listener is even interested in what he or she is saying (Simmons & Baltaxe, 1975).

The second influence on development concerns the effects of impairments in the perception and elicitation of contingent social responses. Autistic children's need for a high degree of predictability and lack of visual attention to other persons may make it difficult for them to perceive contingencies between their own behavior and that of others. Moreover, they fail to display a variety of behaviors that typically elicit predictable responses from parents. Given these deficits, the child may fail to acquire specific expectations of others and a more general sense of effectance and intentionality (Lamb, 1981). Also, since contingent responding may be a primary means whereby social and nonsocial objects are distinguished (Watson, 1967, 1979), a preference for persons as opposed to other objects may fail to develop.

Third, the social deficits of autistic children impede the acquisition of socially transmitted knowledge. This includes the basic knowledge of self and others, in terms of both unique and shared characteristics, of the variety of facial and other nonverbal expressions used to convey and interpret feelings and needs, and of the human symbol system, including the use of gesture, pretend play, and so on. Studies of the early-developing cognitive capabilities of young autistic children (e.g., Curcio, 1978; Dawson & Adams, 1984; DeMyer *et al.*, 1972; Hammes & Langdell, 1981; Ricks & Wing, 1975; Riquet, Taylor, Benaroya, & Klein, 1981; Sigman & Ungerer, 1984; Ungerer & Sigman, 1981; Wing, Gould, Yeates, & Brierly, 1977) consistently report impairments in symbolic play, motor imitation, use of gesture, and vocal language. In contrast, these children typically exhibit relatively good skills in areas such as object permanence and spatial relationships. This profile of cognitive strengths and weaknesses is characteristic of autism and not characteristic of mentally retarded children (e.g., Riquet *et al.*, 1981; Sigman & Ungerer, 1984; Wing *et al.*, 1977).

Wolf and Gardner (1981) suggest that imitation, gesture, symbolic play, and language are all part of the *symbolic* system, whereas object permanence and knowledge of space are aspects of another, independently developing system, which they refer to as *representational*. In their words,

> Representation, the ability to reconstruct or recall information to guide behavior, seems to occur earlier and gives rise to a number of phenomena: object permanence, anticipations in problem solving, and stored knowledge of space. Symbolization is a process that is different from this ability to remember and to guide behavior via an internal image or plan; it is the ability to convert such information into observable forms that refer to, rather than simply guide, experience. (p. 295)

We suggest that the early social deficits of autistic children have a particularly adverse effect on the symbolic system while the representational system is relatively intact, as evidenced by their often excellent rote memories and knowledge of spatial relationships. On the basis of a longitudinal study of young infants and children, Wolf and Gardner (1981) further argue that symbolic abilities evolve out of the early social interactions and reciprocal play between young infants and their caretakers. At about 18 months of age, children begin to conceptualize and adopt the diverse roles involved in social play—for example, they are able to play both hider and seeker in a game of peekaboo (Bruner & Sherwood, 1976). According to Wolf and Gardner, these concepts, called role structures, form a basis for the development of symbolic play and language. The Wolf and Gardner model thus provides a framework for understanding the link between autistic children's early social handicaps and their impaired symbolic abilities.

A DEVELOPMENTAL APPROACH TO INTERVENTION

So far, we have focused on the use of a developmental perspective for understanding the social deficits of autistic children. We turn now to the application of this perspective to a model of intervention. First, we discuss the features of such a model; then we illustrate them with an example from our own work. Finally, we discuss possible criticisms and limitations of this approach.

A developmental approach is necessarily a sequential or hierarchical one: The attainment of later developmental goals depends upon the successful attainment of earlier ones. Consideration of this logical progression is a hallmark of a developmental intervention. One seeks to build upon existing competencies and to address deficits that preclude further development. For instance, the ability to recognize people as social objects logically precedes the development of later social skills and cognitions, such as reciprocity in play. Facilitation of prerequisite functions should precede attempts to model, instruct, or train more advanced forms of social interaction.

The efficacy of a developmental treatment program depends upon the fit between the child's abilities and the demands of the intervention. To ensure that the acquired behaviors are meaningful to the child, the intervention must be within the child's cognitive reach. Experiences that are at or slightly above the child's capacity to comprehend them will be optimally stimulating. Brazelton (1982) and his colleagues have described the continual process of matching social interactions to the developing capacities of the infant in such a way that further development is anticipated. Bruner (1982) has similarly conceptualized the processes he calls "scaffolding" and "raising the ante," referring thereby to the contextual support provided by the mother, staying always a step ahead and guiding the child's development. This process is so commonplace that it is easily overlooked. For instance, in the game of peekaboo, no sooner has the child grasped the nature of this recurring appearance and disappearance than a more sophisticated game of hide-and-seek ensues, drawing the child on to further discovery. In raising an autistic child, the parent is at a great disadvantage in attempting to provide this "scaffolding." First, the young autistic child shows indifference or aversion to social stimuli. Second, the autistic child gives little outward expression of his or her internal world and little of the feedback that typically elicits social interaction. Initially, the intervention must address this basic lack of social relatedness. A developmental approach toward this goal is to build an "augmented scaffold" to facilitate this capacity. This augmented scaffold entails gearing social experiences to the child's developmental competencies and highlighting and simplifying the relevant aspects of normal interactions so as to render them more salient and assimilable for the child.

The ecological or naturalistic validity of this approach is also reflected in the assumption that the child must take an active role in social interactions for them to be fully meaningful. In normal social development, the child is an active participant, both initiator and responder. Spontaneous social behavior has been difficult for therapists of autistic children to train. The social behavior of even the more sophisticated autistic child tends to be passive, mechanical, and under external stimulus control.

A key feature of a developmental approach is the structuring of interactions so as to ensure an active, initiative role by the child. The therapist utilizes the child's spontaneous behavior to begin the interactive sequence, thus placing the child unknowingly in the role of the initiator. Eventually, the child assumes the role intentionally (recall the Kaye and Wells, 1980, "jiggle–suck" dialogue described previously). The therapist must creatively utilize behaviors in the child's repertoire and ensure that, whenever possible, the child's initiations are responded to positively.

Implicit throughout this discussion has been that the goal of a developmental intervention is to effect changes in the child's understanding of the social world. The intervention assumes that the problem is not simply a lack of skills but a more basic lack of sociability, including an awareness of others as social entities and an interest in interacting with them. Behavioral changes are expected to follow from changes in understanding and are not directly trained (though, to be sure, behavioral and developmental approaches may be used concurrently). Changes in the child's understanding of the social world should facilitate generalization of the behaviors acquired and preparation for further development.

We have discussed several of the key features of a developmental model of intervention: (1) its sequential nature, (2) the matching of intervention to the needs and abilities of the child, (3) the use of "augmented scaffolding," (4) the active role of the child, and (5) the emphasis on social understanding as the basis for behavioral change. Together these features constitute a coherent model, but individual features can be integrated with other approaches. For example, a behavioral program might be potentiated by consideration of the child's developmental level and by tailoring target behaviors to meet his or her needs.

ILLUSTRATION OF A DEVELOPMENTAL INTERVENTION

The first author recently completed a study in which a developmental approach was used to facilitate motor imitation and social responsiveness with a group of 15 young (4 to 6 years) autistic children (Dawson & Adams, 1984). The goal was to provide a structured, facilitative context in which the child would be more likely to spontaneously exhibit the desired behaviors, in this case imitation and other social behaviors. We focused on imitation since research on normal development in infancy suggests that imitation is prerequisite for symbol formation (Piaget, 1952), as well as an early opportunity for communication and social interaction (Uzgiris, 1981a, 1981b).

Three different interactive conditions were used that varied in the level of ability required of the child. In the first condition, the experimenter simultaneously imitated the child's toy play with a set of identical toys. This condition is similar to what Piaget (1952) termed "mutual imitation," characteristic of Stage II of imitation development. It is also similar to, though more structured than, the early interactions of normal young infants and their mothers, namely, the "coactional" strategy (Rosenthal, 1982). In the second condition, the experimenter modeled an action known to be in the child's behavioral repertoire, using a toy identical to one available to the child. This condition parallels Stage III of Piaget's theory of imitation development, during which infants are able to imitate only familiar behaviors. In the third condition, novel actions with a toy were modeled by the experimenter (Piaget's Stages IV and V). The child was not prompted to imitate or reinforced for doing so. Rather, we were interested in eliciting *spontaneous* imitation as well as other social behaviors, such as eye contact.

The children's imitative abilities were previously assessed using the Uzgiris-Hunt Scale (Uzgiris & Hunt, 1975). Autistic children with a low level of imitative ability (Piaget's Stages II and III) responded more favorably when the experimenter simultaneously imitated their actions than when she modeled a familiar or novel scheme. When the experimenter imitated their behavior, these children were significantly more socially responsive (for example, touched and vocalized to the experimenter more frequently), showed more eye contact, and played in a less perseverative manner. When the experimenter modeled a familiar as opposed to a novel scheme, these children were more likely to imitate the experimenter spontaneously. In contrast, the social behavior and spontaneous imitation of the children with more highly developed imitation skills did not differ significantly across conditions.

We were particularly interested in the finding that imitating the child led to increased eye contact and general social responsiveness, and facilitated toy exploration (that is, the child played with more toys, more creatively). Similar findings have been reported by Tiegerman and Primavera (1981, 1984). They found that, compared to two other interactive strategies, imitating autistic children's play with objects led to the greatest increase in eye contact and object manipulation.

Imitating a young autistic child's behavior may be effective in facilitating social responsiveness for several reasons. First, according to our assessments, as well as those of others, it appears that many preschool-age autistic children function socially at a level similar to that of 1- to 4-month-old infants. Thus, by adopting a very early interactive strategy, we may provide social experiences that are appropriate for, and meaningful to, the child. Second, this particular strategy allows the child to take active control of the interaction. The child learns that he or she can effectively and predictively elicit a response from another person. Furthermore, because the interaction is led by the child, he or she can regulate the amount and type of stimulation received from the other person, thus ensuring that the interaction will not be overstimulating or too complex.

Lamb (1981) has suggested that three components of early parental response to their infant's behavior are necessary for the infant to perceive contingencies: (1) The responses must be *contingent* and *predictable*, (2) the responses must be *behaviorally consistent*, and (3) the responses must be appropriately *salient* and *reinforcing*. Simultaneously imitating the child incorporates all of these components.

A critical feature of the simultaneous imitation procedure is that several important elements of normally occurring early interactions are exaggerated and simplified for the autistic child. The procedure is carried out in a structured, distraction-free setting. The child's ability to associate his or her behavior with the partner's is facilitated by the partner's responses being highly predictable and identical to the child's actions. Thus, although this interaction is similar to that which occurs naturally, its augmented features may help overcome the attentional and perceptual deficits of the autistic child.

We are currently investigating the effectiveness of this simultaneous imitation strategy with young (3 to 5 years) autistic children when it is performed at home by mothers on a daily basis. We hope that the effects will be cumulative (as found by Tiegerman and Primavera in a laboratory setting) and that increases in social responsiveness will generalize to new settings and stimulus materials. We expect to confirm the earlier finding that this intervention is most appropriate for children with low imitative skills, which we consider to be one indicator of social ability.

In our view, such an interactive strategy would provide the first step in a series of structured play strategies increasing in level of sophistication. For example, a next step might involve alternating rather than simultaneous imitation, and varying degrees of similarity between the child's and partner's actions. Reciprocal interaction, in which the child is both recipient and initiator of a response, such as in ball play, would be an eventual goal.

LIMITATIONS OF A DEVELOPMENTAL APPROACH

Two major criticisms of a developmental approach have been discussed by Bloom and Lahey (1978) in reference to the treatment of language disorders. First, if the normal developmental sequence has failed to occur in the context of normal interactions, what cause is there to believe that more of the same will be beneficial? Second, the concept of "developmental level" loses some of its meaning in the case of abnormal development. What is the "developmental level" of a child with the motor skills of a 4-year-old, the linguistic ability of a 2-year-old, and the social skills of an infant?

In response to the first criticism, there is the definite possibility that "megadoses" of a particular type of experience may prove remedial when normal amounts have failed to promote normal development. This is especially true for autistic children, given their inattention to, and difficulty in, processing social stimuli. Furthermore, we have suggested that in order to be facilitative, the intervention strategies must differ qualitatively from normal interactions. In particular, the relevant factors of the interactions are highlighted and simplified to accommodate the perceptual limitations of autistic children. In the procedure described above, the similarity between self and other and the contingent nature of social interactions are emphasized. The presence of distractions or "cognitive noise" is minimized and the target stimuli are enhanced. The result is a fortified or augmented interaction, more assimilable by the autistic child. Thus, what we propose is not "more of the same" but, rather, a carefully modified version of the normal experience.

In response to the second criticism, given the wide variability among the skills of an autistic child, developmental level must be defined relative to the particular skill being considered. It should be kept in mind that the treatment is not necessarily a literal copy of the typical developmental interactions, but a functional and logical substitution. In designing the intervention there is considerable flexibility, and an effort must be made to find the most suitable interaction *for this particular child*. In facilitating turn taking, for instance, one would not seek to recreate a "jiggle–suck" dialogue with a 4-year-old but would find a more appropriate activity, such as throwing a ball or vocalizing. The intervention must not only suit the child but also be acceptable to the adult who will implement it. Baby-type play may be unacceptable to the mother of an older child. But this is no great obstacle since the specific content of the interaction is not as important as its structure.

The fact that there are instances in which the developmental sequence in autism does not duplicate that of normal children limits this model but does not invalidate it. In such cases, while the *normal* sequence may not form a basis for treatment, the child's attainment of therapeutic goals nevertheless depends upon the attainment of prerequisite skills and sensitivity to the developmental level of the child. Whenever possible, the child's spontaneous behavior is utilized as a basis for treatment, regardless of whether that behavior is typical of the normal development sequence. For example, echolalic speech is not considered a normal stage in language acquisition. However, Prizant (1983a, 1983b; Prizant & Rydell, 1984) has demonstrated how echolalic speech can be utilized to facilitate the later acquisition of spontaneous, creative speech. Several features of Prizant's method of language intervention closely parallel features of the approach described in this chapter. His work demonstrates how the principles of a developmental intervention can be used even when the child's behavior does not follow the typical developmental sequence.

A possible limitation of a developmental approach to treatment is its applicability to a restricted age range. Younger children may be more likely than older individuals to respond to a developmental intervention. Autistic adolescents and adults, though their social experiences have been limited for many years, have nevertheless developed and elaborated a set of cognitive and affective structures and social strategies based on this experience. Although they may have difficulty comprehending social cues, they have had to develop other, perhaps quite complex, strategies for coping with the social world. Because these strategies have been at least somewhat effective and have become habitual, changes at more fundamental levels may not occur as readily as they might in younger children. Some "unlearning" may need to accompany new acquisitions.

Because this model is developmental, it is subject to universal constraints on development. Among these is the possible existence of sensitive periods. It is conceivable that the period in which normal social relatedness develops is limited (Immelmann & Suomi, 1980; Scott, Stewart, & DeGhett, 1974). On the one hand, this limitation argues for the earliest possible implementation of a developmental intervention; on the other, it suggests a real constraint on the applicability of this approach.

Ideally a developmental treatment should be integrated with other treatment methods, for example, behavioral interventions. A developmental intervention does not offer solutions for the severe behavioral problems of autistic children, such as self-abuse. Nor does this approach include specific teaching of social conventions (for example, how to introduce oneself) that are needed to function smoothly in the social world. These approaches are complementary and can, together, form a comprehensive treatment program.

The model of intervention presented here is based on limited empirical—though considerable theoretical and some clinical—support. Yoder and Calculator's (1981) language intervention model and the TEACCH program directed by Eric Schopler at the University of North Carolina are both examples of successful interventions with autistic children that are based on developmental principles. Yoder and Calculator's "transactional-developmental approach" emphasizes the necessity for considering the social context in which language is acquired and the applicability of a normal model of development in designing language interventions for developmentally disabled children. The TEACCH program (see Reichler & Schopler, 1976) uses a comprehensive diagnostic procedure that includes assessment of developmental levels in several skill domains. The focus of treatment in each domain is on skills that are assessed to be "emerging" rather than absent. In this way the treatment is sensitive to the profile of current capabilities of each child.

Although intuitively it seems that facilitation of spontaneous behaviors, rather than specific training of those behaviors, would enhance the likelihood of increased social relatedness and generalization, this may not, in fact, be the case. Answers to questions such as this one will depend on outcome research that assesses both the generalizability and the maintenance of therapeutic changes. Furthermore, careful studies of the social behavior of young autistic children in natural, interactive contexts (e.g., Bollea, Bonaminio, Carratelli, & DiRenzo, 1983) as well as systematic experimental research are needed. Research strategies similar to those used to study normal infants may be productively applied to the study of autism. Sophisticated methods for coding parent–infant interaction now exist that could be adapted to observational research with autistic children and their parents. The experimental paradigms that have evolved to study young infants may be especially useful since the behavioral repertoires of infants and autistic children are similarly limited. An understanding of the nature of autism and the development of therapeutic approaches that address these children's basic social deficits ultimately depend on such research.

ACKNOWLEDGMENTS

We greatly appreciate the comments and suggestions of Barbara Lawrence, Harriet Rheingold, Meredith West, and John Weisz, who read earlier drafts of this chapter. We also thank Mary Lynn Eckert and Sue Wilson for their secretarial and editorial assistance.

REFERENCES

Abravanel, E., & Sigafoos, A. (1984). Exploring the presence of imitation during infancy. *Child Development, 55,* 381–392.

Als, H. (1982). The unfolding of behavioral organization in the face of a biological violation. In E. F. Tronick (Ed.), *Social interchange in infancy: Affect, cognition, and communication* (pp. 125–160). Baltimore: University Park Press.

Amsterdam, B. K. (1972). Mirror self-image reactions before age two. *Developmental Psychology, 5,* 297–305.

Anderson, B. A., Vietze, P. M., & Dokecki, P. R. (1977). Reciprocity in vocal interactions of mothers and infants. *Child Development, 48,* 1676–1681.

Bemporad, J. (1979). Adult recognition of a formerly autistic child. *Journal of Autism and Developmental Disorders, 9,* 383–396.

Bernard, J. A., & Ramey, C. T. (1977). Visual regard of familiar and unfamiliar persons in the first six months of infancy. *Merrill-Palmer Quarterly, 23,* 121–127.

Bloom, L., & Lahey, M. (1978). *Language development and language disorders.* New York: Wiley.

Bollea, G., Bonaminio, V., Carratelli, T., & DiRenzo, H. (1983). La relation mère–enfant dans la première année de la vie et la relation autistique mère–enfant. *Enfance,* 31–44.

Bower, T. G. R. (1977). *Development in infancy.* San Francisco: Freeman.

Brazelton, T. B. (1982). Joint regulation of neonate–parent behavior. In E. F. Tronick (Ed.), *Social interchange in infancy: Affect, cognition and communication* (pp. 7–22). Baltimore: University Park Press.

Brazelton, T. B., Koslowski, B., & Main, M. (1974). The origins of reciprocity: The early mother–infant interaction. In M. Lewis & L. A. Rosenblum (Eds.), *The effect of the infant on its caregiver* (pp. 49–76). New York: Wiley.

Bruner, J. (1982). The organization of action and the nature of the adult–infant transaction. In E. F. Tronick (Ed.), *Social interchange in infancy: Affect, cognition and communication* (pp. 23–35). Baltimore: University Park Press.

Bruner, J., & Sherwood, V. (1976). Peekaboo and the learning of rule structures. In J. S. Bruner, A. Jolly, & K. Sylva (Eds.), *Play: Its role in evolution and development* (pp. 277–285). London: Penguin Press.

Caron, A., Caron, R., Caldwell, R., & Weiss, S. J. (1973). Infant perception of structural properties of the face. *Developmental Psychology, 9,* 385–399.

Carpenter, G. (1974). Visual regard of moving and stationary faces in early infancy. *Merrill-Palmer Quarterly, 20,* 181–194.

Castell, R. (1970). Physical distance and visual attention as measures of social interaction between child and adult. In S. J. Hutt & C. Hutt (Eds.), *Behavior studies in psychiatry* (pp. 91–102). Oxford: Pergamon Press.

Church, J. (1970). Techniques for the differential study of cognition in early childhod. In J. Hellmuth (Ed.), *Cognitive studies* (Vol. 1, pp. 1–23). New York: Brunner/Mazel.

Clark, P., & Rutter, M. (1981). Autistic children's responses to structure and to interpersonal demands. *Journal of Autism and Developmental Disorders, 11,* 201–217.

Cohen, S. E. (1974). Developmental differences in infants' attentional responses to face-voice incongruity of mother and stranger. *Child Development, 45,* 1155–1158.

Curcio, F. (1978). Sensorimotor functioning and communication in mute autistic children. *Journal of Autism and Childhood Schizophrenia, 8,* 281–292.

Dawson, G., & Adams, A. (1984). Imitation and social responsiveness in autistic children. *Journal of Abnormal Child Psychology, 12,* 209–226.

Dawson, G., & McKissick, F. (1984). Self-recognition in autistic children. *Journal of Autism and Developmental Disorders, 14,* 383–394.

DeCasper, A., & Fifer, W. (1980). Of human bonding: Newborns prefer their mothers' voices. *Science, 208,* 1174–1176.

DeMyer, M. K. (1976). Motor, perceptual-motor, and intellectual disabilities of autistic children. In L. Wing (Ed.), *Early childhood autism* (2nd ed., pp. 169–196). Oxford: Pergamon Press.

DeMyer, M. K., Alpern, G. D., Barton,S., DeMyer, W. E., Churchill, D. W., Hingtgen, H. N., Bryson, C. Q., Pontius, W., & Kimberlin, C. (1972). Imitation in autistic, early schizophrenic, and nonpsychotic subnormal children. *Journal of Autism and Childhood Schizophrenia, 2,* 264–287.

Dirks, J., & Gibson, E. (1977). Infants' perception of similarity between live people and their photos. *Child Development, 48,* 124–130.

Dixon, J. C. (1957). Development of self-recognition. *Journal of Genetic Psychology, 91,* 251–256.

Fernald, M., & Dawson, G. (1985). *Perspective-taking ability and its relationship to social behavior in autistic children.* Manuscript submitted for publication.

Ferrara, C., & Hill, S. (1980). The responsiveness of autistic children to the predictability of social and nonsocial toys. *Journal of Autism and Developmental Disorders, 10,* 51–57.

Ferrari, M., & Matthews, W. (1983). Self-recognition deficits in autism: Syndrome-specific or general developmental delay? *Journal of Autism and Developmental Disorders, 13,* 317–324.

Field, T. M. (1979). Visual and cardiac responses to animate and inanimate faces by young and preterm infants. *Child Development, 50,* 188–194.

Field, T. M., Woodson, R., Greenberg, R., & Cohen, D. (1982). Discrimination and imitation of facial expression by neonates. *Science, 218,* 179–181.

Fraiberg, S. (1974). Blind infants and their mothers: An examination of the sign system. In M. Lewis & L. A. Rosenblum (Eds.), *The effect of the infant on its caregiver* (pp. 215–232). New York: Wiley.

Freedle, R., & Lewis, M. (1977). Pre-linguistic conversation. In M. Lewis & L. A. Rosenblum (Eds.), *Interaction, conversation and the development of language* (pp. 157–186). New York: Wiley.

Garvey, C. (1977). *Play.* Cambridge, MA: Harvard University Press.

Haith, M. M. (1966). Response of the human newborn to visual movement. *Journal of Experimental Child Psychology, 3,* 235–243.

Haith, M. M., Bergman, T., & Moore, M. J. (1977). Eye contact and face scanning in early infancy. *Science, 198,* 853–855.

Hammes, J., & Langdell, T. (1981). Precursors of symbol formation and childhood autism. *Journal of Autism and Developmental Disorders, 11,* 331–346.

Hermelin, B., & O'Connor, N. (1963). The response and self-generated behavior of severely disturbed children and severely subnormal controls. *British Journal of Social and Clinical Psychology, 2,* 37–43.

Hermelin, B., & O'Connor, N. (1970). *Psychological experiments with autistic children.* Oxford: Pergamon Press.

Hobson, R. (1984). Early childhood autism and the question of egocentrism. *Journal of Autism and Developmental Disorders, 14,* 85–104.

Hutt, S. J., & Hutt, C. (1970). *Behavior studies in psychiatry.* Oxford: Pergamon Press.

Hermelin, B., & O'Connor, N. (1970). *Psychological experiments with autistic children.* Oxford: Pergamon Press.

Hobson, R. (1984). Early childhood autism and the question of egocentrism. *Journal of Autism and Developmental Disorders, 14,* 85–104.

Hutt, S. J., & Hutt, C. (1970). *Behavior studies in psychiatry.* Oxford: Pergamon Press.

Hutt, S. J., Lenard, H. G., & Prechtl, H. F. R. (1969). Psychophysiological studies in newborn infants. In L. P. Lipsitt & H. W. Reese (Eds.), *Advances in child development and behavior* (Vol. 4, pp. 127–172). New York: Academic Press.

Hutt, C., & Ounsted, C. (1970). Gaze aversion and its significance in childhood autism. In S. J. Hutt & C. Hutt (Eds.), *Behavior studies in psychiatry* (pp. 103–120). Oxford: Pergamon Press.

Hutt, C., & Vaizey, M. J. (1966). Differential effects of groups density on social behavior. *Nature, 209,* 1371–1372.

Immelmann, K., & Suomi, S. J. (1980). Sensitive phases in development. In G. Barlow, K. Immelmann, M. Main, & L. Petrinovich (Eds.), *Early development in animals and man.* New York: Cambridge University Press.

Jaffe, J., Stern, D. N., & Peery, J. C. (1973). "Conversational" coupling of gaze behavior in prelinguistic human development. *Journal of Psycholinguistic Research, 2,* 321–329.

Kagan, J., Henler, B., Hen-Tov, A., Levine, J., & Lewis, M. (1966). Infants' differential reactions to familiar and distorted faces. *Child Development, 37,* 519–532.

Kanner, L. (1943). Autistic disturbances of affective contact. *Nervous Child, 2,* 217–250.

Karmel, B., Hoffman, R., & Fegy, M. (1974). Processing of contour information by human infant evidenced by pattern dependent evoked potentials. *Child Development, 45,* 39–48.

Kaye, K., & Wells, A. (1980). Mothers' jiggling and the burst-pause pattern in neonatal feeding. *Infant Behavior and Development, 3,* 29–46.

Kendon, A. (1967). Some functions of gaze direction in social interaction. *Acta Psychologica, 26,* 22–63.

Kessen, W., Haith, M., & Salapatek, P. (1970). Human infancy: A bibliography and guide. In P. Mussen (Ed.), *Carmichael's manual of child psychology* (Vol. 1, pp. 287–445). New York: Wiley.

Lamb, M. E. (1981). The development of social expectations in the first year of life. In M. E. Lamb & L. R. Sherrod (Eds.), *Infant social cognition: Empirical and theoretical considerations* (pp. 155–176). Hillsdale, NJ: Lawrence Erlbaum.

Lamb, M. E., & Easterbrooks, M. A. (1981). Individual differences in parental sensitivity: Origins, components, and consequences. In M. E. Lamb & L. R. Sherrod (Eds.), *Infant social cognition: Empirical and theoretical considerations* (pp. 127–154). Hillsdale, NJ: Erlbaum.

Lewis, M. (1969). Infants' responses to facial stimuli during the first year of life. *Developmental Psychology, 1,* 75–86.

Lewis, M., & Brooks-Gunn, J. (1979). *Social cognition and the acquisition of self.* New York: Plenum Press.

Lewis, M., & Rosenblum, L. A. (1978). *The development of affect.* New York: Plenum Press.

McCall, R., & Kagan, J. (1967). Attention in infancy: Effects of complexity, contour, perimeter, and familiarity. *Child Development, 38,* 939–952.

Meltzoff, A. N., & Moore, M. K. (1977). Imitation of facial and manual gestures by human neonates. *Science, 198,* 75–78.

Mirenda, P., Donnellan, A., & Yoder, D. (1983). Gaze behavior, a new look at an old problem. *Journal of Autism and Developmental Disorders, 13,* 397–409.

Neuman, C.J., & Hill, S. D. (1978). Self-recognition and stimulus preference in autistic children. *Developmental Psychobiology, 11,* 571–578.

O'Connor, N., & Hermelin, B. (1967). The selective visual attention of psychotic children. *Journal of Child Psychology and Psychiatry, 8,* 167–179.

Oster, H. (1981). "Recognition" of emotional expression in infancy? In M. E. Lamb & L. R. Sherrod

(Eds.), *Infant social cognition: Empirical and theoretical considerations* (pp. 85–126). Hillsdale, NJ: Erlbaum.

Papousek, H., & Papousek, M. (1977). Mothering and cognitive headstart: Psychobiological considerations. In H. R. Schaffer (Ed.), *Studies in mother–infant interaction* (pp. 63–85). New York: Academic Press.

Piaget, J. (1952). *The origins of intelligence in children.* New York: Norton.

Piaget, J. (1962). *Play, dreams and imitation.* New York: Norton.

Polak, P., Emde, R., & Spitz, R. (1964). The smiling response to the human face: I. Methodology, quantification, and natural history: II. Visual discrimination and onset of depth perception. *Journal of Nervous and Mental Disorders, 139,* 103–109, 407–415.

Prizant, B. M. (1983a). Echolalia in autism: Assessment and intervention. *Seminars in Speech and Language, 4,* 63–77.

Prizant, B. M. (1983b). Language acquisition and communicative behavior in autism: Toward an understanding of the "whole" of it. *Journal of Speech and Hearing Disorders, 48,* 296–307.

Prizant, B. M., & Rydell, P. J. (1984). Analysis of functions of delayed echolalia in autistic children. *Journal of Speech and Hearing Research, 27,* 183–192.

Reichler, R. J., & Schopler, E. (1976). Developmental therapy: A program model for providing individual services in the community. In E. Schloper & R. J. Reichler (Eds.), *Psychopathology and child development.* New York: Plenum Press.

Rheingold, H. L. (1961). The effect of environmental stimulation upon social and exploratory behavior in the human infant. In B. M. Foss (Ed.), *Determinants of infant behavior* (Vol. 1, pp. 143–177). New York: Wiley.

Richer, J. (1978). The partial noncommunication of culture to autistic children—An application of human ethology. In M. Rutter & E. Schopler (Eds.), *Autism: A reappraisal of concepts and treatment* (pp. 47–61). New York: Plenum Press.

Ricks, D. (1979). Making sense of experience to make sensible sounds. In M. Bullowa (Ed.), *Before speech* (pp. 245–268). Cambridge: Cambridge University Press.

Ricks, D., & Wing, L. (1975). Language communication, and the use of symbols in normal and autistic children. *Journal of Autism and Childhood Schizophrenia, 5,* 191–221.

Riquet, C., Taylor, N., Benaroya, S., & Klein, L. (1981). Symbolic play in autistic, Down's, and normal children of equivalent mental age. *Journal of Autism and Developmental Disorders, 11,* 439–448.

Robson, K. S. (1967). The role of eye-to-eye contact in maternal-infant attachment. *Journal of Child Psychology and Psychiatry, 8,* 13–25.

Rosenthal, M. K. (1982). Vocal dialogues in the neonatal period. *Developmental Psychology, 18,* 17–21.

Rovée-Collier, C. K., & Lipsitt, L. P. (1981). Learning, adaption, and memory. In P. M. Stratton (Ed.), *Psychobiology of the human newborn* (pp. 147–190). New York: Wiley.

Rutter, M. (1978). Diagnosis and definition. In M. Rutter & E. Schopler (Eds.), *Autism: A reappraisal of concepts and treatment* (pp. 1–25). New York: Plenum Press.

Rutter, M. (1983). Cognitive deficits in the pathogenesis of autism. *Journal of Child Psychology and Psychiatry, 24,* 513–531.

Schaffer, R. (1977). *Mothering.* Cambridge, MA: Harvard University Press.

Schopler, E., Brehm, S., Kinsbourne, M., & Reichler, R. J. (1971). Effect of treatment structure on development in autistic children. *Archives of General Psychiatry, 24,* 415–421.

Scott, J. P., Stewart, J. M., & DeGhett, V. J. (1974). Critical periods in the organization of systems. *Developmental Psychobiology, 7,* 489–513.

Sherrod, L. (1979). Social cognition in infants: Attention to the human face. *Infant Behavior and Development, 2,* 279–294.

Sigman, M., & Ungerer, J. (1984). Cognitive and language skills in autistic, mentally retarded, and normal children. *Developmental Psychology, 20,* 293–302.

Simmons, J., & Baltaxe, C. (1975). Language patterns of autistic adolescents. *Journal of Autism and Childhood Schizophrenia, 5,* 333–351.

Spelke, E. (1976). Infants' intermodal perception of infants. *Cognitive Psychology, 8,* 53–60.

Spelke, E. S., & Cortelyou, A. (1981). Perceptual aspects of social knowing: Looking and listening in infancy. In M. E. Lamb & L. R. Sherrod (Eds.), *Infant social cognition: Empirical and theoretical considerations* (pp. 61–84). Hillsdale, NJ: Erlbaum.

Sroufe, A. L. (1979). Socioemotional development. In J. D. Osofsky (Ed.), *Handbook of infant development* (pp. 462–518). New York: Wiley.

Stern, D. (1971). A micro-analysis of mother–infant interaction: Behavior regulating social conduct between a mother and her 3-1/2 month old twins. *Journal of the American Academy of Child Psychiatry, 10,* 501–517.

Stern, D. N. (1974). Mother and infant at play: The dyadic interaction involving facial, vocal, and gaze behaviors. In M. Lewis & L. A. Rosenblum (Eds.), *The effect of the infant on its caregiver* (pp. 187–214). New York: Wiley.

Stern, D. (1977). *The first relationship: Infant and mother.* Cambridge, MA: Harvard University Press.

Stern, D., Jaffe, J., Beebe, B., & Bennet, S. (1975). Vocalizing in unison and in alternation: Two modes of communication within the mother–infant dyad. *Annals of the New York Academy of Sciences, 263,* 89–100.

Tiegerman, E., & Primavera, L. (1981). Object manipulation: An interactional strategy with autistic children. *Journal of Autism and Developmental Disorders, 11,* 427–438.

Tiegerman, E., & Primavera, L. (1984). Imitating the autistic child: Facilitating communicative gaze behavior. *Journal of Autism and Development Disorders, 14,* 27–38.

Tinbergen, E., & Tinbergen, N. (1972). Early infantile autism: An ethological approach. *Advances in ethology,* Vol. 10. Berlin and Hamburg: Verlag Paul Perry.

Tinbergen, N., & Tinbergen, E. (1983). *"Autistic" children: New hope for a cure.* London: George Allen and Unwin.

Trevarthen, C. (1977). Descriptive analysis of infant communicative behavior. In H. R. Schaffer (Ed.), *Studies in mother–infant interaction* (pp. 227–270). New York: Academic Press.

Tronick, D., Als, H., & Adamson, L. (1979). Structure of early face-to-face communicative interaction. In M. Bullowa (Ed.), *Beyond speech* (pp. 349–372). Cambridge: Cambridge University Press.

Ungerer, J., & Sigman, M. (1981). Symbolic play and language comprehension in autistic children. *Journal of the American Academy of Child Psychiatry, 20,* 318–337.

Uzgiris, I. C. (1972). Patterns of vocal and gestural imitation in infants. In F. J. Monks, W. W. Hartup, & J. deWitt (Eds.), *Determinants of behavioral development* (pp. 467–471). New York: Academic Press.

Uzgiris, I. C. (1981a). Two functions of imitation during infancy. *International Journal of Behavioral Development, 4,* 1–12.

Uzgiris, I. C. (1981b). Experience in the social context: Imitation and play. In R. L. Schiefelbusch & D. D. Bricker (Eds.), *Early language: Acquisition and intervention* (pp. 139–168). Baltimore: University Park Press.

Uzgiris, I., & Hunt, J. McV. (1975). *Assessment in infancy.* Urbana: University of Illinois Press.

Watson, J. S. (1967). Memory and "contingency analysis" in infant learning. *Merrill-Palmer Quarterly, 13,* 55–76.

Watson, J. S. (1970). Perception of contingency as a determinant of social respnsiveness. In E. B. Thoman (Ed.), *The origins of the infant's social responsiveness* (pp. 33–64). Hillsdale, NJ: Erlbaum.

Wickelgren, L. (1969). Ocular response of human newborns to intermittent visual movement. *Journal of Experimental Child Psychology, 8,* 469–482.

Wilcox, B. (1969). Visual preferences of human infants for representations of human faces. *Journal of Experimental Child Psychology, 7,* 10–20.

Wing, L. (1978). Social, behavioral, and cognitive characteristics. In M. Rutter & E. Schopler (Eds.), *Autism: A reappraisal of concepts and treatment* (pp. 27–46). New York: Plenum Press.

Wing, L. (1981). Language, social, and cognitive impairments in autism and severe mental retardation. *Journal of Autism and Developmental Disorders, 11,* 31–44.

Wing, L., & Gould, J. (1979). Severe impairments of social interaction and associated abnormalities in children: Epidemiology and classification. *Journal of Autism and Developmental Disorders, 9,* 11–29.

Wing, L., Gould, J., Yeates, S., & Brierly, L. (1977). Symbolic play in severely mentally retarded and in autistic children. *Journal of Child Psychology and Psychiatry, 18,* 167–168.

Wolf, D., & Gardner, H. (1981). On the structure of early symbolization. In R. Schiefelbusch & D. Bricker (Eds.), *Early language: Acquisition and intervention* (pp. 287–327). Baltimore: University Park Press.

Yoder, D., & Calculator, S. (1981). Some perspectives on intervention strategies for persons with developmental disorders. *Journal of Autism and Developmental Disorders, 11,* 107–123.

IV

Programs for Developing Social Behaviors in Autism

13

A Cognitive Program for Teaching Social Behaviors to Verbal Autistic Adolescents and Adults

GARY B. MESIBOV

INTRODUCTION

It is widely accepted that social skills deficits are among the most pervasive and characteristic of the difficulties confronting individuals with autism (American Psychiatric Association, 1980; Ritvo & Freeman, 1978; Rutter, 1978). From Kanner's (1943) original description of the autism syndrome onward, investigators have been both puzzled and fascinated by this inherent lack of sociability. More recently, those working with autistic adolescents and adults have been encouraged by the realization that these social deficits show marked improvement as autistic people grow older (Mesibov, 1983; Rutter, 1970). However, social problems still persist and are among the most difficult of the many troublesome aspects of this disorder.

Given the extent and importance of the social deficits in autistic youngsters, surprisingly few programs have been developed to remediate these deficiencies (Schopler & Mesibov, 1983). Perhaps the extent of the problem has immobilized workers with this population. In any event, research and clinical programs serving children with other developmental disabilities have been applying cognitive social skills training models to the teaching of social behaviors for some time with encouraging results. Work with mentally retarded youngsters (Morris & Dalker,

GARY B. MESIBOV • Division TEACCH, University of North Carolina, Chapel Hill, North Carolina 27514.

1974), learning-disabled children (LaGreca & Mesibov, 1979, 1981), and children with behavioral problems (Strain & Timm, 1974) has demonstrated the applicability of such models. This chapter will describe the application of a cognitive-behavioral model to our social skills work with autistic adolescents and adults and the ways in which it is evolving.

TARGETED DEFICITS

Because of the pervasiveness and intensity of social skills deficits in autistic children, any program designed to remedy these deficits must first establish priorities. In order to establish priorities for our intervention program, we have set up the following criteria: (1) The behaviors should be problems that appear frequently in the literature and significantly interfere with the social relationships of autistic youngsters. (2) The behaviors should be amenable to remediation and not an immutable consequence of the autistic syndrome. On the basis of these two criteria, the following deficits have been targeted for our intervention program: (1) lack of interaction, and especially reciprocal interaction, with others, (2) difficulties in comprehending rules, (3) difficulties with attention, (4) problems with communication, and (5) lack of positive social experiences. Each of these problem areas will be described in greater detail, with specific emphasis on how it meets our two criteria.

Lack of Interaction

Defined as a condition of being "immured within the self," the term *autism* is synonymous with lack of interaction. DSM-III (American Psychiatric Association, 1980) identifies the pervasive lack of responsiveness to other people as a major characteristic of the syndrome. The tendency of autistic infants and children to prefer objects to other people has been widely described and well documented (Rutter & Schopler, 1978). Virtually every accepted definition of autism has included this interactional deficit as well (Creak, 1963; Kanner, 1943; Ritvo & Freeman, 1978; Rutter, 1978; Rutter & Schopler, 1978).

Related to their lack of interaction is the lack of reciprocity that these youngsters show when they do interact. Reciprocity refers to the adjusting of one's own behavior to relate with what another person is doing. This is one of the most important aspects of being interpersonally effective because it enables one to individualize her actions to the needs, skills, and interests of the other person.

As with interactions, reciprocity is an area of extreme difficulty for autistic people. They seem unable to monitor the impact of their conversations or behaviors on other people, making them less sensitive to when others are annoyed, bored, or uninvolved in what they are saying or doing. This probably relates to the difficulties autistic people have with empathy, which has been described by several investigators (Caparulo, 1981; DesLauriers, 1978). According to Hobson (1981), a more specific statement of the problem is a lack of experience empathy. Because of a postulated cognitive deficit in autistic people, the expressions of other people's emotions lack the impact that they have for the rest of the population. Langdell (1978) suggests that this might be because autistic people do not utilize the same interpersonal information as others. In his studies he finds that autistic people, as compared with nonhandicapped controls, are more likely to focus on lower portions of other people's faces. This strategy is less efficient because of the greater informational value concerning feelings and emotions that is contained in the upper portion of the face (eyes).

To summarize, there is considerable evidence that problems with interaction and reciprocity are frequently found in the literature on autism and significantly interfere with social relationships. There is also evidence that these behaviors fit our second criterion in that they appear amenable to remediation.

The strongest indication that these interactional deficits are amenable to remediation during adolescence and young adulthood is the strong desire that these young adults develop for social interaction. This social interest and desire represents a strong foundation for building new interactional skills and behaviors. The increased social interest was first observed in Kanner's original sample (Kanner, Rodriguez, & Ashenden, 1972) and was described by Katherine Stokes (1977) in discussing her son, "but he needs someone to hug occasionally as well as someone to comfort him when he is troubled" (p. 292). Clara Park's (1983) description of her daughter Jessy shows how this interest in others evolves and becomes quite strong by young adulthood:

> She wants companions now. She is even able to say that she is bored or lonely. She no longer tells people to go away as she did in the years when she sat by the hour and sifted her "silly business," the bits of paper—often her own pictures—she had made into confetti. She says of an absent sister, "I am missing her"; when she hears a friend is delayed, "Oh no! When will Joan come back?" If autism retains its root meaning of "immured within the self," Jessy is not autistic any more. Recently we looked down from a plane and saw a small island with one house on it. We had been talking about the meaning of the word "isolated," for Jessy had become very interested in the words on her school vocabulary lists. So I said the house was isolated and that it would be lonely living there, but that it would be nice if you didn't like people. To which Jessy replied that she *did* like people.
>
> And she does. When siblings or friends come back she is all smiles and hugs. She would hug acquaintances too, and the people who sometimes come to the house to meet her—hug them regardless of age and gender. She has had to be taught that a smile and a handshake is more appropriate. For all her progress, her comprehension

> of language, of gestures, of the social world is still in most ways simpler than that of a normal seven-year-old. (p. 282)

Comprehension of Rules

Many investigators have noted the difficulties that autistic people have in comprehending rules, especially those that are more subtle, situational, or abstract (Lord, 1985; Rutter, 1983). Hermelin and O'Connor (1985) have suggested that the inability to understand information through appropriate categorizations or rules and redundancies is one of the basic problems in autism. Rutter (1983) has argued similarly, suggesting that this is the most fundamental deficit related to the autistic syndrome. More recently, Lord and Allen (1979) have suggested that the problem could be rule use as easily as rule knowledge, and that empirical studies have not adequately separated the two. However, in either case the problem of comprehending and/or acting upon rules or conventions is especially debilitating in social situations.

The problem is that most of our rules governing social and interpersonal functioning are especially subtle, situational, or abstract. In addition, they are not generally articulated but rather deduced by most nonhandicapped people during their developmental years. Simple rules like how far one should stand from another person when talking are easily deduced by most people. However, the autistic youngster, already deficient in rule-governed concepts, finds understanding these many social conventions to be extremely overwhelming. Humor, another important social and interpersonal process that often involves suddenly altered expectations and conventions, is also difficult for autistic people for the same reason. For those who do not have a firm grasp on these conventions in the first place, the humor in many situations is quite elusive.

Although difficulties with rules is pervasive in autistic people, there is some indication that they might benefit from remediation. Although abstract and conceptual rules are difficult, structure has proven to be a most effective intervention technique with these youngsters (Schopler, Brehm, Kinsbourne, & Reichler, 1971). In this study, attending behaviors, on-task performance, and inappropriate behaviors all showed significant improvements in a structured, as compared to an unstructured, learning situation. The structured teaching approach has been incorporated into Division TEACCH's widely recognized statewide program (Schopler, Reichler, & Lansing, 1980) and is now the basis for most educational programs for autistic children around the country (Rutter & Schopler, 1978). The key seems to be in generating specific and very structured rules that autistic people can learn and follow. There is also evidence that practice and role playing can be helpful adjuncts in the acquisition of these concepts (Mesibov, in press; Rutter, 1970).

Attention Difficulties

Attention difficulties have been noted more frequently in autistic children than in the nonhandicapped population by several investigators (Rutter & Schopler, 1978). The aspects of these difficulties that are especially problematic in social interactions are the generally short and inefficient attention span and tendency to focus on atypical aspects of the environment. Hermelin and O'Connor (1970) noted several causes of visual inattentiveness in these youngsters, including disorders of eye movements, scanning, and visual avoidance behaviors. Others postulating neurological bases for the autism syndrome have suggested that autism is frequently accompanied by related neurological dysfunctions such as hyperactivity and inattention (Boucher & Warrington, 1976; Hutt, Hutt, Lee & Ounsted, 1964; Ornitz & Ritvo, 1968). The inability of autistic people to sustain their attention for periods of time can be especially troublesome in social situations. This inability causes them to lose important information about what others are communicating both verbally and nonverbally.

A second attention problem with implications for social relationships is that autistic people generally attend to atypical aspects of the environment. Some investigators have described this as stimulus overselectivity (Lovaas & Schreibman, 1971; Reynolds, Newsom, & Lovaas, 1974), defined as responding on the basis of only one component out of a complex stimulus array. This pattern is in contrast with nonhandicapped people, who customarily take more of the situation and its complexity into account.

Another example of attention to atypical aspects of the environment is an autistic adolescent who visited me at my office for an interview several years ago. When asked about that experience six weeks later, he reported about the dimensions of my office (accurately, I might add) and the color of my shirt rather than about the content of our discussion or the purpose for our meeting. Along similar lines is Barbara Caparulo's (1981) description of an autistic adult during testing:

> An item on the Leiter International Performance Scales requires one to match photographs of women's faces showing extreme emotional states such as joy, shock, and horror with five photographs of men's faces showing similar emotions. One twenty-five year old, with superior non-verbal intelligence, studied the arrays for several minutes, placing first one and then another of the men's pictures next to the women's pictures, finally becoming agitated. He said, "There's something wrong here. There's an error on this test," and he indicated that he could only match three of the five photos. When questioned about what criteria he was matching them on, he explained, "I was sure they went together according to where they were looking—to the right or to the left. But if I do it that way I still have two pictures left." After being told that the photos matched each other for a different reason he developed a new hypothesis that height of the forehead was the critical factor. After many minutes we suggested that he consider how the people in the photos felt. Slowly, and with great thoughtfulness, he replied, "They probably felt soft."

The tendency of autistic people to perceive atypical aspects of the environment is a serious limitation. Much of our social behavior is based on sharing similar ideas and communicating about them. The inability of autistic people to understand and experience the perspectives of others compounds this difficulty as well.

The success of individualized educational models for autistic children (Rutter & Schopler, 1978) suggests that attentional skills can be significantly improved in academic settings. Bartak (1978) demonstrated that academic progress and the attentional skills required to achieve this progress generally result from more structured and better organized teaching situations. Lansing and Schopler (1978) report a similar connection in the TEACCH Program's public school classrooms. Callias's review of the education literature (1978) is also optimistic about the potential of behavioral approaches to improve the attentional and academic skills of autistic students. Given the effectiveness of these approaches in the academic realm, it seems reasonable that they should improve attention to social stimuli as well. However, it might be expected that autistic youngsters will have more difficulty attending to social cues because of the greater difficulty they experience with social meanings (Rutter, 1983).

Although autistic people frequently focus on different aspects of their environment from their nonhandicapped peers, this can probably be altered with a structured approach as well. There is no reason to believe that the autistic person's inability to remember the content of our conversation was inevitable; his attention to the room dimensions seemed more a personal preference than an inability to focus on other aspects. Highlighting more generally observed and understood aspects of the environment and interpersonal interactions should make these more salient and understandable to autistic people.

Communication Difficulties

Communication difficulties are central to the autism syndrome. Virtually every definition of autism includes communication and language problems as being significant and debilitating (Creak, 1963; Kanner, 1943; Ritvo & Freeman, 1978; Rutter, 1978). Although these difficulties are severely handicapping for autistic children and adults in most situations, communication problems are especially significant in social relationships because so many of these are dependent upon the ability to communicate, either verbally or nonverbally, with another person.

Although the pervasiveness of their communication deficits presents significant problems in interpersonal relationships for autistic people, certain aspects are especially crucial. Among these are their flat affect, lack of emotional expression, disfluencies, and abnormal patterns of rhythm, stress, and intonation (Rutter, 1970; Simmons & Baltaxe, 1975). These problems make autistic people seem uncaring and further dissociate them from other people. Semantic deficits, defined as using words in a concrete and literal manner and tying word meanings to specific situations (Lord & O'Neill, 1983), also set these youngsters apart. Autistic people are also impaired in their ability to perceive rules of social dialogue and to distinguish speaker–hearer roles (Cromer, 1981). Beisler and Tsai (1983) view this problem as their inability to take turns as part of a social exchange.

In spite of the number and pervasiveness of their social deficits, some intervention programs have been able to demonstrate the potential for significant improvement in communication skills. Several investigators have shown that training in natural environments in the context of everyday activities can result in significant gains (Beisler & Tsai, 1983; Goetz, Schuler, & Sailor, 1979). Beisler and Tsai (1983) have improved turn-taking behavior as well. The TEACCH language curriculum (Watson, 1985) is another example of significant improvement resulting from language instruction in meaningful, naturalistic settings.

Lack of Positive Social Experiences

Developmentally, autistic children do not seem to be programmed for social interaction in ways similar to other children. Their attachment, cuddling, and other interactive behaviors are quite deficient, as has already been described (Rutter, 1983). Therefore, at relatively young ages these children quickly fall behind everyone else in the development of their social interactions, and this gap widens as they grow older.

This gap in social ability plus the well-documented unusual behaviors manifested by these children (American Psychiatric Association, 1980; Kanner, 1943) leads to many unpleasant experiences in social situations. This is especially pronounced for higher-functioning autistic children and adolescents who are typically mainstreamed in educational programs without the skills or abilities to relate socially and are consequently victims of harassment and rejection from other children (Bemporad, 1979; Schopler & Mesibov, 1983). These unpleasant experiences cause autistic children to further withdraw from social situations, thus increasing the gap in social skills between them and nonhandicapped children. Many negative social experiences can cause autistic youngsters to develop negative attitudes that can become as important a factor in their asocial behavior as their lack of social skills.

There is evidence that social experiences can be made positive and rewarding for autistic children and adults. Kanner *et al.* (1972) noted in their sample an increased desire to have positive social relationships with others: "Again and again we note a felt need to grope for ways to compensate for the lack of inherent sociability" (pp. 29–30). Rutter (1970) writes, "In these children the failure to make friends was a source of distress and unhappiness . . ." (p. 439), and suggests that the possibility for positive peer experiences exists if appropriate skills are taught. Bemporad (1979) also writes about the expressed need for friendships and the potential for these if the proper people and situations can be found or created. To summarize the review of the literature on the social relationships of autistic people, several areas were identified representing crucial problems with the potential for remediation. These include lack of interaction with others, comprehension of rules, attentional difficulties, communication, and a negative social set. The following program was designed to address each of these critical areas in providing a social experience for a group of autistic adolescents and adults.

PROGRAM

Overview

Our TEACCH social skills training program has been designed to specifically and directly remedy the targeted deficits. During the past 2 1/2 years we have worked with 20 older adolescents and young adults with autism (16 males and 4 females), ranging from 14- to 35-years-old. All were diagnosed as autistic in major medical centers and fit the DSM-III diagnostic criteria for Infantile Autism, Residual State. This diagnosis requires the individual to have met the criteria for Infantile Autism during early childhood but to show only some of the signs after adolescence such as oddities of communication and social awkwardness. Recent IQ scores for each client ranged from 55 to 100. Clients were residing in either their parents' homes or group homes that were primarily designed for mildly mentally retarded citizens. Some were not involved in any day activities while others were in public school or sheltered workshop programs. One woman worked parttime in a university library.

In order to work on their social skills, we set aside a 1 1/2-hour block of time for one evening each week. The first half hour of each session is devoted to one-on-one individual work, followed by a 1-hour group session. During the individual time, the major lessons for the day are practiced with each client. The balance between individual and group sessions allows our participants time first to learn the targeted skills in the individualized situations where they learn best (Lansing & Schopler, 1978), and then to practice them in realistic settings with peers. Our groups meet throughout the year with winter and summer breaks. Our group routines are regularly extended into the community through activities such as eating out, holiday and birthday parties, bowling trips, or other similar social activities. In addition, our entire group takes a weekend overnight trip each fall and spring.

A typical group session consists of the following: individual time, snacks, dyads, role playing, and joke time. Each of these will be discussed in detail.

Segments of Group Sessions

Individual Time. Each group meeting begins with a 1 1/2-hour individual session between a trainer and an autistic client. The purposes of this one-on-one segment are to facilitate the development of personal relationships and to use these as a means of teaching appropriate social skills. Because of the well-documented difficulties experienced by autistic people in group learning situations (Schopler *et al.*, 1980), this individual time was designed for the teaching of the basic concepts that might later be applied in the group session. For example, when our day's lesson was asking appropriate questions, this was explained and modeled by the trainer in the one-on-one segment before it was practiced with another autistic person during the larger group meeting.

Snacks. Each session begins with a snack because we find this to be an effective motivator for our participants. In addition, our early evening meeting time makes it important for all the clients to have some food to help carry them over until dinner. Our snack time is not as highly structured as the other parts of our group because we want everyone to feel comfortable talking about whatever interests or concerns he or she might have. We also see this as a time when our participants can be more spontaneous. Our snack discussions are generally about issues of mutual interest or concern such as holidays, upcoming events, or sports. Because several members of our group are living in group home environments, that has been another popular topic of conversation. Other common issues are jobs and sheltered workshops, school, popular music, political elections, and our general group activities.

During snack time we focus specifically on interactive skills, attentional skills, and communication. In addition, this is an extremely positive time for most of our participants. The interactive nature of the snack time is facilitated by our staff, who direct the conversations in turn to each of the participants. In particular, questions are directed to participants as they relate to areas of individual interests. We also identify common themes such as sports, group homes, and popular music and try to involve everyone in conversations about these. In addition we identify topics of interest on a given day during our individual 1/2-hour sessions and bring these up in the context of the larger group during snack time.

Snack time is also useful for focusing on attention skills. Because autistic people have trouble concentrating in group settings, we feel these are important vehicles for learning attention skills. Having topics of general interest is one of the strongest motivating factors for accomplishing this. In addition, as our groups meet together for longer and longer periods, a certain attachment and sense of group identity have emerged. This seems to increase attention to other group members on the part of our autistic participants.

Our spontaneous discussions during snack time are also obvious avenues for developing communication skills. The spontaneous communication skills practiced during snack time nicely complement the more structured communication training that occurs during other parts of our group sessions. One nice result that several families have observed from their children's participation in our social skills program has been an increased interest and effectiveness in communicating with others.

Our snack time is also extremely positive for the participants and helps to make social involvement feel more desirable and therefore more motivating. Food is one of the strongest motivators for our group of autistic youngsters, and the opportunity to eat during our group sessions is extremely positive, making the entire experience more desirable for them. In addition, they do seem to enjoy talking with our staff and the other participants about topics that interest them. The fact that we do not reprimand or correct them in any way during this spontaneous discussion time is also viewed favorably by them and adds to the overall experience.

Dyads. The dyads are designed for smaller group activities within the context of our larger social skills group. During this time we usually split up into 2- to 4-person groups consisting of 1 or 2 staff people and 1 or 2 autistic clients. The dyads allow us to practice interacting with others, attending, and communicating, and these often can be extremely positive social experiences.

Our dyads generally involve small group activities after which a report is made back to the larger group. These activities are always interactive, involving talking, playing simple games, or rehearsing short skits. The skits began during our discussions of emotions and became a good vehicle for working on these concepts. A dyad acted out an emotion and the larger group had to guess what the emotion was. These started quite simply with emotions such as happy or sad and with practice evolved into more sophisticated concepts such as frustrated or confused.

We develop attending skills in the dyad by having each person report back to the larger group what the other has said. For example, if two people are describing what makes them annoyed, each one will report the other's response to the large group. This requires each participant to pay close attention and to report accurately their partner's feelings or perceptions.

The dyads also focus intensively on communication skills. Most of the dyadic activities involve talking about feelings and emotions, areas that are quite difficult for individuals with autism. The combination of being able to practice these communication skills and having our staff model more appropriate behaviors has led to considerable improvement in these abilities.

Finally, as with all of the activities in our social skills group, we try to make the dyads as positive as possible. We have accomplished this in several ways. First, the individualized attention that the clients get in these groups is extremely reinforcing to them. In addition, they seem to enjoy the skits that we have used to act out appropriate emotions and the games we have planned to stimulate interaction. Finally, the dyads combine both smaller and larger group experiences in degrees that our autistic participants find manageable and rewarding.

Role Playing. Role playing is our most effective structured teaching format, allowing us to practice the many skills that we work on during our group sessions. Role playing generally includes identifying a skill, explaining it, and practicing with feedback. For most skills the first practice session is between a staff person and an autistic participant, but our goal is to have the group members progress so they can practice these skills with one another. During the role playing we primarily practice reciprocal interactions and communication, and we try to accomplish these in a positive and supportive atmosphere.

Reciprocal interactions, defined as adjusting behavior to what the other person is doing, is one of the most subtle, yet important, of the social skills lacking in autistic people. In targeting any interactive deficits, a decision must be made as to whether a specific skill can be meaningfully improved or whether it is so fundamentally a part of the autistic syndrome that progress can only be minimal and not especially significant. We generally use role playing to teach those skills that have the most potential for future progress but try to restructure the environment to accommodate other areas that realistically appear beyond the capabilities of our group members. For example, in trying to teach our clients how to stay on a topic of conversation, we soon learned that their lack of reciprocity and difficulties in assuming the perspectives of others made this quite difficult. Basically, they would have a topic of conversation in mind and would not be able to adjust this to the needs and interests of their conversation partner. Our way of dealing with this was to teach each participant to say, "I am interested in talking about baseball. Are you interested in talking about that?" An affirmative response would be a signal to proceed and a negative response would be a signal to say, "What are you interested in talking about?" Although this technique did not directly teach reciprocity to our group participants, it did provide a satisfactory way for them to communicate more appropriately despite their deficits.

Communication skills are the most important ones that we practice during the role playing situations. On the basis of our pregroup assessments, we have targeted staying on topics of mutual interest, asking questions, and following up on what another person is saying as the most important conversational skills for our group. Having staff model appropriate behaviors and providing the group members with extensive practice opportunities have both been helpful. As our group members have become better acquainted with one another, their motivation to communicate has increased along with their skills.

Role playing is at times the most difficult aspect of our group sessions for the participants because it focuses on their deficit areas and requires what is so hard for them. For this reason we have tried to make it a positive experience as well. One technique has been to allow them to practice a skill the "wrong way" after mastering our lesson for the day. This has proven to be a positive outlet. Although our participants have at times become quite silly, they seem to enjoy the pressure-free opportunity to do whatever they want without any expectations or requirements. We also make role playing more attractive by practicing what we will be doing during group field trips. Activities such as going out to eat, bowling, or weekend trips are among the most positive aspects of the group. Therefore, our participants find it extremely reinforcing and exciting to practice these activities. The amount of excitement and enthusiasm they exhibit toward our field trips is somewhat contagious for our staff as well.

Role playing also allows us to practice rule-governed behavior. In describing a skill or a situation, we explicitly state the rules with an explanation. For example, when we were preparing for a trip to a cafeteria, we explained the need to wait in line, state your order quickly and clearly, order one item from each group, and hold onto the ticket to pay at the end. Articulating and practicing these rules was a helpful activity for the group participants.

Jokes. Our participants have enjoyed the joke time in our groups enormously. Although we did not know initially how this would go over, we thought it would be worth trying because of the importance of humor in interpersonal relationships and the difficulties that autistic people have with the subtle social meanings involved. Although our early efforts were mixed and most of the initial jokes were told by our staff, the group members have become more and more enthusiastic about the joke time and many now identify this as the most enjoyable part of the group situation.

Our joke time obviously involves interaction and communication among the members. During this period they are constantly talking to one another and often asking for explanations and clarifications. In addition, the attention of our group members seems to be at its highest point during joke time and everyone seems to be thoroughly involved.

The most positive aspect of the joke time is that everyone enjoys it so much. Although some were slower to become involved than others, everyone now participates frequently and enjoys laughing at one another's jokes. The level of sophistication varies enormously, but the most popular jokes among our group members appear to be "knock-knock" jokes and simple riddles.

OTHER ASPECTS

This chapter has included a description of the need and theoretical bases for our social skills training program as well as the program itself. Our clinical impressions and research data suggest that we have been extremely successful in providing positive experiences, developing skills, improving the quality of life, and giving support and a much-needed service for parents (Mesibov, in press). Although these are significant and important reasons to have a social skills program, there are several other benefits of this program as well. Our social skills training program serves as an excellent model demonstration program for Division TEACCH as well as a training program for students learning about autism.

Model Demonstration

Because of the lack of information available in the area of autism, any program effectively serving these youngsters gets attention from others interested in the field. This is especially true of the TEACCH program because of our long history (Runck, 1979), numerous publications (Mesibov & Schopler, 1983; Schopler & Mesibov, 1983, 1984; Schopler & Reichler, 1979; Schopler *et al.*, 1980; Schopler, Lansing, & Waters, 1983), and the demonstrated effectiveness of our programmatic techniques (Schopler, Mesibov, & Baker, 1982; Schopler, Mesibov, DeVellis, & Short, 1981; Short, 1984). The attention and interest our program generates make it extremely desirable to have opportunities for observation and participation, and our social skills training model meets these needs very nicely.

Since our social skills program began in the fall of 1982, we have had approximately 30 to 40 visitors attend individual sessions or activities. These have included parents and siblings of autistic people as well as professionals from North Carolina, around the country (New York, Florida, Indiana, South Dakota), and around the world (Japan, Denmark, Belgium, and Abu Dabi). Observing the social skills program is an excellent way to get an overview of our TEACCH philosophies and approaches in a relatively short time period (1½ hours) because one can observe our planning process, individual work, how we interact with clients and each other, and the parent participation process.

More specifically, there are several reasons why this program serves especially well as a model demonstration. First, it provides observers with the opportunity to see a large number of clients (10–14) in a relatively short period of time. Many of these clients have been with the TEACCH program for over 10 years, so it also provides the opportunity of observing the outcomes of our intensive program efforts. The social skills training program also allows an observer to interact extensively with families. Many families transport their children long distances to our social skills program and sit in a conference room where coffee is provided while the social skills group is in session. Interested observers can sit and discuss our program and its impact on these families. We also have had several observers attend the family parties held at least twice a year. The advantage of interacting with so many clients and parents at one time is extremely helpful for observers.

Our social skills training program also serves well as a model demonstration program because the observers can actually participate if they wish. Because our goal in this program is to develop social skills, it is helpful for our group participants to meet new people and interact with them. Making observation a participatory experience not only is more interesting and enjoyable for the observers but helps our clients as well. Finally, this program represents an excellent model demonstration because of the recent interest in social skills training and the lack of adequate models in the area of autism (see pertinent chapters in this volume). Therefore, many visitors find it extremely helpful to observe our strategies for developing these most important skills.

Training

Our social skills group is also an excellent vehicle for training students in working with autistic clients. Since we began in 1982, we have trained more than 50 professionals and students in our social skills training model. Trainees have included postdoctoral fellows and interns in psychology, doctoral students in school psychology and special education, master's students in rehabilitation counseling, special education, and therapeutic recreation, undergraduate students, as well as professionals working in the field such as teachers, mental retardation specialists, and therapists within our own program.

There are several reasons why our social skills program represents a good training experience. As was already described in relation to the visitors, it provides a comprehensive series of important experiences such as planning, individual work with clients, working and coordinating efforts among staff, and communicating and relating with families. Extensive prior experience in the area of autism is not required. Because we have an intensive staff-to-client ratio, several staff members with minimal experience can participate. In addition, the cognitive modeling approach to training is as helpful to our new staff as it is to the clients because they have the opportunity of observing others doing training and this facilitates their learning of the training process.

Finally, the weekend trip taken each semester has been described by several trainees as one of the most valuable training experiences in their entire careers. This enables them to better understand the ongoing demands and joys of an autistic child than they could ever appreciate in a clinic setting. The 24-hour experience, including staying up much of the night and not getting many breaks, provides a new understanding of the problems facing parents and the needs of their clients. It also enables them to experience some of the joys and positive possibilities as progress, however slow, is noted.

Another training advantage is that this program provides a model for teaching social skills after the students leave us. Many of our trainees have found this extremely useful because of the great need for such programming and the lack of appropriate models. Several social skills training programs have been set up in other parts of the country and the world, on the basis of the experiences of trainees in our program.

SUMMARY AND FUTURE DIRECTIONS

This chapter has described the evolution of the TEACCH program's cognitive social skills training model over the past 3 years. The major deficits that have been targeted for remediation have been described as well as our evolving program model. Uses of this program as a model demonstration and training site have also been discussed. Along with a continuation of these goals and activities, several new directions are being pursued at this time.

The first involves including in our group a small number of mentally retarded adults without autism who have good social skills. Several visitors have suggested this as a way of stimulating the social development of our clients, and our own positive experiences with high-functioning autistic people in group homes for mildly mentally retarded adults (Mesibov & Shea, 1980) make this arrangement seem viable. Therefore, very shortly we will be including in our groups two mildly retarded young adults with good social skills. The two young adults we have selected are living in a group home with younger children, so the social skills group will also be beneficial for them by providing much-needed same-age peer experiences.

The second new direction will probably be evolving over the next few years. Work with autistic people, especially those who are higher functioning such as our group members, is recently focusing more on training for vocational skills (Mesibov & Schopler, 1983; Schopler & Mesibov, 1983) because of their peak skills and the lack of appropriate opportunities for autistic people in many sheltered workshop situations. However, one of the major problems in vocational settings has been the behavioral and social problems that autistic people present. These, like many other problems, result from their difficulties in relating to other clients and understanding the social expectations of most job situations.

Another future goal for our group therefore will be to discuss vocational possibilities and issues in more detail with our group members. We are hopeful that discussions of these issues with comparisons of experiences will be helpful in developing appropriate understandings that can be translated into more positive work behaviors. In addition, the positive feelings that our clients have developed about the group and their participation in it should be motivating factors. Most of our clients are becoming more and more aware of each other and seem desirous of each other's attention and approval. By establishing vocational effectiveness and competence as group goals, we hope to improve the motivation of our participants in vocational areas. In addition, we hope that discussions of these important issues will result in greater understanding of vocational expectations and therefore more effective job performances.

In conclusion, our social skills training program, beginning with the needs of our individual clients, has evolved into a model for working with verbal autistic adolescents and adults on developing and improving their social relationships. In addition, a major goal continues to be meeting their social needs. As our program has evolved, it has also proven quite useful as a model demonstration as well as for the training of a wide variety of professionals and families. Future plans include continuing and expanding this much-needed service as well as moving into new and promising areas.

Acknowledgments

The author gratefully acknowledges the invaluable assistance of Janet Martin, Bruce Schaffer, Amy Woods, Rhoda Landrus, Joanne Honeycutt, Marie Bristol, Pat Fennell, and the other TEACCH staff and students who have participated in the groups and helped to conceptualize the program.

REFERENCES

American Psychiatric Association. (1980). *Diagnostic and statistical manual* (3rd ed.). Washington, DC: Author.

Bartak, L. (1978). Educational approaches. In M. Rutter & E. Schopler (Eds.), *Autism: A reappraisal of concepts and treatment* (pp. 423–438). New York: Plenum Press.

Beisler, J. M., & Tsai, L. (1983). A pragmatic approach to increase expressive language skills in young autistic children. *Journal of Autism and Developmental Disorders, 13*, 287–303.

Bemporad, J. R. (1979). Adult recollections of a formerly autistic child. *Journal of Autism and Developmental Disorders, 9*, 179–197.

Boucher, J., & Warrington, E. K. (1976). Memory deficits in early infantile autism: Some similarities to the amnesic syndrome. *British Journal of Psychology, 67,* 73–87.

Callias, M. (1978). Educational aims and methods. In M. Rutter & E. Schopler (Eds.), *Autism: A reappraisal of concepts and treatment* (pp. 453–461). New York: Plenum Press.

Caparulo, B. (1981, July). *Development of communicative competence in autism.* Paper presented at the annual meeting of the National Society for Children and Adults with Autism, Boston.

Creak, E. M. (1963). Childhood psychosis: A review of 100 cases. *British Journal of Psychiatry, 109,* 84–89.

Cromer, R. (1981). Developmental language disorders: Cognitive processes, semantics, and syntax. *Journal of Autism and Developmental Disorders, 11,* 57–74.

DesLauriers, A. M. (1978). Play, symbols, and the development of language. In M. Rutter & E. Schopler (Eds.), *Autism: A reappraisal of concepts and treatment* (pp. 313–326). New York: Plenum Press.

Goetz, L., Schuler, A., & Sailor, W. (1979). Teaching functional speech to the severely handicapped: Current issues. *Journal of Autism and Developmental Disorders, 9,* 325–344.

Hermelin, B., & O'Connor, N. (1970). *Psychological experiments with autistic children.* Pergamon: Oxford.

Hermelin, B., & O'Connor, N. (1985). Logico-affective states and nonverbal language. In E. Schopler & G. B. Mesibov (Eds.), *Communication problems in autism* (pp. 283–310). New York: Plenum Press.

Hobson, R. P. (1981, July). *The autistic child's concept of persons.* Paper presented at the annual meeting of the National Society for Children and Adults with Autism, Boston.

Hutt, S. J., Hutt, C., Lee, D., & Ounsted, C. (1964). Arousal and childhood autism. *Nature, 204,* 908–909.

Kanner, L. (1943). Autistic disturbance of affective contact. *Nervous Child, 2,* 217–250.

Kanner, L., Rodriguez, A., & Ashenden, B. (1972). How far can autistic children go in matters of social adaptation? *Journal of Autism and Childhood Schizophrenia, 2,* 9–33.

LaGreca, A. M., & Mesibov, G. B. (1979). Social skills intervention with learning disabled children: Selecting skills and implementing training. *Journal of Clinical Child Psychology, 8,* 234–241.

LaGreca, A. M., & Mesibov, G. B. (1981). Facilitating interpersonal functioning with peers in learning disabled children. *Journal of Learning Disabilities, 14,* 197–199, 238.

Langdell, T. (1978). Recognition of faces: An approach to the study of autism. *Journal of Child Psychology and Psychiatry, 19,* 255–268.

Lansing, M. D., & Schopler, E. (1978). Individualized education: A public school model. In M. Rutter & E. Schopler (Eds.), *Autism: A reappraisal of concepts and treatment* (pp. 439–452). New York: Plenum Press.

Lord, C. (1985). *Autism and the comprehension of language.* In E. Schopler & G. B. Mesibov (Eds.), *Communication problems in autism* (pp. 257–281). New York: Plenum Press.

Lord, C., & Allen, J. A. (1979, May). *Comprehension of simple sentences in autistic children.* Paper presented at the meeting of the Midwestern Psychological Association, Chicago.

Lord, C., & O'Neill, P. (1983). Language and communication needs of adolescents with autism. In E. Schopler & G. B. Mesibov (Eds.), *Autism in adolescents and adults* (pp. 57–78). New York: Plenum Press.

Lovaas, O. I., & Schreibman, L. (1971). Stimulus overselectivity of autistic children in a two-stimulus situation. *Behaviour Research and Therapy, 9,* 305–310.

Mesibov, G.B. (1983). Current perspectives and issues in autism and adolescence. In E. Schopler & G. B. Mesibov (Eds.), *Autism in adolescents and adults* (pp. 37–53). New York: Plenum Press.

Mesibov, G. B. (in press). Social skills training with verbal autistic adolescents and adults: A program model. *Journal of Autism and Developmental Disorders.*

Mesibov, G. B., & Schopler, E. (1983). The development of community-based programs for autistic adolescents. *Children's Health Care, 12,* 20–24.

Mesibov, G. B., & Shea, V. (1980, March). *Social and interpersonal problems of autistic adolescents and adults.* Paper presented at the meeting of the Southeastern Psychological Association, Washington, DC.

Morris, R. J., & Dalker, M. (1974). Developing cooperative play in socially withdrawn retarded children. *Mental Retardation, 12,* 24–27.

Ornitz, E. M., & Ritvo, E. R. (1968). Perceptual inconstancy in early infantile autism. *Archives of General Psychiatry, 18,* 76–98.

Park, C. C. (1983). Growing out of autism. In E. Schopler & G. B. Mesibov (Eds.), *Autism in adolescents and adults* (pp. 279–295). New York: Plenum Press.

Reynolds, B. S., Newsom, C. D., & Lovaas, O. I. (1974). Auditory overselectivity in autistic children. *Journal of Child Psychology, 2,* 253–263.

Ritvo, E. R., & Freeman, B. J. (1978). National Society for Autistic Children definition of autism. *Journal of Autism and Childhood Schizophrenia, 8,* 162–167.

Runck, B. (1979). Basic training for parents of psychotic children. In National Institute of Mental Health Science Monograph, *Families today* (Vol. 2, pp. 767–809). (DHEW Publication No. ADM 79–815). Washington, DC: U.S. Government Printing Office.

Rutter, M. (1970). Autistic children: Infancy to adulthood. *Seminars in Psychiatry, 2,* 435–450.

Rutter, M. (1978). On confusion in the diagnosis of autism. *Journal of Autism and Childhood Schizophrenia, 8,* 137–161.

Rutter, M. (1983). Cognitive deficits in the pathogenesis of autism. *Journal of Child Psychology and Psychiatry, 24,* 513–531.

Rutter, M., & Schopler, E. (Eds.). (1978). *Autism: A reappraisal of concepts and treatment.* New York: Plenum Press.

Schopler, E., Brehm, S., Kinsbourne, M., & Reichler, R. J. (1971). The effect of treatment structure on development in autistic children. *Archives of General Psychiatry, 24,* 415–421.

Schopler, E., Lansing, M., & Waters, L. (1983). *Individualized assessment and treatment for autistic and developmentally disabled children (Vol. 3.). Teaching activities for autistic children.* Baltimore: University Park Press.

Schopler, E., & Mesibov, G. B. (Eds.). (1983). *Autism in adolescents and adults.* New York: Plenum Press.

Schopler, E., & Mesibov, G. B. (Eds.). (1984). *The effects of autism on the family.* New York: Plenum Press.

Schopler, E., Mesibov, G. B., & Baker, A. (1982). Evaluation of treatment for autistic children and their parents. *Journal of the American Academy of Child Psychiatry, 21,* 262–267.

Schopler, E., Mesibov, G. B., DeVellis, R. F., & Short, A. (1981). Treatment outcome for autistic children and their families. In P. Mittler (Ed.), *Frontiers of knowledge in mental retardation: Social educational and behavioral aspects* (pp. 293–301). Baltimore: University Park Press.

Schopler, E., & Reichler, R. J. (1979). *Individualized assessment and treatment of autistic and developmentally disabled children (Vol. 1): Psycho-educational profile.* Baltimore: University Park Press.

Schopler, E., Reichler, R. J., & Lansing, M. (1980). *Individualized assessment and treatment for autistic and developmentally disabled children (Vol. 2). Teaching strategies for parents and professionals.* Baltimore: University Park Press.

Short, A. B. (1984). Short-term treatment outcome using parents as co-therapists for their own autistic children. *Journal of Child Psychology and Psychiatry, 25,* 443–458.

Simmons, J. Q., & Baltaxe, C. (1975). Language patterns of adolescent autistics. *Journal of Autism and Childhood Schizophrenia, 5,* 333–351.

Stokes, K. S. (1977). Planning for the future of a severely handicapped autistic child. *Journal of Autism and Childhood Schizophrenia, 7,* 288–297.

Strain, P. S., & Timm, M. A. (1974). An experimental analysis of social interaction between a behaviorally disordered preschool child and her classroom peers. *Journal of Applied Behavior Analysis, 7,* 583–590.

Watson, L. R. (1985). The TEACCH communication curriculum. In E. Schopler & G. B. Mesibov (Eds.), *Communication problems in autism* (pp. 187–206). New York: Plenum Press.

14

A Model for Mainstreaming Autistic Children

The Jowonio School Program

PETER KNOBLOCK and ROBERT LEHR

Systematic teaching of children with autism is relatively new, and teaching these students with their nondisabled peers is a very recent innovation. Jowonio School,* located in Syracuse, New York, was begun in 1970 by parents seeking an alternative to public education for their normal children. Gradually, children with social and academic problems were taken into the school, and in 1975 three young children with autism were accepted. Thus, Jowonio School was one of the first schools to design a curriculum for such a wide range of learners.

Jowonio's history as an alternative school utilizing humanistic principles and practices facilitated the integration of these students (Knoblock & Barnes, 1979). As integration proceeded, the school maintained its emphasis on the importance of creating a warm and caring environment while expanding the curriculum to incorporate teaching strategies appropriate for more disabled students (Knoblock, 1983).

JOWONIO SCHOOL DESIGN

Combining warmth and structure in the preschool and kindergarten classrooms at Jowonio School is a major objective of the teaching staff. They have attempted to create a classroom structure that resembles regular school

**Jowonio,* in Onondaga Indian language, means "to set free."

PETER KNOBLOCK • School of Education, Syracuse University, Syracuse, New York 13210. ROBERT LEHR • Department of Psychology, State University of New York, Cortland, New York 13045.

environments, with the added emphasis of designing activities, materials, and interventions that contribute to the skill attainment and acquisition of *all* children, nondisabled and disabled. Classroom composition and staffing patterns are two major aspects of the school structure.

Classroom Composition. Children of varying ages (usually a 3-year-age span) and abilities are placed into groups of 16. Care is taken to distribute those children who present the most severe management and learning problems across the four classrooms. Once they are placed, a rather elaborate daily schedule is developed to provide each child with opportunities for social interaction and skill development. For example, a 5-year-old autistic child may function, in certain areas, much like his 3-year-old classmate, thus providing a way for the teacher to group them. On the other hand, some children require individual attention by language therapists, physical therapists, and other resource persons. These adults may work within the classroom, but at times a child may be seen in the resource room individually or accompanied by one or more of his nondisabled peers who enjoys the activity and can be of assistance to the adult. Many other grouping considerations are important, such as building on the friendship patterns that may have developed between nondisabled and disabled children and placing them in the same classroom. To maintain flexible grouping options each classroom must have an adequate number of nondisabled students. Despite the lack of research reporting on the appropriate balance within classrooms, a ratio of 2:1—disabled to nondisabled—has been maintained over the years. We began with nine children in a class, but teachers have advocated an increase in class size to maximize the availability of normal peer models for the disabled children.

Cross-age grouping has been an important aspect of the program at Jowonio School. It responds to the variations in development found in any mixed-ability group, but at the same time it places unique demands on the staff to design instructional and social experiences that respond to such diversity.

Staffing Pattern. Each classroom has a lead teacher and an assistant teacher. The goal is to foster a climate of teamwork in which the paid staff, one or two student interns, and volunteers will share the duties and decisions. Toward this end the lead teacher provides leadership and training for classroom staff. In turn, another school staff member functions as a support person to that lead teacher and classroom teaching group. Another function of both the lead teacher and the support person is to monitor the quality of each child's instructional program. Each team has regularly scheduled planning meetings at which individual and group objectives are decided upon and responsibility for implementation is assigned. Skill groups are taught by staff members, and university trainees may function as assistants. In that role, the trainee can support a special child or two in an integrated group while the teacher is responsible for the group lesson. There may be portions of the day when adults are assigned to specific duties. For example, managing transition times between activities is one important responsibility. Teacher behaviors at those times could include alerting each group that the activity will end in 3 minutes, monitoring the needs of children who may have particular difficulties with transition times, and prompting other staff members, if necessary, to attend to management issues that arise.

These examples of school structure and staffing patterns stem from several beliefs upon which the Jowonio program is based: the value of diversity, individualization, taking a social systems perspective, and using an empirically based approach.

EMPHASIZING DIVERSITY

For many advocates of mainstreaming, a most important concept is diversity. At Jowonio, it is assumed that a range of abilities and learning needs exist whenever children are grouped for purposes of instruction and that interaction with nonhandicapped peers can contribute to the development of social skills in children with autism (Voeltz, Johnson, & McQuarter, 1983). Further, a growing body of research and observations supports the contention that nonhandicapped children *also* profit from systematic contact and ongoing interactions with disabled peers (Odom, Deklyen, & Jenkins, 1984). These findings, and our own experiences, have encouraged us to design an intake policy that accepts a wide range of children. We make every effort not to exclude a child on the basis of severity of needs if we can balance our groups so that teachers and nondisabled children can experience less disabled children as well.

In addition to accepting a range of children labeled autistic and broadening our admission criteria to include mulitiply handicapped children, we are often asked to admit nonlabeled typical children who may have mild to moderate learning and behavior problems. Their parents often share similar concerns for their children with parents of disabled children, namely, finding an environment that will respond to their child's cognitive, social, and emotional needs. Hence, we may be seeing an increasing number of families, often single-parent families, hoping to find a safe place for their child. These may be children under stress for a variety of reasons, all of whom can profit from a carefully structured program to meet their needs.

The emphasis on a diverse student population brings many strengths to a school: Skilled children are available for disabled students to imitate, language is used appropriately throughout the day, nondisabled children are available as peer tutors, and opportunities exist to learn play skills and other social interactions, to cite just a few advantages for disabled children. Nondisabled students also receive a great deal of individualized attention for their academic and social needs. In addition, they have an opportunity to make contact with a range of disabled peers. Ideally, they will learn to value differences and maintain such an orientation as they mature. And finally, many teachers appreciate the opportunity to use their range of skills. With an integrated group they can teach high-functioning nondisabled children phonics, for example, and use sensory stimulation activities with disabled students. In this way, a teacher can employ the full range of teaching skills that constitute a teaching repertoire.

A belief in diversity, reflected in the selection of a wide range of children, necessitates certain practices, and hiring a diverse staff is a major one.

Staff Diversity. Selecting a diverse staff is important in a mainstreamed school. The varied nature of children's needs commented upon above highlights the importance of recruiting adults with diverse skills and backgrounds. What does it mean to select a staff for its versatility and skillfulness? To begin with, we now actively search for teachers with backgrounds in early childhood education and elementary education as well as those trained to teach children with autism. We have learned to value such diversity in training and experience. One of the first teachers hired was trained in elementary education and was particularly interested in teaching reading. While she had no prior teaching experience with autistic children, she believed strongly that all children could be taught to read. She helped a 5-year-old autistic child learn to read by assisting him to learn the alphabet with magnetic letters on the refrigerator, by helping him look through books, and by reading to him on a regular basis. The teacher viewed the child as ready to combine letters and to learn a sight vocabulary. In other words, she processed some of his needs through her elementary education perspective and did not perceive herself as a teacher whose training was irrelevant to the learning needs of an autistic child. That teacher became a resource to other staff members, just as those with an early-childhood background have encouraged the development of play skills and a play curriculum to foster symbolic thinking (Uline, 1982).

A diverse staff can include those with physical disabilities, as long as they are capable teachers. A Jowonio teacher who uses a wheelchair has children riding in it as a reward, or a nonverbal child sitting on her lap in her wheelchair must make the sign for "go" before the teacher moves. In play situations children were observed playing school, with the "teacher" sitting in the wheelchair and others grouped around her. Another adult volunteer was deaf and a fluent user of sign language. She joined the staff at a time when we were exploring sign language training for several children, and she was a marvelous teacher. These people, and others, provide role models for children who may be disabled, they can respond to questions and concerns that children and adults may have about disability, and they can present themselves as functioning persons who are capable of making adaptations.

The presence of staff members who are disabled challenges others to clarify their questions and concerns about disability: Will this person be able to do everything other teachers can do, or will special accommodations need to be made? One person (physically disabled or able-bodied) will not be able to do everything, and it is important to have a range of staff members who can provide particular skills. Also, some environmental changes may be needed such as providing close-in parking spaces for your staff and for visitors who are disabled. The goal is to assist adults to become comfortable with each other, and this goal parallels that for children. Diversity, then, is one ingredient of a mainstreamed school that offers children and adults a tangible opportunity to learn to value each individual.

A second practice made necessary by an emphasis on diversity is that of problem solving. The importance of finding ways to capitalize on the strengths and experiences of staff members is a challenge to a learning environment.

Problem Solving. Our emphasis on diversity facilitates another important concept in our school, problem solving. At Jowonio almost all problem solving is, in fact, group problem solving. There are advantages and disadvantages associated with solving problems in groups, and time must be devoted to learning the skills and attitudes in order to be effective at this task. The two main advantages of group, as opposed to individual, problem solving are (1) that a greater diversity of knowledge and perspectives can be brought to bear on the problem, and (2) that by involving the people who will be carrying out the plan there will be greater investment by all in making the new methods work (Maier & Verser, 1982). The group members should be open-minded and committed to changing the environment rather than people, and they should agree on their goals and that no single person will dominate the meeting (Maier & Verser, 1982). Emphasis at Jowonio is placed on the active and equal participation of all members of the classroom team. No solution is automatically excluded and a wide range of opinions are welcomed (Davis, 1973). The focus is on the problem, not on assigning blame either to the child ("he is not trying") or to the parent ("the home situation is terrible").

There are several levels of group discussion and problem solving at Jowonio, starting with informal discussions at lunch or after school each day. There are also two or three formal meetings each week after school that deal with planning and problem solving. One of these meetings is specifically directed toward planning activities for the following week (e.g., where will the field trip be, what is the theme of the week). The second meeting covers supervision of students in the class where the teacher gives feedback to the student teachers on the classroom team. The third meeting is called the support meeting and involves an administrator, the language person, and the other resource people (e.g., occupational therapist, physical therapist) all sitting together to discuss issues that have come up during the week. At these meetings staffing patterns (e.g., who is responsible for Jim at each transition) and how particular interventions will be carried out by all of the staff (e.g., we will ignore Jeff when he bites and will redirect him; or, when Jim hits we will ignore him) are discussed and agreed upon. The support meetings are specifically directed at solving behavior and curriculum problems.

At Jowonio, by having everyone who works with the child involved in the decision process, the intervention program is carried out more uniformly: The administrators, language therapists, and resource staff are all committed to the same program that the classroom staff is trying to implement.

In addition to these regular meetings, over the last several years clinical teams have been formed to provide additional perspectives. At the clinical team meetings that are held each week (each classroom is involved once a month), specific problems the classroom staff raises are discussed by this larger group. The team involves as many different experts as possible so as to elicit the widest possible set of ideas relevant to the problem. In addition to the classroom staff and their support people, language therapists, psychologists, other teachers, administrators, consultants, and others who might help (parents, foster parents, social workers) participate in clinical team meetings. The clinical team was first set up to deal with specific problems of particular children. Some examples included screaming and biting, hitting, and self-injurious behavior, but also included were decisions about what type of alternative communicative system to use with a particular nonverbal child (Schubert, 1982). Over the last several years these meetings have frequently dealt with more general problems, such as how to integrate nonverbal children into reading or math groups, what is an appropriate play activity for a 3-year-old who is severely handicapped, how to deal with the feelings of the typical children, and how to support their emotional needs. It should be mentioned that all problems are not exclusively related to handicapped children.

An example of a recent situation that was dealt with by the clinical team will illustrate this process. A child labeled autistic who had a history of being abused was hitting teachers and other children. Preliminary analyses showed that the hitting seemed to serve several goals; sometimes it was an escape response ("I want out of here") (Carr, Newsom, & Binkoff, 1980) while at other times it seemed to be simply aggressive or the result of too much stimulation. An attempt by the classroom staff to deal with these different types of hitting was unsuccessful, so a clinical team meeting was called to address this problem. One week before the meeting, a set of questions was drawn up by the classroom staff and distributed to all the people who would be involved. This provided an opportunity for each participant to observe the child. The foster parent of the child was invited to the meeting and in the discussion of the hitting she reported that the behavior did not occur at home. From this it was clear that the child was capable of controlling the hitting, and therefore, the question was how to set up a situation in school in which the hitting would not occur. After input from a variety of people, an intervention was decided upon that involved changing the schedule and many activities to reduce the child's frustration. In addition, times that may have been boring were made more interesting and some activities were geared to a more appropriate level. For example, at group meeting time, a particularly hard time for this child, more gross motor activities were planned for the whole group, such as group games to help them identify body parts, and some parallel activities that this particular child could enjoy were included. When the group was doing the calendar and weather, this child was given a matching task—a task in which he was particularly skilled—that included the same numbers and pictures that the whole group was dealing with. Finally, each time the child hit another child or a teacher he was seated in a chair separated from the group (a consequent time-out procedure). All children in the class were made aware of the time-out contingency, which was carried out in as neutral a way as possible since the child enjoyed teacher attention. The total approach of avoiding situations that were frustrating, the introduction of more appropriate activities, and the contingent sitting were consistently applied across the child's day (in the gym, in the speech therapy room, with quite successful results). After 1 week, hitting dropped from 25 to 30 times per day to no hits for 3 days. The input from many people resulted in the intervention program, and they carried out the program with consistent success.

Each person's input is valued and all people have a common goal of helping the child. This problem-solving process is used at several levels and results in a range of programming changes including changes in schedules, personnel, behavioral interventions, special activities, and any combination of these and other interventions that are appropriate. At Jowonio the problem-solving approach involves a variety of people working on a problem, and parents can contribute greatly to such staff efforts.

A belief in individualizing instruction facilitates the implementation of the problem-solving process outlined above. Jowonio's position on individualization and its practices are described in the next section.

INDIVIDUALIZING INSTRUCTION

The unique learning and social needs of these children requires a highly individualized instructional approach. Jowonio's belief in the potential of all children, including those with autism, to change has guided the school in designing practices to accomplish such growth.

From its inception, Jowonio's program has enacted this belief in children's potential to change by (1) communicating respect and caring for them, (2) teachers' willingness to hold themselves accountable for children's development in school (as opposed to blaming the child for lack of progress), (3) collaborating with other professionals and parents to strengthen a child's program, and (4) maintaining realistic expectations for their development.

Designing practices that are responsive to the children's individual needs in a mainstreamed program requires an extraordinary degree of planning. The range of children—disabled and nondisabled—and the goal of maximizing positive social interactions between these students necessitates teacher behaviors that reflect intensity and relevance of functioning and curriculum practices that embody such intensity. These are discussed in the following sections.

Intensity and Relevance of Programming. According to Wolfensberger and Glenn (1975), the level of challenge presented by a staff to its clients can be measured by the intensity of relevant programming: "Is the program relevant (regardless of intensity to the person, group, or problem? And is it of the high intensity that is relevant to the service needs of the clients? Is there a strong commitment to move the client along a developmental continuum, and if possible, to graduate him/her to independence, or at least to more advanced demands and services?" (p. 41).

In order to maintain such a high level of interaction with children of varying abilities and need levels, it is necessary to focus on several ingredients in the environment, including administrative support, setting objectives, providing a safe environment, maintaining expectations, and evaluating progress.

Jowonio administrators recognize that every effort must be made to facilitate the work of classroom teachers and resource personnel. These efforts range from finding the money that enables teachers to provide their classrooms with learning materials and equipment to assisting them in developing instructional approaches for individual children and classroom groups. Every effort is made to protect front-line personnel from the "administrivia" that plagues every organization. On the other hand, equally strenuous efforts are made to involve staff members in the decisions that affect their school lives, thereby fostering a feeling of psychological ownership.

Teaching by objectives is imperative in a mainstreamed setting because of the range of learners in each classroom. Each activity must be tailored to the needs of each participant including nondisabled children. Short-term objectives must lead to the eventual achievement of long-term objectives. The consistent use of goal-setting instruments like developmental therapy (Wood, 1975), whose objectives in the areas of behavior, socialization, communication, and academics are incorporated into each special child's individual education plan, provides our teachers with a rich pool of goals, activities, and materials.

Every child learns best in a climate of safety and trust. For autistic children this means having teachers who can respond accurately to their communications and needs, and who can ease them into the environment, helping them to learn the expectations, and how to become comfortable first with adults, then with children. For all children it means having schedules and learning goals that accurately reflect their needs. Teaching communication and interaction with peers should be the priorities. There may be behaviors that are scary or worrisome to the nondisabled students, and teachers will need to help the handicapped children to modify them. It is important to control behaviors against others or drooling at the lunch table, or to provide nondisabled peers with positive techniques of their own to use when approached by special children.

Deficits in autistic children's social, communication, and cognitive development are viewed as deficits in skill development and as such can be taught and remedied. This perspective has greatly energized our teachers and fostered a climate of careful optimism. This enthusiasm is translated into practice by teachers' willingness to devote adequate time to teaching skills on the assumption that teaching makes a difference. Despite the fact that many of these children are management concerns—that is, they may require persistent direction and redirection—a variety of positive interventions can be used (LaVigna & Donnellan, 1985).

The evaluation process in a mainstreamed environment must include systematic and ongoing diagnosis and evaluation procedures for all children. At Jowonio we strive to collect information that can be useful in the classroom for planning and teaching purposes. There is a timetable of assessment procedures used throughout the school year that also includes reviews of nondisabled children's development. In essence, the evaluation process can provide teachers with data they might not otherwise obtain. This information should serve as a transfusion for the teacher, enabling him to restructure classroom schedules and practices.

It is of interest to note that the above program ingredients match those identified by Edmonds and Fredericksen (Fiske, 1984) as qualities important in a "good school": principal and administrative support and leadership, setting clear teaching objectives, providing a safe and orderly learning environment, maintaining high and realistic expectations of students, and evaluating children's progress on a regular and ongoing basis. The point is that a mainstreamed learning environment can be designed and its program implemented according to currently assumed characteristics of effectiveness. The development of sound curricular approaches is facilitated when these quality indicators are emphasized.

A Curriculum for Disabled and Nondisabled Children. In a recent analysis of programmatic factors that contribute to social interactions in mainstreamed settings, Guralnick (1982) considers it essential when determining the feasibility of integrated programs that "(a) the fundamental structure and philosophy of a particular educational program's model remains intact despite the heterogeneity of the children in the classroom; (b) the developmental and educational needs of all children are met; (c) the program is compatible with certain humanistic and social goals of integrated education" (p. 72). The Jowonio program is responsive to each of these factors.

Curriculum. The curriculum approach at Jowonio focuses on the following goals: (1) to maximize each child's development through an individualized curriculum emphasizing behavior, communication, socialization, and (pre) academics; (2) to maximize each child's potential for independence through functional skills and tasks; (3) to maximize each child's participation in normalized settings by relating the child's firsthand, daily experiences to classroom activities and instructional content; (4) to maximize each child's integration with typical peers by maintaining a balance between normal development programming and intensive psychoeducational procedures.

These goals reflect the humanistic perspective that assumes each individual is capable of learning and can be motivated or assisted to change. Jowonio School is designed to meet these goals by caring about each child and by communicating that concern through the program's structure.

In contrast to Guralnick's (1982) notion that integrating disabled chldren into a program should not disrupt the ongoing nature of that program, Jowonio School begins with the premise that a learning environment can be designed to include disabled students from the outset. The implication is that disabled children do not have to earn their way into "regular" programs but rather all classrooms and programs are "special" (Reynolds & Birch, 1977). When we apply a "ready to fit" criterion to the admissibility of autistic children into programs, we penalize those children by requiring them to meet certain standards. In contrast, at Jowonio the teachers change their behaviors; the procedures and school structure can be modified, and the match between child and program is improved by focusing on environmental change and not by blaming the children for their behaviors.

The programming philosophy at Jowonio further assumes that, if a special intervention program seems warranted, the teaching staff has first considered the situational/environmental factors that may explain why a child is not progressing or why a problem behavior is continuing. In addition, the teaching staff will document the rate of progress of problem occurrence to demonstrate that the special intervention is warranted.

Teachers are required to plan extensively in order to implement a daily program for the wide range of abilities in each classroom. Their planning combines normalization theory principles (Flynn & Nitsch, 1980) and current practices in teaching severely disabled students.

Normalization theory seeks ways to expose disabled children to the same opportunities experienced by all students. At Jowonio these opportunities include arranging transportation using yellow school buses and adhering to the same hours and vacation schedule as other schools in the Syracuse school district. Because all of our children move into the public schools at the kindergarten or first-grade level, it is necessary to guarantee, as best as we can, that all children are prepared to meet public school achievement standards. Accomplishing this might involve administering school district level tests, using equivalent reading and mathematics materials, and methods of feedback (report cards, progress reports) to children and parents that prepare them for public school procedures. At Jowonio School we are actively seeking ways to involve disabled children in challenging and difficult activities that are essential to their future success in regular classrooms. For example, the majority of our special children have difficulty participating in group meetings but we maintain they should be part of that process. A staff member may hold a child on her lap or position himself next to a disabled child for support, or a child is expected to remain at the meeting for a minute, with the time increased as behavior becomes more appropriate. In other words, rather than avoiding group situations, we consider it essential that children learn to function appropriately in groups. Conversely, teachers also assume responsibility for designing some group activities that are geared expressly to the interest level and enjoyment of the disabled children.

In addition to these emphases, our instructional process is tied to our positive responses to the following questions, which combine principles and practices of teaching severely disabled students and normalization theory (Altieri, 1983): Are disabled children taught chronologically age-appropriate skills? Is there a conscious effort to design opportunities for interaction between nondisabled and disabled peers? Is there an acceptable level of coherency to the ways in which the many program variables are organized to meet each child's needs? Can the child participate in any aspect of the task now? Are skills and tasks taught in natural environments? Are children taught in environments that are related to future functioning?

Jowonio School's curriculum approach encompasses more than teacher–child interactions. It relies on home and community involvement. This belief in a broader perspective is described next.

A SOCIAL SYSTEMS PERSPECTIVE

Jowonio School is committed to a perspective that includes collaborating with parents and area schools and agencies. A social systems perspective attempts to focus on all aspects of a child's life. This "whole child" orientation recognizes that many curriculum decisions involve families. If the goal is to foster generalization skills from school to home, then school tasks must be feasible for parents to attempt at home, parents must be assisted in developing the needed skills, and on the other hand, teachers will need to solicit information from parents about their child's functioning at home. The coordination of data from many sources is essential for a child's continued growth. Active collaboration with schools and agencies is another important aspect of social systems perspective. Children leaving to enter public school programs benefit from ongoing communication between Jowonio and the receiving school. Other examples include efforts to assist families in finding respite services and after-school recreational opportunities. A major aspect of a social systems perspective is the concept that changes in any part of a child's world will have an impact on other parts. Certainly this is seen when home conditions change and a child's school behavior is affected, when staff changes have an impact on a family's response to the school, and when agencies are unable to find suitable respite situations and parents buckle under the pressure of caring for a severely disabled child without supportive services. These examples and others serve to remind us of the importance of coordinating all aspects of a child's life to the extent possible.

Parent Involvement. Parents have become a valuable and even necessary part of the education of disabled children (Harris, 1983; Kozloff, 1979; Schopler & Reichler, 1971) and their participation can occur in school and at home. Parents of disabled children have a wide variety of needs (Featherstone, 1980; Murphy, 1981), and the development of positive relationships between professional educators and parents is essential (Gliedman & Roth, 1980; Turnbull & Turnbull, 1978). At Jowonio there is a commitment to involving parents in all of the school activities. The school is operated on the assumption that all aspects of the child's life can be coordinated, and therefore, collaboration between home and school, where it is appropriate, is stressed. Over the years a number of structures, based on needs of the parents and availability of resources, have been used to accomplish these goals. There have been a variety of parent groups and parent–school interaction arrangements (Kuglemass, 1982). Initially the school had social workers who visited the home and assisted the parents. Later there were parent workers who were special education teachers and who also worked in the classroom. Today each classroom teacher is released at least one half-day a week to work with the parents.

Classroom Staff Involvement. The most important factor in Jowonio's support and encouragement of parents' participation in the education of their child involves the classroom staff. Each teacher makes several home visits during the school year depending on the needs of the parents and child. Teachers communicate with the parents of our disabled children on a daily basis. The telephone and a notebook sent back and forth in the lunch box are the basic forms of this two-way communication. For students who are nonverbal or who have severe language problems this is absolutely essential. Each day after school, or during school, teachers are talking with parents on the phone about the activities of the day, the plans for tomorrow, or the doctor visit next week. Each part of the child's life is considered important and our staff is regularly involved in helping parents obtain services, receive information, and find respite services.

One of the teachers described her involvement with parents as helping them on three levels (Donovan, 1984). In the classroom, in addition to other goals, she attempts to teach the child skills that will help the family to live better (self-control, specific words, self-help skills). At the home, through modeling, role playing, even direct instruction, she attempts to teach the parents skills that will help them cope with their child and the problems associated with having a disabled child (e.g., how to handle a tantrum, how to record behaviors, how to talk to the school committee). The third level is getting other agencies and support groups involved with the family. Involving the family with other parent groups or therapists or welfare agencies can help them immensely and therefore results in a better life for the child.

Parent Groups. Parent groups can be an effective part of the family–school interaction (Auerbach, 1968; Hereford, 1963). In addition to open-house meetings and potluck suppers for all parents, formal parent groups for those with handicapped children have always been a part of Jowonio's program. The form and content of the groups vary from year to year on the basis of the needs of the parents involved. There have been groups for single parents, groups directed at sharing of common experiences, groups focused on parent problems, and groups primarily directed at educating parents about parenting skills and behavior management in the home. Involvement of the parents in their child's education, their personal growth, and their skill development are consistently emphasized. At present there are two parent groups, one meeting at night and one meeting during the day. The topics range from helping parents enjoy their child to advocacy, information sharing, and future planning. In each group the two half-time workers try to deal with each individual parent and respond to his/her individual needs. The Jowonio staff feels that parents often have difficulty dealing with the societal problems associated with bringing up a disabled child (Gliedman & Roth, 1980) and therefore, the staff may be involved in some unconventional ways. For example, staff activities may include how to get professional services (doctors, dentists), behavioral interventions to reduce obnoxious behaviors, how to deal with school committees, how to treat siblings (we also have a sibling group that meets once a month), how to deal with neighbors, how to deal with one's own feelings, and what kind of Christmas presents to buy.

The commitment of our staff to work with families is illustrated by the following example. One child came to school with welts and bruises on his body. The teacher documented the abuse and tried to talk to the parent in order to stop the apparent beatings. At the same time the appropriate authorities at child protective services were informed and, as a result, the parent was required to attend meetings with the child protective staff. The classroom teacher reminded the parent of the meetings and arranged transportation to the meetings. In addition, respite care for the child was obtained so that the parent would not have to deal with the child so much of the time. The point is that the teacher tried to help the parent cope with the problem rather than assigning blame. Not all parents require such intensive interventions, but some do.

Parental involvement, while important, is just one dimension in an effort to seek out additional persons to staff classrooms. The next section describes the school's role in training persons and outreach efforts to attract resources.

Providing Human Resources. Mainstreamed environments require additional teaching and support services to respond to the many social and academic needs of disabled and nondisabled students. Existing school budgets often preclude hiring sufficient staff, and creative ways of involving skilled persons must be found. Jowonio School has responded to the need for additional human resources by developing relationships with Syracuse University, Onondaga Community College, and other area schools. To do this it has been necessary for Jowonio administrators and teachers to make a commitment to training preservice teachers. This commitment requires staff time and energy if student teachers and volunteers are to achieve sufficient skill levels to be helpful with the children. This expenditure of energy has long-term benefits for Jowonio School's recruitment of future teachers and teacher assistants. In addition, Jowonio School now attracts a variety of persons from the community who bring expertise in music, drama, arts and crafts, and recreation, and every effort is made to take advantage of such a rich pool of resource persons.

This commitment to training a range of persons is a complicated matter because it is not necessarily an integral part of most environments that have a direct service emphasis. At Jowonio, the willingness of teachers to share their time and energy with trainees, assuming that the children and they, as teachers, would eventually benefit, began as an article of faith. Through hard work and growing confidence administrators and teachers have become increasingly committed to offering training to others. Now, for example, a summer practicum experience is available for experienced public school teachers interested in learning more about autism and mainstreaming, and for those teachers who will be integrating Jowonio children into their regular classrooms at a later time. These changes have occurred because of the school's long-standing focus on program evaluation resulting in the restructuring of existing aspects of the program and creating new emphases and directions.

AN EMPIRICAL APPROACH

In addition to the basic philosophical positions stated above, Jowonio School operates on the assumption that effective educational practices (those that work) should be used irrespective of their theoretical bases. We assume that effective empirically demonstrated practices should not be excluded on purely theoretical grounds, and that careful empirical observations and evaluations are a necessary part of any quality program. The overall curriculum is based on methods that were developed from a variety of theoretical orientations (e.g., psychodynamic, behavioral); the only criterion is that they work. While Jowonio is not a research or laboratory school, some careful empirical research has been and is being carried out and data are continually being collected on student progress.

Evaluation. Evaluation of each child's progress is a regular and continuing part of the Jowonio program. Fundamental to the evaluation process is that the goals be clearly defined. Most of the children at Jowonio have been labeled autistic; the average score on the Autism Behavior Checklist is 98.2 (Krug, Arick, & Almond, 1980), and they fit most definitions of severely handicapped children. However, diagnostic tests rarely translate directly into classroom programs.

The first month of school is the time when each child's skills are systematically assessed, for the most part in the classroom setting, and a detailed IEP is developed. These IEPs, which become the working plans for the children, are generally based on goals and objectives described in Developmental Therapy (Bachrach, Mosley, Swindle, & Wood, 1978; Wood, 1975), the Learning Accomplishment Profile (Glover, Preminger, & Sanford, 1978), the Vulpe Assessment Battery (Vulpe, 1978), and the Behavior Checklist Progression (1973). These developmentally arranged goals are the pool from which particular tasks are selected on the basis of the individual child's needs.

Throughout the year, each activity planned for a child is based on the IEP, and progress or lack of progress is continually noted. At midyear (January) and at the end of the year (June) each IEP is carefully reviewed by the whole classroom staff, and a formal update, with appropriate revisions based on the child's development, is written. The initial IEPs this year (1984–1985) average 16 typewritten pages of goals, activities, and projected dates of accomplishment, and the updates average 15 pages. The teachers do the majority of writing, which is a skill that has to be developed in our younger staff.

Promoting social interactions between disabled and nondisabled children is a major focus. Barnes and Isaacson (1982), using direct observations (specimen recording and coded observations), have shown that disabled children at Jowonio interact with nondisabled children at about the same rate as with other disabled children (i.e., they "don't seek out their own kind"). They also found that the overwhelming majority of the interactions between disabled and nondisabled children were positive. They reported differences in the amount of interactions based on the type of task, classroom, and time of year as expected. More social interactions occurred during play and lunch times and fewer during teacher-directed "work" activities.

In addition to collecting direct observational data, Barnes and Isaacson

(1982) did sociometric analysis. They asked children to pick out the children that they "liked" and "disliked" and to rank the children in each category. The disabled children received "like" votes in about the same proportion as their numbers in the classes. When disabled children were "disliked," the main reason was that they were aggressive. In a more recent study (Accetta & Berres, 1983), children in one room were asked to pick the picture of the child that they liked the best and would like to play with most, from pictures of all of the children. On the basis of the ranks obtained by repeating this process they found that disabled children were distributed throughout the range. They then took the lowest-ranked disabled child and asked the classroom staff to try to change the other children's perceptions of this child. The child was given extra teacher attention (e.g., he was made "student of the week") and in general was responded to more positively by the staff. The ranking was repeated in 2 months, and this particular child had moved up from the bottom to the middle of the class. Positive effort by the staff had changed the other children's perception of this disabled child.

This year videotaping was done at the beginning and end of the year. Children were taped in a variety of settings throughout the day (e.g., one-on-one, small groups, meeting time) and the tapes are being coded to assess child change, particularly in the areas of social interactions and play development.

A model program in mainstreaming severely disabled children must be evaluated by how effective the model works as well as how often the program, or a modification of it, is copied. A follow-up study on the placement of our children after they leave Jowonio is currently being carried out. Preliminary results indicate that approximately 90% were in mainstreamed settings for at least 1 year after leaving Jowonio.

Jowonio's "graduates" often continue in integrated settings because parents are convinced that this is an appropriate placement for their children. Another reason is that the Jowonio staff has helped local school systems to develop integrated options that ensure students the opportunity to develop functional life, social, and language experiences that are necessary for their development (Brown *et al.*, 1979). Some children are integrated into regular classrooms with the assistance of an aide or by utilizing a resource room teacher. Others are mainstreamed into special subjects (music, art, gym), often with an aide.

The Edward Smith Elementary School in the Syracuse City School District has developed a program for the full integration of autistic children into regular classrooms. Based on the Jowonio model and with the assistance of the Jowonio staff, a single classroom was started with 5 severely handicapped children, 25 nonhandicapped children, and two teachers, one with a background in autism. At a later time Jowonio located one of its classrooms in a regular elementary school in order to further demonstrate that the model would work in the "real world." As a result of these positive experiences, Syracuse has designed kindergarten-through-grade-5 classes where severely handicapped children are integrated on a full-time basis. Thus, one school district has a program that allows for the full-time integration of severely disabled children into regular classrooms throughout the whole elementary school experience. We believe that this will have lasting effects on the disabled as well as the nondisabled children.

The success of transporting the Jowonio model into the Syracuse City School District has led to the development of additional technical assistance efforts; these are described in the following section.

Disseminating Information and Technical Assistance. Jowonio School is increasingly committed to sharing its expertise and experiences with others. This outreach effort is now supported by a 3-year grant from the Handicapped Children's Early Education Program to offer assessment and consultation services to families and service providers for young children with developmental delays and behavior disorders. The goal is to facilitate the placement of young autistic and emotionally disturbed children into integrated preschools and primary schools. A consultation staff comprising a special education teacher, a speech and language therapist, and a school psychologist receives referrals from school personnel, physicians, and clinics, and from parents directly. This technical assistance can include (a) visits for teachers and administrators to see the mainstreaming program at Jowonio; (b) an initial meeting with parents and service providers to discuss a consultation plan; (c) observation of the child in his or her own environment; (d) observation and assessment of the child in a Jowonio classroom; (e) recommendations for further assessment and/or referral to appropriate agencies; (f) referral for placement in an appropriate preschool or primary program, or help in creating one, by working with teachers and administrators to develop an effective placement; (g) help in designing individual service plans (methods, activities, and materials); (h) consultation on a continuing basis; (i) in-service training for receiving programs and school districts in such areas as behavior management, facilitating language in classroom, individualizing instruction, and working as an interdisciplinary team.

Jowonio School has reached a stage in its development as an integrated learning environment that allows staff members to share their expertise with others. We hope, as other schools accept students with autism into their programs, that they, too, will reach out to other professionals and parents so we can expand opportunities for integrated education.

SUMMARY

This chapter has described ingredients of the Jowonio model that reflect its philosophical, educational, and community orientation to mainstreaming. These include an emphasis on valuing the presence of diverse students and staff members, designing a daily program that reflects intensity and relevance of programming, building a curriculum responsive to the learning needs of all pupils, utilizing a problem-solving orientation, including parents and others in planning children's programs, staffing classrooms with sufficient numbers of skilled adults, and designing ongoing program evaluation and child-change data-gathering procedures. All of these emphases have encouraged the Jowonio staff and parents to engage in an increased level of dissemination activities that includes providing technical assistance to area schools and parents.

REFERENCES

Acetta, M. L., & Berres, M. (1983). *A sociometric study of a mainstreamed classroom.* Unpublished manuscript.

Altieri, E. (1983). *Developing functional goals and objectives.* Unpublished manuscript.

Auerbach, A. B. (1968). *Parents learn through discussion: Principles and practices of parent group education.* New York: Wiley.

Bachrach, A. W., Mosley, A. R., Swindle, F. L., & Wood, M. M. (1978). *Developmental therapy for young children with autistic characteristics.* Baltimore: University Park Press.

Barnes, E., & Isaacson, D. (1982). Evaluating peer interactions in an integrated setting. In P. Knoblock (Ed.), *Teaching and mainstreaming autistic children.* Denver: Love.

Behavior Checklist Progression Observation Booklet. (1973). Santa Cruz Special Education Management System. Palo Alto, CA: VORT Corp.

Brown, L., Branston, M. Hamre-Nietupski, S., Pumpian, I., Certo, N., & Gruenwald, L. (1979). A strategy for developing chronological-age appropriate and functional curricular content for severely handicapped adolescents and young adults, *Journal of Special Education, 13,* 81–90.

Carr, E. G., Newsom, C. D., & Binkoff, J. A. (1980). Escape as a factor in the aggressive behavior of two retarded children. *Journal of Applied Behavior Analysis, 13,* 101–117.

Davis, G. A. (1973). *Psychology of problem solving.* New York: Basic Books.

Donovan, E. (1984). *A model for teachers as parent advocates.* Paper presented at the meeting of Sequin Community Services, Syracuse, NY.

Featherstone, H. (1980). *A difference in the family.* New York: Basic Books.

Fiske, E. B. (1984, April 15). New look at effective schools. *New York Times Education Spring Survey,* pp. 1, 35, 36, 55, 56.

Flynn, R. J., & Nitsch, K. E. (Eds.). (1980). *Normalization, social integration, and community services.* Baltimore: University Park Press.

Gliedman, J., & Roth, W. (1980). *The unexpected minority: Handicapped children in America.* New York: Harcourt Brace Jovanovich.

Glover, M. E., Preminger, J. L., & Sanford, A. R. (1978). *Early LAP.* Winston-Salem, NC: Kaplan Press.

Guralnick, M. J. (1982). Programmatic factors affecting child–child social interactions in mainstreamed preschool programs. In P. S. Strain (Ed.), *Social development of exceptional children* (pp. 71–91). Rockville, MD: Aspen System Corp.

Harris, S. L. (1983). *Families of the developmentally disabled.* New York: Pergamon Press.

Hereford, C. F. (1963). *Changing parental attitudes through group discussion.* Austin: University of Texas Press.

Knoblock, P. (Ed.). (1982). *Teaching and mainstreaming autistic children.* Denver: Love.

Knoblock, P. (1983). *Teaching emotionally disturbed children.* Boston: Houghton Mifflin.

Knoblock, P., & Barnes, E. (1979). An environment for everyone: Autistic and nondisabled children learn together. In S. J. Meisels (Ed.), *Special education and development* (pp. 207–228). Baltimore: University Park Press.

Kozloff, M. A. (1979). *A program for families of children with learning and behavior problems.* New York: Wiley.

Krug, D. A., Arick, J. R., & Almond, P. J. (1980). *Autism screening instrument for educational planning.* Portland, OR: ASIEP Education Company.

Kuglemass, J. (1982). Parent–school partnership: The essential component. In P. Knoblock (Ed.), *Teaching and mainstreaming autistic children.* Denver: Love.

LaVigna, G. W., & Donnellan, A. M. (1985). *Alternatives to punishment: Non-aversive strategies for solving behavior problems.* New York: Irvington Press.

Maier, N. R. F., & Verser, G. C. (1982). *Psychology in industrial organization* (5th ed.). Boston: Houghton Mifflin.

Murphy, A. T. (1981). *Special children, special parents.* Englewood Cliffs, NJ: Prentice-Hall.

Odom, S. L., Deklyen, M., & Jenkins, J. R. (1984). Integrating handicapped and nonhandicapped preschoolers: Developmental impact on nonhandicapped children. *Exceptional Children, 51,* 41–48.

Reynolds, M. C., & Birch, J. W. (1977). *Teaching exceptional children in all America's schools.* Reston, VA: Council for Exceptional Children.

Schopler, E., & Reichler, R. J. (1971). Parents as cotherapists in the treatment of psychotic children, *Journal of Autism and Childhood Schizophrenia, 1,* 87–102.

Schubert, A. (1982). Alternative communication methods. In P. Knoblock (Ed.), *Teaching and mainstreaming autistic children.* Denver: Love.

Turnbull, A. P., & Turnbull, H. R. (1978). *Parents speak out.* Columbus, OH: Charles E. Merrill.

Uline, C. (1982). Teaching autistic children to play: A major teacher intervention. In P. Knoblock (Ed.), *Teaching and mainstreaming autistic children* (pp. 94–119). Denver: Love.

Voeltz, L. M., Johnson, R. E., & McQuarter, R. J. (1983). *The integration of school-aged children and youth with severe disabilities: A comprehensive bibliography and a selective review of research and program development needs to address discrepancies in state-of-the-art.* Minneapolis: University of Minnesota Consortium Institute.

Vulpe, S. G. (1978). *Vulpe assessment battery.* Toronto: National Institute on Mental Retardation.

Wolfensberger, W., & Glenn, L. (1975). *Program analysis of service systems: A method for the quantitative evaluation of human services.* Toronto: National Institute on Mental Retardation.

Wood, M. M. (Ed.). (1975). *Developmental therapy.* Baltimore: University Park Press.

15

Social Skills Training for Elementary School Autistic Children with Normal Peers

MARIAN WOOTEN and GARY B. MESIBOV

INTRODUCTION

The passage of Public Law 94-142, mandating public education for all handicapped children in the least restrictive environment, has brought about many changes in education for these children (Aloia, Beaver, & Pettus, 1978). No longer automatically isolated in schools for the handicapped, they are more frequently in regular school settings with nonhandicapped peers (Egel, Richman, & Koegel, 1981; Halpern, 1970). The amount of contact between handicapped and nonhandicapped children differs markedly from school to school but in general has increased significantly over the past decade. Although the placement of handicapped children in normal schools increases the potential for them to learn appropriate social skills and adaptive behaviors, this is not always realized in practice. The problem is that handicapped children, and especially those with autism, often require specialized training programs in order to develop social skills. Such training programs are not always provided.

Gresham (in press) has presented an astute analysis of the problems with mainstreaming to date. He points out that rather than facilitating the social integration of handicapped people, current mainstreaming practice has more often

MARIAN WOOTEN • Millbrook Elementary School, 1520 Millbrook Road, Raleigh, North Carolina 27609. GARY B. MESIBOV • Division TEACCH, University of North Carolina, Chapel Hill, North Carolina 27514.

resulted in poor social acceptance of handicapped children, negative rates of social interaction between handicapped and nonhandicapped peers, poor self-concept of many handicapped children, and a generally negative attitude toward mainstreaming by most regular educators. The reasons for this are many but are generally the result of the simplistic philosophy that successful mainstreaming only requires placing handicapped and nonhandicapped children together in normal settings.

Although mainstreaming as practiced has not been very effective in achieving its desired goals, this does not mean that there cannot be potential advantages for handicapped children in interacting with nonhandicapped peers (Mesibov, 1984; Chapter 13, this volume). However, the evidence to date suggests that simple exposure to appropriate behavior is not enough. Because individualized teaching is still the rule with handicapped youngsters, and especially those with autism, a one-to-one teaching approach is as necessary with these social skills as with the academic components of their educational environment. Therefore, the problem with mainstreaming is not that nonhandicapped children have little to offer but rather that we have not found the best method to utilize these youngsters (Campbell, Scaturro, & Lickson, 1983; McHale, Olley, Marcus, & Simeonsson, 1981). The following chapter presents a classroom model in the TEACCH program for using nonhandicapped peers to teach social skills to autistic students. This program comes from one of the 55 classrooms for autistic youngsters around the state of North Carolina that are affiliated with the TEACCH program. Many of the approaches and techniques developed and refined in this classroom are being used in other TEACCH-affiliated classrooms around the state as well.

SETTING

The classroom is located in a fifth-grade hall in a 1000-student elementary school for kindergarten-through-fifth-grade students. The self-contained autistic classroom included six autistic males between the ages of 8 and 12 years. The levels of functioning ranged from severe mental retardation to mild mental retardation and the range of autism was also from mild to severe, according to the diagnostic criteria of the Childhood Autism Rating Scale (CARS; Schopler, Reichler, DeVellis, & Daly, 1980).

Typical of autistic children, the students in the classroom lacked responsiveness and interactive skills with other children. Even those with verbal ability were unable to carry on a conversation or interact socially in an appropriate manner, appearing egocentric to others and unable to become involved in a conversation or to relate effectively. In a normal school environment with children constantly talking and interacting, these problems were especially evident.

CONCEPTS

Given the deficits of the autistic children and the presence of nonhandicapped peers who interacted easily and effectively, it seemed logical to use these strengths to teach appropriate social skills to the autistic students. The typical mainstreaming model involves sending autistic children into classrooms of nonhandicapped children for brief periods of the day. This seemed inappropriate to us for reasons well described by Gresham (in press) as well as others noted by us. First, the difficulties autistic children have with changes in their routine and environment would make these disruptions in their schedule difficult to tolerate. In addition, the activities would be structured by the teachers in the nonhandicapped classrooms and might not be appropriate for the skills and abilities of the autistic students. Therefore, we decided to use "reverse mainstreaming" to accomplish our interaction goals (Poorman, 1980). As the name implies, this involves bringing nonhandicapped students into our autistic children's classroom to work with our students.

Reverse mainstreaming fits very nicely with a general concept that is commonly used in teaching autistic children. When teaching a new objective, it is usually best to keep consistent as many aspects of the situation as possible. For example, if a new skill is being taught, it should be done with setting, structure, and materials remaining familiar. On the other hand, if the setting is new, it should be introduced with familiar skills and materials. For example, if you are teaching sorting (a new skill), it should be done with familiar materials in a familiar place and in a previously encountered learning situation. On the other hand, if you are going to teach in a different environment, this would not be the time to introduce a new skill. Therefore, because the nonhandicapped peers in reverse mainstreaming are new, they should be introduced into a familiar classroom with familiar materials.

We expected that bringing normal peers into our classroom and having them practice already acquired skills with the autistic children might facilitate the eventual generalization of these skills outside of the classroom. Practicing skills with nonhandicapped peers is a step toward generalization and the spontaneous use of these skills. However, it has taken us 7 years of structuring and experimenting to develop this model to its present form. It is probably worthwhile to describe the early stages of our play groups because it has been through these past experiences that we have been able to learn and to eventually develop our existing model.

INITIAL STAGES OF THE PLAY GROUP

When this group began 7 years ago, we had six nonhandicapped children come into our classroom for free-play activities with the autistic children. Materials such as balls, wagons, blocks, cars, trucks, and similar play objects were available for the children to use. Each session lasted for approximately 30 minutes, with the hope that forced interactions would stimulate our autistic children to respond and play with their normal peers. It was expected that new play skills would be developed as a result of communicating and responding to peers.

Unfortunately, these initial objectives were never met. Instead, the autistic children became more adept at avoiding and rejecting these intrusive peers. They either ignored the nonhandicapped children, had tantrums, or engaged in their own self-stimulatory activities. The nonhandicapped children began to play with each other rather than forcing themselves upon the autistic children.

In retrospect, the reasons for these initial failures seem obvious. Our initial objectives for the children in the class were neither specific nor clear. "Developing play skills" or "increasing communication" are worthy goals but not specific enough for autistic children to learn or for nonhandicapped peers to teach. We have since learned that "bouncing and catching a ball" or "cooperatively putting a puzzle together" are the kinds of objectives more likely to achieve results. Moreover, the initial setting of 12 children in a large play area with lots of toys was not as conducive to learning as we might have thought. A one-to-one setting with a single set of materials and clear objectives is far more productive. The goal of playing with another child was far too advanced developmentally for our autistic children. However, if an autistic child is able to put a puzzle together, then doing it cooperatively with another child is practical and more realistic. This notion is consistent with the concept of using an acquired skill in a highly structured one-to-one setting with known materials and then adding a new element, which in this case is the peer. A great deal was learned through these initial "play groups," even though the outcomes were not as successful as we had hoped. Actually, the main problem was in thinking of these as play groups because the children were not actually learning to play in a group. In fact, free-play activities are probably one of their weakest areas. These are situations that have the least organization, the highest level of self-stimulation and inappropriate behaviors, and the least amount of understanding. Rather than trying to teach autistic children to play in groups, we learned that it is far more productive to teach them to play in a one-on-one setting with specific materials and then to help them carry this learned skill into larger group situations. The next section will describe the current play groups and show how the children go through this developmental process.

CURRENT PLAY GROUPS

Following our early notion that interaction required only the presence of nonhandicapped children, we eventually learned that setting, structure, materials, preparation, and every other aspect of the mainstreaming experience is extremely important if interaction and social skills development are to result. In organizing our group, of particular importance are the objectives, teacher and peer preparation, group structure, activities, rules, and follow-up. In developing each of these aspects of our play groups, we have learned that the groups have benefits beyond those initially anticipated. Each of these aspects, including additional benefits, will now be discussed in turn.

OBJECTIVES

The objectives for this group are twofold in that we want both the autistic and the nonhandicapped peers to gain from the play group. The objectives for each autistic child vary as they are individualized to meet current needs. These objectives are very specific and developmentally appropriate. A new skill would never be introduced in the play group, but as described earlier, acquired skills are generalized into this setting. For example, if a child can play Bingo with the teacher in a one-to-one setting, playing in a group with two nonhandicapped peers would be the developmentally appropriate objective. A later step might be attending to the game with conversations proceeding at a faster pace. Starting with these basic skills, one of our children is now able to go out for family Bingo night with his family and play the game in a room full of strange people. This would not have been possible a year ago, even though he had the skills to play the game. The process began by having this youngster play the game with a peer who came into the classroom for table games. This was an easy step for him. However, when we added two more peers and the distractions of conversations and laughter, it took this youngster several weeks to learn how to concentrate and play the game while ignoring the distractions. The next step was to have him actually reply to some of the conversation around him. This was done by systematically having him imitate the others by saying, "I have that one" or "One more and I have Bingo." After several months of Bingo in this setting, he was able to play the game regardless of the distractions and actually to participate in the conversation. More and more children were added until he was playing the game with 12 children at the table. One last step before sending him out with his family was for us to accompany the family and add the additional structure of the teacher to remind him of the appropriate rules in the new setting.

Other objectives may range from taking turns to learning how to lose. For low-functioning children, objectives may be simply tolerating another child in their presence, such as in putting a puzzle together. Learning to work cooperatively is another possible objective, as in helping to finish a puzzle. It is important to have objectives that might carry over into the home in structured play with a sibling or in simply tolerating the intrusiveness and distractions of having other people around.

As with all appropriate objectives, those for this group should be specific and easily observable. This is especially important for the nonhandicapped peer students who need positive feedback and the feeling that they are really accomplishing something. It is this feeling that they are helping and teaching the other children that keeps them coming back. It is quite exciting to hear the nonhandicapped children bragging in the halls about teaching an autistic child to play Horse on the basketball court or finishing an entire game of Go Fish with a deck of cards.

TEACHER AND PUPIL PREPARATION

Our school year begins with several teacher workdays before the students arrive. We use these days to meet with all of the teachers in the school to talk about our autistic program. Our goals for these sessions are to give them some understanding of our children, their handicaps, and their educational goals. We also want to help them to answer anticipated questions from their students and to impress upon them the role their classes can have in the social development of autistic children. In these sessions we discuss the characteristics of autism in general and the specific strengths and weaknesses of our children. We try to anticipate behaviors they might see in the cafeteria, bathrooms, or halls and how to explain these to their students. We talk about the autistic children's families and what their futures might hold. This also enables us to emphasize the importance of language and social skills and how this program can have a meaningful impact on their lives, using examples such as the family night Bingo discussed earlier.

We also try to explain how much the nonhandicapped children can gain from these interactions, such as a general awareness of handicapped people, fulfilling a need to help others, and increased self esteem. We strongly emphasize how much these children will gain and learn from interacting with handicapped people and seeing them as individuals with needs and assets to offer, just like everyone else. If teachers understand this, their commitment to the play group program is much greater. Their commitment is important because it involves their willingness to change the classroom routine and allow their children up to an hour each week out of their classroom. Although this was sometimes an issue early on, so many nonhandicapped children in our school have participated in the program, and their teachers have seen so much growth in maturity and understanding in them, that we now have very little problem with teacher support and cooperation.

Early in the school year, we visit each classroom to talk about the autistic program. As with the teachers, we emphasize situations where these children will encounter the autistic students, such as the cafeteria, hallway, or bathroom. We begin with a general discussion of handicaps and then focus on autism in particular. The main objective is to allay their fear of a child having a tantrum and their tendency to ridicule a person who cannot talk or use the bathroom unaided at the age of 10. In these meetings we hope to develop an understanding of why autistic children have these problems and how they can be taught. In discussing deficits of autistic children, we focus mainly on the language deficits, social withdrawal, and inappropriate behaviors because these are the ones that the nonhandicapped children are most likely to encounter. We try to help them to understand the relationships between these deficits and the behaviors that the nonhandicapped children will see in the school or our classroom. We also discuss the importance of learning appropriate behavior and how this can affect their future. We emphasize the role that these nonhandicapped children can have in this process. This initial discussion is followed up by sessions at the middle and end of the year to talk about their observations and answer their questions.

Because the fifth-grade classes will participate in the play groups, they have these discussions in more detail. This age group was selected for several reasons. First, they are similar to our autistic children in age and size and are able to accept more responsibility and have greater understanding than the other students in our school. They are also mature enough to empathize and want to help our children and less likely to ridicule their problems. Our experience has been that these students become very involved in meeting our objectives and take great pride in the progress that is made.

In the initial discussion with the fifth-graders, we inform them they might be involved in the play groups if they desire. We describe the various groups and what each will be doing. We also pass around a picture of each child and discuss his or her basic skills and communications, academic functioning, social skills, and behavior. We then talk about how the play groups can help these children to learn more effectively. We discuss the importance of interaction and having experience with nonhandicapped peers. We emphasize the importance of these experiences for the future development and prospects of the students in our class.

We also explain how the nature of autism makes it difficult to teach and help these children. We prepare them for being ignored and possibly provoking tantrums because interactions with new people are different and difficult. We try to explain why this may occur and how to deal with it. We follow this up with specific discussions as these situations arise in our classroom. In this initial session the nonhandicapped students are also reassured that the teacher will be with them at all times to help them deal more effectively with these autistic students. Our goals with the fifth-graders in these initial sessions are to elicit a desire to help, to give them an understanding that they can help, and to describe some specific ways in which they might help.

PLAY GROUP STRUCTURE

We have three play groups per week for 45 minutes each. The play groups, to be described in detail shortly, are cooking, outside games, and table games. Nonhandicapped children enjoy all of these activities and this makes the play groups even more appealing. Each autistic child and nonhandicapped peer tutor has specific individualized objectives for each activity. For example, a cooking objective for a nonhandicapped fifth-grader might be to teach the handicapped peer how to stir the batter. The objective for the autistic child might be to imitate stirring, take turns stirring, follow a verbal command to stir, or some related target behavior.

Three fifth-grade classes participate in the three play groups, each class sending six children for 1 month apiece. Each month six new children are sent so that everyone who wants to participate will have the opportunity. Teachers have various selection processes from having children earn the right to go, to drawing names, to following a random list made up at the beginning of the year. The three play groups (cooking, outside games, table games) are rotated every 3 months so that each class gets an opportunity to participate in each of the three groups. The time slots for each fifth-grade teacher stay the same and the groups rotate every 3 months as illustrated (see Table 1).

Prior to their arrival in our classroom, each of the six peers knows what activity to participate in that day. At the beginning of each month we introduce

Table 1. Sample Schedule

	Ms. Ferguson's class Monday 1:00–1:45	Ms. Kaufman's class Wednesday 1:00–1:45	Ms. Wilder's class Thursday 1:45–2:30
September–November	Table games	Outside games	Cooking
December–March	Outside games	Cooking	Table games
April–June	Cooking	Table games	Outside games

each autistic child (or have the child introduce her or himself, if possible) and briefly discuss language levels and effective teaching techniques. The fifth-graders then pick a partner for that day from the six children. For the first 3 weeks of the month, the fifth-graders pick their partners. By the last week of the month, the autistic children are familiar enough with the fifth-graders to pick their own partners. We allow the children to switch partners each week if they desire so that everyone will have the opportunity of working with different children. This enables them to see different learning styles, note various ways of communicating, and gain a broader perspective of the handicap. There are also some autistic children who are more difficult to work with, or less appealing, so the switch gives the nonhandicapped children assigned to them a chance to work with others.

Along with allowing the children to switch partners, we encourage the nonhandicapped fifth-graders to pass on information gained in working with an autistic child. It is fascinating to hear their descriptions of their work. One child first described how an autistic child could not catch a ball from 3 feet but could do so from 1 foot, and then recounted beginning play at 1 foot and backing off a step at a time after each successful catch until reaching 3 feet. Another fifth-grader explained how a child who could not make an overhead pass after only seeing it done did so successfully after the ball was placed in the child's hand and moved physically with the entire arm and body through the correct motions.

In addition to wanting our nonhandicapped peers to have a positive experience and to feel successful as teachers, we also want them to develop respect for autistic children as people who have thoughts and feelings. We want them to be aware that handicapped people also have something to contribute. To accomplish this goal we have sessions each month in which the autistic children teach their nonhandicapped peers specific skills such as sign language or individual craft projects.

ACTIVITIES

Once the initial partner selection process has been completed, we then discuss the activity for the month. As indicated earlier, the specific activities we focus on are cooking, table games, and outside games.

Cooking. Cooking is one of the most desirable groups for our children because the end results can be eaten! After the fifth-graders select a partner, they go to their partner's desk. Introductions are made, with everyone practicing each other's name. The nonhandicapped peers are then given written objectives for teaching their partners during the cooking group. These may range from having a lower-functioning child read a recipe in sequence to appropriately carrying out each step. Each activity has a social objective as well. For example, the child who imitates stirring is learning to copy an appropriate peer, while the child reading a recipe must read it loud enough for all to hear, direct instructions to specific people, and wait until an instruction is carried out before reading the next step. The teacher works on the social objectives, prompting as necessary. Once again, the skills are skills that the autistic children have acquired in the classroom but are now learning to use under the direction of nonhandicapped peers. The additional variables, including new people, more people, more distractions such as conversations, and same-aged peers, make this an entirely new context for producing these known skills. We often find that children who can follow picture directions have no idea how to do this in the context of this larger group. However, they can learn to apply their skills in this setting with practice.

In the case of those children in our class who can communicate verbally, we encourage the nonhandicapped peers to engage them in conversation as much as possible. Questions about what they have done during the day, what they ate for lunch, and related issues are asked while the child is working on the cooking activities. The nonhandicapped peers seem more spontaneous in their conversation and can create a setting more conducive to conversation than the teachers are able to do. We help prepare our children for these conversations in a one-to-one setting by teaching them to initiate and respond to conversations, to stay on a topic of conversation, and to identify topics they are able to talk about.

Recipes for the cooking class come from books of recipes for children. All objectives are written down clearly for the nonhandicapped peers and are selected to maximize the possibility of observable improvements. From opening boxes, collecting and putting in ingredients, chopping, stirring, or shaking, to watching something boil, bake, or chill, a cooking project is finally produced. This is generally an enjoyable and productive activity for everyone involved.

Table Games. The table game session also begins with the choosing of partners, introductions, and going to a designated area. These games may be played one-to-one as partners, in small groups of 4, or with as many as 12 people. The objectives given to the peers for these games involve their actually playing with their autistic partners. All of the selected table games are those that the autistic children can play already. The objectives for their autistic partners are further broken down for the peers into (a) knows whose turn it is, (b) waits for turn, (c) moves one game piece only, and so forth. As with many of these activities, the carrying over of already learned skills into the play group setting is one of our major objectives. In addition, the added dimensions of conversation, background noise, and the presence of other children may become distracting to our autistic youngsters and make them unable to use the skills they have. By starting with one child at a time and gradually expanding into larger groups, we see our children become better able to use the skills they already have. As with all of the groups, our objectives for the children range from following directions and responding to peers to the social aspects of conversing and having fun while playing the games.

Games that involve taking turns, are based on simple strategies, and have clear endings are the most successful. Trouble, Bingo, Candy Land, and The Money Game have been excellent board games. Games that involve more conversation and social skills, such as Uno, Go Fish, Crazy 8's, Old Maid, and Twister have helped increase the social aspects of table games. The spontaneity of interaction and excitement that occurs between the children during these games is irreplaceable.

For our lower-functioning children, Candy Land, Bingo, Pick a Pair, and Slap Jack have been good games. These games involve the ability to match and to take turns. For the child unable to engage in table games, we have a series of play activities. Games such as building blocks, throwing Velcro dart balls, catching, throwing, and rolling balls, play dough, and imitating the use of musical instruments have been quite useful. These involve playing with a peer by taking turns or working cooperatively to finish an activity such as a puzzle or a Lincoln Log house. Activities must be short, from 1 to 5 minutes each, so that the children will not lose interest. It is also important for these games to have a clear ending, such as when all the blocks are stacked or all the play dough has been made into balls.

We change games at least once during each table game period. Forty-five minutes at one game is too long for our children. During each 45-minute session we try to include a one-to-one game for each child along with a group game.

Outside Games. The format for the outside games is slightly different. The games we use include basketball, kickball, croquet, soccer, and baseball. We work on a single game at a time and switch every 2 months. At the beginning of a month the targeted game is broken down into its component skills. For example, the skills in basketball include catching and throwing a chest pass, catching and throwing a bounce pass, dribbling, shooting, dribbling then passing, dribbling then shooting, and stealing. These skills are then broken down further for the nonhandicapped peers, such as catches a bounce pass from 2 feet.

After choosing partners, the children go outside. Although our children have trouble outside because of additional distractions, we feel this is a good learning environment. Six centers are set up, one for each of the above skills. The children spend 5 minutes at each center, working on their child's objectives before rotating to the next center. This format is used for the first 3 weeks and then we play the game during the last week. The games can be a little chaotic because most of the children do not really understand the rules. However, everybody still seems to have fun. The nonhandicapped children are responsible for getting their handicapped partners to use their skills in the games. This emphasis on having the nonhandicapped peers responsible for their handicapped partner's performance of skills is stressed throughout. We emphasize that this is much more important than doing something for their handicapped partners.

GENERAL PLAY GROUP RULES

General rules are used in all three of our play groups. The first is always to introduce the handicapped and nonhandicapped peers to one another and require them to use each others' names throughout the group period. This is especially helpful for our autistic students, who actually begin to recognize the fifth-graders and to greet them around the school. We always know when our children have arrived in the morning because the "Hello Dwaynes" follow them down the hall.

The first 5 minutes of each play group are spent in reviewing the individual autistic children's language and how to communicate with them, restating individual objectives, and discussing how to teach each of them. We then review the teaching sequence of starting with a verbal request, then showing the autistic youngster if the verbal request is not understood, and finally using physical prompting if this fails.

The teachers supervise the play groups quite closely and step in to show the fifth-graders how to better communicate if they observe difficulties. As with many professionals, the nonhandicapped peers often expect too much and frequently use language that the autistic children cannot comprehend. Teacher guidance and direction is critical so that the autistic children and their peers do not become frustrated.

While the groups are in progress, a major rule is to have the autistic children do things for themselves. Doing things for them will not teach them, but showing them how to do something will. Initially we see the nonhandicapped peers trying to help too much, but as they begin to see what autistic children can do and how they learn, they begin to pull back. Outside the bathroom one day I heard a child tell a friend that Charlie could fix his pants by himself. The child was observed putting Charlie's hand on each of the snaps on his pants and telling him to push and snap them. This was ultimately more helpful for Charlie than having the peer do it.

After a play group is finished, about 5 or 10 minutes are left at the end for less structured activities. We allow the children to do something with their partners at this time if they like (e.g., art project, reading a book, building blocks) or to go out and play on the playground. This adds a more spontaneous element to the groups because the children are not as directly under the supervision of the teachers and can talk and play together as they wish.

Before the children leave to return to their classrooms, we have a brief discussion. The autistic children go back to their desks with one teacher while the peers stay with the other teacher. The nonhandicapped peers are encouraged to discuss their successes and problems and how they dealt with various situations. They frequently pass very helpful information on to one another.

Although some of our fifth-graders may come into our groups without any understanding of autistic children and with slightly unrealistic expectations and demands, they leave having learned quite a bit. They generally learn how to communicate nonverbally through modeling, gesture, and physical guidance. They also learn to break tasks down and to take steps back into lower levels of communication when language is not understood. Above all, they develop a deep respect for these autistic children, who, despite severe handicaps, can still play games, cook, and have fun with appropriate assistance.

FOLLOW-UP

Follow-up is continuous throughout the year since we are constantly answering questions and leaving time at the end of our play groups for discussions. We also visit each fifth-grade classroom an additional two times during the school year to get feedback, hear stories about their work, and answer questions. At the end of the year we give a questionnaire to each of the students involved in the program including general questions on autism, communicating with autistic children, and the future prospects for these youngsters. Most of the children receive extremely high scores, suggesting that they have learned quite a bit about our autistic children. They also write about their favorite experiences, favorite children, worst experiences, and why they think these occurred. These responses generally reflect a very positive attitude and genuine caring for the autistic children. Favorite experiences include an activity that an autistic child learned to do, an especially successful cooking project, or just helping the children to learn. The fifth-graders really seem to feel they have accomplished something, which was well expressed by one youngster, "I taught them a thing or two, and they taught me, too." Tantrums and times when the autistic children were sent away from the groups for inappropriate behaviors usually rated as the worst experiences. Some of the students remark on the teachers' firmness by saying that the autistic children are not allowed to "get away with nothing." However, the majority of the worst experiences are nothing at all: "Nothing was bad. I loved it all."

Interestingly enough, the nonhandicapped children are generally divided in terms of their favorite children, although there is a tendency to prefer those who can talk and interact. However, even our lowest-functioning children are the favorites of some: "I like teaching him to do things" or "He smiled at me in the hall." Every child in the classroom ranks as someone's favorite partner and for every reason possible. It might be because they talk, or like to play games, or greet people, or simply because the fifth-graders were able to help them and feel good about it. Whatever the case, the experience is positive for all. If we had any lingering doubts about the benefits of our play group, the questionnaires were able to lay them to rest.

ADDITIONAL BENEFITS

There have also been additional benefits from the play group experience that we had not initially anticipated. Many children in the school drop into our classroom each morning to play with our students and see how they are doing. Nonhandicapped fifth-graders love to become a friend our children recognize. Although they initially may feel pity and think our children bizarre and strange, they come to develop respect and sincere affection for them. At lunch time they often ask to sit with our children or ask if one of our students can sit with them. We also do an annual Christmas play with the six autistic children and six fifth-graders. It is a Christmas musical play given once for the school and again for the families and friends at night.

A result of teaching the autistic children some interactive, social, and play skills and exposing them to experiences with nonhandicapped students is that greater integration into the community and school system has become a realistic objective. Although it is on a limited basis, we have children who can be sent out with their safety patrol friends to raise the flag. One particular child is on the "serve our school" committee with three fifth-graders, delivering supplies to teachers and staff. We also send children out with their friends to art, gym, the library, and music. When they go to these activities with a partner in the class, they are more comfortable and generally much better behaved. This makes their mainstreaming activities more meaningful and effective.

CONCLUSIONS

Our peer groupings with handicapped and nonhandicapped students in our classroom have definitely promoted more appropriate social behaviors and interactive skills in our autistic students. Although we can teach autistic children in one-to-one settings to have eye contact, follow directions, add a topic sentence to a conversation, initiate change, and end conversations, we cannot always teach them to generalize these skills and use them more spontaneously. However, as a result of bringing nonhandicapped children into our classroom and structuring the desired interactions, our students have learned to use their skills in a meaningful way in naturally occurring situations. This had led to the acquisition and generalization of these skills and their use in a variety of settings. In addition, it has provided a desirable and extremely rewarding experience for our children, the nonhandicapped peers, the families, and our school. To us, our program represents the true intent of Public Law 94-142, which is to provide meaningful and mutually enriching experiences for both handicapped and nonhandicapped students.

REFERENCES

Aloia, G., Beaver, R., & Pettus, W. (1978). Increasing initial interactions among integrated EMR students and their nonretarded peers in a game-playing situation. *American Journal of Mental Deficiency, 82*, 573–579.

Campbell, A., Scaturro, J., & Lickson, J. (1983). Peer tutors help autistic children enter the mainstream. *Teaching Exceptional Children, 15*, 64–69.

Egel, A. L., Richman, G. S., & Koegel, R. L. (1981). Normal peer models and autistic children's learning. *Journal of Applied Behavior Analysis, 14*, 3–12.

Gresham, F. M. (in press). The effects of social skills training on the success of mainstreaming. In J. Meisel (Ed.), *The consequences of mainstreaming handicapped children*. Hillsdale, NJ: Erlbaum.

Halpern, W. I. (1970). The schooling of autistic children: Preliminary findings. *American Journal of Orthopsychiatry, 40*, 665–671.

McHale, S., Olley, J. G., Marcus, L., & Simeonsson, R. (1981). Nonhandicapped peers as tutors for autistic children. *Exceptional Children, 48*, 263–264.

McHale, S., & Simeonsson, R. (1980). Effects of interaction on nonhandicapped children's attitudes toward autistic children. *American Journal of Mental Deficiency, 85*, 18–24.

Mesibov, G. B. (1984). Social skills training with verbal autistic adolescents and adults: A program model. *Journal of Autism and Developmental Disorders, 14*, 395–404.

Poorman, L. (1980). Mainstreaming in reverse with a special friend. *Teaching Exceptional Children, 12*, 136–142.

Schopler, E., Reichler, R. J., DeVellis, R. F., & Daly, L. (1980). Toward objective classification of childhood autism: Childhood autism rating scale (CARS). *Journal of Autism and Developmental Disorders, 10*, 91–103.

16

A Guide for Developing Social and Leisure Programs for Students with Autism

JOYCE HENNING and NANCY DALRYMPLE

OVERVIEW

The lack of social, social communication, and leisure skills appears to be a major reason for autistic people to fail in their families, schools, and jobs. Clearly, if autistic people are to be kept in our communities, the teaching of these skills must be a priority. If age-appropriate leisure skills are not taught and generalized in real community environments, then the myth of incompetence that surrounds severely handicapped people will be perpetuated (Wehman, Schleien, & Kiernan, 1980). This chapter presents suggestions from a guide that has been developed for teaching social, social communication, and leisure skills to autistic students.

Autistic people's problems in mastering social and leisure skills hamper their successful adjustment in the family. Parents have cited as a major problem the inability to take their child out and have family recreational activities. This inability can greatly contribute to the stress of having an autistic person in the home (DeMyer & Goldberg, 1983).

Successful vocational performance of handicapped persons may depend on their adapted behaviors. Many employers maintain that inappropriate interpersonal behavior is a major contributor to job failure among handicapped workers

---

JOYCE HENNING and NANCY DALRYMPLE • Developmental Training Center, Indiana University, Bloomington, Indiana 47405.

(Kochany & Keller, 1980). Sheltered workshop productivity has been significantly related to "personal independence" and low productivity associated with "social maladaption" (Cunningham & Presnall, 1978).

Autistic students are capable of learning social and leisure skills, if these skills are assigned a high priority and instruction is adapted to the learning needs of these students. Fredericks, Buckley, Baldwin, Moore, and Streml-Campbell (1983) assert that age-appropriate and functional skills can be taught in natural environments. Voeltz and Evans (1983) state that instruction ought to occur in relevant contexts during acquisition, and evaluation data should be collected evenly across situations, persons, and environments to ensure that the skill is being generalized. Teachers and other professionals who work with the severely handicapped must include recreation and leisure educational objectives in the students' individualized educational programs. Furthermore, these skills must be taught in a sequential and systematic manner, with a plan to generalize them into the students' repertoires of free-time behaviors (Horst, Wehman, Hill, & Bailey, 1981). Schools will have to stretch their concept of education to include functional, integrated, and longitudinal training in life skills (Donnellan, 1981).

Wuerch and Voeltz (1982) have identified some general factors to consider in choosing appropriate objectives for severely handicapped students. They emphasize choosing skills that are chronologically age-appropriate and utilized by the nonhandicapped population. Family preference, community resources, developmental levels, learning style, and sensory preference should be considered.

Recent research in social learning theory suggests that handicapped children can imitate appropriate social behavior if modeling is carefully planned and sequenced (Gresham, 1982). Autistic youth often learn a skill in a structured lesson but then cannot apply it in a social or leisure situation. Strain, Kerr, and Ragland (1979) assessed the relative effectiveness of two intervention procedures for improving social behaviors. While both were successful, neither intervention generalized or resulted in change beyond the direct intervention setting. Learning is best accomplished by teaching and practicing skills simultaneously in both structured and natural settings. Concurrent instruction is the best strategy for instruction of severely handicapped students under the age of 18 (Brown *et al.*, 1983). Finding appropriate motivation may be a primary factor in generalizing social skills (Kelly *et al.*, 1983).

Understanding the need for appropriate reinforcers may be one of the most difficult aspects of teaching people with autism (Koegel, Rincover, & Egel, 1982). Reinforcing social and leisure skills is particularly complex. One can never assume that what is fun and pleasurable for most people is necessarily reinforcing for an autistic student. By definition, social and leisure activities are thought to be intrinsically motivating (Iso-Ahola, 1980), but autistic persons often need extrinsic rewards to motivate them to learn these kinds of activities. Reinforcements used in teaching social and leisure skills should be as natural as possible; an activity that the student likes should be incorporated as a reward for something less desirable. Margaret Dewey (1973) suggests, "An imaginative adult can abstract the enjoyed elements of an activity, then encourage a child to diversify and expand his interest along progressively advanced lines" (p. 3). The familiarity and routine of a leisure or social activity can become reinforcing. Sometimes being in a community environment can be a strong reinforcer for an autistic person if he feels safe and supported, thus eliciting more socially appropriate behavior.

Structure and routine must be incorporated into teaching techniques. A learning sequence must be provided with set cues and expectations and control of environmental factors. Organizing the student's activities in a structured way and exposing him to interpersonal situations are profitable strategies (Clark & Rutter, 1981). Skills must be practiced often enough for the student to recognize them as routine, and ample time must be allowed for practice. Social and leisure situations rarely occur in an orderly or predictable manner; therefore, service providers often have to plan some situations. Activities and routines can be changed if the student has enough preparation and support. However, too many changes at one time usually result in negative behavior. Carefully planned steps are often needed for the student to accept new activities, new people, or new places.

Voeltz, Wuerch, and Bockhaut (1982) caution that skill gains by severely handicapped learners may be small by comparison to community expectations and yet may be highly functional and meaningful for adjustment in integrated community settings. They suggest that people must come to value behavior changes—however small—that are important for the severely handicapped person's quality of life.

The remainder of this chapter presents specific strategies for teaching self-care and functional academic skills, interpersonal skills, social communication skills, leisure skills, and community skills. These strategies are presented in greater detail in the sourcebook *Teaching Social and Leisure Skills to Youth with Autism* (Henning, Dalrymple, Davis, & Madeira, 1982).

This book was written to provide practical suggestions for residential or group home programmers, parents, recreation staff, and educators about teaching social and leisure skills to autistic youth. This guide is designed for autistic students who are 10 to 15 years old and who have gained some basic social readiness skills, such as imitative movements, eye contact, response to one-step direction, basic self-care skills, and understanding of a simple, immediate contingency.

The guide includes representative samples of social and leisure objectives, but it is not a sequential or comprehensive curriculum for a total program. Rather, it presents a rationale and process for making decisions and designing individualized programs in the area of social and leisure skills. The sourcebook speaks specifically to the special needs of the autistic student and should be used in conjunction with other curriculum materials on communication, academics, vocational programming, and self help skills.

TEACHING SELF-CARE AND ACADEMIC SKILLS

Learning the skills that accompany social or leisure activities is necessary for students to function as independently as possible in their environments. These related skills can be grouped into two categories: (1) *self-care*, including grooming, care of belongings, manners, social-sexual awareness, and mobility, and (2) *functional academics*, including reading, money and time skills, and giving and requesting information.

A cluster of related skills should be identified to accompany a social or leisure objective. Learning to care for belongings may accompany a goal of increasing independence; this skill may also be necessary in order to use a YMCA locker successfully. If an objective is to follow procedures in a restaurant, the following skills may be practiced in a classroom setting: (1) matching coins to written prices, (2) relating times to specific events, and (3) reading menus. In a home-type setting, the student may work on (1) performing a grooming routine, (2) mealtimes, and (3) riding in a car with others. All of these related skills would be used when going out to a restaurant. As much as possible, something in the social situation should be used to motivate students to learn related skills. If a student completes a grooming checklist, let her go on a favorite outing; if she recognizes the correct coins, let her use them in the soda machine.

Providing materials that help the student remember rules and expectations prevents students from relying excessively on adults. Labeling drawers and shelves for belongings, making individual calendars and schedules, listing rules, and writing checklists for self-care routines all contribute to independence.

Some sample related skill objectives are that the student will (a) transport belongings from one location to another and keep them in locations where they belong, (b) sit in close proximity to others in a car or bus with appropriate behavior, (c) match combinations of penny, nickel, dime, and quarter to a sample on a card and use the money to buy something, (d) relate the time on the clock to events that occur during the day.

TEACHING INTERPERSONAL SKILLS

Selecting Objectives

Autistic youth seldom receive and process the social messages that could help them correct their behavior (Bemporad, 1979). Social interaction is a complex, ever-changing skill area. Personal interaction is often unpredictable, depending on an interrelationship of complex variables such as personality, mood, and setting. There are very few concrete rules; rather, many subtle and elusive guidelines apply. Therefore, it becomes important to create some structure, certainty, and rules that can be used in a variety of situations and applied in natural settings.

Assessment of the student's existing interaction skills sometimes requires detective work and careful analysis of antecedents and consequences. Often attention focuses on the autistic student's inappropriate behavior, rather than analyzing the cause of the behavior.

Helping the student learn alternative behaviors is often more important than using direct interventions when the student interacts negatively. For example, if a student is aggressive toward her classmates during recess, staff must observe carefully to see why. What is the student getting out of this behavior? Does she really want to interact or to communicate something? Can she learn to do so in a positive way? Objectives that focus on social communication and on cooperative play may be important for this student. Likewise, if a student always screams upon arriving at school, the antecedent must be identified. Each autistic student will have her own unique problems in relating to others, which must be targeted in her interpersonal skills objectives. Some sample interpersonal objectives are that the student will (a) use touching, hugging, and cuddling in appropriate ways to interact with others, (b) accept regular times he has adult's full attention, and times to be quiet and leave the adult alone for minutes, (c) participate in a familiar small group activity with peers.

Motivating the Student to Interact

The autistic youth will need to develop a feeling of security and trust in the people around her. This will take time, but only then will the autistic student begin to reach out and respond to others in positive ways. Initially, the student will have to depend heavily on persons she trusts as she begins interacting with those around her.

Another prerequisite to successful interaction is a positive self-concept. The student must hear strong messages that she is a likable, competent, and important human being. Since the autistic person can seldom articulate how she feels about herself, her self-concept may not be considered. However, the perceptive observer will discover that her feelings are revealed in her behaviors and her willingness to risk social interaction with others.

Sometimes autistic youth do want to interact with others around them, even when they appear not to care. This impression usually stems from the students' long-standing pattern of failure in past interactions. They have received repeated negative messages that they are wrong, bad, and very different from others as a response to their attempts at interaction. Autistic persons learn to use isolation and bizarre, negative, or aggressive interactions in order to cope or to get what they need.

After a trust relationship has been established, the adult will need to demand responses and set expectations. Rules and expectations should be taught through simple, clear statements: "You need to stop and listen when I talk to you" or "Answer my question." Teaching must be firm, but never negative or sarcastic. At the same time, it is essential that all appropriate interaction attempts be reinforced. All environments will need to be consistent in their expectations and reinforcement if the student is going to learn to enjoy interacting. Natural situations must be arranged so that a student needs to interact acceptably with others to get what is wanted. For example, the adult can refuse to move when pushed by the student but can move immediately if the student says or signs, "Please move." Expectations must depend on what the student can handle. With one, just "using words" to get what is wanted should be reinforced; another may be expected to ask for something in a polite tone.

Expressing Feelings

Autistic students need an outlet for expressing their feelings. Typically, acceptable outlets must be taught, since many autistic persons have large apparent deficiencies in emotional expression (Lovaas, 1979). Acceptable outlets can include shouting, pounding a pillow, stamping feet, or telling somebody, "Stop it!" or "I'm mad!" There are times when adults must be willing to accept and even encourage angry and negative talking as an alternative to destructive or aggressive behavior. It may be hard for some adults to accept this necessity. Students may also need to learn to express positive feelings, such as "I like Randy" or "I'm happy" or "This is fun." We all get positive reactions from others with such expressions.

Prior to expressing feelings in real situations, it is useful to teach labeling of feelings. This abstract concept requires interpretation of multiple, different stimuli. Modeling these expressions and actions and talking about what situations make people feel a certain way may help. At the same time, this instruction must be carried over to other settings by helping students label their own feelings when they occur, and by adults' modeling expression of their own feelings.

Facilitating Interactions with Peers

There is increasing evidence that the autistic person benefits from sociable peer models (Egel, Richman, & Koegel, 1981). Social interaction skills are difficult to teach to autistic youth when they are grouped with other handicapped students who do not initiate or respond appropriately to sociable behavior. Being around nonhandicapped peers suggests that the autistic student is a competent person who can be like others. This message can enhance self-concept. However, interaction with peers usually does not "just happen" for autistic people. If they are not prepared and supported, they may react negatively. Peers and siblings find it difficult to keep trying to interact with the autistic student. Integration without planning and preparation often results in others disliking and avoiding the autistic students. Familiar adult support is almost always necessary, at least initially.

Interest and motivation of peers probably determines the success of the relationship more than anything else. Adults may need to realize that peers will need and want recognition and credit for their efforts. Most of all, the peers have to *want* to be involved. Peers need to be mature and self-confident enough to initiate interaction and not be overly concerned with what others think of them. Peers who are socially insecure themselves may be intolerant of the autistic student's odd behaviors. A peer with high status in his group can be extremely valuable in modeling a positive, accepting attitude that others will follow. The more the peers "adopt" the student and feel personally responsible, the more successful the integration.

Peers need information about autism that is presented at their level, along with opportunities to express their ideas, misconceptions, or fears about autistic people. They also need information about the individual autistic student. An adult should be sensitive to times when too much preparation makes peers unduly wary of the autistic student or unnecessarily changes their normal ways of interacting.

Once the autistic student begins participating with peers, the adult can provide support by modeling interactions and through regular "debriefing" sessions where peers discuss reactions or problems. Some peers have described the great effort it takes to maintain interactions with autistic youth. They have also listed mannerisms that particularly bother them, such as (1) continued repetition of phrases, (2) talking loudly, (3) insisting on their own way, and (4) odd movements. At the same time, peers are often quite understanding and perceptive of the autistic person's unique characteristics. Peers can be encouraged to be direct with the autistic student when her bothersome behavior directly affects them.

Adults need to be creative in involving sociable peers in the autistic student's regular routine. Peers can be used as tutors, for modeling skills, or to fill the role of friend and companion. One peer has a difficult time filling all roles. Peers should be more than "little adults" directing the autistic student.

TEACHING SOCIAL COMMUNICATION SKILLS

Selecting Objectives

As children grow older in our society, social expectations demand an increasingly sophisticated use of language. Autistic people of all ages and levels rarely understand and apply the full function and use of language (Tager-Flusberg, 1981). Even autistic youths who are highly verbal have difficulty using language effectively at times of high emotion or stress. This problem can prevent a student from participating in social or work activities within his intellectual capabilities and greatly limit his ability to function meaningfully in the community. Therefore, increasing the functional and social use of language should be a primary goal early in an autistic child's program and remain a central focus throughout his life.

In order to teach functional social communication skills, each training program must be student-specific. Lessons should be based on the individual's favorite materials, foods, and interests. They need to be success-oriented, starting at the student's present level and gradually challenging him to higher levels of achievement. The communication program must include adults in all settings, so that parents, teachers, and other staff will be consistent in their objectives and cues. Finally, functional skills must be taught in context (Goetz, Schuler, & Sailor, 1979).

Objectives are based on an accurate descriptive assessment as well as ongoing observation and analysis. From these findings, staff and parents set priorities as they determine the student's most important communication needs. Staff look not only at a student's language skills but also at the relationship between communication and behavior, social skills, problems at home, and ability to function outside the home.

For example, if a student has an outburst every time another student touches something that belongs to him, a logical objective for instruction could be learning to tell other students, "Leave my records alone." Careful observation of the student's skills in social relationships might reveal that he knows how to play some games, but in his recreation program he may stand around and decline to participate. This student could learn how to ask peers to join him in games or ask if he can join games. Another student may become confused and angry when given directions containing certain prepositions. She will benefit from specific instruction on prepositions and their application in natural settings.

Sample objectives: The student will (a) say "hi" or "bye" when greeting or when he or another person is exiting, (b) use familiar people's names to greet them and to gain their attention, (c) ask permission to use or obtain items that do not belong to her, and accept a refusal, (d) address a directive or question to a peer when wanting some information or object from that peer.

Using Social Communication Skills

After objectives are established, the instructor identifies the situations in which the skill will be used. If a student is learning to use the word *no*, staff can identify situations in which he usually refuses something and can be allowed to say no. The student may say no to food at snack time or no to playing a game. If a student is learning to respond appropriately to a social introduction, the lesson can be planned on a day when someone new is visiting, so the skill is practiced and then immediately used.

Realistic situations may be set up in order to work on functional skills during lessons. The most effective teaching materials are concrete objects, especially familiar items the student deals with daily. Role-playing situations are better than using pictures, but using real-life situations as they arise will be most effective. For example, when working on describing emotions, pictures of people displaying various emotions will probably be less effective than role playing a situation where something has made the teacher or student angry. However, the student will understand that concept most fully when he or another student is feeling angry, and the teacher helps the student label and describe the feeling.

After training has begun, the student should be helped to use the skill throughout the day. Imperfect attempts should be rewarded at first, since he will learn where and why he uses a social communication skill by experiencing positive results from using language. Articulation or sign execution can be improved later.

Motivation for Using Social Communication

Since communication is difficult for autistic students, planning for effective motivation is vital. The logical outcome of a situation should be used whenever possible. A youth who wants to use another student's bicycle may need a model or prompt to ask the owner for permission. Ideally, this request will be rewarded by a positive response, and the autistic student will see that his talking was effective. If the response is "no," the adult will need to provide reinforcement for "good asking" and perhaps suggest alternative activities.

External motivators, such as charts, points, or tokens, may be necessary at times. If they are used, the challenge is to make the reward system motivating enough to elicit appropriate communication without being the sole reason for the communication. Autistic young people need to learn that communication is necessary and functional in itself even when not tangibly rewarded.

TEACHING LEISURE SKILLS

Selecting Objectives

Students with autism may isolate themselves or, conversely, demand constant attention. They may engage in continuous repetitive, stereotypic behaviors, which can be very wearing on those around them. They seldom use available play materials symbolically, as other children do, either because they do not understand how to use the materials or because they do not understand the intent of the play material (Riquet, Taylor, Benaroya, & Klein, 1981). They can be taught to use play materials appropriately.

Since autistic students have such difficulty interacting with others, it is essential to give them a medium for interaction such as card or ball games. An autistic student who is unable to approach and interact conversationally with a peer may be able to learn a board game well enough to play with that peer.

Leisure activities can provide excellent opportunities for experiencing success, mastery, acceptance, and a sense of well-being. Leisure settings can provide a relaxed, accepting atmosphere with little pressure. The "fun" aspect can be emphasized. Such an atmosphere can give adults a chance to accept the students as they are and to establish a caring relationship with a whole person. Mastering a leisure skill can be thrilling for an autistic youth! These experiences help students feel valued and competent.

Selection of activities must be individualized, on the basis of an assessment of the student and the environment. The student should be assessed in terms of (1) interests and previous experiences, (2) social interaction skills, (3) fine and gross motor skills, and (4) cognitive skills. It is also essential to assess the student's environmental situation: (1) What leisure skills would allow this student to function more independently during free time? (2) What leisure skills would give the student a means for interacting with others? (3) What leisure skills would allow this student to participate more fully in her family, community, and extracurricular school activities? (4) What are the resources of the family, school, and community?

In addition, it is important to analyze the leisure activity in terms of the cognitive, motor, and social skills required. A common mistake is to underestimate the complexity of skills needed to participate successfully in leisure activities. For example, few people realize the complexity of the cognitive skills involved in softball: the rules, decision making, score keeping, the concepts of "safe," "out," and winning.

Problems of motivation can be greatly reduced by creative selection of activities to teach. Adults should look for elements in a leisure activity that may be motivating to the student and should emphasize those. Repetitive manipulation of objects, visually stimulating objects, music, putting things in order, intense sensory stimulation, or fitting objects into spaces are typically motivating for autistic persons. The structure inherent in some activities, such as an aerobic exercise routine, may be motivating for some autistic youth. On the other hand, these students often tend to have problems with symbolic, open-ended, pretend, or more creative play activities.

Some sample leisure objectives are that the student will (a) play Uno, following the game rules with an adult or a sociable peer, (b) make cookies independently and share with peers, (c) when presented with three different familiar play materials, choose one and play with it for 10 minutes, with initial cues, (d) ride a bike independently in an area without traffic.

Independent Leisure Skills

For independent leisure activities, it is best to select something that the student can learn to do quickly and easily. Most students will do best if the activity has built-in structure and has a clear point of completion. Activities that require filling in a set pattern, such as rug hooking or Lite Brite, can provide the structure needed for a student to do them independently. If the objective is to do the skill independently, fading assistance and cues should be planned. A minimum of help should be given while still ensuring success. New leisure skills need to be taught within a structured routine before working on independence. If possible, a specific place should be provided for one-to-one instruction and another place where the same activity is expected to be done independently. The location will then cue the student to expect to do an activity with minimal assistance.

Sports, Fitness, and Movement Skills

At a time when so much emphasis is placed upon athletic activities during leisure time, sports should be included as a means to social acceptance. The gross motor skills learned in school or in recreation programs need to be shaped into meaningful activities that can become enjoyable during leisure time. If an autistic student is to participate in a sport or game with a group of sociable peers near her age, additional one-to-one instruction in that skill should be provided.

Since autistic youth do not readily generalize skill concepts, instructors need to make certain the student knows what game is being played and exactly what each skill means in that game or sport. For example, if the student is told to dribble the ball when playing soccer, she may pick it up and bounce it as in basketball, rather than using her feet. Students need visual demonstrations to help them process the correct movement or skill. Using a series of pictures or a written list of fitness or sports skills can help the student to go through a physical routine more independently once it is learned. Lead-up activities are expecially useful in sports and movement (Blake & Volp, 1964), allowing a student to work on part of the skill and to experience success more quickly. Care should be taken early to ensure that the student understands how the skill fits into the whole game.

Most autistic persons have great difficulties with the concepts of cooperation and competition needed in team play (Dewey, 1976). Organized team games are usually overwhelming. Selecting activities in which students participate with others without the requirement of complex interactions is more beneficial. Individual sports activities such as bowling, swimming, jogging, or skating can benefit students both physically and socially if taught at the student's own pace. These activities have fewer inherent rules, allowing students to make attempts without risking failure.

Leisure Awareness

Autistic students often do not differentiate between play and work activities. Furthermore, they may not understand the concept of making choices and will need to be taught decision making. Frequently they are so closely directed and structured that they are seldom given choices. As a result, when a choice is presented they are unable to cope with it. Leisure time is a natural setting to learn to make choices. Teaching a student the concept of choice may range in difficulty from choosing between two games that are right in front of her to selecting activities to do for an entire Saturday. Adults need to establish cues that help the student distinguish free time, when choices are available, from work time, when choices are not available. The cue may be a time, place, written schedule, person, or activity; however, the cue must be clear and specifically taught.

Some students may benefit from basic leisure education lessons (Joswiak, 1975) such as learning to categorize activities commonly thought of as play or work. They can also learn simple explanations of why an activity is commonly considered work or play and can learn when and where people usually play and work. A student can be taught to identify "free time" and can learn that "we can play and do fun things during free time." These concepts are often commonly shared values rather than absolutes. However, for the autistic student, the idea of work and play will have to be simplified and made more black-and-white than it really is for understanding. At the same time, these concepts must be applied concretely to the student's own activity schedule, such as identifying which activities on the schedule are work and when there is free time to play. Most autistic youth do not consciously think about or express how they feel about an activity. Adults can help students become more aware of preferences and positive ways of expressing choices in a leisure context.

TEACHING COMMUNITY SKILLS

Selecting Objectives

As the autistic youth ventures outside the familiarity of the home or school environment, the world becomes more and more unpredictable. Many students have great fears about going to new places; frequently these fears are expressed by outbursts or other inappropriate behaviors. They may react to the complexity and lack of familiar structure in community settings. Behaviors stemming from sensory overstimulation are common. At other times, the autistic person simply may not understand the behaviors expected in specific public places; for example, he may not modulate his voice level inside a store. Furthermore, he will not learn appropriate behaviors by observation, as most of us do, but must be specifically taught. Community socialization is an experience necessary for all, and participation in a life of dignity includes taking risks (Brown *et al.*, 1983).

Teaching students to be in the community and to follow expected procedures in public places is not traditionally a part of educating or training the severely handicapped. However, failure to teach autistic children these skills may sentence them to a life of isolation and segregation from their community. This outcome is an unnecessary loss on both sides; not only can autistic persons learn to cope with public places, they can also learn to truly enjoy outings. For the family, a child's ability to function in the community may relieve some of the burden and stress of having an autistic child who is at home a great deal of the time.

If skills are to be generalized to the community, that is where they should be taught. Playing "store" or pretending to ride a bus in the classroom is of limited value to autistic students. However, they can benefit from rehearsing specific skills that they apply immediately in a specific community setting.

Learning community skills also means learning how to behave in public. The best place to learn to control behavior in public is in public. This is not to say that unacceptable behavior should be tolerated or that a youth in a tantrum should not be kept home or removed from a public place; rather, the possibility that a youth might misbehave in public is not a good reason to keep him home. However, adults should have a well-tested intervention for dealing with unacceptable behavior *before* a student is taken out in public.

There are three levels of learning to function in the community: (1) becoming familiar with a community setting and learning to feel comfortable there, (2) learning to participate in an activity in a community setting, and (3) learning to interact with people and with groups in the community (Henning *et al.*, 1982).

Some sample community objectives are that the student will (a) order food and eat with a sociable peer and an adult with no more than three directions, (b) follow commonly used procedures when using a commercial bowling alley, with occasional direction, (c) participate in selected Girls' Club activities on a regular basis, with peer support, (d) make a single purchase in a convenience store independently.

Steps in Teaching Community Skills

Autistic youth typically need a great deal of initial support in order to experience success in the community. The following steps make success in a community setting possible.

Preparation. A new outing may need to be talked about as much as every day for a week, and usually no less than the day before. The student should be told as much about the outing as he is able to tolerate, even if he doesn't understand all of it: *where* he is going, *who* will be going along, *when* he will go, *how* he will get there, and *what* he will do when he gets there. Language should be at the student's level and kept simple. Many students will benefit from having a photograph of the place to help them understand where they are going. Higher-functioning youth can discuss and rehearse procedures such as ordering food or asking for bowling shoes. This practice should be done right before the actual outing.

Manageable Steps. A lengthy program of desensitization and shaping may be planned, beginning with looking at the car, touching the car, sitting in the car, driving past the place, then a brief visit to the place. Preparation may mean ordering by phone ahead of time so that the youth has a short waiting time in a restaurant, and then gradually increasing that waiting time. The difficulty of outings can be modified by several variables: (1) length of time on the outing, (2) size of crowd and/or space in the setting, (3) amount of stimulation in the setting, (4) level of participation expected, (5) familiarity of the setting.

Routine. Autistic students typically derive little benefit from special events or field trips until they have reached a comfortable level of functioning in the community. The same outing should be planned several times consecutively. Some students may need to go daily, while others can recognize once or twice a week as being routine.

New Skills. Once a student feels comfortable in a community setting, the adult should begin to prioritize skills that need to be worked on to increase independent participation and acceptable behavior. Since the skill deficits of an individual and the social skills demanded by an environment will never be entirely predictable before an outing, this assessment must be an ongoing process. In order to plan for success, some behaviors may need to be tolerated and little participation expected. For example, distracting stereotypic hand movements may be ignored in a restaurant while the student concentrates on using an appropriate voice level. Later, he can concentrate on table manners or ordering food and paying the cashier independently. He may work on *some* of these things simultaneously as long as he is not so overloaded with expectations that he finally decides going to a restaurant is not worth the trouble!

Supervision. One-to-one supervision is often needed, especially on new outings or in places where it is undesirable to give information to those who will come into contact with the autistic student. Going to places where there is a low tolerance for atypical behavior without adequate supervision may result in a feeling of failure on all sides. Trained volunteers may be needed to provide extra supervision. However, without a plan for fading one-to-one supervision, the student may never move toward independence in the setting. Sometimes adults continue giving cues rather than expecting independence, even when the outing has become familiar. Letting the salesperson repeat the cues or waiting for the student to realize he needs to get out his money before he can have his treat often provides a better learning experience.

Some autistic persons may handle fairly high expectations when they are in the community, but when they return to a more familiar environment a reaction to this effort appears to set in. This reaction may be in the form of regression, inappropriate behaviors, or just "tuning out" behavior after the student returns. This result could mean that expectations should be reduced, or it may mean that adults need to allow the student some extra space, time, and support to work through this reaction following outings.

Preparing and Educating the Community

One mistake commonly made in mainstreaming efforts is putting all resources into changing the autistic person and demanding he fit into the environment as it is. "Environment" refers to an ecosystem that includes individual persons, groups, and their expectations, as well as physical characteristics (Beare & Lynch, 1983). Some autistic persons may experience success only if the community environment is modified slightly or is prepared to tolerate some atypical behavior. Adults providing programs for autistic persons must determine if the community environment can be changed and must work closely with community persons. Often, giving basic information on autism and individual needs to the community group involved will increase their acceptance and understanding.

The environment should be analyzed in terms of possible advantages and disadvantages for autistic persons. Variables to be considered are size and division of space, crowded or uncrowded times, age of persons in the environment, cohesiveness and leadership of peer groups, noise or other stimuli, expected behavior, procedures for participating in activities, and tolerance of deviance from normal behavior. The impact of one autistic person on a community environment is very different from the effect of a group of autistic persons. Careful consideration of environmental impact must precede the introduction of groups of autistic students. Going out individually or in pairs will be a much more normalizing experience.

Providing Information. If community persons need information, the first step is to provide a general explanation of autism. Discussion should include a description of common difficulties autistic students may have in the community and an explanation of why this community experience is beneficial to them. Persons having more extensive interactions with students, such as youth club staff, need specific information on individual students. Interests, skills, language problems, behaviors that may occur, and interventions that will be used can be included.

Establishing Communication Channels. Communication must be ongoing. If someone in the community reacts negatively, the problem should be discussed with him or her as soon as possible and usually without the student. If an autistic youth behaves inappropriately, and an adult deals with the behavior effectively and immediately, people will usually accept the situation. At other times, direct explanations may be needed. Problems sometimes can be avoided by asking beforehand for special procedures if they are needed. For example, disappointment can be avoided if a check is made to ensure the availability of the right size pair of skates, or a favorite soft drink.

Giving recognition and appreciation to people and organizations who are cooperative helps in establishing a community support system. This effort may include taking the time to mention the enjoyment and benefits students are experiencing, writing a letter, or arranging publicity in the local paper.

SUMMARY

People with autism do not need to remain separate from the mainstream of life. They do need specific, individualized training in social and leisure skills, including (1) interpersonal, (2) social communication, (3) leisure, (4) community, and (5) related skills. These must be functional skills students can use in their everyday routines. Teaching techniques should consider the special needs of autistic people. Finally, service providers must develop community support systems if they are to reach the goal of keeping young people with autism in their home communities.

ACKNOWLEDGMENTS

This chapter has been adapted from the book *Teaching Social and Leisure Skills to Youth with Autism*, by Joyce Henning, Nancy Dalrymple, Kim Davis, and Shelley Madeira, available from the Indiana University Developmental Training Center, 2853 East Tenth Street, Bloomington, Indiana 47405. The training videotape by the same title is available from the Indiana University Audio Visual Center.

EXAMPLES

Representative samples of social and leisure objectives and teaching procedures for each one follow as they appear in the sourcebook. Individualization and adaptation will be necessary. Modification and lead-up activities, a plan for motivation, and precautions are specified.

GOAL: Increase independence in performing self-care skills

Skill area: Grooming

Skill: Grooming Routine

Objective: Will independently perform a set or routine within ten minutes when getting ready to go out.

Modifications and Lead-up Activities

- Following more simple routines independently.
- Practice making adjustments in front of the mirror and identifying items which make up a neat appearance.
- Work on consistently and independently fastening fasteners like zippers and snaps before leaving bathroom or bedroom.
- Student will need to be familiar with and motivated to go on outings if outings are used as reinforcer.

Associated Objectives

- Will independently follow a bath or shower routine daily.
- Will wash and dry hair independently three times a week.
- Will use personal care items such as deodorant, perfume, and creme rinse as part of a routine.

Plan for Motivation: Plan contingencies so that when a student follows a grooming routine she:

- Realizes she looks nice.
- Enjoys the security of the routine.

  Sample contingency: "Get washed up and we'll go to Spaceport," or "Do your checklist all by yourself then we'll stop by the park on the way home."

Rationale

For many autistic youth, learning a grooming routine will need to come before they understand why it is important to look nice. Usually they have no awareness of the social impact their appearance may have on others. Learning to assume the responsibility for being well groomed must be taught.

Teaching Procedures

- Set the timer or note the time on the clock.
- Assemble materials, including washcloth, towel, soap, hairbrush, and handbrush, if needed.
- A sequential list will be prepared using pictures, words, or sentences the student can understand. This will serve as a "check" and reminder.
  - Wet washcloth and rub on soap
  - Scrub face
  - Rinse face
  - Rinse washcloth and hang up
  - Scrub hands with soap
  - Dry face and hands with towel
  - Brush hair
  - Look in mirror and make clothing adjustments: Shirt tucked in, clothes are clean, zippers closed, belt on, underwear not showing.
- Have student or adult check off items on the list, using laminated paper or daily or weekly lists.
- Establish a way to go back and fix each "No."
- Do a final self-check.

Precautions

- Make sure some flexibility is built in as the routine is learned so the student does not become overly obsessive with routine and unable to adjust to changes. This could be done by combining several steps, changing the kind of soap, or adding a step like curling hair.
- Avoid adult attention during the routine when possible. Reward completion and help with adjustments.
- Use interventions that promote independence rather than reliance on adult.

GOAL: Increase independence in performing self-care skills

Skill area: Mobility: Walking

Skill: Staying with a group

Objective: Will stay with a small group with verbal cues only.

Modifications and Lead-up Activities

- Learn to walk beside an adult.
- Learn to respond to touch cues that are faded to verbal cues when moving one-to-one with an adult.
- Learn to stop when cued.

Associated Objectives

- Will wait with other people when sitting or in line, 5 minutes when cued.
- Will demonstrate the ability to follow all traffic signals.
- Will respect all safety rules on streets and sidewalks.
- Will demonstrate understanding of the danger of moving cars.
- Will get home safely from __blocks away.

Plan for Motivation: Plan contingencies so that when a student stays with the group he:

- Gets to control his movements.
- Gets to go to fun places.
  Sample contingency: "If you stay with the group you can walk on your own." or "Stay with the group, then we'll go stop for an ice cream cone."

Rationale

Autistic youth often have problems with open spaces, and unfamiliar places. They also tend to want to avoid groups and closeness to people. Walking alone is much more reinforcing. Therefore, staying close to people when moving often must be taught.

Teaching Procedures

- Practice with individuals first to establish responses to cues such as "Walk by me." "Wait," "Stop." Fade touch cues such as a finger on the back of the collar or the shoulder to verbal cues only. Reinforce response to verbal cues by using a primary reinforcer such as a raisin or praise. Establish consequence for nonresponse such as a quick-sit.
- Practice in familiar places having defined borders with the students. Have only two or three familiar peers to a group at first. Reinforce staying with the group.
- Next, practice in community settings when the student feels comfortable and with people he knows.
- When the behavior is well established, generalize to new and unfamiliar places.
- Interventions must be planned for nonresponse since safety demands that there can be no trial or error in many instances. Student gradually earns the right to be a greater distance from the adult and group. Independence must be earned. This can be a good reinforcer.

Precautions

- Know each student well and anticipate individual behaviors such as darting, wandering, or running when more than two feet from an adult.
- Work on skills individually until there is a high level of consistency to learned cues.

GOAL: Increase the use of academic skills in everyday life.

Skill area: Functional reading

Skill: Reading menus

Objective: Will read menus and order food.

Modifications and Lead-up Activities

- Some students may only be able to do a part of this objective. Make it as large or small a job as that student can handle. It may be that the student chooses only the drink at first.

Associated Objectives

- Will read directions in community settings and follow them.
- Will read and follow the daily schedule.
- Will read and follow recipes.
- Will read directions in shop or on audio-visual machines, etc.
- Will read prices on a menu, and compare the price of his selection with the amount of money he has.

Plan for Motivation: Plan contingencies so that when a student reads menus and orders food he:

- Gains independence and control in making choices.
- Gets approval of others.
  Sample contingency: "You choose then you get to eat what you want." or "If you tell the waitress what you want you will get it."

Rationale

Going out to restaurants is something most people do in our country. Having control and a choice of what is ordered gives a person added power. This is something too often done for the autistic youth.

Teaching Procedures

- Teach words found on menus. Start with one type of restaurant and foods the student likes. The student can match words to pictures at first.
- Practice grouping foods into categories such as all sandwiches, all drinks, all desserts. Use pictures and real food.
- Practice giving the order either by verbalizing, manual signing, pointing or reading from a list.
- Borrow menus, or make visual aids that simulate menu boards at the fast-food restaurants. Practice choosing and ordering from these.
- Use the skill in the restaurant after it is learned in school. Initially, find out the main menu choices and have student select his choice just before going to the restaurant. Some may need more structured direction such as, "Choose one meat, one vegetable and one dessert."

Precautions

- Sometimes autistic children get caught in a rut and will always order the same thing. Offering a menu choice as at Sambo's or Denny's may help break this sameness. Making choices is difficult even if you can read.

GOAL: Increase interpersonal skills

Skill area: Social interactions with peers

Skill: Handling teasing

Objective: Will effectively ignore teasing behavior of peers.

Modifications and Lead-up Activities

- Student needs to have positive experiences with one or two non-handicapped peers before he is exposed to small groups of peers.

Associated Objectives

- Will tell an aggressive peer to stop and/or move away or will ask for adult help.
- Will express his feelings to a close peer or sibling who bothers him, such as saying, "I don't like that!"

Plan for Motivation: Plan contingencies so that when the student ignores teasing he:

- Sees that others stop teasing.
- Feels more safe and comfortable in a group.
  Sample contingency: "When you ignore teasing, people stop teasing you." or "When you do something else, you don't notice the teasing as much."

Rationale

In order to be with groups of peers without adult support, autistic youth need help interpreting negative behavior of others and knowing how to react effectively.

Teaching Procedures

- Distinguish teasing from nonteasing. Because autistic youth don't understand humor or when someone is being mean in concrete incidents, teasing is very abstract and difficult to understand. A literal translation is usually made of all communication and interaction. For example: The autistic youth asks, "What time is it?" Fellow student answers "It's way past your bedtime." The autistic youth drops something. Fellow student grabs it and runs away or hides it. The autistic youth says something. Fellow student says, "Shut up, you are so dumb."
- Practice in structured settings with questions like "Is that teasing? Is it real?" "Is it mean?" "How does it make you feel?"
- Practice with strategies for dealing with teasing. The most effective is ignoring. Usually this has to be taught in a specific situation, such as "Pay no attention to Matt when he calls you a baby." Ignoring can be practiced and reinforced in structured situations so that autistic youth understand what it is and how effective it may be. Provide strong support for reinforcements as this skill is practiced. A backup of getting adult or peer support may be necessary when a situation is beyond the student's tolerance level.
- Gradually practice the skill and expand on the concept in natural settings. Peer models and a support group will be very helpful. The autistic student can begin to see that teasing stops when he ignores it, but will continue if everyone enjoys seeing him get upset.

Precautions

This is a tough behavior to learn and will require much interpretation and support.

- Peers may need instruction to help them reinforce the autistic student.
- If the autistic student becomes sophisticated, he can learn to make remarks that may stop the teasing, but this is a very complicated area and the outcome is quite unpredictable.

GOAL: Increase interpersonal skills

Skill area: Social interaction

Skill: Being quiet and leaving adult alone

Objective: Will accept regular times he has adult's full attention and accept times to be quiet and leave the adult alone for __ minutes.

Modifications and Lead-up Activities

- Have the student practice occupying himself with structured activities, gradually increasing the time he can do this independently (see Section on Teaching Leisure Skills)
- When student has a repertoire of independent activities redirect him to activities when the adult requests quiet.

Associated Objectives

- Will wait __ minutes for adult attention.
- Will entertain himself for __ minutes.
- Will appropriately seek adult attention and instruction.

Plan for Motivation: Plan contigencies so that when the student follows directions to leave the adult alone he:

- Gets positive attention after being quiet.
- Is proud of his self-control.
- Knows when he will receive "quality" time from adults.
  Sample contingency: "When I finish reading the newspaper, we'll play your Sorry game" or "When you leave me alone it lets me finish faster."

Rationale

Verbal autistic students often do not monitor their talking and do not sense when they can talk and when others do not wish to talk. They can be very demanding, asking endless questions.

Teaching Procedures

- Adult will cue student with "I'm busy now, be quiet until I'm finished" or "I'm busy—go away for __ minutes." Set the timer or refer to the clock. This explanation can be accompanied by gestures such as fingers to mouth for quiet and hand up for go away. Since autistic students have problems with gestures, these may have to be specifically taught. However, these cues can then replace the explanations.
- Teaching a student what being quiet means may be necessary. If the time he waits is short and he is sitting near you, it may be very difficult for him to refrain from talking anyway. Use of timer for quiet time is useful. State for everyone: "It is quiet time. No noises or talking." Start with thirty seconds and build up the time. Always reinforce on completion. This can be fun.
- Give the student a suggestion of something else to do.
- With a very talkative student it is helpful to give advanced warning, saying, "I will answer two more questions then you must be quiet for ten minutes."
- Make sure you remember to seek the student out at the specified time or when you are finished and give him undivided attention. "Let's talk now. Thank you for waiting."
- It may also be necessary to specify a waiting place if a particular student becomes anxious waiting. Always use the same place. "Wait on the couch."
- Gradually expand the time you expect a student to wait, but provide some help in deciding when something is urgent.

Precautions

- Adults all too often forget the needs of the student and do not get back to him in the specified time. This objective is necessary for all those living with autistic students, but should not be abused or overused.
- An intervention other than talking, scolding, and explaining should be followed when the student does not do as requested. For instance, restate, "It's not time to talk." Reset the timer and say, "When you are quiet for __ minutes then we'll talk."

GOAL: Increase social communication skills

Skill area: Social communication

Skill: Conversation skills

Objective: In a group situation, will respond to conversational comments made by other people.

Modifications and Lead-up Activities

- Answer direct questions with "yes" or "no."
- Answer questions requiring a phrase or sentence in response.
- Practice sticking to a subject for three or four conversational turns that the student introduces.
- Practice continuing a conversation that is not of great interest to student.

Associated Objectives

- Will carry on conversations of several minutes in length on subjects of interest to the student.
- Will converse for one minute on subjects of interest to a conversational partner.
- Will respond to comments made by peers.
- Ask for more information about a subject.

Plan for Motivation: Plan contingencies so that when the student responds to conversational comments by others he:

- Receives positive attention from other people.
- Enjoys a more reciprocal relationship with others.

Sample contingency: "I like it when we talk about my favorite sports. Now, what would you like to talk about?"

Rationale

After students have learned some conversational skills, they frequently fail to continue conversing in response to comments by others. The conversation may end if direct questions are not continually asked of the autistic youth.

Teaching Procedures

- Explain to the student that when we talk to people we answer their questions. We also answer after they tell us something, commenting on the same subject or changing it.
- In a structured conversational group use an arrow to point to the person whose turn it is to talk. This lets him know that he is responsible for saying something. A ball or block could be passed from the speaker to the listener as the speaker finishes talking. This cues him that it is his turn.
- If the youth has difficulty knowing what to say, jot down conversation topics in a list. For example, the teacher says, "I have a six-month old baby at home," and writes down the word "baby." The student then knows he needs to ask or say something about a baby. He needs to think of something on this subject.
- Begin training in language or conversational sessions; then expand to other environments. Use tokens or points as necessary at first.
- If the student always insists on talking about his favorite topic, set up a time for talking about the favorite topic. Then when another topic is introduced, redirect to the topic: "We can talk about what you want to talk about at snack time. Now we're talking about what I want to talk about."

Precautions

- Give the student as many cues as he needs in order to know what to say.
- Allow him to be as creative as he can.
- Give him all the time he needs initially.

GOAL: Increase social communication skills

Skill area: Social communication

Skill: Conversation skills

Objective: Will initiate conversations with familiar adults and peers, introducing appropriate subjects.

Modifications and Lead-up Activities

- Practice engaging in short conversations with adults and peers when initiated by others. Have student practice responding to questions of others and discussing daily routine and other very familiar topics.
- Practice greeting people with "Hi" and "Bye" and using people's names.
- Some students may respond best to writing out conversation openings and reading them as he rehearses at first.

Associated Objectives

- Will open conversations appropriately with peers that the student has recently met.
- Will ask other students to join an activity.
- Will ask if he can join in an activity or game.
- Will ask for help in the community from appropriate community helpers.

Plan for Motivation: Plan contingencies so that when the student initiates conversations he:

- Receives positive reactions.
- Receives information that is interesting to him.
- Recognizes he is liked by his peer group.
  Sample contingency: "When you talk to Jim, he really feels like being your friend." "When you told Jim he's a good basketball player, he smiled."

Rationale

After students enjoy conversation, they may still not know how to initially engage someone in a conversation. Sometimes an inappropriate behavior is used to gain attention or a stereotyped utterance is used to start someone talking.

Teaching Procedures

- Practice some specific conversation openers, "Hi, _____. What's new?" or "Hi ______. How are you doing?" At this point, the burden of the topic of conversation is on the other person.
- Move to "Hi, ______. Guess what happened at school today?" or "Hi, ______. I had a busy week.
- List some things the youth can talk about. Begin with an appropriate opener and converse in special conversation time. The student may need to make lists of possible topics in his notebook. Books on making friends may be useful for some children.
- Cue the youth to appropriate conversation openers and topics as he moves from his conversation time to the next environment on his schedule. Have the adult present with whom he has practiced to cue him, if needed. Fade cuing as quickly as possible, and the first adult can fade out as well. Move to cuing him before he goes to the next setting. The adult in the next setting will cue as needed by asking open-ended questions and letting the student suggest the topic, as in "Hi, Dan. What's new?"
- Before the youth goes home he can write down a list of topics that he wishes to tell his family.
- Have student rehearse ideas for conversations before specific situations like outings, visiting, and having quests.
  Examples: "What did you do today that you can tell Jim about when you get to the Boys' Club?" "Could you think of a question to ask Jim?"

Precautions

- Avoid leaning on stereotypic uses of conversation openers. Perhaps start with one, but quickly encourage students to use several different ways to initiating conversations.
- Be careful not to reinforce the one stereotypic opener too strongly.

GOAL: Increase social communication skills

Skill area: Social communication

Skill: Talking about activities

Objective: Will make one or two comments about activities in which the student is or was involved, given cues as necessary.

Modifications and Lead-up Activities

- Student will need to be taught basic vocabulary necessary for describing the activities. Teach vocabulary first if necessary, including people's names, action verbs, basic descriptive words, names of objects and activities at home, school, and recess.
- Establish a daily communication group to practice skills.

Associated Objectives

- Will comment on activities spontaneously to an adult.
- Will describe events after they occur to others.
- Will comment on activities to peers.

Plan for Motivation: Plan contingencies so that when a student comments on his activities he:

- Receives positive attention.
- Receives information that is interesting to him.
- Realizes he can share important events in his life with others.

  Sample contingency: "Tell me where you went on your trip, then I'll tell you what's for snack."

Rationale

Some autistic youth use their language skills only to talk about concrete things, what will happen next, or to repeat a question of great concern. They may require specific training to expand their use of language.

Teaching Procedures

- Begin by talking about present events, about things as they occur. Model appropriate descriptions of activities and ask the students simple questions.
- Then talk about the events immediately afterwards, this time using past tense.
- Talk about very concrete things that just happened, asking specific questions as necessary, such as "What did you eat for lunch?" rather than general questions like "What did you do today?"
- Have the student carry a notebook. Jot activities down in his notebook so that when he gets to the next setting the adult can refer to the book and see specific items the student might discuss.
- Draw pictures of events that occur and discuss them afterward. Write out descriptions of events with the student's help.
- Use real photos of the student doing activities. Use these as memory joggers to help him discuss things that happened.

Precautions

- Autistic students need to understand the worth of communication before they need to use syntactically correct sentence construction. Do not get bogged down with grammar. Rather, let the student learn joy and value of sharing with and talking to others. Once he understands this, he will be in a better position to understand why we use standard forms of grammar.
- Initially, adults will need to know the answers to the questions they ask so they can provide prompts and model if needed.

GOAL: Increase leisure skills

Skill area: Leisure education

Skill: Making choices during leisure time

Objective: When presented with three different familiar play materials, will choose one and play with it for ten minutes, with initial cues.

Modifications and Lead-up Activities

- If needed, provide regular one-to-one instruction for using play materials until the student becomes familiar with a variety of them; then fade adult assistance.
- For non-verbal students, have students respond by pointing to their choice. Next, have students point to a picture of the object with one object beside it. Then, have the student choose from pictures of objects only.

Associated Objectives

- Will choose one play material and play with it for ten minutes when given a verbal choice of three.
- Will choose one play material from a toy box or shelf and play with it for ten minutes.
- Will respond to familiar choices presented, "You may do this or you may do that" by selecting a choice, in all environments.

Plan for Motivation: Plan contingencies so that when the student chooses and plays with play materials he:

- Enjoys having a choice and more control over his time.
- Enjoys the routine of having a scheduled play time.
- Comes in contact with some reinforcing quality of play materials.
  Sample contingency: "If you can choose the toy, you can have the one you want."

Rationale

Autistic persons frequently have trouble making open-ended choices and initially need some structure to learn to make decisions. Many autistic youth will not use play materials spontaneously.

Teaching Procedures

- During a regular playtime scheduled once or twice daily, present two familiar toys by putting them on the table in front of the student. Ask, "What do you want?" then, "Do you want the paints or the Lite-Brite?" Point in an exaggerated manner at each toy as it is named. If the student reaches for a toy model a verbal response: "Tell me paints.' Good. You picked paints." Youth or adult can then put the unselected toy away.
- Provide directions and cues as needed for the student to use the chosen play material for five minutes.
- When the student appears to have the concept of choosing between two, add one more choice.
- Fade directions and cues needed for the student to select and play with the toy. Gradually increase the time the student uses the toy to 10 minutes.
- Vary the three choices as students become familiar with new play materials. If progress is being made on independent materials include some interactive activities such as board games.

Precautions

- Some students may not understand the concept of "or." It is best to know this before starting so that the concept can be worked on separately.
- A student who seldom uses play materials will probably depend a good deal on the routine; therefore a routine playtime should be established before introducing choices.
- Avoid the youth's becoming too dependent on the adult by selecting play materials he eventually will be capable of using independently and by fading the adult.

Name: ______________________

Code: 0–Does not do
1–Model and/or directions
2–Cues and prompts
3–Independent with adult nearby
4–Independent

PROCEDURES FOR FAST-FOOD RESTAURANT

STEPS DATES			
Enters restaurant			
Finds a place in line or finds the place to give order			
Waits in line appropriately (quiet, keeps hands to self)			
Gives order to cashier when asked			
Uses "please" and "thank you" appropriately			
Uses polite tone and acceptable voice level			
Gives money to cashier when cashier announces total bill			
Holds hand out and accepts change			
Carries tray/food to a table and seats self			
Uses acceptable table manners when eating (small bites, eats slowly, food remains on tray)			
Carries tray to trash and empties tray			
Places tray in correct place			
Leaves restaurant			
Other			

PLAN FOR MOTIVATION:

Name: ______________________________

Code: 0–Does not do
1–Model and/or directions
2–Cues and prompts
3–Independent with adult nearby
4–Independent

PROCEDURES FOR USING A FITNESS CENTER

STEPS DATES			
Waits in lobby appropriately			
Shows card at counter to staff			
Enters door when buzzer rings			
Undresses and places clothes in locker			
Remains in pool area during swimming, follows pool rules (no running, splashing, etc.), gets out of pool when told			
Dresses in locker room, keeps track of own belongings			
Uses gym area appropriately (basketball courts, soccer, etc.)			
Uses jogging track appropriately			
Uses equipment in weight room correctly—List			
Leaves Y-Center when activities completed			
Other			
Other			
Other			
Other			

PLAN FOR MOTIVATION:

REFERENCES

Beare, P. L., & Lynch, E.C. (1983). Rural area emotional disturbance service delivery: Problems and future directions. *Behavioral Disorders, 8*,(4), 251–257.

Bemporad, J. (1979). Adult recollections of a formerly autistic child. *Journal of Autism and Developmental Disorders, 9*, 191–193.

Blake, O. W., & Volp, A. (1964). *Lead up games to team sports*. Englewood Cliffs, NJ: Prentice-Hall.

Brown, L., Nisbet, J., Ford, A., Sweet, M., Shiraga, B., York, J., & Loomis, R. (1983). The critical need for nonschool instruction in educational programs for severely handicapped students. *Journal of the Association for the Severely Handicapped, 8*(3), 71–77.

Clark, P., & Rutter, M. (1981). Autistic children's responses to structure and to interpersonal demands. *Journal of Autism and Developmental Disorders, 11*, 201–217.

Cunningham, T., & Presnall, D. (1978). Relationship between dimensions of adaptive behavior and sheltered workshop productivity. *American Journal of Mental Deficiency, 82*, 386–393.

DeMyer, M., & Goldberg, P. (1983). Family needs of the autistic adolescent. In E. Schopler & G. B. Mesibov (Eds.), *Autism in adolescents and adults*. New York: Plenum Press.

Dewey, M. (1976). The autistic child in a physical education class. *Physical education, recreation, and related programs for autistic and emotionally disturbed children*. Washington, DC: American Alliance for Health, Physical Education, and Recreation.

Dewey, M. A. (1973). *Recreation for autistic and emotionally disturbed children*. (ERIC Document Reproduction Service No. ED 094 495), p. 3. Rockville, MD: National Institute of Mental Health.

Donnellan, A. M. (1981). An educational perspective of autism: Implications for curriculum development and personnel preparation. In B. Wilcox & A. Thompson (Eds.), *Critical issues in educating autistic children and youth*. Washington, DC: NSAC, The National Society for Children and Adults with Autism.

Egel, R., Richman, G., & Koegel, R. (1981). Normal peer models and autistic children learning. *Journal of Applied Behavior Analysis, 14*, 3–12.

Fredericks, H. D., Buckley, J., Baldwin, V., Moore, W., & Streml-Campbell, K. (1983). The educational needs of the autistic adolescent. In E. Schopler & G. B. Mesibov (Eds.), *Autism in adolescents and adults*, New York: Plenum Press.

Goetz, L., Schuler, A., & Sailor, W. (1979). Teaching functional speech to the severely handicapped: Current issues. *Journal of Autism and Developmental Disorders, 9*, 325–343.

Gresham, F. M. (1982). Misguided mainstreaming: The case for social skills training with handicapped children. *Exceptional Children, 48*, 422–433.

Henning, J. H., Dalrymple, N. J., Davis, K. J., & Madeira, S. S. (1982). *Teaching social and leisure skills to youth with autism*. Bloomington:Indiana University Developmental Training Center.

Horst, G., Wehman, P., Hill, J. W., & Bailey, C. (1981). Developing age-appropriate leisure skills in severely handicapped adolescents. *Teaching Exceptional Children, 14*, 11–15.

Iso-Ahola, S. E. (1980). *The social psychology of leisure and recreation*. Dubuque, Iowa: Wm. C. Brown.

Joswiak, K. F. (1975). *Leisure counseling program materials for the developmentally disabled*. Washington, DC: Hawkins.

Kelly, W. J., Salzberg, C. L., Levy, S. M., Warrenteltz, R. B., Adams, T. W., Crouse, T. R., & Beegle, G. P. (1983). The effects of role-playing and self-monitoring on the generalization of vocational social skills by behaviorally disordered adolescents. *Behavioral Disorders, 9*, 27–35.

Kochany, L., & Keller, J. (1980). Analysis and evaluation of the failure of severely disabled individuals in competitive employment. In P. Wehman & M. Hill (Eds.), *Vocational training and placement of severely disabled persons*. Richmond: Virginia Commonwealth University.

Koegel, R. L., Rincover, A., & Egel, A. L. (1982). *Educating and understanding autistic children*. San Diego: College-Hill.

Lovaas, O. (1979). Contrasting illness and behavioral models for the treatment of autistic children: A historical perspective. *Journal of Autism and Developmental Disorders, 9,* 315–323.

Riquet, C. B., Taylor, N. D., Benaroya, S., & Klein, L. S. (1981). Symbolic play in autistic, Down's, and normal children of equivalent mental age. *Journal of Autism and Developmental Disorders, 11*, 439–448.

Strain, P. S., Kerr, M. M., & Ragland, E. V. (1979). Effects of peer-mediated social initiations and prompting/reinforcement procedures on the social behavior of autistic children. *Journal of Autism and Developmental Disorders, 9,* 41–53.

Tager-Flusberg, H. (1981). On the nature of linguistic functioning in early infantile autism. *Journal of Autism and Developmental Disorders, 11*, 45–56.

Voeltz, L. M., & Evans, I. M. (1983). Educational validity: Procedures to evaluate outcomes in programs for severely handicapped learners. *Journal of the Association for the Severely Handicapped, 8*(1), 3–15.

Voeltz, L. M., Wuerch, B. B., & Bockhaut, C. H. (1982). Social validation of leisure activities training with severely handicapped youth. *Journal of the Association for the Severely Handicapped, 7*(4), 3–13.

Wehman, P., Schleien, S., & Kiernan, J. (1980). Age-appropriate recreation programs for severely handicapped youth and adults. *Journal of the Association for the Severely Handicapped, 5*(4), 395–407.

Wuerch, B., & Voeltz, L. (1982). Longitudinal leisure skills for severely handicapped learners. In *The Ho'onanea curriculum component*. Baltimore: Paul H. Brooks.

17

The TEACCH Curriculum for Teaching Social Behavior to Children with Autism

J. GREGORY OLLEY

Problems in relating to others or in the social aspects of any task are such familiar components of the autism syndrome that they are included in all definitions of the disorder (e.g., American Psychiatric Association, 1980; National Society for Autistic Children, 1978; Rutter, 1978). In fact, the term *autism* is an expression of these very problems. Thus, the need to teach social skills is a familiar and fundamental issue for those concerned with autism.

Although such problems are less frequent and far less severe in the average school-age population, children's social skills have been the focus of a great deal of research in recent years. The concept of social skills has been reviewed by McFall (1982), and approaches to teaching social skills have recently been critiqued by Beck and Forehand (1984), Michelson, Sugai, Wood, and Kazdin (1983), and others. These reviews reveal a remarkable growth industry in teaching social skills to children, and they raise many issues and problems. This chapter will refer to these issues only as they apply to autistic and other severely handicapped children. This extensive literature on the nature of social skills and their measurement has led to the development of several social skills curricula for children. From this background of research and need, the TEACCH Social Skills Curriculum developed. In this chapter the TEACCH curriculum is described. Beginning with a background of related work, the chapter provides the rationale and the procedures used to develop individualized social skills teaching activities for students with autism.

J. GREGORY OLLEY • Division TEACCH, University of North Carolina, Chapel Hill, North Carolina 27514.

One way to make the current viewpoints on the nature of social skills clear is to examine the measurement strategies used. The recent interest in this topic has led to an extraordinary number of review articles on measurement or assessment of children's social skills (e.g., Asher & Hymel, 1981; Connolly, 1983; Foster & Ritchey, 1979; Greenwood, Walker, & Hops, 1977; Gresham, 1981, 1983; Gresham & Elliott, 1984; Michelson, Foster, & Ritchey, 1981). The many assessment methods cited reflect three general approaches to social skills (Gresham, 1985).

In the first approach, social skills are measured by peer acceptance. Those children who are accepted by their peers, as measured by sociometric techniques (peer nominations, peer ratings, teacher nominations, teacher ratings), have good social skills. Research within this approach deals with refinements or innovations in measurement, such as self-assessment (reviewed by Michelson *et al.*, 1981), or with those categories of behavior that are associated with acceptance by peers (e.g., cooperation).

Although acceptance by peers is one reasonable goal when teaching social skills to autistic students, this approach has severe limitations. Measurement strategies such as asking peers to identify the four children they like best do not yield useful information about autistic children, whose social deficits are severe. It is virtually assured that autistic students will not be among the most popular in a class. Nevertheless, this approach has value if it can direct us toward measures of tolerance and understanding toward autistic classmates, instead of popularity.

A second approach noted by Gresham (1985) is based on a behavioral definition. From this viewpoint social behaviors are those in interaction with others that lead to the greatest probability of positive or negative reinforcement or the lowest probability of punishment or extinction. In other words, social skills are the ones that get positive responses from others—the ones that keep social interactions alive. This approach defines social skills empirically but does not give any other guidance in deciding what to teach.

The third approach, as described by Gresham (1985), is the most helpful in choosing skills to teach an autistic student. This "social validity" approach emphasizes social skills that lead to or predict outcomes that are important or valued by others. These outcomes include (a) acceptance by peers, (b) social skills valued by parents, siblings, teachers, or others, and (c) skills in interaction with others that lead to socially valued adult status (e.g., independence, employment, responsibility).

The popularity of the social validity approach is a reflection of changes in measurement (Wolf, 1978) and educational priorities (Voeltz & Evans, 1983) to recognize the importance of teaching skills that are valued by the student's family, the community, and society at large. This approach has influenced the development of many aspects of the TEACCH curriculum.

SOCIAL SKILLS CURRICULA AND AUTISM

In keeping with the general growth of interest in social skills, there has been a growth of research and teaching of social skills in handicapped populations (Wacker, 1984). For example, Walker (1983; Walker *et al.*, 1983) developed the ACCEPTS program to teach handicapped students the social skills needed for successful mainstreaming. It includes an individualized assessment leading to teaching social skills in five areas ranging from specific classroom skills (e.g., following teacher instructions) to coping skills (e.g., what to do when someone teases you.)

Another example of a curriculum oriented toward social skills is Wehman's (1976) system of four levels of skill for severely handicapped learners. In this approach, lower levels (e.g., personal care) are viewed as prerequisites for learning higher levels (e.g., initiative, cooperation), and social skills are broadly conceived to include related skills such as money management. A similar approach is the Benhaven curriculum (Simonson, 1979) for autistic and severely handicapped children, a behaviorally oriented approach that focuses on many functional skill areas, specifies many detailed steps in teaching, and includes procedures for program evaluation.

Whereas the above two curricula provide detailed task analyses of traditional school skills, more recent approaches emphasize the social skills that are most likely to be needed in postschool environments. For instance, the Assessment of Social Competence (Meyer *et al.*, 1983) is a method for assessing a severely handicapped person's abilities in 11 areas of social competence. This information is combined with evaluations of possible social activities to determine appropriate curricula (Meyer, McQuarter, & Kishi, 1985). The emphasis is upon those social skills that will enable students to participate fully or partially in community life. This is accomplished, in part, by teaching social skills with social validity, that is, skills that are valued by parents and members of the community.

Another recent curriculum was developed at Indiana University (see Henning & Dalrymple, Chapter 16, this volume; Henning, Dalrymple, Davis, & Madeira, 1982) for 10- to 15-year-old students with autism who already have some basic skills. The curriculum contains strategies for teaching social, communication, and leisure skills in school and community settings. These and other curricula have helped teachers significantly in designing appropriate instructional activities for students with autism.

DEVELOPMENT OF THE TEACCH CURRICULUM

Division TEACCH at the University of North Carolina at Chapel Hill provides direct services to children with autism and their families as well as staff training and consultation for classrooms, group homes, and other services. The teaching of social skills has been a central part of the comprehensive statewide program for many years. During the TEACCH clinic-based assessments, information regarding social skills is gathered through administration of the Psychoeducational Profile (Schopler & Reichler, 1979) as well as through parent interviews and informal observation. The information gathered in this way is the basis for consultation with families and teachers regarding social activities at home, at school, or in other community activities.

As TEACCH-affiliated classrooms in North Carolina have increased to their present number of 60, teachers have recognized the need for a more formal and systematic approach to teaching social skills in schools. In response to this need, and with the aid of a contract with the Office of Special Education and Rehabilitative Services of the U.S. Department of Education, TEACCH initiated the development of a social skills curriculum for students with autism and a companion curriculum emphasizing communication skills (Watson, 1985; Watson & Lord, 1982). The remainder of this chapter will describe the rationale and the development of the TEACCH Social Skills Curriculum, emphasizing the ways in which it addresses the unique social difficulties of autism and its use of assessment in the classroom and other social settings to develop individualized teaching activities.

This emphasis on social skills is important for two broad reasons. First, the ability to engage in appropriate social interaction enhances the quality of life for all individuals. In addition, social skills are of critical importance in adult adjustment (Greenspan & Shoultz, 1981). Teaching social skills at an early age prepares students to live and work in the least restrictive environment throughout their lives.

Despite the teachers' high awareness of these issues and of the social problems of autistic students, work in the TEACCH-affiliated classrooms revealed that currently available curricula for autistic students have some serious limitations. The TEACCH curriculum was developed to address a perceived need for a tool that could be helpful to autistic students at all ages and all functioning levels. The curriculum was intended primarily for classroom use but recognizes that social skills must be used in a wide variety of circumstances outside of schools. It is intended to be practical and feasible for teachers but to include a form of measurement that allows progress to be tracked and program revisions to be made.

The curriculum is intended to be broad enough to address social problems encountered by many handicapped children but at the same time to have a unique focus on the social characteristics of autism. All TEACCH services take into consideration also the perspective of the child's family. Similarly, this curriculum seeks to assure social validity by involving parents in setting teaching priorities and guiding teachers toward outcomes that will truly be valued by the family, by those whom the student will encounter often, and by our society. This orientation is essential, because the success of our efforts will be judged not on the basis of good school performance but on adjustment outside of school and throughout life.

Autistic and other severely handicapped individuals have difficulty in generalization of nearly all skills, but generalization of social skills is particularly troublesome. Social rules are often specific to circumstances, and the natural cues for social behavior can be quite subtle. Thus, even a person with extensive social skills must use considerable judgment before acting. The cognitive ability that we call social judgment is often one of the areas of greatest difficulty for people with autism. Thus, a curriculum that guides the teaching of social skills must assure not only that skills are taught in school settings but that they are practiced in other common settings. By the teaching of social rules and social behaviors and through opportunities to practice these skills and their subtle variations in various settings, students can learn to acquire, generalize, and spontaneously use social behavior that will make a practical difference in their lives.

With these considerations in mind, experienced teachers in North Carolina were consulted in order to develop a draft curriculum. Early versions of both curricula were field-tested in two classes in Raleigh, North Carolina, and later in two classes in Winston-Salem, North Carolina. Both formal evaluation based on student progress and informal evaluation based on teacher suggestions provided the basis for many revisions. During the early stages of development, it became clear that the curriculum should not simply be a compendium of activities, each with task analyses with many steps. Further, it should not advocate one rigid method or sequence of teaching each activity. Instead, the curriculum should be a strategy for developing activities that are both individualized and useful. The resulting curriculum in many ways parallels the TEACCH approach to developing individualized programs in other areas (Schopler, Reichler, & Lansing, 1980).

Individualized teaching activities are developed in a four-step process. The first step involves assessment of social skills based on naturalistic observation in the classroom or other settings. This procedure yields a picture of the student's strengths and weaknesses in six social characteristics that can take place in five different social contexts.

The second step is an interview with the child's parents to determine their view of their child's social skills and their priorities for change. This information is used in the third step to set priorities for change and to express these priorities in the form of written objectives. In the final step, these objectives form the basis for designing individualized social skill training activities.

A Working Definition of Social Skills

In keeping with the considerations stated above, the TEACCH curriculum has adopted a view of social skills that emphasizes social validity and the practical value of the social skills to be taught. Thus, social skills are those behaviors in interaction with others or which lead to interaction with others that have social value and are associated with successful adjustment during both school years and adulthood.

The curriculum is intended to aid the development of social skills and provide alternatives for behaviors that interfere with good social outcomes. For instance, appropriate social initiation is a social skill. Related behaviors, such as posture, grooming, being on time, and a pleasant facial expression, are traits that lead to positive social interactions. Inappropriate personal habits (e.g., spitting, nose picking, hands in pants) are behaviors that interfere with social interaction. In order to plan for all autistic students, these broad aspects of social skills must be considered.

The TEACCH Social Skills Curriculum emphasizes social skills which can reasonably be taught in schools but which have wide application in home, work, recreation, and other community settings. This emphasis upon independent functioning does not mean that all or even a substantial portion of autistic adults are expected to live independently. Good social skills make even partial participation in adapted tasks with supervision more feasible, and they surely make acceptance by members of the community more likely.

ASSESSMENT OF SOCIAL SKILLS

The first of the four steps in developing teaching activities is the observational assessment of social skills in the classroom and/or other social settings. The assessment is intended to describe how independently the student can perform social activities in five common social contexts. This information provides a picture of the student's social strengths and weaknesses on a continuum from independent use on the upper end to a lower level at which the student actively resists the activity. Between these extremes lie several intermediate levels of ability in which the child needs help or prompting in order to succeed.

In addition to observing degree of independence in these social contexts, the assessment considers the social characteristics of autism and the ways that they affect social behavior. An understanding of the curriculum can best begin with a description of these social characteristics.

Observation of Social Characteristics

Many writers have described the syndrome of autism and its associated characteristics. Several of these characteristics are related to social behavior and must be considered when assessing social skills. The following six social characteristics of autism affect social behavior and must be considered in the assessment. They are separate but somewhat overlapping characteristics, and, thus, they can be observed as they naturally occur without regard to sequence. Remember, each of these social characteristics is observed in five different contexts, and level of independent functioning is recorded. Given this information, social teaching activities can be designed to help students to move to a level requiring less assistance.

Proximity. Individuals with autism often encounter problems in social interaction because they do not observe the usual rules of proximity to others. In Kanner's (1943) original account of autism, he noted that the children averted their gaze from others. Later observations (Richer, 1976, 1978) described other problems of proximity, such as turning away, hanging one's head, moving away, facing the wall, and standing on the periphery of an area. Appropriate proximity is an important aspect of nonverbal communication (Shah & Wing, Chapter 8, this volume), and those who violate such social conventions are impaired in social interactions.

Observation of proximity requires that the observer note whether the student is in the right place for that social context. Is the child performing the task in the right place? Is he/she too close or too far from the person or materials? Is the student facing in the right direction? Can the student walk down a corridor on the right without zigzagging or rubbing against the wall? If the student can independently observe rules of proximity in all social contexts, proximity is not a problem and need not be a target for social teaching activities. On the other hand, if proximity is a problem requiring teacher intervention in several contexts, it may be an appropriate target for charge.

Object/Body Use. Another social characteristic that may make students with autism seem odd is their inappropriate use of objects. Many writers (e.g., Rutter, 1978; Wing, 1969) have noted autistic children's lack of spontaneous use of materials for play and related lack of play skills. Autistic children may have strong attachments to objects and routines (Wing, 1969) that limit social interaction and play. In social contexts in which no objects or material are required, autistic students may use their bodies inappropriately. For instance, Wing (1969) described problems such as jumping, grimacing, and spinning. Odd posture or use of hands also limit many social interactions.

Observation of object/body use refers to the way in which the student uses materials or toys relative to the demands of the task. Can the student choose the correct object for the social situation and use material appropriately? Does the student self-stimulate with material (even if it does not interfere with completion of the task)? If the social context requires no material, does the student use his/her body appropriately?

Social Initiation. Autistic children's failure to initiate social interaction has been described by many writers (e.g., Richer, 1976, 1978). When initiations are tried, they may be inappropriate. Wing and Gould (1979) described several variations on problems of social initiation and response that they observed in children with autism and other social impairments. Such children cannot begin, maintain, or end social interactions effectively.

When observing social initiation as part of this curriculum, one must look for the extent to which the student tries to begin an interaction. For instance, asking for, or even pointing to, materials, asking for help, or inviting a peer to participate in play are forms of appropriate initiation.

Social Response. When another child or an adult approaches an autistic student and initiates social interaction, the student may not respond appropriately or may not recognize this form of turn taking that we call social exchange (Duchan & Palermo, 1982). The result is likely to be that the social contact ends abruptly, and those who experience this lack of appropriate response will not approach the autistic student again. Such an unfavorable outcome can be avoided by teaching autistic students to recognize and respond to social approaches.

Observation of social response involves noting whether the child answers or otherwise responds to initiation by others. Does the student comply with requests in a socially appropriate manner? Does he/she reply to another's greeting or to another's initiative to play? Is the timing of response appropriate, or is it too quick or too delayed? Does the student move away when others make social approaches?

Extent of Interfering Behavior. Many students with autism engage in repetitive, stereotyped behaviors (Eisenberg & Kanner, 1956; Rutter, 1978) that make them appear very socially odd and may interfere with work or learning. It is important when planning teaching activities to note the extent to which the student's odd behaviors interfere with the task at hand. Some behaviors, such as body rocking, may not interfere with some school tasks or with work productivity but are quite likely to deter social interactions, particularly outside of sheltered settings.

The observation of interfering behavior should note in specific social settings whether the student self-stimulates in a manner that interferes with the social aspects of the task. When presented with a social opportunity, does the student injure him/herself, run away, or aggress toward others? Observation focuses on the extent of structure or prompting needed to overcome these interfering behaviors and interact appropriately.

Adaptation to Change. The result of autistic individuals' insistence on rituals and quite rigid cognitive style is that they often become upset or disruptive when aspects of their environment are changed. This "insistence on preservation of sameness" was noted in many early descriptions of the syndrome by Kanner and others (e.g., Eisenberg & Kanner, 1956). Rutter (1978) also included "insistence on sameness" as part of his definition of the disorder.

These problems in dealing with changes in routine or insistence that certain aspects of the environment must stay just so (e.g., the door must be open just 2 inches; the light across the street must stay on) contribute to a larger educational problem. That is, students with autism do not generalize their skills easily (Carr, 1980). Even though a student may seem to have a skill well established, changes in people, setting, materials, time of day, or other factors often disrupt performance. Since people with autism have, by definition, difficulties in social skills, and social cues vary widely by circumstances, the task of learning and using social skills across settings and when the routine has been altered is very important.

Unlike the above five social characteristics, adaptation to change cannot be observed on one occasion only. The observer must know how the student performs in the familiar routine and also observe social behavior when systematic changes have been made. The highest level of skill occurs when the student can generalize skills or use judgment in choosing the appropriate social behavior in new circumstances. At the lowest level the child actively resists new tasks, new people, or changes in general. The observer must note each social context and the extent to which the student needs help, structure, prompting, or other interventions to perform appropriate social behavior in the face of change.

Observation of Each Social Context

The above six social characteristics of autism must be observed in context because the nature of the student's difficulty is often related to the setting or context in which it occurs. Thus, the observational assessment in the TEACCH social skills curriculum stresses five social contexts that commonly occur both in schools and in other settings. The following is not an exhaustive list of social settings, and others could be added, but observation of social characteristics in these contexts provides a standard format that makes the results easier to use when choosing priorities for later teaching.

Observation during Structured Time. Although structured time constitutes most of the school day in the typical program for autistic students, it is often not thought to be social. In fact, it involves many social considerations. In traditional classrooms the interaction during this time is primarily with the teacher, but in many classes structured periods also include group interactions

Table 1. Scoring Guidelines for Structured Time

Social characteristic	Level of independence				
	Inappropriate-resistant	Physical prompt	Specific prompt	General prompt	Independent
Proximity	Not in appropriate area; refuses to come or remain even with physical prompt	Goes to and remains in work area with physical assist/prompt	Goes to work area with partial motor prompt or specific prompt (e.g., "John go to your desk"); may need repeated prompts to remain	Goes to work area given general prompt ("Work time everyone"); remains without further reminders	Goes to work area independently (e.g., Signal such as bell may ring); student reads clock or follows daily schedule card
Object/Body use	Nonfunctional use of object or body; self-stimulatory, destructive; resists prompts	Uses object only with continued physical assist/prompt; hands down with physical assist	Uses appropriate object with partial motor prompt or specific prompt; hands down with specific prompt	Uses appropriate object and/or keeps hand down with general/abstract prompt to organize	Uses appropriate objects independently following a schedule or other natural, age-appropriate cues
Social initiation	No initiation, loud verbal self-stimulation, no awareness, tantrums	Inappropriate initiation, requires physical prompt to initiate need for materials or assistance	Appropriate initiation requires specific prompt ("John, ask for help." "John, ring your bell if you need more materials.")	Initiates with a general/abstract prompt ("John, tell me what you need." "When you finish work, what do you do?")	Makes appropriate initiation to natural cues (e.g., when finished requests new task)

Social response	Unaware, resists prompts, tantrums	Responds after long delay, inappropriate response, needs physical assist to comply with teacher request	Requires specific prompt to respond (e.g., "Tim asked for a pencil; give him one.")	Requires general/abstract prompt to respond (e.g., "John, Tim asked for something.")	Makes appropriate response to natural cues
Extent of interfering behavior	Verbal and physical self-stimulation, aggressive, withdrawn, uncooperative, resists prompts	Physical prompt/assistance needed to curtail interfering behaviors	Partial motor prompt or specific prompt necessary to curtail interfering behaviors	General/abstract prompt curtails interfering behaviors (e.g., "It's work time!")	No interfering behaviors present
Adaptation to change	Given a change in people, place, schedule, materials, or task, behavior is inappropriate and student resists prompts	Given a change in people, place, schedule, materials, or task, student complies only with full physical prompt	Given a change in people, place, schedule, materials, or task, student complies with specific prompt	Given a change in people, place, schedule, materials, or task, student complies with general/abstract prompt	Given a change in people, place, schedule, materials, or task, student works independently

or two children working on the same task. Examples include taking turns in a structured group, two handicapped students cooperating in a complex assembly task, or a tutoring session with an autistic student and a nonhandicapped peer.

Social interchanges during structured times may involve following teacher instructions, requesting help, or helping another. It is also important to know when *not* to be social—to work independently and alone when appropriate. Structured time is the classroom analogue of work. Students who learn the social aspects of work are more likely to succeed in real work settings.

Observation of each context must take into consideration each of the six social characteristics and the extent to which skills can be performed independently. Examples of each of the social characteristics during structured time appear in Table 1.

Observation during Play or Leisure. When most people think of social behavior, leisure activities come readily to mind. Observation of children during play or leisure reveals that some activities are quite social (e.g., cooperative or competitive games, conversations), others involve individual activities in a social setting (e.g., video games in an arcade), and others are appropriately done in isolation (e.g,, listening to records). Adherence to social rules in all of these leisure settings is important. Observation of leisure time focuses also on the six social characteristics.

Observation during Travel. Many severely handicapped children's first steps toward independence involve travel. The activity may simply be moving from one section of the classroom to another, or it may be walking to the office or to the school bus, or using public transportation. Any movement requires social skills and judgment. Travel may be alone or with others. It may require asking others for help or avoiding strangers. It requires avoiding danger and acting appropriately in the presence of others. Again, all six social characteristics must be considered.

Observation during Eating or Mealtime. Meals are a very common context for social exchange for everyone. Mastering the self-help aspects of meals is important because few people want to interact with a person who eats inappropriately. However, observation for our purposes includes only the social aspects of eating. Social opportunities associated with meals include food preparation, deciding what to order in a restaurant, interacting with cafeteria or restaurant employees, and social exchanges while dining. Since travel is often involved in mealtime, both social contexts can usually be observed conveniently by the teacher.

Observation during Meeting Others. Although meeting others or greeting friends does not happen as often or last as long as the activities in other social contexts, they are important skills that convey a strong impression to others. Problems in proximity, use of body, initiation, and response are common when meeting or greeting others. Several types of meetings with others can usually be observed in a school day, and some can be arranged (e.g., meeting a visitor) during the observation period.

Summary of Observational Data

The purpose of the observation is to assess in natural social settings the pattern of social strengths and weaknesses for the individual student. The goal of instruction in social skills (or in any other area) is to help the student to use that skill independently and appropriately in natural social settings—in other words, to use social skills and to use social judgment to generalize those skills.

Therefore, our observational data should tell us the areas in which the student is most nearly independent and the areas in which help (structure, prompting) is required to use social skills. Further, our summary should note how much and what type of help the student currently needs. Such a summary can guide teachers and others to set priorities for change that will result in more independent use of functional social skills.

In order to form a summary of the observation, level of independence is rated for each social characteristic in each social context. A summary score is entered in a matrix illustrated in Table 2. Field testing of the curriculum has shown that this summary of a student's social strengths and weaknesses usually shows a pattern across social characteristics and across contexts, and this pattern is seen as subjectively valid by the teacher. For instance, a child may have difficulties in social initiation that exist in all contexts (row 3 in Table 2) or problems in meeting others that involve all social characteristics (column 5 in Table 2).

Ratings of independence are recorded in five steps. Examples from structured time are in Table 1. At one extreme (Independent), the student has mastered that social characteristic in that context. For example, in Table 1 a student who can independently judge the appropriate proximity during structured time with no help other than the natural social cues available would be scored at the Independent level.

At the other extreme (Inappropriate/Resistant), a student is not in the correct proximity and actively resists the teacher's efforts (e.g., physical prompts) to get him/her into the correct proximity. In between lie three intermediate levels of social independence. Those at the Physical Prompt level will comply with a teacher's physical prompt. Those at a Specific Prompt level will comply with the teacher's request if less than full physical prompting is used or if some other type of very clear, specific prompt is given. Continued work after the initial prompt may be very poor at this level.

A student at the General Prompt level still needs structure and reminders but has better independent work skills. The prompts are general verbal instructions (e.g., "It's work time") or nonverbal instructions (e.g., pointing to the

Table 2. Summary Form for Observation Assessment of Social Skills

Social characteristic	Context				
	Structured time	Play/Leisure	Travel	Eating/mealtime	Meeting others
Proximity					
Object/Body use					
Social initiation					
Social response					
Interfering behavior					
Adaptation to change					

schedule). At the highest (Independent) level, the student spontaneously acts in the presence of natural cues for social behavior.

These five steps represent a continuum of independence, and although they are not intended to have psychometric precision, they give a relative picture of the student's social independence with regard to five contexts and six social characteristics. The summary information entered in Table 2 is the basis for setting priorities and developing activities.

INVOLVING PARENTS

In all aspects of TEACCH services, a strong effort is made to involve parents, although the form of that involvement may vary with the interest and resources of the individual parents (Schopler & Olley, 1982). Because the Assessment of Social Skills is the basis for the later development of instructional activities, the involvement of parents or parent surrogates in the assessment is very important.

The extent of parent involvement in assessment may vary widely. A very interested parent may wish to learn the observational system and conduct an observation at home. Comparison of parent and teacher observation can reveal the extent of problems in both home and school. In a more typical case, parent involvement may take the form of an interview in which the teacher asks the parents about usual social behavior considering the five contexts and six social characteristics.

In a case in which parents wished to have only minimal involvement in assessment, the teacher could discuss the results of the classroom observation and ask the parents to what extent these observations were accurate summaries of the child's behavior at home or in other social settings. This parent interview allows the opportunity either to confirm the findings or to learn that a different pattern holds outside of school.

The interview is intended to be brief, clear, and nontechnical and to emphasize the child's strengths, weaknesses, and areas of interest. Areas of common concern at home and at school are important in narrowing down the assessment data to a few reasonable priorities.

SETTING PRIORITIES

Following the parent interview, the findings from the observational assessment must be organized to indicate teacher and parent priorities. Although there is a social aspect of most activities, and teaching social skills should be combined with other efforts, not all social problems can or should be worked on at once.

Priorities must be set that reflect shared parent and teacher goals. Even if the teacher does not agree with many parental priorities, some activities should be included in the curriculum that reflect parent preferences. This consideration of parental wishes is important for home–school cooperation and for the development of social skills that have value outside the classroom.

In addition to the involvement of parents, setting priorities must take into consideration many other factors.

1. When beginning any new effort, it is important to have some success quickly (even a modest success). Early success generates energy and enthusiasm to continue for teachers, parents, and students and lays a good foundation for later, more difficult tasks. Thus, when reviewing the assessment summary (Tables 2 and 3), the child's area of greatest difficulty is probably a poor starting place. Contexts or social characteristics in which the child already has some skills (perhaps at the level of requiring specific prompts) would make better priorities. Next teaching steps could then involve movement toward general prompts—a more independent level.

2. The student's interest should be considered. Although children with autism may indicate their interest in tasks in odd ways, teachers and parents (and especially siblings) usually have a clear understanding of what activities, settings, people, materials, or times of day a particular student likes. If priorities for teaching take into consideration the student's interests, they are more likely to lead to success. If all elements of the situation are of low interest, the resulting activity may be a struggle for all concerned.

3. An exception to the above points may occur if a crisis exists in one context or regarding one social characteristic. If a problem involving danger, destruction of materials, or major disruption of activities exists, that problem must become a priority. However, this curriculum is not an approach to crisis intervention; it is a long-term plan for teaching social skills. Fundamentals of classroom management (e.g., Sulzer-Azaroff & Mayer, 1977) should be in place before priorities are set for this curriculum.

4. When setting priorities, one should also consider that most autistic students learn slowly and generalize poorly. Thus, social priorities should be skills that, once acquired, will have use in many settings and be valuable as the student gets older. By these criteria, social rules unique to a certain school building or social activities appropriate only to small children would be poor priorities.

5. Priorities that involve activities that can be carried out at home and in which the parents are interested are likely to be practical and aid generalization.

6. Priorities are preferred if they can be met through activities that are practical for teachers or other supervisors, if they are reasonably inexpensive, if they do not require materials that are not available anywhere else, and if, in general, they enhance the chances of others interacting with the autistic student.

In general, it is useful to keep in mind that the purpose of the curriculum is to design individualized activities to teach the social aspects of tasks. Many task analyses of self-help skills, for example, already exist. The TEACCH Social Skills Curriculum is intended to complement, rather than replace, such information. Because social experiences are necessary in order to learn and generalize practical skills, the social aspects of tasks should be high priorities and should be taught as an integral part of all activities.

DESIGNING ACTIVITIES

The final steps in the curriculum process are the development and implementation of individualized social skill teaching activities. These activities should not simply be chosen from a list of more or less appropriate activities but should be developed for each child. The observational assessment, parent involvement, and setting of priorities that have already occurred provide the needed information for designing activities.

Planning the activities can be most systematic if each priority is written in the form of an instructional objective. For instance, if the priority is for the student to improve proximity in the context of travel, and the observational assessment noted difficulty in walking independently throughout the school, an objective could be written as follows:

> When given a note in the classroom and verbal instructions to take the note to the school secretary, Theresa will walk directly to the office and deliver the note and return directly to the classroom. The criterion for mastery is 18 correct out of 20 opportunities.

If Theresa were functioning at a lower level of independence, her objective would involve more teacher assistance. This information leads directly to activities that give Theresa an occasion to travel throughout the school. Teacher assistance in travel should, of course, be faded as independence is gained, and new opportunities for independent travel in other practical settings should be introduced.

The development of activities is thus a matter of applying the priorities to create or enhance social learning opportunities throughout the day. The priorities are the guide for where the existing curriculum needs revision. Revisions may be as simple as offering more social opportunities in the priority areas. Other revisions may be difficult or administratively complex, such as generalizing social skills to recreation times when no recreation program exists. On such occasions, the priorities can be very helpful in determining what is needed for the student's future programming both in and out of school.

Having established a set of social skill teaching activities for a student, the teacher must continue to observe and make revisions as required. The framework of the curriculum lends itself to continuing formal and informal observation. As the child progresses in social skills, priorities can easily be revised toward the goal of greater independence.

EXAMPLE

In order to illustrate the process of individualized curriculum development in social skills, a brief example follows.

Harry was a 9-year-old boy with the characteristics of autism. He had good motor skills but was nonverbal. His communication was limited to a few signs and gestures.

Harry attended a class for autistic and related communication-handicapped children in a regular elementary school in his community and lived at home with his parents and a 6-year-old sister. His classroom program was generally well organized, and Harry did not present crisis behavior problems. The teacher had begun to teach Harry some vocational skills but noted that improvement in social skills was needed to complement his other work skills and improve his long-term prospects for more independent functioning. The social skills observational assessment conducted by his teacher indicated that the context in which Harry's skills were strongest was Structured Time. A summary of the assessment is in Table 3. When activities were in the classroom and had a familiar routine with clear teacher direction, Harry could perform appropriately with general prompts. The social characteristics in which he was strongest were Proximity and Object Use. When presented with his work schedule in the form of a picture of each activity, he could select the correct materials and do his work in sequence. With the teacher present, Harry would stay at his work space and complete academically oriented work sheets at the first-grade level. He used pencil, paper, and a finish box appropriately and did not show odd behaviors that interfered with his or other students' work.

The area of greatest difficulty for Harry was Adaptation to Change. Virtually any change in people, place, schedule, materials, or task led to tantrums or other disruptive behavior, although Harry accepted physical assistance and calmed down quickly. This made it difficult to introduce new tasks and difficult to teach generalization of new skills. Another problem area was Initiation. Harry seldom initiated activities, even activities he seemed to like. But once he got started, he could continue many activities independently. In Structured Time, presentation of the schedule and a sign to work (a general prompt) were sufficient to get Harry started, but in the context of Play or Leisure, Harry did not initiate, or he repeated inappropriate sounds while pulling his hair. A physical prompt

Table 3. Completed Summary Form for Initial Observational Assessment of Harry

Social characteristic	Context				
	Structured time	Play/leisure	Travel	Eating/mealtime	Meeting others
Proximity	General prompt	General prompt	Specific prompt	General prompt	General prompt
Object/body use	General prompt	Specific prompt	Specific prompt	General prompt	General prompt
Social initiation	General prompt	Physical prompt	Physical prompt	Physical prompt	Physical prompt
Social response	General prompt	Physical prompt	Specific prompt	Specific prompt	Specific prompt
Intefering behavior	General prompt	Physical prompt	Specific prompt	Specific prompt	General prompt
Adaptation to change	Specific prompt	Physical prompt	Physical prompt	Physical prompt	Physical prompt

(often through most of the activity) was required to get Harry started and keep him involved in many activities. Harry seemed generally to like play or leisure time. His favorite contexts were Play and Travel, but he lacked independent skills in both settings.

Interviews with Harry's parents revealed a similar pattern at home. They were very interested in improving Harry's ability to cope with change because they were unable to take him to church or to participate in other family activities. They also wished to see more Social Initiation because Harry required a great deal of supervision. They hoped that appropriate initiative would lead to greater independence. On the basis of this information, highest priority was given to initiative, because it could be prompted successfully and would lead to desired activities. The next priority involved adaptation to change. This problem was so pervasive and disruptive that it was seen as important, but reality dictated that it be worked on in small steps.

Activities were devised to prompt Harry by modeling signs and gestures to initiate play and travel. When Harry got started in some favorite play and travel activities, he would continue the activities appropriately. He enjoyed using the record player and taking notes to the office, both familiar activities. Because he was strong in proximity and object use, he could be trusted to follow through on his initiations. In the presence of playtime and the record player or a note to be taken to the office, Harry quickly responded to the teacher's sign. Eventually the teacher waited a bit before giving the sign, and Harry began to initiate in the presence of these favorite activities. Later steps involved signs to prompt other activities of interest to Harry and the fading of the signs to allow Harry to initiate those activities. He learned to initiate a wide variety of classroom activities, and the teachers prompted initiation of similar activities in other settings (e.g., use of the record player in the recreation room). Because this program began with areas of interest and strength, Harry began to take initiative in new activities and to tolerate other changes in his routine.

Harry's teacher was successful in using the curriculum development strategy to design new activities and to evaluate Harry's progress. As he improved in the initial priorities, Harry's educational program moved toward more independent functioning in several social areas that he was able to practice at school and in a variety of other settings.

CONCLUSION

Difficulties in the social aspects of many activities are universally regarded as part of the syndrome of autism. Teachers and other service providers recognize this difficulty, but most curricula for handicapped children and youth emphasize self-help, motor skills, basic academic skills, or other areas that do not explicitly help the teachers plan activities to improve social behavior. The TEACCH social skills curriculum is intended to complement curricula in other areas by focusing planning on the social aspects of many activities.

The curriculum reflects the long-standing priorities of the TEACCH program, such as assessment, parent involvement, and highly individualized instruction. The application of this approach to social skills is intended to help individuals with autism, regardless of age or ability level, to function with a greater degree of independence in a wider variety of settings.

ACKNOWLEDGMENTS

Preparation of this chapter was supported in part by contract number 300-80-0841 between Office of Special Education and Rehabilitative Services, U.S. Department of Education, and the University of North Carolina. The development of this curriculum occurred with the help of many people, including Patricia Fullagar, Janet Martin, Eric Schopler, Catherine Lord, Jack Wall, Gary Mesibov, and the many teachers of autistic children in North Carolina.

REFERENCES

American Psychiatric Association. (1980). *Diagnostic and statistical manual of mental disorders* (3rd ed.). Washington, DC: Author.

Asher, S. R., & Hymel, S. (1981). Children's social competence in peer relations: Sociometric and behavioral assessment. In J. D. Wine & M. D. Smye (Eds.), *Social competence*. New York: Guilford Press.

Beck, S., & Forehand, R. (1984). Social skills training for children: A methodological and clinical review of behavior modification studies. *Behavioral Psychotherapy, 12,* 17–45.

Carr, E. G. (1980). Generalization of treatment effects following educational intervention with autistic children and youth. In B. Wilcox & A. Thompson (Eds.), *Critical issues in educating autistic children and youth* (pp. 118–134). Washington, DC: U.S. Department of Education, Office of Special Education.

Connolly, J. A. (1983). A review of sociometric procedures in the assessment of social competencies in children. *Applied Research in Mental Retardation, 4,* 315–327.

Duchan, J. E., & Palermo, J. (1982). How autistic children view the world. *Topics in Language Disorders, 3*(1), 10–15.

Eisenberg, L., & Kanner, L. (1956). Early infantile autism 1943–55. *American Journal of Orthopsychiatry, 26,* 556–566.

Foster, S. L., & Ritchey, W. L. (1979). Issues in the assessment of social competence in children. *Journal of Applied Behavior Analysis, 12,* 625–638.

Greenspan, S., & Shoultz, B. (1981). Why mentally retarded adults lose their jobs: Social competence as a factor in work adjustment. *Applied Research in Mental Retardation, 2,* 23–38.

Greenwood, C. R., Walker, H. M., & Hops, J. (1977). Issues in social interaction/withdrawal assessment. *Exceptional Children, 43,* 490–499.

Gresham, F. M. (1981). Assessment of children's social skills. *Journal of School Psychology, 19,* 120–133.

Gresham, F. M. (1983). Social skills assessment as a component of mainstreaming placement decisions. *Exceptional Children, 49,* 331–336.

Gresham, F. M. (1985). Strategies for enhancing the social outcomes of mainstreaming: A necessary ingredient for success. In C. J. Meisel (Ed.), *Mainstreaming handicapped children: Outcomes, controversies and new directions.* Hillsdale, NJ: Erlbaum.

Gresham, F. M., & Elliott, S. N. (1984). Assessment and classification of children's social skills: A review of methods and issues. *School Psychology Review, 13,* 292–301.

Henning, J., Dalrymple, N., Davis, K., & Madeira, S. (1982). *Teaching social and leisure skills to youth with autism.* Bloomington: Indiana University Developmental Training Center.

Kanner, L. (1943). Autistic disturbances of affective contact. *Nervous Child, 2,* 217–250.

McFall, R. M. (1982). A review and reformulation of the concept of social skills. *Behavioral Assessment, 4,* 1–33.

Meyer, L. H., McQuarter, R. J., & Kishi, G. S. (1985). Assessing and teaching social interaction skills. In W. Stainback & S. Stainback (Eds.), *Integration of students with severe handicaps into regular schools* (pp. 66–86). Reston, VA: Council for Exceptional Children.

Meyer, L. H., Reichle, J., McQuarter, R. J., Evans, I. M., Neel, R. S., & Kishi, G. S. (1983). *Assessment of social competence functions.* Minneapolis: University of Minnesota Consortium Institute for the Education of Severely Handicapped Learners.

Michelson, L., Foster, S. L., & Ritchey, W. L. (1981). Social-skills assessment of children. In B. B. Lahey & A. E. Kazdin (Eds.), *Advances in clinical child psychology* (Vol. 4, pp. 119–165). New York: Plenum Press.

Michelson, L., Sugai, D. P., Wood, R. P., & Kazdin, A. E. (1983). *Social skills assessment and training with children: An empirically based handbook.* New York: Plenum Press.

National Society for Autistic Children. (1978). National Society for Autistic Children definition of the syndrome of autism. *Journal of Autism and Childhood Schizophrenia, 8,* 162–167.

Richer, J. M. (1976). The social-avoidance behaviour of autistic children. *Animal Behaviour, 24,* 898–906.

Richer, J. M. (1978). The partial noncommunication of culture to autistic children—An application of human ethology. In M. Rutter & E. Schopler (Eds.), *Autism: A reappraisal of concepts and treatment* (pp. 47–61). New York: Plenum Press.

Rutter, M. (1978). Diagnosis and definition of childhood autism. *Journal of Autism and Childhood Schizophrenia, 8,* 139–161.

Schopler, E., & Olley, J. G. (1982). Comprehensive educational services for autistic children: The TEACCH model. In C. R. Reynolds & T. B. Gutkin (Eds.), *The handbook of school psychology* (pp. 629–643). New York: Wiley.

Schopler, E., & Reichler, R. J. (1979). *Individualized assessment and treatment for autistic and developmentally disabled children: Vol. 1. Psychoeducational profile.* Baltimore: University Park Press.

Schopler, E., Reichler, R. J., & Lansing, M. (1980). *Individualized assessment and treatment for autistic and developmentally disabled children: Vol. 2. Teaching strategies for parents and professionals.* Baltimore: University Park Press.

Simonson, L. R. (1979). *A curriculum model for individuals with severe learning and behavior disorders.* Baltimore: University Park Press.

Sulzer-Azaroff, B., & Mayer, G. R. (1977). *Applying behavior-analysis procedures with children and youth.* New York: Holt, Rinehart & Winston.

Voeltz, L. M., & Evans, I. M. (1983). Educational validity: Procedures to evaluate outcomes in programs for severely handicapped learners. *Journal of the Association for the Severely Handicapped, 8,* 3–15.

Wacker, D. P. (1984). Training moderately and severely mentally handicapped children to use adaptive social skills. *School Psychology Review, 13,* 324–330.

Walker, H. M. (1982). The social behavior survival program: (SBS) A systematic approach to the integration of handicapped children into less restrictive settings. *Education and Treatment of Children, 6,* 421–441.

Walker, H. M., McConnell, S., Holmes, D., Todis, B., Walker, J., & Golden, N. (1983). *The Walker social skills curriculum: The ACCEPTS program.* Austin, TX: Pro-Ed.

Watson, L. R. (1985). The TEACCH communication curriculum. In E. Schopler & G. B. Mesibov (Eds.), *Communication problems in autism* (pp. 187–206). New York: Plenum Press.

Watson, L. R., & Lord, C. (1982). Developing a social communication curriculum for autistic students. *Topics in Language Disorders, 3*(1), 1–9.

Wehman, P. H. (1976). Toward a social skills curriculum for developmentally disabled clients in vocational settings. *Rehabilitation Literature, 36,* 342–348.

Wing, L. (1969). The handicaps of autistic children—A comparative study. *Journal of Child Psychology and Psychiatry, 10,* 1–40.

Wing, L., & Gould, J. (1979). Severe impairments of social interaction and associated abnormalities in children: Epidemiology and classification. *Journal of Autism and Developmental Disorders, 9,* 11–29.

Wolf, M. M. (1978). Social validity: The case for subjective measurement or how applied behavior analysis is finding its heart. *Journal of Applied Behavior Analysis, 11,* 203–214.

Index

Academic achievement, 70
ACCEPTS program, 353
Adolescence
  autistic development, 86–87
  compliance/noncompliance, 171–172
Affect
  attribution of, 161–162
  autistic behavior and, 109
  autistic deficits and, 246
  communication and, 159
  emotional cue recognition behavior, 112–113
  friendships and, 72–74
  infancy and, 242
  nonverbal communication comprehension, 138
  social and leisure program, 326–327
  social skills definition and, 103
Age at onset, 26–27
Age level
  autism and, 3
  friendships and, 66
  interpersonal relations and, 5
Aggression
  communication skills and, 52
  social reciprocity and, 18
Analogue tasks, 106
Animal studies, 26
Asperger's syndrome, 156–157
Assessment
  behavior, 104–107, 110
  Jowonio School program, 299–301
  learning handicaps, 107–108
  nonverbal communication comprehension, 139
  readiness, 217
  social skills, 353
  TEACCH program, 356–365
Assessment of Social Competence, 353
Athletic activities, 331–332
Attachment behaviors, 110–111
Attention
  autistic behavior, 111
  cognitive program, 269–270
Autism
  communication skills and, 53–56, 133
  compliance/noncompliance, 176–178
  developmental limits in, 96–98
  friendship and, 69
  gaze patterns, 244–245 (*See also* Gaze behavior)
  historical perspective on, 2–6
  imitation and, 246–247
  intelligence and, 154–156
  intelligence tests and, 155–156
  interest in, 1–2
  language development and, 84–86
  language production and, 142–144
  mainstreaming and, 196–205 (*See also* Mainstreaming)
  parent's perspective on, 81–99
  play behavior and, 46–47 (*See also* Play Behavior)
  social developmental theory and, 25–29
  social skills development and, 36–37
  vocalization and, 245
  See also Behavior (autistic)
Awareness, 3

Behavior (autistic), 103–131
  assessment, 104–107, 110
  attachment behaviors, 110–111
  attention behavior, 111
  cognitive deficits and, 153–169
  emotional cue recognition and, 112–113
  gaze behavior, 113–115 (*See also* Gaze behavior)
  interpretation of, 121–123

Behavior (autistic) (*Cont.*)
learning handicaps assessment, 107–108
negativism, 116
older children, 117–123
peer relationships, 68–69, 117–118
physical withdrawal, 115–116 (*See also* Withdrawal)
play behavior, 118–121 (*See also* Play behavior)
self-recognition, 111–112
social deficit in, 108–109
social skills definition and, 103–104
treatment implications of, 123–125
young children, 110–116
See also Autism
Behavioral interviews, 106
Behaviorism, 4–5
Behavior modification, 86–89, 213–236
Biology
structure-function bidirectionality and, 18–19
See also Psychobiology
Brain, 156–157

Cairns, Robert B., 15–33
Classroom
friendships and, 65
Jowonio School program, 286
peer instruction, 306–307
treatment programs and, 124
See also Mainstreaming; Social skills development; TEACCH program
Coaching, 229–230
Cognition
communication skills and, 5
compliance/noncompliance and, 172, 177, 182
infancy, 166
mainstreaming and, 199–201
negativism, 182
social deficits and, 248–249
Cognitive deficits, 153–169
social behavior and, 154–158
specific areas of, 161–165
specific social impairments, 158–161
speculations on, 166
Cognitive program, 265–283
attention difficulties, 269–270
communication difficulties, 270–271
demonstration of, 277–278
Cognitive program (*Cont.*)
friendships and, 70–71
future directions for, 279–280
group sessions segments, 273–277
overview of, 272–273
positive social experience in, 271–272
rules comprehension in, 268
social interaction deficits, 266–268
targeted deficits in, 266–272
training program for, 278–279
Commitment, 75–76
Communication, 133–150
affect and, 159
autism and, 109, 117, 133
behavioral intervention, 215
childhood content in, 135–136
cognitive program and, 270–271, 275–276
community skills instruction, 336
comprehension and, 136–142
defined, 133
infancy, 241
intentional versus nonintentional, 144–146
learning handicapped, 107–108
nonverbal comprehension, 137–139
nonverbal production, 146–148
social and leisure program, 328–330
social relations and, 134–135
social skills definition and, 103
synchrony in, 160
verbal comprehension, 139–142
verbal production, 142–144
See also Nonverbal communication
Communication skills, 47–54
autism and, 53–56
cognitive deficits and, 5
developmental overview of, 47–48
elementary school children, 51–53
infancy/toddler years, 48–50
preschool children, 50–51
Community skills instruction, 333–336
Competence
friendship and, 67
social skills definition and, 103
See also Social skills
Compliance/noncompliance
autism and, 176–178
child development research and, 173–175
definitional issues in, 171–173
intervention strategies, 182–184
oppositional syndromes, 175–176

Compliance/noncompliance (*Cont.*)
research studies, 178–182
theoretical questions in, 184–185
Comprehension
nonverbal, 137–139
verbal, 139–142
See also Communication
Context
cognition and, 164–165
observational assessment and, 359–363
Criminality
friendships and, 67–68, 71
intimacy and, 75
cross-cultural studies, 26–27
Curriculum
integrated approaches, 219
Jowonio School program, 293–295
social skills development, 216
See also TEACCH program

Dalrymple, Nancy, 321–350
Dawson, Geraldine, 237–261
Delinquency. *See* Criminality
Developmental model, 237–261
autistic deficits, 244–247
implications of deficits in, 247–249
intervention approach, 249–251
intervention illustration, 251–253
limitations of, 253–255
normal child development, 239–244
theories in, 238–239
Developmental theory. *See* Social developmental theory
Discrimination (cognitive), 162, 246
Division TEACCH. *See* TEACCH program
Donnellan, Anne M., 213–236
Down's syndrome, 160
Dramatic modeling. *See* Modeling

Echolalia, 142, 177
Electric shock therapy, 214
Elementary school children
autistic development and, 85
communication skills and, 51–53
hierarchies of play, 45
play behavior among, 41–43
Embeddedness. *See* Social embeddedness
Emotion. *See* Affect
Entry strategies
autism and, 117
Entry strategies (*Cont.*)
peer groups and, 41–42
TEACCH program and, 358
Errorless learning, 230–231
Ethological theories, 15–16
Eye contact. *See* Gaze behavior

Face recognition
infancy, 174
nonverbal comprehension, 137
Facial expression, 159, 246
Family, 20
See also Parents
Friendships, 61–79
affective qualities variations, 72–74
autism and, 69
cognitive program, 267–268
commitment variations, 75–76
content variations, 71
defined, 61–63
diversity variations, 71–72
importance of, 63–65
individual differences, 65–69
intimacy variations, 74–75
qualitative variations, 69–76
social skills development and, 76
See also entries under Peer

Galpert, Larry, 237–261
Gamble, Wendy C., 191–212
Garfin, Deborah G., 133–150
Gaze behavior
autism and, 113–115, 158, 244–245
communication skills and, 52
compliance/noncompliance, 171
infancy and, 174, 240–241
interpretation of, 122
Gesture
autism and, 158–159
context and, 147–148
See also Nonverbal communication
Group leader, 228–229
Group therapy
cognitive program, 273–277
psychoanalysis and, 4
See also Peer instruction

Hartup, Willard W., 61–79
Henning, Joyce, 321–350
Heterochrony, 21–23

Howlin, Patricia, 103–131

Imitation
  autistic deficits, 246–247
  developmental model, 252
  infancy, 242–243
Individual differences
  behavioral approach, 227
  compliance/noncompliance, 176
  friendships, 65–69
  Jowonio School program, 287–295
  mainstreaming and, 194
  TEACCH program, 367
Infancy
  autistic development, 82–83
  communication skills, 48–50
  compliance/noncompliance, 171, 173–174
  gaze and, 158 (*see also* Gaze behavior)
  hierarchies of play and, 44
  normal developmental model, 239–244
  play behavior and, 38
  social skills in, 166
  synchronous communication, 160
Information processing, 162–163
Integration, 21–23
Intelligence
  autism and, 154–156
  friendships and, 67
  See also Cognition
Intentional communication, 144–146
  See also Communication
Intentionality, 243–244
Interpersonal relations
  aging and, 3, 5
  autism and, 2–3, 108–109, 117–118
  behavioral interventions, 214
  centrality of, 213
  cognitive development and, 162
  cognitive program, 266–268, 271–272
  communication and, 134–135
  developmental model for, 237–261
  learning handicaps and, 107–108
  mainstreaming and, 196, 201–205
  negativism in, 116
  nonverbal communication and, 146–147
  ontogenetic functionalism, 23
  play behavior and, 39, 136
  social and leisure program, 325–328
  social reciprocity and, 18 (*See also* Reciprocity)

Interpersonal relations (*Cont.*)
  social skills definition and, 103
  structure-function bidirectionality and, 19
  treatment and, 124
  verbal communication and, 140–141, 143–144
  See also Friendships
Intervention strategies. *See* Treatment
Intimacy, 64, 66, 74–75
  See also Friendships
Isolation
  autism and, 2, 82
  See also Withdrawal

Joining strategies. *See* Entry strategies
Jowonio School program, 285–303
  design of, 285–287
  diversity and, 287–291
  empirical approach in, 298–302
  individualized instruction in, 291–295
  social systems perspective in, 295–298
  See also Mainstreaming
Juvenile delinquency. *See* Criminality

Kilman, Beverly A., 213–236
Knoblock, Peter, 285–303

La Greca, Annette M., 35–60
Language
  autism and, 83, 84–86, 91–92, 157, 159
  compliance/noncompliance and, 172–173
  pretend behavior and, 39
  social developmental theory and, 28–29
  social skills development and, 95–96
  See also Communication
Learning
  assessment of, 107–108
  social reciprocity and, 27
  social skills development and, 157
Learning theory, 322
Least restrictive environment, 191–192
Lehr, Robert, 285–303
Leisure programs. *See* Social and leisure programs
Lord, Catherine, 133–150

Mainstreaming, 191–202
  autistic children, 196–205
  efficacy of, 193–205
  enhancement of, 205–207

Mainstreaming (*Cont.*)
peer instruction, 305–319
programs in, 192–193
rationale for, 191–192
unpleasant social experiences, 271
See also Peer instruction; Social skills development
Maternal–infant relationship
compliance/noncompliance, 174
developmental model, 252–253
friendships and, 70, 73
gaze patterns, 240–241 (*See also* Gaze behavior)
social developmental theory, 26–27
synchronous communication and, 160
vocalizations, 241
McHale, Susan M., 191–212
Mental retardation, 154–155
Mesibov, Gary B., 1–11, 265–283, 305–319
Modeling
behavioral approach, 230
effectiveness of, 16
mainstreaming and, 202
social and leisure programs, 322
Motivation
autistic development and, 87–88
communication instruction, 329–330
compliance/noncompliance, 183–184
prognosis and, 3
social and leisure programs, 325–326
Motivational theories, 4
Movement skills, 331–332

Negativism
autistic behavior, 116
centrality of, 178
definitions of, 172, 173
withdrawal and, 177
See also Compliance/noncompliance
Noncompliance. *See* Compliance/noncompliance
Nonintentional communication, 144–146
Nonverbal communication
autistic behavior, 109, 118, 158–159
comprehension, 137–139
elementary school children, 51–52
emotional cue recognition, 112–113
learning handicapped and, 108
learning of, 157
preschool children, 51

Nonverbal communication (*Cont.*)
production of, 146–148
See also Communication

Object relations, 2–3
Objects
infant play behavior and, 38
social attachment and, 27
TEACCH program and, 357–358
Observational assessment
behavior assessment, 104–106
interpretation of, 121–122
TEACCH program, 356–365
Obsessiveness
play behavior and, 46
social developmental theory and, 29
TEACCH program and, 358
Olley, J. Gregory, 351–373
Ontogenetic functionalism, 23–24
Oppositional syndromes, 175–176
Outcomes
behaviorism and, 4–5
theory and, 16

Parents
attachment behavior, 110–111
compliance/noncompliance, 176
Jowonio School program, 295–298
mainstreaming and, 207
TEACCH program and, 365
See also Maternal–infant relationship
Park, Clara Claiborne, 81–99
Passive aggressive personality disorders. *See* Oppositional disorder
Peer groups
autism and, 117–118
behavior assessment and, 104
mainstreaming and, 200–201
social and leisure program, 327–328
See also Friendships; Social skills development
Peer instruction, 305–319
activities in, 313–316
concepts in, 307–308
current play groups, 309
effectiveness of, 28
follow-up in, 317–318
initial play group, 308–309
Jowonio School program, 287
objectives in, 309–310

Peer instruction (*Cont.*)
  play group rules, 316–317
  play group structure, 312–313
  preparation for, 310–312
  setting for, 306–307
  unanticipated benefits of, 318
  See also Play therapy
Physical proximity. *See* Proximity
Plasticity of interchanges, 20–21
Play behavior, 37–47
  autism and, 46–47, 117, 118–121
  communication and, 134, 135–136
  developmental overview, 37
  elementary school children, 41–43
  friendships and, 66, 71
  hierarchies, 43–45
  importance of, 37
  infants/toddlers, 38
  mainstreaming and, 203
  observational assessment, 362
  preschool children, 39–41
Play therapy, 214
  peer in, 215
  psychoanalysis and, 4
  See also Peer instruction
Positive social behavior
  play behavior and, 39
  reinforcement of, 40
Predictability, 247
Preschool children
  autistic development, 83–84
  communication skills, 50–51
  compliance/noncompliance, 175
  friendship and, 62
  hierarchies of play, 43–44, 45
  play behavior and, 39–41
Pretend play
  autistic children, 46
  hierarchies of play and, 44
  play behavior and, 39
Prognosis
  motivation and, 3
  See also Outcomes
Prompts, 229
Proximity
  behavioral approach, 227
  TEACCH program, 357
  teaching of, 46–47
Psychoanalysis
  persistence of view of, 15
Psychoanalysis (*Cont.*)
  self-recognition and, 111–112
  view of, 3–4
Psychobiology
  social developmental theory and, 17–18
  See also Biology
Public schools. *See* Mainstreaming
Punishment, 223–224

Race differences, 66
Readiness assessment, 217
Reading ability, 163
Reality, 24–25
Reciprocity
  autistic behavior, 109, 117
  centrality of, 247–248
  cognitive deficits, 153
  cognitive program, 267
  communication and, 49, 134
  developmental theory and, 18
  friendships, 61, 73–74
  infancy, 243–244
  interpretation problems and, 122
  learning process and, 27
  role play behavior and, 40
  social skills definition and, 103
  treatment and, 124
Reinforcement
  behavioral approach, 223, 229
  effectiveness of, 16
  mainstreaming, 202
  positive play behavior, 40
  social and leisure programs, 322–323
  social skills definition and, 103
  social skills development and, 214
Retarded children. *See* Mental retardation
Role playing
  behavior assessment, 106
  cognitive program, 275–276
  play behavior and, 39–40
  play hierarchies and, 43

Sameness. *See* Obsessiveness
Sancilio, Michael F., 61–79
Schizophrenia, 3
Schopler, Eric, 1–11
Self-awareness, 93–95
Self-care, 324
Self-concept, 24–25
Self-disclosure. *See* Intimacy

Self-recognition, 111–112
Self report inventories, 106
Sensitivity, 112–113
Sex differences
  compliance/noncompliance, 176
  friendships, 63, 66, 71, 75
  play behavior and, 45
Sexuality
  appropriate behavior and, 27
  friendships and, 64, 75
  structure-function bidirectionality, 19
Shah, Amitta, 153–169
Shaping techniques, 229
Situation, 103
Social and leisure programs, 321–350
  communication skills, 328–330
  community skills instruction, 333–336
  interpersonal skills, 325–328
  leisure skills instruction, 330–333
  overview of, 321–324
  representative samples for, 338–348
  self-care and academic skills, 324
Social cognition, 161
  See also Cognition
Social-cognitive tasks, 106
Social developmental theory, 15–33
  autism and, 25–29
  eclecticism in, 16–17
  integration/heterochrony, 21–23
  ontogenetic functionalism, 23–24
  plasticity of interchanges, 20–21
  psychobiology and, 17–18
  self-concept and, 24–25
  social embeddedness, 20
  social reciprocity and, 18
  structure-function bidirectionality, 18–19
Social embeddedness, 20
Social learning theory, 15
Social relations. *See* Interpersonal relations
Social skills
  autistic behavior and, 117–118
  brain and, 156–157
  cognitive deficits and, 155
  definitions of, 103–104, 356
  learning handicaps and, 107
  specific impairments, 158–161
  treatment and, 135
Social skills development, 35–60, 213–236
  autism and, 36–37, 92–95
  behavioral approaches, 216, 217, 219–224
Social skills of development (*Cont.*)
  behavioral considerations, 226–231
  communication skills, 47–54 (*See also* Communication skills)
  curriculum development triad, 216
  developmental approaches, 217, 218, 224–225
  friendships and, 76
  functional approaches, 216, 218, 225
  infancy, 166
  integrated approach, 218, 219
  language and, 84–86, 95–96
  learning and, 157
  mainstreaming and, 201–205
  peer instruction, 305–319
  play behavior and, 37–47 (*See also* Play behavior)
  TEACCH program, 351–373
  treatment and, 124
Sociodrama. *See* Role play
Socioeconomic class, 67, 68
Sociometric assessment, 104
  See also Assessment
Speech. *See* Communication; Language
Sports, 331–332
Stone, Wendy L., 35–60
Stress, 64
Structure-function bidirectionality, 18–19
Synchrony, 160

TEACCH program, 196–197, 201, 255, 351–373
  activities design, 367–368
  development of curriculum, 353–356
  example of instruction in, 368–370
  parental involvement in, 365
  priority setting in, 365–367
  social skills assessment in, 356–365
  social skills curricula, 353
  See also Cognitive program
Teacher rating scales, 106
Teachers
  behavioral approach, 221–223, 228–231
  Jowonio School program, 285–286, 288–289, 294, 296–297
  mainstreaming and, 205–206
  peer instruction and, 310–312
Theory
  developmental model, 238–239
  friendships and, 70–71

Theory (*Cont.*)
  outcomes and, 16
Toddlers
  autism and, 46, 83
  communication skills, 48–50
  compliance/noncompliance, 171–172, 174
  hierarchies of play and, 44
  play behavior, 38
  See also Infancy
Treatment
  behavioral approaches, 213–236
  behavioral implications for, 123, 125
  cognitive program, 265–283
  communication and, 134
  compliance/noncompliance, 182–184
  developmental model, 237–261
  nonverbal communication and, 139, 147
  social and leisure programs, 321–350
Treatment (*Cont.*)
  social skills program, 135
  verbal communication comprehension, 141
  See also TEACCH program

Visual regard
  autistic children, 46
  infant play behavior, 38
  See also Gaze behavior
Vocalizations, 241, 245
Volkmar, Fred R., 171–188

Wing, Lorna, 153–169
Withdrawal
  autistic behavior, 115–116
  cognitive deficits and, 155
  negativism and, 177
Wooten, Marian, 305–319